THE WORLD OF HERODOTUS

Aubrey de Sélincourt was born in 1896 and educated at Rugby and University College, Oxford. One of the finest classicists of his generation, he specialised in the history of the ancient world, translated a number of works by Herodotus and Livy, and spent many years as a schoolmaster. Aubrey de Sélincourt lived in retirement on the Isle of Wight from 1947 until his death in 1962.

Also by Aubrey de Sélincourt

Six Great Playwrights
The Channel Shore
Horatio Nelson
Isle of Wight
Nansen

As editor or translator

The Book of the Sea
The Campaigns of Alexander, Arrian
The Life of Alexander the Great, Arrian
The Histories, Herodotus
The Early History of Rome, Livy
The War with Hannibal, Livy

THE WORLD OF HERODOTUS

Aubrey de Sélincourt

PHOENIX
PRESS

5 UPPER SAINT MARTIN'S LANE
LONDON
WC2H 9EA

A PHOENIX PRESS PAPERBACK
First published in Great Britain
by Secker & Warburg in 1962
This paperback edition published in 2001
by Phoenix Press,
a division of The Orion Publishing Group Ltd,
Orion House, 5 Upper St Martin's Lane,
London WC2H 9EA

I should like to express my thanks to the Oxford University Press
for permission to quote a passage from Alfred Zimmern's *The Greek
Commonwealth*, and to Penguin Books Ltd. for permission to reproduce a
number of passages from my translation, *Herodotus: the Histories*. A good
deal of the matter in my chapter on Greek drama has already appeared
in my book *Six Great Playwrights*, published by Hamish Hamilton,
who have kindly allowed me to reproduce it here.

A CIP catalogue record for this book is
available from the British Library.

Printed and bound in Great Britain by
Clays Ltd, St Ives plc

ISBN 1 84212 458 7

TO MY WIFE

In winter, on your soft couch by the fire, full of food, drinking sweet wine and cracking nuts, say this to the chance traveller at your door: 'What is your name, my good friend? Where do you live? How many years can you number? How old were you when the Persians came . . . ?'

Xenophanes

Contents

Preface

THE RELATIONSHIP WHICH GROWS UP BETWEEN A TRANSLATOR AND the author whose work he is translating is a peculiarly intimate and personal one, and is apt to turn either to irritation or to a firm and lasting affection. The two years I spent in translating Herodotus were happy ones, and I soon came to feel that here, if anywhere in antiquity, was a man whose attitude to life was, in spite of basic differences, immediately intelligible to the modern world.

When, therefore, my publishers asked me to write a book about Herodotus, my first impulse was to consent. But misgivings followed, for I felt that such a book, if it was to be worthy of its subject, called for scholarship much wider and deeper than mine, which is merely the result of having browsed for some fifty years past in the literature of ancient Greece with no conscious purpose beyond the pleasure it gave me.

Gradually, however, I came to persuade myself that my amateur status (so to call it) might not, after all, be a serious disqualification; indeed, it might even be an advantage in writing a book of a certain kind, which now began to take shape in my thoughts: a book, that is, not for professional scholars, but for readers who, like myself, enjoy venturing both for instruction and amusement into new regions of intellectual experience, where, if they are lucky, they will have the odd sensation, amidst an unfamiliar landscape, of having 'been there before'.

So the book was written. For most of the facts it contains I have been dependent upon the labours of others. Within the framework of those facts, which is as solid as I have been able to make it, I have tried, in the course of following Herodotus' story, to give some expression to what for so long has interested, or delighted, or horrified me in the civilisation and culture of antiquity, and to the sense I have that men in the passage of centuries, though they have changed their clothes much and often, have but little and seldom changed themselves.

9

Herodotus was a universal historian. I have followed his narrative pretty closely from country to country—to the Near East, to Egypt, to North Africa, to southern Russia—filling in for the modern reader certain details which recent research has revealed. All this tends to discursiveness and to the attempt, perhaps, to say too much in too small a space; but it is essential to my purpose, because Herodotus' own book is much more than a history of Greece: it is a history of the then known world with Greece as its focal point. Herodotus sees the brilliant cultural and political achievement of Greece against the background of the ancient empires of Persia, of Egypt, of Assyria; and it is precisely this breadth of view, this universality, this delighted and uncensorious interest in cultures other than his own, which makes Herodotus the greatest of Greek historians, and one of the greatest of all historians. The work of his younger contemporary Thucydides, estimated more highly both by ancient and, until a hundred years ago, by modern scholars, is by comparison parochial, dealing, as it does, with a single episode, the war between Athens and Sparta. Thucydides' book is undoubtedly a work of genius; but it is narrow in scope and conception and obsessed with a single idea—the betrayal by Athens of the Periclean ideal—and has nothing in it comparable to the sheer range and capacity of intellectual insight and interest which give to Herodotus' work its unique power and charm.

In my title *The World of Herodotus* I use the word 'world' in a double sense: the geographical, to describe how Herodotus saw it in the course of his travels; and the figurative, to describe that complex of thought, feeling and tradition—that culture—which made the emergence of a Herodotus possible, and which he himself so signally crystallised. Thus, though I have written a good deal about other countries, the core of my book is Greece, and my chief concern has been to give some picture of that extraordinary civilisation from which we have inherited so much. I have put together the picture in the only way I could—piecemeal, with such cross-lights and shadows as I could supply from my miscellaneous reading both of Greek and of other literatures. I have often digressed, when this or that aspect of Greek life and thought has suggested some contrast or comparison in the modern world; but I hope my readers will accept my digressions, as for me, at any rate, they are a necessary part of my theme.

Finally, has what I have said all been said before? In a way, I suppose it has; nevertheless in discussing so vast a subject as ancient Greek civilisation no man can very well avoid contributing a mite of his own—not indeed of fact, but by way of value and interpretation. In describing Greek life I have not attempted to gloss over its darker and more disagreeable elements, and the reader will not find in my treatment of Greek literature that indiscriminate admiration which so often in the past has served it ill. Lastly all that I have written tends to the rejection of the common, but, to my mind, erroneous view that the consummation and crown of Greek civilisation is to be found in the Athens of Pericles. That brief period, brilliant though it was, I see as the beginning of the end of much that was most characteristic and most precious in the history of this remarkable race.

Table I

Date B.C.	Egypt	Asia	Greece and Mediterranena
2600–2500	4th dynasty. Building of pyramids of Cheops and Chephren		Early Bronze Age. Immigrants from Asia Minor settle in Crete and Cyclades
2000–1600		Rise of Hittite Empire	Minoan Civilisation
1600–1400			Height of Crete's prosperity. Contact with Mycenaean centres of mainland Greece. Greek Dynasty of Cnossus *c.* 1450
1400–1300			Flowering of Mycenaean culture
1300		Rise of Assyrian Empire	
1183		Fall of Troy	
1100			Dorian invasion of Peloponnese
900 approx.			Phoenician alphabet adopted in Greece
800		Fall of Hittite Empire	
700		Phrygians in control of Lydia	
672	Conquest of Egypt by Assyria		
650 approx.		Invention of coinage in Lydia	Coinage adopted in Greece

13

TABLE I

Date B.C.	Egypt	Asia	Greece and Mediterranena
645	Egypt regains independence under Psammetichus		
640	Foundation of Greek trading colony of Naucratis on the Nile		
612		Fall of Assyria	
560		Croesus, King of Lydia	Death of Solon
546		Defeat of Croesus by Cyrus of Persia	
540			Rise of Peisistratus in Athens
538		Cyrus captures Babylon	
524	Conquest of Egypt by Cambbyses		
523			Death of Polycrates of Samos
521		Accession of Darius	Sparta predominant in Greece
508			Cleisthenes in Athens
499			Ionian revolt against Persian domination
498		Burning of Sardis by Athenians and Eretrians	
490			Battle of Marathon
490-80			Athens under Themistocles becomes a sea power
485		Death of Darius, accession of Xerxes	

Table I 15

Date B.C.	Egypt	Asia	Greece and Mediterranena
480			Battles of Thermopylae, Artemisium and Salamis.
479			Battle of Plataea
478			Confederacy of Delos and beginning of Athenian Empire
466			Rise of Pericles in Athens
432			War between Athens and Sparta
404			Defeat of Athens
336			Death of Philip of Macedon and accession of Alexander the Great

Table II

Third Millenium B.C.	Greeks begin to penetrate into Greece.
13th and 12th centuries	Achaean age in Greece.
9th(?)-6th century	Period of Greek colonisation in Asia Minor, Thrace, Black Sea coast, Italy, Sicily and North Africa.
7th and 6th centuries	So-called 'Age of Tyrants' in Greece. Flowering of Greek lyric poetry. Beginnings of science and philosophy in Ionia.
5th century	Rise of democracy. Gradual extinction of lyric poetry. Rise of the drama in Athens.
5th and 4th centuries	Age of Athenian philosophy. (Plato: 429-347, Aristotle: 384-322).

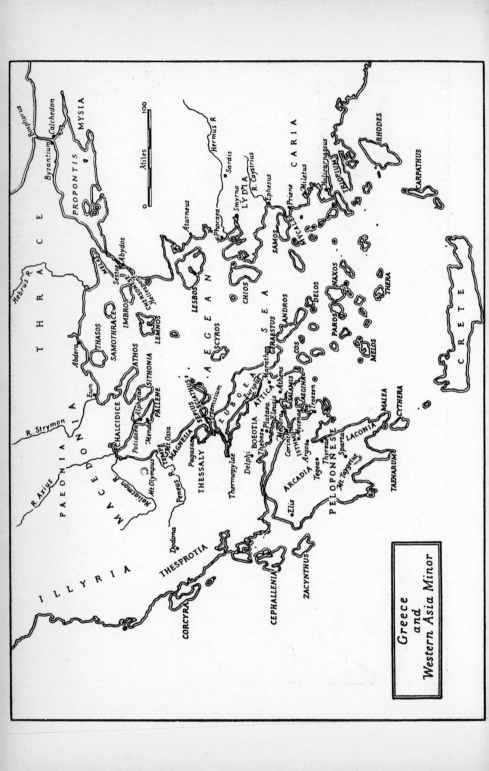

Greece
and
Western Asia Minor

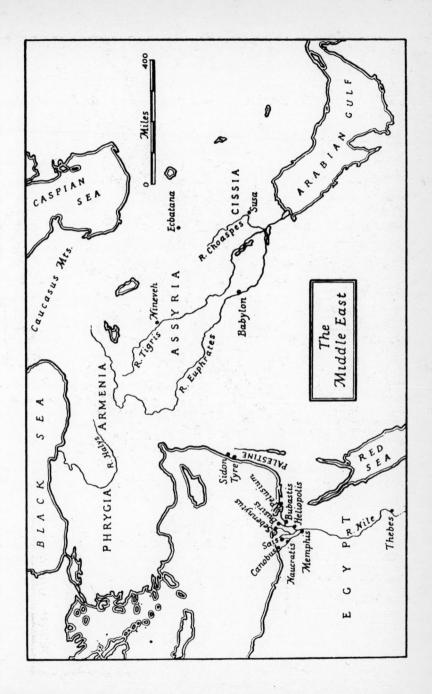

The Middle East

PART ONE

Herodotus the Historian

The Greek Feeling for History

GREEK LITERATURE, THE RICHEST IN THE WORLD AFTER OUR OWN, IS comparatively poor in the department of history. Only two Greek historians have a title to greatness: Herodotus, first in time and incomparably the greater, and Thucydides. Xenophon, who continued the story of Greece where Thucydides left it, was a second-rate historian; he did indeed write one good book, his account—a splendid piece of first-hand reporting—of the expedition of a Greek mercenary army deep into the interior of Asia on a wild adventure in the service of the Persian prince, Cyrus; and he left some amiable tracts, in the manner of a country gentleman, on hunting and the management of an estate; but his major historical work few nowadays can bring themselves to read. Polybius, the fourth and last, was a writer of eminence, but though his long work included much Greek history, he was primarily a historian of Rome, telling the eventful story of her wars with Carthage. These four—unless we include Arrian, who wrote in the second century of our era a pious and competent history of Alexander the Great—complete the list of the Greek historians whose work has survived in anything but a fragmentary state and has quality above the mediocre.

Survival, indeed, is not a proof of quality, but it is some indication at least, and we can be pretty sure that neither accident nor time nor the judgement of the old Alexandrian scholars, has deprived us of any Greek histories of first-rate importance. Chroniclers of second—or fourth-rate-importance, and laborious compilers of historical facts and fictions, such as Diodorus the Sicilian who wrote a work in 144 books on world history from the Trojan War to the death of Julius Caesar, can be reckoned in hundreds; but to us these men themselves are not even names, and even of the hundreds I mentioned before, the great majority are little more than names. For the fact is that the brilliant lead of Herodotus and Thucydides was not followed. Herodotus, the

Father of History, had an undistinguished family. This makes his own achievement only the more remarkable, as all the evidence forces us to the conclusion that historical writing of a high order was, unlike poetry, philosophy and the visual arts, in some way alien to the subtle and inventive genius of the Greeks. Poetry was in their blood: they were born poets, seeing what they saw with passion and immediacy, never, in the great early centuries before their decline, misting it with sentiment or wrapping it in rhetoric. They were born philosophers, too, with their devotion to first principles and insatiable curiosity about the workings of the sensible universe, of man in society and of their own minds; but they were not, it seems, by temperament or inclination, historians. Thus Herodotus, a native of Caria, part of that region on the Eastern shores of the Aegean where the first great impulse towards free speculation began in the sixth century before Christ —though a Greek of the Greeks in his habitual attitudes, and representative of much that was wisest and most civilised in that brilliant people whose civilisation was yet never separated by anything but the thinnest wall from savagery and barbarism, was nevertheless, in one important respect, untypical of his race. Homer (as we now believe) wrote the first great poem, and from that fount of poetry flowed innumerable streams. Men like Thales and Anaximander broke through the age-long darkness of superstition and the universal tyranny of myth to use their wits and their senses upon the fundamental problems of science and cosmology ('where does the visible universe come from, and how was it made?') and were followed throughout the six centuries of Greek intellectual pre-eminence by a succession of thinkers and speculators who built upon that priceless foundation of the freedom of thought; but Herodotus, who wrote the first great History in Greek, wrote also the last; Thucydides indeed, his younger contemporary, wrote a history which is still very much alive today and thus justifies its author's claim to make it a 'possession for ever'; but compared with Herodotus, Thucydides' book is tendentious in matter, parochial in scope, and difficult to read from the violences it does to the beautiful and perspicuous Greek language.

Homer, then, and the earliest Ionian thinkers, did what other Greeks with a similar intellectual endowment were potentially capable of doing, once they had been shown the way; Herodotus, on the contrary, did what others of his countrymen could never learn to do, or never wished to do. He was able (surely the first quality of a good historian) to see his subject as part of a larger process and to be constantly aware of the threads which linked his country with the vast and mysterious lands of Egypt and Asia. He was able to keep before his reader the sense that Greece, the centre of his interest, was still only one country in an immense and diverse world which it was yet to dominate by virtue of certain qualities which that world lacked, above all by that passion for independence and self-determination which was both her glory and her bane; to be aware of the past, not only the immediate but the most remote, as a living element in the present; and to find—unlike, in this, most historians writing today—a continuing moral pattern in the vicissitudes of human fortune all the world over. That pattern was simple enough: too simple for modern criticism, which tends to reject moral causes in tracing changes in the power-patterns of human society. It was formed from the belief that men, as men, are subject to certain limitations imposed by a Power—call it Fate or God—which they cannot fully comprehend, and that any attempt to transcend those limitations is met by inevitable punishment. In the search for a principle one might, after all, go farther and fare worse; such as it is, it has, in one form or another, lived on beside our newer notions. We still believe I suppose, that men are bound by the necessity of obedience. The only point of debate is obedience *to what?*

Perhaps I have suggested that the fact that Herodotus had no worthy successors during the period of Greek intellectual supremacy is a matter for surprise. This is not so. It is Herodotus himself who is surprising; for the study of history, in Herodotus' sense and in our own, was alien to the whole temper and circumstances of the ancient world. The priests in Egypt kept records stretching back to the remotest antiquity; but records are not history. Even the book of Thucydides, in many ways a noble one, is only an essay in history, dealing as it does, except for an introductory sketch, the validity of which has lately been called into question, only with contemporary events, and attempting the delineation, memorable indeed, of the contemporary political behaviour of men under the stresses of a civil war. But free and far-ranging inquiry into the past, either for its own intrinsic interest or in the search for a fuller understanding of the present, is an activity more natural to the modern than to the ancient world. Nor is this a question merely of techniques, which for Herodotus were almost totally non-existent; it is also, and predominantly, a question of the different direction of interest fostered by a comparatively primitive and a highly complex and artificial civilisation. The Greeks, most inquisitive of peoples, were not, on the whole, much interested in the past simply because they were too intensely occupied with the present. A civilisation like our own, though it liberates a man from many of the pressures of living, at the same time softens the impact of the basic realities. Perforce nowadays we live largely at second hand, not knowing, or wishing to know, the processes which supply our needs, and not understanding, or wishing to understand, even if we could, the evidence upon which most of our current beliefs rest. The enormous amount which we take on trust must be obvious to anyone. The ancient Greek world was a small world, in which a man counted for something: he counted for something even if the tiny community in which he lived was governed by a despot; for there was always the hope that an opportunity might arise to stick a knife into the despot and have a revolution. And because it was a small world, what went on in it came home to a man's business and bosom in a way which is hardly possible for us today. Moreover it was not afflicted with the curse, unavoidable in modern conditions, of departmentalism. Every man had his public duties to perform, at least in the democratic communities, as politician and soldier. The Greeks had a word for those who avoided these duties: the word was 'idiot'. To all this we can add the extreme uncertainty amongst the ancients of the physical bases of life, the imminence of death by hunger, disease or violence, and the continual internecine feuds between neighbouring communities and between rival political parties within the same community, the whole sunlit scene shading off into a spirit-haunted darkness and a horror of the unknown—conditions of living which the Greeks seem to have accepted sometimes with a fierce joy, sometimes with a gloomy resignation to life's inevitable ills. It is not hard to see why they had little inclination to bother themselves with the past. The present filled them, and, if they did look to the past, it was through legend and myth, mainly local and particular, by which a community might connect its origin with a divine founder or a family with a divine ancestor.

Another reason why the Greeks were comparatively poor in historical writing is that they had no sense of the general march or development of human society. This difference between the Greeks and ourselves is important, and not easy to grasp. Time, for us, has been enormously extended by modern accretions of knowledge; our ability by means of geology, anthropology and other sciences to see, however dimly, into its dark backward and abysm, has necessarily affected our views of the development of man during the comparatively brief period he has been upon this earth. Evolution, in one form or another, is a part of our common mental furniture, and even the notion of progress, so fervently entertained in the hopeful years of the later 19th century, is not yet dead. At any rate we still believe that humanity is moving somewhere, even if not towards a better state. The odd identification of progress with material improvement has had, no doubt, to be seriously questioned recently; but we still know that our species is on the march, and that is progress of a kind; for one cannot but march forward even when the road leads back. The Greeks, when they looked back at all, looked back to a mythical Golden Age, since when they had steadily declined; nor did they fancy that Golden Age as very different in essentials from their own, except that men then were, so to put it, better at being men. The heroes who so splendidly walked the earth, sometimes in company with the gods, were but heightened images of themselves—better fighters, lustier lovers, bigger eaters and drinkers able to consume whole chines of beef and swallow honey-sweet wine by the barrelful, cunninger thieves, like the god Hermes, more ingenious tricksters in love or war. In short, they were fine fellows compared with their degenerate children. But any conception of a movement of humanity from primitive savagery to civilisation was absent from Greek thought, and when they looked at the future the Greeks saw it in the same terms as the present. In the political thought of the classical period, the City-state, for instance, had come to stay; and stay it did, till Alexander the Great left it in ruins. It is amusing to remember that Aristotle, who was Alexander's tutor, and whose reputation as a philosopher is still, I suppose, as high as most, laid it down in his *Politics* that no state should ever consist of more than 100,000 people; elsewhere, I believe, he said that a really satisfactory community should be small enough to allow everyone to know everyone else by name. That lesson, at any rate, his young pupil did not learn.

Lastly, the Greeks in general were not very much interested in countries and civilisations other than their own. They were aware, indeed, that the world was full of men, but the men were of two kinds only: Greeks and barbarians. The word 'barbarian' is itself a measure of their lack of interest: it means people whose unintelligible lingo sounds to a Greek ear like *bar-bar-bar*—or to borrow a more agreeable and imaginative comparison from Herodotus, like the twittering of birds. Unlike the Romans, who spoke Greek familiarly, the Greeks never seem to have bothered to learn a foreign language.

Herodotus overcame the disabilities imposed by time and place with astonishing success. Anyone can read his book with pleasure and profit, but the magnitude of his achievement can be grasped only by an imaginative reconstruction of the circumstances in which it was written. He was the first European historian and remains, in many respects, amongst the greatest; he was also—an achievement hardly less important—the first European writer to use prose as an artistic medium. The *art* of Greek prose was Herodotus' invention. English literature began, fully grown, with Chaucer; but Herodotus' achievement was greater than Chaucer's, because, unlike the Englishman who built his work on the solid foundation of the already long tradition of European literature, Herodotus had nothing to build upon at all. Prose had indeed been written before his time, and by others contemporary with him, 'logographers', as they were called—chroniclers, that is, of collections of facts in history and geography, the best known of whom were Hecataeus of Miletus, whom Herodotus often quotes, and Hellanicus; but the work of these men, only fragments of which survive, had no literary pretension. They were pioneers, seeking a form which would express what could not be satisfactorily expressed in poetry, and what they did was valuable; but it was left for Herodotus to take the strange, new medium of language freed from the lilt and melody of verse—verse, which is so easily memorised, so well adapted to recitation which, in those days when solitary reading was seldom, if ever, indulged in, was the only form of 'publication'—and to mould it into an instrument of the subtlest and most delicate art. Herodotus' prose has the flexibility, ease and grace of a man superbly talking, and it is the easiest Greek, with the possible exception of Homer's, for anyone with modest pretensions to scholarship to understand. That it should have the grace of heightened and superb speech is, moreover, no accident, for Herodotus, like the poets, wrote his book to be read aloud, not to be perused in the privacy of a man's study.

CHAPTER 2

Biographical

LITTLE IS KNOWN OF HERODOTUS' LIFE. HIS BIRTH-PLACE WAS
Halicarnassus, the modern Bodrum, originally a Carian town on
the south-west coast of Asia Minor; it was later occupied by
Dorian emigrants from Troezene, and became in time, like the
other Greek settlements on the eastern coast of the Aegean,
subject first to the Kings of Lydia and then, after the conquest
of the Lydian Kingdom by Cyrus the Great in 546 B.C., to the
Persian Empire. It was governed in Herodotus' time by a woman,
Artemisia, who was responsible to the local Persian satrap for
tribute in money and for the supply of troops on demand.

The date of Herodotus' birth was round about 480 B.C. or
perhaps a few years earlier, between, that is, the two Persian
attempts at the subjugation of Greece. The best, though not very
precise, evidence for this is an anecdote which Herodotus recounts
of a dinner-party given by a wealthy Theban called Attaginus to
fifty Persian grandees and fifty of his fellow-countrymen on the
eve of the battle of Plataea. Amongst the Greek guests was one
Thersander, a native of Orchomenus, and he was surprised and
much moved when a Persian, his neighbour at table, suddenly
said to him: 'You see these countrymen of mine eating and
drinking here—and the great army we have left in camp along
by the river? In a day or two from now, few of them will be left
alive.'

'I heard this story,' Herodotus adds, 'from Thersander himself.'
Thus Herodotus was old enough at any rate to have spoken
with men who took an active part in the war, though too young
to have been himself involved either in the fighting of 490 B.C.,
the year of Marathon, or in the campaigns of the second Persian
invasion, ten years later, under Xerxes.

He came of a good Halicarnassian family. Suidas, an only
moderately trustworthy information-monger, tells us that he was
related to a certain Panyasis, now forgotten, but apparently in

his day a man of letters not without repute, writing epic poetry and—which was perhaps more important for the young Herodotus—attempting rational explanations of dreams, portents and other phenomena which popular belief attributed to gods. Not that Herodotus was ever to become a rationalist; but the atmosphere of free inquiry was a natural and necessary element for his growing mind. Of far greater weight for his future development than his kinsman Panyasis, was the general intellectual climate of that portion of the Asiatic coast, especially of Miletus, a town some forty miles to the northward, founded long before by Ionian settlers from Attica. Asiatic Ionia was the true cradle of what was to prove most vital and permanent in the development of Greek and consequently of European civilisation; a man's right, namely, to inquire into, and to speculate upon, the enveloping mystery of his situation. Once reason, acting upon the data of the senses, is recognised as being one of the avenues towards truth and not in itself a forbidden or impious activity, a necessary consequence is the recognition of the individual as a person instead of a unit. Every thinker stands upon the shoulders of his predecessors, and though Anaximander, Anaximenes, Thales and the rest may have nothing directly to tell us today, with their guesses at water, or air, or 'the unlimited' as the first principle of the physical universe, yet they are the men who started Europe on its march away from the static and ant-like civilisations of the East. Their belief in the human intellect, a belief which in their own age was a revolutionary one, led to what we now know, for better or worse, as Western Man. Athens always felt a strong bond, not only of blood but also of the spirit, with Miletus; Herodotus relates that after its capture by the Persians in 494 B.C., the playwright Phrynichus produced at the Great Dionysia a tragedy on the theme of its fall. The Athenian spectators are said during the performance to have burst into tears. The play was banned, and Phrynichus fined a thousand drachmas for reminding his fellow-citizens of *their own* sorrows.

There is no means of knowing if the education of boys in grammar, gymnastics and music, which was generally accepted in Greece a few years later, had any equivalent in Halicarnassus during Herodotus' boyhood; but it is obvious from his History that he had a wide and deep knowledge of all available literature, both ancient and contemporary. He quotes or familiarly refers to in the course of his work such names as Hesiod, Sappho, Aeschylus and Pindar, with many others of less note, while his knowledge of the Iliad and Odyssey was evidently so much a part of his mind as to be almost unconscious. Such details, however, though dear to scholars, may perhaps be taken for granted, as it is not likely in any age that a man of letters will be ignorant of literature. Herodotus' real education—that part of it which differed from the education of his contemporaries—consisted in his travels, during which he saw, like Odysseus, 'many cities of men' and came to know their ways. To judge by the extent of these travels and the fact that they were over by the time he was forty, he must have begun them at an early age. The precise limits of the regions he visited have been disputed, but it is certain that he went to Babylon, penetrated deep into Upper Egypt, knew Thrace and parts of Scythia (southern Russia) as far East as the Crimea, and visited Cyrene on the north African coast. He was familiar with most of the Greek mainland, with southern Italy, the other countries of Asia Minor in addition to his native Caria, and all the more important islands of the Aegean, including, probably, Crete. So wide a first-hand knowledge of the world was a rare thing in Herodotus' day; indeed, I suppose it was unprecedented, except in the travels of Scylax, who left a book, now lost, in which he told, amongst other odd things, of certain Indian peoples whose ears were so big that they wrapped themselves up in them to sleep, and of others who, finding the heat of the sun inconvenient, used their large flat feet as parasols. Herodotus himself enjoyed a tall story; but he apparently drew the line at Scylax, for he made no use of his book.

About the year 447 B.C., when Herodotus was in his late thirties, he left Halicarnassus for good and went to live in Athens, then the intellectual centre of the Greek world. Halicarnassus had recently gone through one of the political revolutions which were endemic to Greek life, and had joined the Athenian confederacy, having got rid of her 'tyrants', as they were called, or irresponsible rulers, as Artemisia and her grandson Lygdamis had been. It was thus easier for Herodotus to find a welcome—though Athens always tended to be hospitable to strangers, especially to strangers who had something to give her. He had already written much of his *History*, and we are told that he gave public readings of it in Athens, and probably in other towns as well. Athens, under the leadership of Pericles, though her actual power, after the defeat at Coronea, had declined, was at the height of her glory and influence. Herodotus identified himself with what she stood for—political and intellectual liberty. He seems to have been admitted into the group of distinguished men of whom Pericles was the recognised leader, and he became a friend of Sophocles who (if we may believe Plutarch) wrote a poem in his honour. In all likelihood it was while he was in Athens that the final form of his *History* became clear in his mind; he had begun it as separate accounts of the manners, geography, monuments and antiquities of the various countries—Lydia, Egypt, Scythia and the rest—which he had visited, a work similar in kind to that of the Ionian logographers though larger in scope, and enriched by far more first-hand observation and direct inquiry; but now, caught up as he was by admiration of the Athenian spirit and of Athenian institutions, he determined so far as he could to make his wide and various researches subserve a master plan. This plan was to tell the story of the Persian wars, and in the course of the story to celebrate the decisive contribution of Athens to their successful outcome. Inevitably this left large portions of his work as merely episodical and digressive; but, happily for us, Herodotus was a superb digressor: the digressions are in themselves nearly always of fascinating interest, and he had the knack of beguiling his reader into a belief that some sort of thread, however slender, does, after all, connect them with the leading theme.

After four years in Athens he left for Italy, to return to Athens only once during the remainder of his life. Guesses have been made at the reasons for this removal: perhaps his funds were running low and he no longer felt able to maintain himself in the sort of Athenian society to which he had become accustomed; possibly he was irked at his political position—or rather *no* position, for it was not the Athenian custom to grant full citizenship to strangers. In any case, it so happened that just at this time Athens was determined to found under the auspices of Pericles a new settlement at Thurii on the gulf of Taranto in southern Italy, close to the site of the ancient town of Sybaris which half a century previously had been destroyed by its neighbours and rivals in Crotona. Herodotus went with the settlers and made

Thurii his home. Readers of Plato's dialogue the *Republic* will like to remember that amongst the settlers were the two sons of Cephalus, the old man so delightfully described in that book as reversing the common Greek attitude to old age by the declaration that to him, at any rate, as to the poet Sophocles, it was a sweet and welcome refuge from the savage tyranny of physical desires.

In Thurii Herodotus lived for the next fifteen years or so, travelling a little in Sicily and Italy, visiting Cyrene in North Africa, polishing his *History* and bringing it as near as he could to completion. Some time between 430 and 425 B.C. he died. The exact year cannot be determined, but that it was after 430 is proved by the mention in his book of certain events in the Peloponnesian war which occurred at or after that date, notably the betrayal of the Spartan and Corinthian ambassadors into the hands of the Athenians. Some commentators have tried to give him a much longer life; but it is hardly conceivable that, had he lived even to as late as 415, the year of the Athenian expedition to Sicily, he would have made no mention at all in his work of that irretrievable disaster to his beloved Athens. His tomb in Thurii had the inscription: 'This dust hides the body of Herodotus, son of Lyxes, and prince of old Ionian history. He sprang from a land of Dorian men, but fleeing from their scorn made Thurii his home.' It is a puzzling epitaph—but there are many puzzles, or rather blanks, in the life of Herodotus for us, who know so little. Why did the Dorian men of Halicarnassus scorn Herodotus? The word I have translated as 'scorn' might mean merely 'blame', and there was, to be sure, a story once current that Herodotus got into trouble with Lygdamis, the town's political boss, under the Persians, and was forced to take refuge in the island of Samos, before he finally went westward to the Greek mainland and Italy. The story goes on to say that he subsequently led an expedition back to his native town and expelled the despot, Lygdamis. What, then, of the 'scorn' or 'ridicule'? Rawlinson, one of the best nineteenth-century commentators on Herodotus, suggested that the whole Lygdamis tale was a myth to account for the dislike of despotic government which is everywhere apparent in Herodotus' book, and that the 'ridicule' of the epitaph was aroused, if it was aroused at all, by certain religious credulities revealed in the *History*: such credulities would not have been to the taste of the rising generation of free-thinkers in that part of the world.

With this meagre collection of biographical facts, and of even less satisfying bits of guess-work, we must be content. None the less, I suppose we are not content, requiring, as we have learnt to do of late, a kind of biography of famous men and women which would have made the ancients stare. The ancients did not feel—nor perhaps did the moderns before Rousseau wrote his *Confessions*—that there could be any permanent or public interest in the minutiae of personal life. A man's work, or his large acts on the world's stage, were all they thought worth remembering; and, if they wanted more, they were apt to invent a myth which would satisfy their fancy or their sense of fitness, like the story of Herodotus reading his *History* at the Olympic Games and of the boy Thucydides, as he listened, bursting into tears of admiration.

Let us admit, then, that we know less of Herodotus, in the way of biographical detail, even than we know of Shakespeare. Perhaps it does not matter; for, like Shakespeare, Herodotus might well say to any one of us,

> *My spirit is thine, the better part of me;*

for that spirit looks out from and greets us familiarly in every page of his book.

CHAPTER 3

Methods and Characteristics

THE WORD 'HISTORIA' MEANS IN GREEK AN INQUIRY, AND IT MIGHT be better if we kept for Herodotus' book the title which he himself gave to it: *The Inquiries of Herodotus*. To do so would at least remind us of one remarkable fact, that he gathered a great deal of the information which his book contains by asking questions. It would also suggest another fact: namely, that his book contains much which is not properly history at all.

Herodotus, like Lord Bacon though in a very different spirit, took all knowledge to be his province and pursued his inquiries into a great many different things, the results of all of them finding a place in his pages. He is concerned, for instance, not only with the events in a nation's past, but also with such diverse matters as the cause of earthquakes, boat-construction on the Euphrates, the height and thickness of the walls of Babylon, the size of the cables used for Xerxes' bridge across the Hellespont, the soundings thirty miles off the mouth of the Nile, and why mules cannot be bred in Elis. He is interested in geography and climate; he has an inkling of geological time, describing how Egypt, which he calls 'the gift of the Nile', has been built up by river silt during the course of ages; his curiosity leads him to investigate the substratum of fact in many legends, the cultural interrelationship of nations, the salient national characteristics of Egyptians, Persians or Greeks. For practical matters he has a quick and appreciative eye, describing with accuracy and gusto such things as the method of ship-building on the Nile, the raising into position of the enormous stone blocks used in the construction of the pyramids, the engineering common sense of the Phoenicians who were the only people to know how to dig Xerxes' canal through the promontory of Athos without letting the sides fall in. The odd fact never fails to fascinate him, whether it is the burial customs of the Kings of Scythia, a detail of religious observance in Egypt, how certain northern savages for lack of

34

wine intoxicate themselves with the fumes of hemp-seed, or what the goat did to the woman in the streets of Mendes. He loves a tale, and tells it like a master.

All this heterogeneous stuff, this mass of observed or reported detail collected over the years by his indefatigable researches and unflagging interest in what men do, and how they live, in every part of the known world, he has recorded with consummate art like a brilliant talker who, though seeming to be led out of his way by the incidence and associations of some chance idea, is yet revealed to a careful listener to have kept the thread of his discourse. He has worked his miscellaneous material, like the coloured threads of a tapestry, in with the epic story of a crucial period of European history, told not only with a marvellous approximation to truth but also with a transforming moral passion and a sense of life—of the actual immediacy of the words and doings of men—seldom surpassed in any literature.

I suppose all historical writing might be called an approximation to truth, for the past must always remain, in a very real sense, unknowable. A man's least act, let alone a nation's, is precipitated by a thousand interanimating impulses in himself and his surroundings; we can know the act, or what we call the act, as a thing-in-itself or isolated phenomenon; but isolate any phenomenon, and you kill it: it becomes at once insignificant and dead. The living act is an integral part of the passions and impulses which led to it, and upon which it is only a sort of brusque and hurried commentary. History is compelled to deal with those commentaries and to make the best of them. The life behind remains elusive and beyond its grasp. Much historical writing has the same sort of relation to the past as the sludge left in a net which has been trailed behind a boat at sea has to the actual life of the moving and generative waters: the algae and the animalcules are there, caught, isolated, inspectable, and dead. It is this which brings about the necessity for an art, as well as a science, of history, if the past is, in any real sense, to live for us again. It is fashionable today to give the science of history pre-eminence, mainly, no doubt, because of the vast accumulation of knowledge made possible by modern techniques and methods of research; it can hardly be otherwise in an age which trusts the specialist as implicitly as ours does, but it also drives some of us, who are not specialists, into revolt and a longing for something of a different quality. We may be grateful for the facts and know that they are indispensable; but we also look around for somebody who will animate them for us, and put them back so to speak, into those generative waters from which they were drawn up by the drag-net. Just as poetry, according to Aristotle, is the most philosophic of the arts, so history is, or can be, the most poetic of the sciences.

Thus, if we want knowledge *about* the ancient world, we must turn to the scientific historians, to the archaeologists and palaeographers, to the decipherers of Linear B and the devoted men who have found Mycenaean pottery at Acragas and Syracuse, or established trade-relations in the neolithic age between Crete and the Aegean islands by evidence of the export of obsidian from Melos; but if we want knowledge *of* the ancient world, we must turn to historians of a different kind. Of these the first and best is Herodotus, in whose pages we get, over and above a mass of historical and legendary information, an immediacy of impression and a sense of life in the actual living of it, which scientific history cannot give. In any estimate of Herodotus this should be the starting point. De Quincey, I remember, divided literature into what he called 'books of knowledge' and 'books of power'; Herodotus' *History*, though it contains in its five or six hundred pages as much factual knowledge of the ways of his world as they can well hold, belongs unquestionably to the second category. It is a book of power, in that Herodotus was able to enter imaginatively—that is, with sympathy and delight—into the doings of men, fellow-countrymen or foreigners, in this fascinating, mysterious and half-intelligible world, and had at the same time in full control the art which would open the doors into that world for us, his readers. It is this that makes Herodotus a great figure not only amongst European historians but in European literature generally.

Until recently it was a commonplace of criticism to contrast the severely intellectual Thucydides with the naïve Herodotus and his charming story-telling. It would be absurd to impugn the intellectual power of Thucydides—though the impression of it is no doubt enhanced by the refusal, in his political disquisitions (or the imaginary speeches in which they are embodied) ever to call a spade a spade, and his determination to cram as much meaning into as small a space as possible, so that his tightly knotted sentences irked the patience even of Quintilian, the Roman critic and man of letters, to whom Greek was as familiar as French, say, is to us; nevertheless no sensitive modern reader, however willing to grant Thucydides his due, could fail to realise that for sheer intellectual stature Herodotus was by far his superior. That Herodotus, with the means at his disposal, should, first, conceive the possibility of a universal history, then gather materials for it, and, finally, organise the whole mass of his information into a great drama—episodical, indeed, but all tending to one end—of the conflict between East and West and their irreconcilable modes of life and thought, was a prodigious feat.

The means at Herodotus' disposal were crude and scanty. Precisely what use, if any, he made of the fairly numerous writers —'logographers', geographers, myth-mongers—contemporary with, or a little older than, himself, is not possible to say. Some of them we know from notices which have come down to us, or from surviving fragments, to have covered ground which Herodotus covered: Charon, for instance, a native of Lampsacus, wrote a history of Persia; Xanthus, a history of Lydia, Dionysius of Miletus another history of Persia. There are many others—to us mere names—who might have recorded information which would have been useful to Herodotus; but it is rash to assume that because a book had been written Herodotus was necessarily acquainted with it. Publication, as I have already said, did not exist in Herodotus' day, except through the act of public recitation, and the copying or multiplication of books was too laborious a process to be undertaken lightly. Herodotus, moreover, was always ready enough to admit indebtedness, (he quotes the poets freely) but the only other prose writer he mentions—mainly to disagree with him—is the historian and geographer Hecataeus.

We can assume, then, that though Herodotus took from other men the *idea* of writing history, a precious theft, he took little of the actual stuff; or, if he did take any, he so transformed it (to judge by the scraps which survive) as to make it unrecognisable. This by itself suggests the chasm which separates the task confronting Herodotus with that which confronts a modern historian, who stands on the shoulders of his predecessors, whose works he may read, while for new information he relies upon the discovery of original documents, or the reinterpretation of known

ones. Herodotus had few predecessors, and few documents apart
from monuments and inscriptions were available to him, at least
so far as the Asiatic parts of his history are concerned. He was
left, therefore, to collect his information by personal and direct
inquiry. It seems a daunting process; but by Herodotus it was
indefatigably pursued over a period of many years. Is it possible
by such methods to gather materials for anything like a reliable
and veracious history? The answer must be, of course, a qualified
no. Herodotus knew no foreign languages, so all his talk with
Egyptians, Assyrians and the rest was through interpreters;
moreover, the kind of information he received—and, no doubt,
expected to receive—bore little resemblance to what our own
times have learnt to regard as history: it was much more akin
to popular tradition. To take an instance, the story of the treasury
of the Pharaoh Rhampsinitus*: this admirable story is hardly
likely to be true; but—and this is the thing to remember—it
was a popular belief current in the streets of Memphis in the
fifth century before Christ, and doubtless for centuries before
that, and as such it has its value. For what men like to believe
about themselves and their country is assuredly a part of history.

Herodotus is usually quite honest in this respect: 'It is said,'
'I was told' are constantly recurring phrases in his book, and
again and again he tells us that he heard two contradictory ver-
sions, or more, of the same story. When that is so, his practice
is to give them both, or all of them, sometimes indicating which
in his own opinion is the more likely to be true, sometimes
leaving the reader to take his choice. Often he tells a tale, and
then adds, with a smile no reader can fail to be aware of: 'But I
don't believe a word of it.' Popular tradition, then, but popular
tradition seen through very acute Grecian eyes: that is the substance of the narrative parts of Herodotus' account of foreign
countries.

Apart from the value and interest of popular tradition for its
own sake, it is worth remembering that for the Greek world,
at any rate, modern research has in many instances confirmed it.
A hundred years ago no scholar believed in the historical reality
of the Trojan war, an incident of primary importance in the
Greek oral tradition of later times. Schliemann's work on the
site at Hissarlik proved beyond a doubt that the old tale was

* See Appendix II for the story in full.

based solidly upon fact. It was the same with the legendary Minos, and the brilliant civilisation in Crete, revealed to modern eyes so spectacularly by Sir Arthur Evans' excavations at Cnossos. It may well be that future archaeological research will prove many a statement of Herodotus, which scholars have hitherto taken as guess-work or fairy-tale, to be substantially true: for instance, his statement that the mysterious Etruscans came originally from Lydia.

The reader, then, should at least be cautious in accepting what Herodotus tells him of the past history of countries not his own, though there is no reason for doubting the veracity of anything which he says he has seen with his own eyes. He is an honest reporter, and, if someone has told him about

> Anthropophagi and men whose heads
> Do grow beneath their shoulders,

he will, as likely as not, pass on the information to amuse us, adding that, in his own view, his informant was a liar. For geographical details of places he has not visited, he usually demands the first-hand evidence of an eye-witness; he will not, for instance, admit the existence of a sea to the north of Europe, because, as he puts it, 'I have been unable to get a report of it from anyone who has actually been there.'

In dealing with Greek history Herodotus is on much firmer ground. Here, too, there is a good deal of legendary matter, for some of which he attempts a rational explanation, but for his main historical narrative, which can be taken as beginning with the accession of Cyrus to the Persian throne—only about a hundred years before his own time—he has a considerable mass of documentary evidence to rely upon. The chief source of this was, first, the lists of priests, kings and victors in the various national games of Greece which were kept in many of the principal Greek cities and shrines, and, secondly, the great number of inscribed votive offerings which were to be found not only at the national shrines in Delphi and Olympia but also in the public squares and temples of countless Greek towns. Often the inscriptions would contain historical details of great value, by which Herodotus could check such accounts as he had received by word of mouth: one example would be the gold and bronze tripod dedicated to Apollo after the victory over the

Persians at Plataea, and having engraved upon it the names of the Greek communities who played a part in the struggle. For such things too as the fabled wealth of Croesus and his pro-Grecian sympathies he could in this way find confirmation; everyone who has read his book remembers the pleasant story of Alcmaeon the Athenian who was invited by Croesus to take from his treasury in Sardis as much gold as he could carry at one time, and of how Alcmaeon put on a large loose tunic with a baggy front and a pair of the widest top-boots he could find, and, thus clad, entered the treasury and proceeded to attack a heap of gold-dust, cramming into his boots as much as they would hold, filling the front of his tunic full, sprinkling the dust in his hair, stuffing more into his mouth, and then staggered out scarcely able to drag one foot after the other and looking, with his bulging cheeks and swollen figure, like (as Herodotus puts it) anything rather than a man. That is one way of telling us of the wealth of Croesus—who burst out laughing at the appearance of his guest, and promptly doubled the gift—and it is very much in Herodotus' manner; but it is good to know at the same time that the point of the anecdote is confirmed by what Herodotus saw with his own eyes at Delphi—the image of a lion in gold weighing 570 lb., amongst other priceless gifts from the Lydian King, including a mixing-bowl of pure silver with a capacity of 5,000 gallons.

Of the more serious errors which Herodotus makes in his history of foreign countries I will speak when I come to describe his accounts of them; but his history of Greece, derived as it was from oral tradition and, in its more recent phases, either from the accounts of eye-witnesses or at second-hand from the fathers and grandfathers of men with whom he had spoken, and checked wherever possible by such records and inscriptions as I have mentioned, can be taken as substantially true. Such accuracy of detail as modern historical criticism expects is of course not to be looked for; for instance, his assessment of numbers is not only inaccurate but often absurd, in particular his assessment of the numbers of Xerxes' army. But perhaps in this he is like most of us, who, when we are not on oath, talk of millions when we mean a great many. The fighting force which accompanied Xerxes into Greece Herodotus puts at something over two and a half million men, and the camp-followers and crews of the provision-ships at another two and a half million, while as for eunuchs (he adds), female cooks and the soldiers' women, no one could attempt an estimate of their number. No wonder in their thirsty passage through Thrace and Thessaly, with their multitudes of horses and Indian dogs, they drank the rivers dry. Such passages one must read in the spirit in which, I suppose, they were written, and allow them their emotive effect. Modern scholars put the number of Xerxes' army at about 300,000 men.

However it was not for this sort of innocent falsification of fact that the Father of History came to be known as the Father of Lies. It was for a much more characteristically human reason, namely, that the tone of Herodotus' book is strongly pro-Athenian, and the enemies of Athens, very naturally, resented what they considered this absurd prejudice and did what they could to discredit the author of it.

CHAPTER 4

The Question of Bias

LUCIAN IN HIS ESSAY 'ON HOW TO WRITE HISTORY' SAID THAT THE ideal historian should be 'fearless, incorruptible and free; outspoken and the friend of truth, calling a spade a spade; uninfluenced by likes or dislikes or any sort of emotional consideration; a fair and impartial judge who will never give to one side more than its due; a man, so far as his writings are concerned, belonging to no country and owing allegiance to no master; king over himself, determined to state not what will please the reader of his choice, but the plain fact only.'

Lucian had Thucydides in mind when he wrote those words, and coming from a Greek they embody a not ignoble conception of the historian's task. Few Greeks were impartial, and no Greek was ever uninfluenced by emotional considerations. Nevertheless it is doubtful if such Olympian impartiality as Lucian looked for, or pretended to look for, would, even if it were possible, really be a desirable quality in a historian who wished to be read. 'The plain fact only' . . . It sounds an honest demand; but the plain fact is, that in the story of mankind there are no plain facts. We know, indeed, that Greece repelled the two Persian assaults upon her territory, and you may call that a plain fact, if you will; but it is of minor interest until we also know, or think we know, the conditions in Greece which made her success possible, and to which of her conflicting, disputatious and mainly self-centred little communities that success was due. Here is matter for opinion and opinion is not impartial, being governed by a host of predilections, prejudices, passions and beliefs which go to make up the temper of a man's mind. And it is the temper of the historian's mind which, other things being equal, ultimately gives value to his history; it is this which wins, or repels, readers.

In this sense, then, Herodotus was not impartial at all. He honoured and admired Athens above any of the other Greek towns; disliking any form of despotic government, he found his sympathies won, and kept, by the democratic institutions and the spirit of free inquiry which underlay the structure of Athenian life. This led him to magnify the part played by Athens in the Persian wars—and he justified his view in a well-known passage of his book: 'At this point,' he wrote, leading up to the magnificently narrated climax of his story, 'I find myself compelled to express an opinion which I know most people will object to; nevertheless, as I believe it to be true, I will not suppress it. If the Athenians, through fear of the approaching danger, had abandoned their country, or if they had stayed there and submitted to Xerxes, there would have been no attempt to resist the Persians by sea; and in the absence of a Greek fleet it is easy to see what would have been the course of events on land. However many lines of fortification the Spartans had built across the Isthmus, they would have been deserted by their confederates; not that their allies would have wished to desert them, but they could not have helped doing so, because one by one they would have fallen victims to the Persian naval power. Thus the Spartans would have been left alone—to perform prodigies of valour and die nobly. Or, on the other hand, it is possible that before things came to the ultimate test, the sight of the rest of Greece submitting to Persia might have driven them to make terms with Xerxes. In either case the Persian conquest of Greece would have been assured; for I cannot myself see what possible use there could have been in fortifying the Isthmus, if the Persians had command of the sea. In view of this, therefore, one is surely right in saying that Greece was saved by the Athenians. It was the Athenians who held the balance: whichever side they joined was sure to prevail. It was the Athenians, too, who having chosen that Greece should live and preserve her freedom, roused to battle the other Greek states which had not yet submitted. It was the Athenians who, after God, drove back the Persian King. Not even the terrifying warnings of the oracle at Delphi could persuade them to abandon Greece; they stood firm, and had the courage to meet the invader.'

'Most people' did indeed object to this eloquent passage, for the obvious reason that most people were not Athenians. And it was this passage together with others in the same spirit which led, understandably enough in the divided Greek world, to calumnies against Herodotus and the general calling into question of his veracity. It would have been quite feasible for a Spartan, relying upon Sparta's part in the victory of Plataea and her noble defeat at Thermopylae, to make out a case for Sparta as the saviour of Greece. However that may be, Herodotus made no bones about it; he came down clearly and firmly on what he knew, when he wrote, would be the unpopular side. For him it was Athens, and Athens alone, to whom Greece owed her survival. If this is partiality then I should venture to say that partiality of a sort is a valuable quality in a historian. From the point of view of historical accuracy, it does not matter a button to which side the historian is emotionally or intellectually committed, provided his commitment does not lead him actually to conceal or falsify known facts; but it does make a great difference to the life and meaning of the story. If Herodotus had by temperament been committed to the Spartan way of life, to that dour and unillumined community of 'military monks', as Pater called them, he could by no possibility have written the book he did. His preference for Athens was a necessary consequence of his general outlook upon life and the world, of his own liberal and inquiring mind. No pro-Spartan writer could have conceived a world history in the spirit in which Herodotus conceived it, so that it is hardly fanciful to say that his marked partiality for Athens—the very thing which caused her enemies and rivals to represent him as a distorter of the truth—was, properly considered, only an aspect of its opposite; for the fundamental impartiality of Herodotus' mind is one of the most remarkable things about him. This is not to say that he did not care: he cared passionately for the Greek tradition, for his own vision of the divine and mysterious governance of things, and for Greek individuality and experimentalism in philosophy and politics as opposed to the ancient and static civilisations of the East. His sense of values was sharp and clear, but at the same time he was slow to judge and still slower to condemn. He never gives the impression of thinking that Greece—or any other nation—is in possession of the whole truth, but conveys his assurance implicitly or explicitly, that all nations, like all individuals, may have contributions to make to the sum of knowledge. The wisdom of Egypt or Babylonia or Persia is not the wisdom of Greece, but let us not suppose, he seems to tell us, that it is therefore nugatory. 'We tend,' wrote Tacitus the

Roman, 'to magnify in fancy what is unknown, to imagine it as something impressive or tremendous;' Herodotus' way was a different one: it was to tackle the unknown in a much more direct and businesslike manner—to go and see it, in fact, fully prepared to discover that it was by no means necessarily either tremendous or impressive, but quite certainly of fascinating interest.

This breadth of sympathy is one of the chief characteristics of Herodotus' work, and it is an uncommon quality in ancient Greek literature, which in general, despite the intrinsic brilliance and seminal power of the best of it, had a certain insularity. Educated Greeks in Herodotus' time were no doubt aware of certain cultural and intellectual debts they owed to foreigners: that Chaldaea, for instance, had set them on the path towards the study of astronomy, and that Egyptians had invented geometry long before the Greeks themselves had even heard of it; and they probably acknowledged a debt to Egypt and Phoenicia in the matter of shipbuilding—if ever they bothered to stop and think about it. Nevertheless in reading Greek literature one is nearly always aware of its separateness, of the wall shutting in the Greek intellectual world from the spaces beyond, of the spectacle of a fervid life played upon a floodlit stage, surrounded by darkness. In that darkness lived—of course—the *barbarians*, strange and ignorant men, menacing at all times in a dark and dangerous way. 'Such are all foreigners,' Euripides makes Hermione exclaim in his *Andromache*; 'fathers lie with daughters, sons with mothers, sisters with brothers; kinsmen murder each other, and they have no law to prevent such things.' It is a somewhat sweeping statement, even if one grants its dramatic propriety. Herodotus' approach is different; he had, to be sure, much to say about the odd practices of foreigners, not excluding the lunatic excesses of Cambyses in Egypt; but his tone is never the tone of indignation, but rather that of the curious and interested observer. 'Now isn't that odd', he seems to say. 'Would you ever have thought that people could behave like that—but they do, you know.' And as he says it, the darkness which surrounded the floodlit stage thins away, and the reader is aware that the 'barbarians' for all their unintelligible twittering, are men and women, subject to the same passions and the same chances as himself. It is a wonderful widening of horizons.

In all his judgements Herodotus is singularly free from the characteristic Greek national arrogance—and 'national' arrogance meant, for a Greek, a sense of the superiority of his own tiny community to those of his neighbours. In spite of his partiality for Athens he is always careful to give every other state its due, wherever it is possible to do so, going out of his way, for instance, to praise the gallantry of the Thebans—no favourites of the Athenians, who popularly referred to them as Boeotian pigs—at the battle of Plataea, and assigning the prize of valour at Salamis (a notably Athenian victory, if ever there was one) to the contingent from Corinth. Still more remarkable is his account of the Persians, the terrible enemy around whose defeat his whole history is constructed; he is full of admiration for their personal qualities, for many of their institutions, and for their courage, laying the blame for their military reverses not upon a lack of bravery or devotion to duty, in which he declares they were fully the equals of the Greeks, but upon their inferior equipment and inadequate training. His own native Caria had been under Persian dominion, yet his whole picture of the Persian character, highly elaborated and delicately shaded, is, for its breadth of sympathy and understanding, a most unusual achievement not only for an ancient writer but for a writer in any age. National prejudices and blimpery are not confined to any one period of history, but Herodotus is innocent of both; it comes, I suppose, from his evident pleasure in the sheer variety and spectacle of life, his almost childlike delight, joined with an exceedingly adult and comprehensive intellect, in the bright immediacy of things, in human character and achievement, in the splendour and folly of men's hopes, in the pathos of their almost inevitable disappointment.

CHAPTER 5

The Greek Feeling for Life

IT WOULD BE INSTRUCTIVE IF WE COULD SUMMON FROM THE underworld an intelligent representative of some of the successive cultures of the ancient world, a Hittite, say, an Assyrian, an Egyptian, an old Minoan, a Lydian, a Persian and a Greek, and ask them what they understood by the word civilisation. They might reply that though they had learned by conversation with the many souls of many races who had joined them since their departure from the upper air, that we of the modern world were much concerned with the word and liked to argue about the various concepts it was supposed to include, for them it was too vague and abstract to have much significance. Even the Greek might tell us that, in his day, his people had no word in their language equivalent to it. Perhaps, then, all we meant to ask them was what they felt the good life to be? How much, if at all, does it depend upon such things as commercial prosperity, or military power, upon material resources and the knowledge and skill to use them? To what extent do moral considerations enter into the composition of it? Does it consist in the effort to make the most of what one has, or in the struggle to get more? To accept one's condition, or to try to improve it? Again, is the foundation of the good life political, or personal? Which should take precedence in it, the individual or the state? Is it more important to get control over circumstances and the inimical forces of nature than over the even more mysterious and recalcitrant enemy, the human psyche? Has mere *size*—the size of a City state, of an empire, of a man's balance at the bank—anything or nothing to do with the good life, or with the satisfaction and sense of fulfilment which must be presumed to accompany it? Is the belief that a man should be his brother's keeper merely an invention of the Christian conscience, or is it an integral part of human goodness in all times and conditions? Is the notion of 'security', of which we in the modern world make such a palaver, in any way connected with the good life, or is it wholly irrelevant?

One could think of many more questions of this sort, which one would like to ask, in spite of the danger of the Hittite, the Assyrian and the Egyptian answering them only with a blank stare. The other ghosts, however, the Minoan, the Lydian, the Persian and the Greek would probably be prepared to do their best to help us. The Greek at any rate would have plenty to say, all of it to the point and much of it surprising. It would be surprising, I think, partly because the values which the Greeks attached to things were so very different from our own, and partly because we have been led by the arrogance of scholars, working in a difficult and highly specialised subject, to accept too readily their generalisations. Moreover the current view of an ancient civilisation is dependent upon a number of contemporary preconceptions: upon the colour, so to say, of the spectacles through which successive generations look at it. To a greater extent than we like to admit, we see what we want to see. Even God, the Greeks said, cannot alter the past; men, however, alter it constantly. For instance, we are not likely nowadays to imitate our great-grandfathers and imagine the citizens of, say, Athens as a godlike race of infinite dignity and calm, like the statues of Pheidias, living a life of philosophic leisure and leaving the dirty work to a horde of unmentioned and unmentionable slaves. We can still be thankful for the art of Pheidias, but we are at least ready to recognise that—as Heracleitus guessed in the 6th century B.C.—a moment of apparent calm may be the result of fierce opposing tensions, and that the Greeks were fond of saying 'Nothing too Much' only because they were naturally given to excess. Even Keats, who was fitted by nature though not by learning to understand the Greeks, misled us by his beautiful description of the little town 'mountain-built with peaceful citadel', for the little town would never even have possessed a citadel had there been any chance of five consecutive days of peace.

There were dark gods in ancient Greece as well as the Olympians; and many a Greek of the great days—indeed most, I fancy—would have split his sides with laughing, as we ourselves do, at Aristotle's absurd and reverential description in his *Ethics*, of the Magnanimous Man or Megalopsych: one remembers

Archilochus, for instance, and the salty verses in which he described the sort of fighter he best liked to lead him into battle: 'Give me,' he cried, 'a stout little fellow, planted firmly on bandy legs, and full of guts.' And one remembers the terror and anguish of the old nurse in Euripides' *Hippolytus*, when she first knows of Phaedra's love: 'Oh that men might care for each other with gentleness and affection—without the passion which pierces to the quick and marrow of our life!' That passion—and nobody has ever known better than the Greeks its power to destroy—that laughter at such things as Aristotle's lapse into humbug and absurdity, that gay and practical rejection by Archilochus of a military leader who was a long-legged dandy in favour of a man who knew his business whatever he might be to look at: these things, added to the ubiquitous evidences in Greek literature of quarrelsomeness, of the passion for notoriety, of zest for doing one's neighbour down, accompanied all the time with a fierce appetite for life's immediacies and a profound and gloomy sense of the precariousness of a man's hold upon all that makes it worth living, are as Greek as the Parthenon; and no doubt, if we had the wit to disentangle them we should see them as elements in the serene perfection of that building. A few ancient Greeks in one of our modern cities might have a number of things to teach us, but they would be uncomfortable companions, playing the catfish to not a few of our cherished beliefs, and asking us, may be, how we can think to change the nature of a thing by changing its name, or why we refuse to admit that self-interest is still the motive of action both in individuals and in nations, or why we shut our eyes to the plain fact that if one scratches a civilised man, one finds him still a savage. Incidentally, such visitants would welcome our moon-rockets and motor cars with wonder and delight, while our absorption in money-making they would laugh off as childish, especially when they discovered that we seldom had very clear notions of what we wished to do with the money when we had made it.

Perhaps we are more restless, more disillusioned than our grandfathers were; less prone to idealise what we only half understand, or to take things on trust; but whatever the reason may be, there is something in the modern temper which drives us to look for, and to find, in what survives for us of the ancient world the kind of qualities which I have, almost at random, suggested. Thanks to the increasing number of translations, more people read Greek books today than ever before—and they read them, moreover, not with the spurious awe due to 'the classics', but simply as books, as the record of certain men's experience. That experience may, to the modern reader, appear now as universally valid and intelligible, now as odd, sometimes as merely shocking; but he reads with sympathy, knowing it was the experience of men. He looks less for the finished perfection of what has been called 'the Greek miracle', and more for the elements, some of them disagreeable enough, which went to compose it. His spectacles (to repeat my metaphor) are like prisms, and break up into all sorts of startling and unexpected colours the white radiance of classicism. And he finds, if he is lucky, that over this infinitely varied world, in spite of its deep fundamental pessimism, its cruelty and bloody-mindedness, its harsh opportunism, its lust and greed, its physical squalor and the poverty which was endured to make such things as the Propylaea and the Parthenon economically possible, and even, perhaps, the magnificent public buildings in the far wealthier cities of the Asiatic coast: he finds, I say, that in spite of these things there lies over the world of the ancient Mediterranean civilisations an indescribable light: a lightness almost, a sort of insouciance and uncloyed zest in the here and now, in the actual and immediate, in what is within the grasp of a man or woman. That lightness I speak of, though the roots of these civilisations went back to an immemorial past, through massacre and blood and the migrations of peoples, through the neolithic age to the age of bronze and the coming of the Dorians in the age of iron, yet seems to belong to a youth which the world will never again know.

This sense of youth is felt by modern travellers even in the ruins of it which survive, like a whispered word of grace out of the past; it flashes out to us continually from Greek literature, even from the hag-ridden magnificences of a tragedy of Aeschylus, or from Sophocles' impassioned brooding upon human destiny. It comes to us most purely, perhaps, in the things which the Greeks made, in their architecture, sculpture, jewellery, pottery, coins, and in the surviving fragments of the lyric poetry of the sixth and seventh centuries before Christ, and one guesses at its presence in the voices of the men and women and children who spoke the Greek tongue. To call it a quality of youth is perhaps a misleading metaphor; it may be that I fell to the use of it only because all the records of that civilisation bring us a sense that the creators of it never suffered from the satiety of declining years; they seem always to have lived within their moment, filling it. Not till the latter years of the fifth century, when the old world was already beginning to crumble, did their delighted curiosity about the physical universe and themselves turn to doubt and self-questioning—both eminently characteristic of modern man. How to 'live well' was a familiar inquiry amongst the later Greek philosophers, but we in our more burdened and disillusioned age cannot but feel that the men of those old civilisations needed no philosopher to tell them the answer. They instinctively knew it; and they knew it, I fancy, for the simple reason that their vitality was unimpaired. They did not know that emptiness of spirit which hopes that tomorrow may bring some gift to fill it. 'Happiness' is amongst the most slippery of words, but these peoples assuredly knew a *kind* of happiness which is lost to us today, and was beginning to darken even when Thucydides wrote his history of the Peloponnesian War. It was beginning to darken with the first coming of doubt in the validity of present experience; and the glad confident morning was never to return.

The old Greeks had their dark superstitions, their hauntings and terrors; but these made the sunlight only the more desirable. Plato with his doctrine of the reality of the unseen belongs to the decadence of the pagan world, which in its vigour loved things passionately for what they were—or as passionately hated them. For the earlier ages there was no division between what is and what seems, no suspicion that mortal life might, after all, be a sham. When Pindar called it the dream of a shadow, he used his beautiful metaphor only to point its brevity, the transitoriness of this gift of God, and not at all to call in question its worth.

This unquestioning acceptance of the actual, whether good or bad, explains another thing—the *unfleshliness* of early Greek love-poetry. For them there was no dichotomy of material and spiritual, and therefore no need either to over-emphasise physical passion or, on the other hand, to idealise it. Modern preoccupation with the physical comes from a failure of power and a sense of guilt. The Greek lyric poets suffered from neither. The excellence of every art, Keats said, is its intensity, making all disagreeables evaporate by being in close contact with beauty and truth. So it was with the Greeks: accepting without question the physical basis of life, they were therefore able to raise and rarefy it. The lyric poet Alcman, by birth a Lydian, left the fragment of a poem lamenting his lost youth. 'Girls,' he says (to translate the lines into bare prose), 'girls with honey-sweet voices which speak of love, my limbs no longer bear me up. Would I were a gull, the sea-dark bird of spring, flying with careless heart over the blossom of the waves.' What makes these lines so essentially Greek, in their passion and restraint—the one being the complement of the other—is the coolness of the imagery, which yet carries its full effect. It is the memory of girls' *voices* which holds for the poet his vanished pleasures: and then, after the first lament, comes the image of the gull, so cool, so remote, so disembodied, yet relevant and revealing. To have this quality of feeling—and it is common in the early Greek poets—is, to borrow an English poet's phrase, to live in eternity's sunrise. The secret of it is irrecoverable today by us, who are so much more civilised than ever the Greeks were. Perhaps we know too much, or too many of the wrong things; perhaps we *have* too much, and consequently get confused in our values; perhaps having discovered more sources of guilt than the Greeks were aware of, we wrap our experiences in so many folds of anxious and half-conscious moralising that they can only with difficulty struggle through. The Greek playwrights have many a song in which the singer prays that love, if it comes, may come benignly and without his destroying fires; but how puzzled they would have been by the theme and treatment of eighty per cent of modern fiction. It would have seemed to them an inordinate fuss about nothing.

'When I wake in the morning,' said D. H. Lawrence, 'and say to myself, "I wish I were rich", I know that my vitality is low.' Lawrence made a number of sensible remarks in the course of his voluminous works, and that is not the least sensible of them. Possibly it might serve as a starting-point for a study of ancient Greece. It is one of the objects of this book to observe this quality, this unimpaired appetite for life, in the Greeks of the ancient Mediterranean world, on the mainland, in the islands, in Sicily and Southern Italy, on the coasts of Anatolia and the Black Sea, and to consider what they achieved by the help of it. Herodotus will be my friendly guide.

CHAPTER 6

Scepticism and Credulity in Herodotus

ONE WAY IN WHICH THE ARTIST DIFFERS FROM THE REST OF US IS
that he knows better than we do what to leave out. A sculptor,
knowing which bits of stone are irrelevant to his purpose, chips
them away. Knowledge of what to leave out makes the difference
between a good talker or a successful raconteur and a bore;
between a good book and a ragbag of information or gossip.
A good book may deal with all sorts of peripheral matters, but
the reader perceives, or comes in the end to perceive, that the
line they follow is indeed a periphery—the circumference of a
circle which, by the nature of things, has a centre.

The Greeks possessed this knowledge in a high degree. We
commonly call it a sense of form, which is as good a term as any.
It was the sense which led their first philosophers to seek a single
principle underlying the bewildering multiplicity of the visible
world; it was the cause of their delight in the beautiful shapeliness of mathematics—NO ONE ADMITTED, said the notice
over the door of Plato's Academy, WHO HAS NOT STUDIED
GEOMETRY. It was one cause, also, and not the least important,
of the excellence of their best literature. The best Greek writers
did not over-elaborate or fluff; they said what they wanted to
say, clearly and directly, and left it at that, assuming that readers
would take their point. The assumption would perhaps be a
rasher one today than it was then, for modern readers are jaded
and need artificial, or artful, stimulus to keep them awake.
They too often want what might be called emotional rhetoric,
as well as verbal rhetoric: it is not always safe for a modern
writer, if he hopes to hold attention, to leave things alone. He is
tempted to make mountains out of what for a Greek would have
been a molehill, a spiced dish for what would have been a plain
Greek loaf. This leads some modern readers to fancy that Greek
literature is cold—a great mistake. It has a cool surface, but that
is a very different thing. The molten earth has a cool surface too.

The moon is down
And the Pleiades;

It is midnight and the hour has passed;
Yet I sleep alone.

In that lyric of Sappho's the irrelevant bits of stone have been chipped away indeed. A single image suffices: moon-set—hope-set.

Herodotus, as I have already said, had no literary guides to follow, and the scope and contents of his book, containing, as it does, such a mass of miscellaneous information on any subject likely to interest an inquiring mind, would tend to make it formless, at any rate in the hands of a less competent artist. All the more remarkable is the skill with which he has succeeded in subduing this heterogeneous material to the service of his central theme. His sun, so to speak, has sufficient power of attraction to keep his unruly planets in orbit. The opening sentence announces his theme: 'In this book, the result of my inquiries into history, I hope to do two things: to preserve the memory of the past by putting on record the astonishing achievements both of our own and of the Asiatic peoples; secondly, and more particularly, to show how the two races came into conflict.' That sentence, though it stands at the beginning, was certainly not the first to be written; for there can be little doubt as I have said that Herodotus began by intending to amplify the work of the logographers and to produce separate accounts of the various countries which he included in his travels. But suddenly, it seems, perhaps when much was already written, by a flash of inspiration, or simply by that innate Greek sense of form and shapeliness which in Herodotus was as vigorous as in any other Greek writer or artist, he saw his work as an organised whole. The unruly planets began in his mind to circle obediently about their sun.

The scheme of the book is very simple. Herodotus begins with an account of Lydia, the first foreign power to come into direct contact with the Asiatic Greeks; the defeat of Croesus, the last King of Lydia, by Cyrus the Great of Persia brings him on to the road which leads straight to the climax of his story—the triumphant struggle of little and divided Greece against the vast resources of the Persian empire under Darius and Xerxes. The description of the rapid growth of Persian power serves a double purpose: first historical, as it enables the historian to tell what he knows of the various countries—Egypt, Babylonia, Scythia (portions of southern Russia), North Africa, the more easterly of the Aegean islands—which were invaded or subdued by the successive Persian Kings; and, secondly, dramatic, as by building up stage by stage in the reader's mind a sense of the sheer physical magnitude of this Empire which controlled half the known world, it thereby increases the impact of the climax of the story, which is the successful resistance to it of the tiny country of Greece. This, the 'more particular' theme of the history, the account, namely, of how the two great civilisations of the East and of the West came into conflict, is worked out in a narrative of beautiful clarity and balance, and at the same time flexible enough to admit subsidiary matter of almost infinite variety and degree of interest. Digression, with Herodotus, is not a vice but a virtue: 'I need not apologise for it,' he says, 'it has been my plan throughout this book to put down odd bits of information not directly connected with my main subject.' Any reader will agree that he had no need to apologise; the 'odd bits of information' may not, indeed, be directly connected with Herodotus' main subject, but—and a reader who fails to see this has not been reading Herodotus as he ought to be read—they form an essential part of the self-revelation which lies behind all truly imaginative writing—behind 'books of power' (to repeat De Quincey's distinction) as opposed to 'books of knowledge.' What a man sees is determined not by his eyes only but by the quality of his mind, and Herodotus' mind was a very subtle as well as a very capacious one. Like all great writers, behind and beyond his ostensible theme, he was writing indirectly of himself, and it is that self—warm, humorous, humane; rational and credulous by turns; curious and kindly, daringly speculative, undismayed by the brutality and beastliness of men, and always *on the side of life*—which gives Herodotus' book its other—its personal—unity. Ultimately this is a question of style. Few writers less resemble Herodotus than the seventeenth century Bishop Burnet; but I am reminded of the bishop because of what Charles Lamb once said in connection with him, when he compared his sort of history favourably with that of Gibbon: 'None,' wrote Lamb to his friend Manning, 'of the cursed philosophical Humeian indifference, so cold, and unnatural, and inhuman! None of

the cursed Gibbonian fine writing, so fine and composite!'
There is no cursed Gibbonian fine writing in Herodotus either.
Herodotus' changes of mood are as subtle as his perceptions of
men; with his beautiful bare narrative he can tickle the fancy,
inflame the imagination, or touch the heart.

Underlying Herodotus' delight in the kaleidoscope of human
life is the characteristic Greek pessimism. Only in Homer, of all
Greek writers, is this fundamental pessimism not discernible,
though even in him the life of men in the sunlit world gets half
its brilliance from the sense of its brevity and the ever-present
darkness of death. In Homer's world, full though it was of death,
violence and blood, men had no speculative burdens; in it there
is an innocence of thought almost childlike. The gods have been
almost wholly humanised. Immortal and powerful, they nevertheless act from motives precisely like those which move ourselves, and a Homeric hero, to get or keep a god on his side, had
to treat him precisely as he would treat a friend or enemy: he
had to pay him the honour that was his due, in word, or in the
giving of a gift, or in acceptable sacrifice. Homer's fighting
chieftains could, one feels, have got on perfectly well without any
gods at all; but, as old tales told them that there were, indeed,
such beings, they re-formed them in fancy to suit their own ardent
unspeculative lives. The Homeric religion, if it can be called a
religion, seems, in its complete divorce from morality, divine
justice and a sense of sin, to have sprung, unlike all other religions,
from a transitory morning of self-confidence and self-sufficiency,
and not at all from the almost universal consciousness of the
mysterious and inexplicable powers which, for good or ill, menace
or sustain the little life of men.

But the morning passed; we see it passing in the poems of
dour old Hesiod; and what I called the characteristic Greek
pessimism took its place. The Greeks were a religious people and
carried religious observance into the commonest acts of daily life
to a degree hardly imaginable by a modern man. Families and
states looked for protection to their special and peculiar gods,
called by local names and often fragmentations, as it were, of the
official Olympian hierarchy. But the Greeks had no established
priesthood and no sacred book, and hence no body of religious
teaching. Their religious observances tended always to be more
in the nature of propitiation than of worship, except perhaps in

the mystery cults of which few details are available to us. Fear of God was universal; of the love of God they knew nothing. The notion of a benevolent and all-powerful deity, the sense found in Judaism and Christianity of the 'everlasting arms', was utterly foreign to Greek thought. Hence their pessimism. Life, for a Greek, was to be enjoyed or endured—if the gods would let him. Orphism, indeed, taught a kind of immortality; but for the Greeks in general death was the end. The recurrent image for death in Greek poetry is the loss of the sunlight—to see the sun no more, to go down into the dark. It is strange that the Greeks with their philosophic passion for first principles did not move more quickly towards monotheism. There is a groping after it in the tragic poet Aeschylus, Herodotus' elder contemporary— 'Zeus, power unknown . . . when I weigh all things, I can guess at nothing but Zeus, if the burden of vanity is to be cast off from my soul . . .'—but Aeschylus' one God, even if his guess is right, is still a harsh and malevolent power, forcing men to learn the truth by pain. It was Plato, early in the fourth century, who with his rejection of the sensible world and his pursuit of the ideal—of 'beauty absolute, separate, simple and everlasting, without diminution or increase or change'—who marked the end of the old classical Greece and offered much which could later be absorbed into Christian theology.

In Herodotus there is nothing of all this, though the religious colouring of his mind is, like everything else in him, full of delicate shades. In religious matters he is at once curious and credulous. Everyone, he says, naturally—and rightly—thinks that the beliefs and observances in which he has been brought up are the best. He himself was no exception, though it should be noted that this very way of putting it suggests a broad tolerance and a refusal to claim absolute validity for any one system of belief, even his own. The gods, in Herodotus' view and in that of his time generally, were not all-powerful; like men they were subject to a mysterious something called Fate—the Greek word, *moira*, means 'the dealer-out of portions'—or to the same thing under another name, Necessity. The power of Fate was unsearchable, though a certain pattern in its operations upon human affairs could be seen. It was Fate, not the Gods, which brought retribution, and the crime which more than any other called retribution down was Pride—that self-exaltation which led a man in the moment of success to 'think more than mortal thoughts'. The idea was deeply characteristic of the Greeks, and sprang, obviously enough, from the insecurity of life in the ancient world, an insecurity more immediate, insistent and universal than any that has until recently menaced the world today, and, at the same time, from the passion which was innate in the Greek character for personal distinction and power. The Greeks knew that they wanted inordinate things—and knew at the same time that such things were dangerous: Fate would see to it that the too prosperous man would one day lose his prosperity. The gods were jealous gods: hence the insistence upon (combined with the very rare practice of) the virtue of 'moderation'—on the necessity for *sophrosyne*, or 'saving thoughts', the kind of thoughts which do not let a man step out of the sphere which is proper to him. If he does, Fate, the Sharer-out, will give him sooner or later what he deserves.

Herodotus' book is full of this sense of Fate, of the watchful and jealous power of this Necessity, which broods like a shadow over the struggles, toils, triumphs and adventures of men and cities. It gives an added depth to the brilliant and varied scene played out on the human stage, linking it with a mystery beyond itself. The whole story of Croesus, one of the most moving and beautiful in the book, is heavy with it—'count no man happy until he is dead.' With a different effect, almost with a touch of implied irony, it is the hinge upon which turns the well-known story of Polycrates of Samos and the ring, his dearest possession, which he proved unable to lose. 'Not God himself,' said the priestess at Delphi, 'can escape Destiny;' and no man, however great, can escape punishment for pride.

Fate, too, is more than the punisher: it is the ultimate power which determines the course of human events; it sets the bounds within which a man can act. A man is free to act, or seems to be free, but the end of his action is ordained. The pattern of life belongs to Fate. 'Now I know,' said the Persian King Cambyses when he was near his miserable end, 'that it is not in human power to avert what is to be.' Yet, with a touch of inconsistency perhaps, we are constantly shown how this same Necessity is prepared to give poor mortals a chance by sending them warnings of coming disaster in the shape of dreams, or portents, or whatever it may be. 'There is nearly always,' Herodotus writes, 'a warning of some kind when disaster is about to overtake a city or a nation'; and he goes on to relate how, before the island of Chios fell to Histiaeus and the Persians, the people of the island had sent a choir of a hundred young men to Delphi, and that all but two of them had died of the plague, while at almost the same time, in the island's chief town, the roof of a school had fallen in and killed all but one of the hundred and twenty children who were learning their letters there. Both these events, Herodotus adds, were acts of God to forewarn the people of Chios. But what could they have done about it, had they taken the warning? The question comes to mind, but it is an idle one, for we are not dealing here with anything like a systematic or philosophical scheme of belief, but only with an inherited and ancient *sense* of things, with a kind of primitive awe which is the stuff out of which theologies come to be made, with a recognition, instinctive rather than reasoned, of the dependence of men upon a shaping power the nature of which is beyond their understanding. It is one of the charms of Greek literature and of Herodotus in particular that it is the work of men whose religious beliefs have not hardened into dogma: of men with quick minds and quicker senses who do not pretend to understand the incomprehensible: who, filled with awe by the invisible, with delight by the visible, can still turn upon human destiny a speculative and wondering eye.

Retribution and the fear of retribution is a recurring idea in Greek literature. Often the retribution is delayed; but punishment for sin, hobbling on its lame foot after its victim, catches him at last, even in the third or fourth generation. The theme of inherited guilt, of the family curse, is frequent in Greek tragic drama; it is a symbol, no doubt, and a powerful one, of what must in the dawn of things have been the disturbing discovery that no fact or act ever is, or can be, isolated; a deed is a pebble dropped into a pond, and the concentric rings spread wide. Croesus was a good man and a good King, friendly on the whole towards Greece; but he came to grief and was dethroned. Why?—because, Herodotus says, he had to expiate in the fifth generation the crime of his ancestor Gyges, a mere soldier in the royal bodyguard, who, tempted by a woman's treachery, murdered his master and stole the crown to which he had no claim. Gyges had long been dead, but his guilt lived after him. Again, in his account of Egypt, Herodotus relates how he heard from certain Egyptian priests a different story from the one which Homer told about the abduction of Helen: according to them, when the Greeks landed in the Troad and sent envoys to King Priam to demand the restoration of Helen, they were assured that she was not in Troy at all but had gone to Egypt. Thinking this to be a merely frivolous answer, the Greeks laid siege to the town and ultimately sacked it. But the story was true none the less, and 'I do not hesitate to declare,' Herodotus wrote, 'that the refusal of the Greeks to believe it was inspired by providence, in order that their utter destruction might plainly prove to mankind that sin is always visited by condign punishment at the hands of God. That, at least, is my own belief.'

The word 'sin' in the last sentence needs some comment. 'Sin' has no word in Greek which exactly corresponds to it. Greek has many words of reproach to express the things which they felt a man should not do, but those things were not by any means in every case what we should describe as sinful. Of the seven deadly sins of Christian doctrine—Pride, Envy, Wrath, Sloth, Avarice, Gluttony, Lust—six, in the Greek view, would have been called *hamartiae*—errors, or 'bad shots'—worthy, perhaps, of reproof from a teacher of virtue, but even so mainly because indulgence in them might spoil the proper balance and satisfaction of a man's life. The only one which a Greek would have recognised as 'sinful' in anything like our sense of the word is Pride—and even that must be understood in a somewhat different sense from ours. The Greeks called it *hubris*, and it meant, as I have already suggested, a failure of that proper subordination, a breaking of that due order of things, upon which life in this world is, and must be, founded. The act of presumption may be against other men, or against the gods: in each case it brings certain punishment.

'Revenge and wrong,' wrote Aeschylus (the translation is Shelley's) 'bring forth their kind

> The foul cubs like their parents are;
> Their den is in the guilty mind,
> And conscience feeds them with despair.'

When Pheron was on the throne of Egypt, it so happened that the Nile, one year, rose too high, and the excessive floods, accompanied by gales, did much damage. In sudden rage Pheron seized a spear and hurled it into the swirling waters—the sacred waters, for all rivers were in part divine. For the act of presumption the Pharaoh lost his sight. Herodotus' book is full of such stories of the perils of pride—pride of wealth, pride of power, pride of success, and, deadliest of all, the pride which leads a man to forget that he is a nothing in the sight of the gods. This is Herodotus' fundamental morality, and it is not ignoble. Incidentally though the Greeks took to most vices (except gluttony) as a duck takes to water, of *accidie*, at any rate, I do not think any Greek before the fourth century would have been capable.

In all this Herodotus was a man of his time, as he also was in his belief in oracles and in the significance of dreams and omens. In a general way, that is: for one can never be sure with Herodotus whether or not, when one is listening to him telling some tale, one is going to catch at the end of it a hint of half-subdued yet mocking laughter. Popular legend comes in for much amused and rational criticism; there is, for instance, his pleasant comment on the supposed origin of the oracle of Zeus at Dodona. The three priestesses—and Herodotus duly records their names— who served the temple told him that two black doves, long ago, flew away from Thebes in Egypt and that one of them alighted at Dodona, the other in Libya. The former, perched on an oak, and speaking with a human voice, told whoever was there to hear that on that spot there should be an oracle of Zeus. The mystic words were understood to be a command from heaven, and were at once obeyed. Similarly the dove which flew to Libya told the Libyans to found the oracle of Zeus Ammon in the Libyan desert. So much for the legend. Herodotus, however, had previously heard from certain Egyptian priests that a party of Phoenician marauders had, in the distant past, carried off two women from the temple of the Theban Zeus; these they sold, one in Libya, the other in Greece, and it was these women who founded the two oracles. Putting the two stories together, Herodotus goes on to suggest that if there is any truth in the Egyptian version, then the woman who was sold in Greece must have been sold to the Thesprotians, in whose territory Dodona lies; later, while she was working as a slave in that part of the country, she built, under an oak which happened to be growing there, a shrine to Zeus, remembering in her exile the god she had served in her native Thebes. Subsequently, when she had learnt to speak Greek, she established an oracle there. As for the doves, Herodotus adds, 'the story came, I should say, from the fact that the women were foreigners, whose language sounded to the local inhabitants like the twittering of birds; later on the dove spoke with a human voice, because by that time the woman had stopped twittering and learned to speak intelligibly. That at least is how I should explain the obvious impossibility of a dove using the language of men.'

It has always to be remembered that ancient Greek legends and myths, like the legends and myths of all ancient peoples, were not fairy stories. They were believed as historically true, and it is precisely this universal popular acceptance of them as historical fact which throws into relief, for us, the first beginnings of a rational criticism of them. To call Herodotus a rationalist would be untrue and absurd; he shared much too deeply in the general temper of his times. Nevertheless, he asked questions; and, as I have said, one never quite knows what direction his questions will take, and the fact that he can keep us in this uncertainty is not the least interesting aspect of his wide-ranging and many-shaded mind. Does he, or does he not, believe in the significance of dreams? I have suggested that he does; and there are plenty of passages in his book where he gravely tells of some dream whose warning was all too true—the very odd dream, for instance, which Astyages dreamed of his daughter Mandane. Suddenly, however, he will appear to take another look at the whole business, and to smile at his own credulity. In the splendid passage of the seventh Book, recording the conversation between Xerxes and Artabanus before Xerxes had decided upon the invasion of Greece, we are told of the King's ominous dream and how, in doubt and fear, he went to Artabanus, his uncle, for advice upon its meaning. In the course of his reply the old man assured him that dreams do not, as men imagine, come from God. 'I, who am older than you by many years, will tell you what these visions are that float before our eyes in sleep: nearly always these drifting phantoms are the shadows of what we have been thinking about during the day; and during the days before your dream we were, you know, very much occupied with this campaign. Nevertheless it is possible that your dream cannot be explained as I have explained it: perhaps there is, indeed, something divine in it . . .'

Those were two Persians, not two Greeks, talking together; but the thoughts are Herodotus' thoughts. It is true, indeed, that the story goes on to tell how Artabanus, persuaded to sleep that night in the king's bed, himself dreamed a dream of similar import and was thereby convinced of its divine provenance. Nevertheless, the question has been slipped quietly in.

Another instance is Herodotus' comment on a popular belief of the Egyptians, a belief quite consonant with ordinary Greek feeling. Cambyses the Persian king after his conquest of Egypt, committed in that country numerous acts of outrageous cruelty and beastliness, which culminated in his wantonly sticking a dagger into the thigh of the sacred bull, Ap 's. The wound festered, the bull died, and Cambyses went mad. According to the Egyptians his madness was a divine punishment for his impious act, and, says Herodotus, perhaps it was; 'nevertheless,' he adds, 'it may have been the result of any one of the many maladies which afflict mankind, and there is, in fact, a story that Cambyses suffered from birth from a serious complaint, epilepsy; there would then be nothing strange in the fact that a serious physical malady should have affected his brain.' Again and again we hear Herodotus quietly putting forward the proposition— sometimes with a smile, sometimes with a hint of irony, most often with the sheer pleasure of intelligent curiosity—that there are, indeed, 'more things in heaven and earth . . .'—and es- pecially, perhaps, on earth, as for him at any rate it was the more interesting place of the two. Is it not, he seems to ask, at least possible, in attempting to account for such or such a phenomenon, to leave the gods out of it for once, and to find, perhaps, some cause in human psychology or in the forces of nature? The case of Thessaly, for instance, which was once a vast lake ringed round by mountains, but is now a plain, good for horses, and drained by the River Peneus flowing out through the gorge of Tempe— *was* it Poseidon, Shaker of Earth, who, as men say, split asunder those enclosing hills? Or could it have been an earthquake?

Herodotus would not at all have approved of the remarks of Xenophanes about the gods; he was happy enough in the religion of his race, though he used to the full the opportunities of in- cidental comment and criticism which a religion like the Greek, lacking as it did any sacred scripture or body of doctrine, rendered available to whoever chose to use them. The nature and accent of these comments, flickering like summer lightning over a mind fundamentally reverential and steeped in tradition, is one of the things which constitute the incalculable originality of Herodotus' book.

Herodotus has been taken to task for his credulity about oracles, and there is some justice in the charge. It is important, however, to clear away a very common misconception about the nature and function of the Greek oracles, especially of Apollo's oracle at Delphi which was the most generally respected. Contrary to what many people suppose, the least important function of the oracle was to foretell the future, or to exercise any sort of magical or superhuman power of prevision. Its responses were, indeed, given by the God, through the mouth of his Priestess inspired by him—or perhaps, at Delphi, inspired by certain gases which are said to have arisen through a cleft in the mountain, or even by some sort of self-induced frenzy aided by the ancient and numinous associations of the place; and they were usually delivered in archaic, and often ambiguous, terms, couched in hexameter verse, all of which no doubt added something to their apparent weight and solemnity. But—and this is the point—behind the imposing façade erected by a very ancient tradition and kept in being by a continuing sense of religious awe, there was, in fact, a highly competent, and wholly human, organisation. The Delphic oracle acted as a kind of Central Information Bureau for the whole of Greece, and even beyond—for we hear of Asiatic princes, Gyges, for instance, and Alyattes and Croesus, sending gifts to adorn the temple at Delphi and asking Apollo for advice. The organisation seems on the whole to have been most efficient, and information on political and other matters from all parts of the civilised world was carefully collected. Precisely how it was collected we do not know; but there were numerous oracles both in Greece and in Asia Minor (Apollo alone had twenty-two), and it seems pretty certain that the officials who served them were in constant touch with each other. The commonest type of question put to the God was not 'What will happen?' but 'What, in the present circumstances, is the best, or safest, course to take?' To consult the oracle meant not so much to ask for a revelation as to seek advice. No colony, or new settlement, for instance, was ever sent out by the parent city until the oracle had been consulted about the suitability of the proposed site; for the 'oracle-service'—if one may use so irreverent a term—was much more likely to have useful and accurate information about conditions in a distant part of the world, say in the far West or on the Black Sea coast or in North Africa, than any of the people at home who had travelled little, if at all. Information of this kind was, quite obviously, of solid value. The oracle was also asked for its advice on procedure in all sorts of tricky situations, both public and private; and in these cases its answer was not dependent upon a body of carefully collected and perfectly genuine factual knowledge, but upon the general acumen and knowledge of the world of its functionaries. Politically the oracle tended to have a stabilising effect—if anything could be called stable in the Greek world—and its influence was normally used to support the existing order. At Delphi it was under the supervision of a group of distinguished Delphian families, and this fact led, naturally enough, to a certain political bias in favour of the Dorian states, of which Delphi was one. In early centuries this was probably harmless enough, but during the struggle between Athens and Sparta, which occupied the last thirty years of the fifth century, the bias became so marked—Sparta being the leading Dorian state—that by the rest of Greece the oracle's authority was no longer taken seriously and fell into general disrepute. In its religious aspect the influence of the oracle was undoubtedly good: it was believed to give its answers to anyone who came to consult it with a pure heart, and no one was supposed, if he had guilt on his conscience, to get a reply until he had made atonement.

On the whole, then, the oracle was a useful institution, and its service was performed efficiently and intelligently. Naturally it made mistakes; and frequently it was forced to express its judgements darkly and ambiguously, in order that the error, if error there was, might be laid to the interpretation of its answer, not to its own failure in knowledge. There was the well-known response, for instance, which was given to the Athenians when the Persian armies were approaching from the north with Xerxes:

'the wooden wall only shall not fail, but help you
   and your children.
Divine Salamis, you will bring death to women's sons
When the corn is scattered, or the harvest gathered in.'

What was the wooden wall? The wall of the Acropolis, or the ships of the Athenian navy? fortunately for Athens, Themistocles guessed right, but not before he had overcome strong opposition from other Athenian leaders, even from those who accepted the interpretation that the wooden wall meant the fleet—for whose sons did Apollo mean were to die at Salamis? Was Athens to fight a naval action in the straits, and be beaten? No, said Themistocles; had Apollo meant that, he would surely not have called Salamis 'divine'. And most people, if they have read Herodotus or not, will be familiar with the classic ambiguity of the Delphic oracle's advice to Croesus, who wanted to know— poor man—if it would be wise for him to make war upon Cyrus of Persia. This was indeed a tricky question, for the abilities of Cyrus had not yet by any means been fully proved. 'Fight him,' said the oracle, 'and you will destroy a mighty empire.' So Croesus did so—and destroyed his own.

I have not met with any remarks of Xenophanes about the oracle, so I do not know if he included it in his general scepticism about the Olympian religion. There is no doubt, however, that belief in the value—and divine authority—of its responses was all but universal in the Greek world, at least until the fifth century was drawing toward its close. Herodotus was no exception, and he cannot, I think, be charged with credulity when one considers the very real services which the oracle performed; on the other hand, the charge cannot be wholly suspended, because he, like most of his contemporaries, was prepared to accept its occasional sillinesses as well as its more habitual wisdom. Herodotus *liked* oracles; and he quotes a large number of them in his book, uncritically and with evident pleasure. He doesn't turn a hair at the absurd story of how Croesus tested the veracity of the various oracles before deciding which one to consult upon his major problem—how he sent envoys to each with instructions to inquire what, exactly, he was doing at a particular pre-arranged moment on a particular day. Several of the oracles, Herodotus tells us, including Delphi, answered that Croesus was boiling a tortoise in a bronze cauldron: and, strange to say, they were right. Second-sight of this sort is not, I suppose, inexplicable, granted a little collusion and hanky-panky, with perhaps the passing of a coin or two; but for Herodotus, apparently, it was second-sight indeed.

Greek religion was based not upon doctrine but upon observances and ceremonial hallowed by ancient tradition. In these matters all Greeks, with the exception of a few philosophers and free-thinkers, were traditionalists. Herodotus himself was a traditionalist, but with a difference. He treasured the tradition, but allowed himself at the same time to question it.

PART TWO

Greece before the
Persian Wars

CHAPTER 7

The Beginnings of Greece

MORE THAN TWO THOUSAND YEARS BEFORE CHRIST GREEK-SPEAKING people first began to filter down from the North-west in scattered bands to absorb or conquer over many centuries the inhabitants of the Aegean world and to impose their language upon them. The Greeks of the classical period had only the dimmest memories of these first beginnings of their race preserved in legend and story. The Ionians of Attica thought themselves to be aboriginals, and the Arcadians believed they had lived amongst their Peloponnesian hills before the birth of the moon.

Yet long before Greece was Greek a brilliant civilisation was flourishing in Crete and the neighbouring islands of the Aegean sea; and to this civilisation the Greeks were to owe much, though they were never fully conscious of the debt. It is not impossible that they wished to forget the debt, like the Romans, who, as some have thought, wished to forget what they owed to their Etruscan conquerors. Everyone knows the story of Theseus and the Minotaur, how seven youths and seven maidens had to be sent each year to be devoured by the bull-headed monster in the Cretan labyrinth. It is not pure fairy-tale—indeed, the Greeks never told fairy-tales; rather it is a memory dimmed by time of a remote past when, it was said, the men of Attica and elsewhere on the Greek mainland had to pay tribute to Minos the lord of Crete. The excavations at Cnossos revealed that the bull was a sacred animal amongst the old Minoans, and they showed us the Cretan double-headed axe, the *labrys*. So the bull and the labyrinth step out of fairyland for us into history, or a kind of history.

Herodotus knew that Crete had once been a great sea power. He tells us that the people of Caria, where he was himself born, came originally from the Aegean islands and were subject to King Minos (nobody knows who Minos was, or if he was one man, or two, or more, or even if he ever existed) aboard whose ships they used to serve, winning thereby fame for themselves, as Minos was a great conqueror and always successful in his wars. He also tells the traditional tale of how Minos came to a violent end in Sicily, after which the Cretans, having fitted out a great expedition and failed to take the town of Camicus, were wrecked on the southern coast of Italy as they were bound homeward again. Here they founded new settlements, and as time went on men of various nations, and especially Greeks, flocked into the deserted island of Crete and made it their home. Here they prospered, but, having gone in force to support Menelaus in the Trojan war, nearly all of them perished on the way home from famine and the plague, so that Crete was a second time stripped of its inhabitants.

The tradition does, indeed, contain a shadow of history, but it needed the work of modern archaeologists to give the shadow substance. Minoan bronze-age civilisation in Crete began in the middle of the third millennium B.C., perhaps a thousand years after the coming from southern Asia Minor of the earliest neolithic settlers and lasted for another thousand years, reaching its peak about 1600 B.C. The remains of it which have been dug out of the earth have revealed not only a maritime empire controlling the islands of the Aegean, in close commercial intercourse with Egypt, sending its products as far West as Sicily and Spain, and settling colonists on the coast of Asia Minor, where they founded the earliest settlement at Miletus and built towns in southern Palestine—an ancient name of Gaza was Minoa—but also a civilisation of grace and charm, acquainted with domestic luxury and highly skilled in the graphic arts, their surviving frescoes rich with beautiful representations of natural objects—flowers, trees, animals—suggesting delighted awareness of their surroundings. The Minoans were a non-Greek people; to what period Herodotus referred, if indeed he knew, or even thought he knew, when he said that Greeks flocked into Crete and made it their home cannot be determined. That Greek was spoken by the rulers of Cnossos as early as 1450 B.C. has been shown by the recent decipherment of the Mycenaean linear script (Linear B), and it is known that about fifty years later the great palaces at Cnossos and Phaestus were destroyed. This catastrophe, whether it was due to an invasion from the Greek mainland or to a sea-raid by the powers of the eastern Mediterranean, brought

Cretan maritime supremacy to an end. The island itself continued to prosper, but what must, from the evidence of archaeology, have been a rare and exquisite civilisation was destroyed for ever.

Nevertheless it was not destroyed before powerful influences from it had spread to Greece. Some time after 1600 B.C. Cretans penetrated to various parts of Eastern Greece and established themselves there, especially in Argolis and Boeotia. Off Megara there is an island called Minoa, a name which suggests a Cretan origin; Europa, in the legend of Cadmus and Europa, the founders of Thebes, is called the mother of Minos, and the tradition that Cadmus invented writing may have arisen from the introduction into Greece of a Cretan script. It was these Cretan settlements which gave rise to, or at least profoundly affected, the parallel 'Mycenaean' civilisation, so called because of the long supremacy of Mycenae, on the Greek mainland and in the Greek islands, a civilisation in many aspects similar to the Cretan, but, with its fortified strongholds and vast Cyclopean walls, somewhat darker and gloomier, and without the gaiety and charm which it is impossible not to associate with the greatest days of ancient Cnossos, who owed her easier life to her unchallenged command of the sea. Greek Mycenaean civilisation was to last for four hundred years, spreading over much of the mainland, to the coasts and islands of the Ionian Sea, and as far east in the Aegean as Rhodes. It perished with the coming of iron and the invasion of the Dorians, when all the great cities were destroyed and a new Dark Age descended upon Greece, about which little is known until the curtain rises again with the Greek migrations to Asia Minor and the beginning of the period when the city-states first came into being.

It is the closing period of the Mycenaean civilisation which is reflected with modifications in the poems of Homer, though for Homer himself it was already far away in the past. Herodotus says that Homer lived some four hundred years before his own time: say about 850 B.C., and Herodotus' guess is as good as most men's. Homer took his theme from the past, as epic poets are wont to do, founding his own poems upon old existing lays, altering many details of the society therein described, to make it intelligible to his contemporaries, and working it all up into a new and beautiful whole.

No fact is significant in isolation; knowledge grows only by seeing the connections between things. As recently as a hundred years ago it seemed to scholars that Hellenism, as it is called, the flowering in one small corner of Europe of a new sort of civilisation distinguished above others for philosophy and the arts, arose suddenly, miraculously, as if from nothing. The threads which linked it with other civilisations—with Egypt, Sumeria, Babylon, Crete, and the vast Hittite empire which for centuries controlled the trade route from Mesopotamia to the Aegean— were revealed only by the devoted labours of modern archaeology. Some of the links are tenuous enough; often they are full of romance, like the discovery in the earliest of the seven cities on the famous hill of Troy of an axe-head made of white jade, which could not but have come there from the far east, perhaps from China. History is continually pushing backward the curtain of darkness which hides our origins, giving an added dimension, as it were, to the significance of the present by linking it with a previously unimagined past. Homer told no fairy-tale when he wrote of Agamemnon and Achilles and their doings at Troy by the Scamander river; he described a society which actually existed and a kind of life still dimly remembered by the people of his day. The sort of houses which Homer's people built, their weapons, household utensils and gear of all sorts, have been dug out of the earth for us to see; and as for the war itself, of which Homer describes what may or may not be an imaginary incident, it takes its place in history as firmly and easily as any other war— as a struggle, namely, for control of the shipping route from the ʒreek mainland to the Dardanelles and the Bosphorus. A strong current—something like four knots—sets out of the Dardanelles into the Aegean, and for a considerable part of the summer sailing-season the wind in that locality is northerly or north-easterly. Hence it was difficult for ships powered only with oars and sail to make the passage, and they frequently were forced to bring up on the coast just south of the straits, perhaps off Tenedos, to wait for the weather. Thus a town situated as Troy was some four miles inland and controlling the surrounding country, had no difficulty also in controlling the sea-borne traffic past her shores. This she did effectively enough; she imposed a toll on all shipping, and grew rich on it. Greece, under the lordship of Mycenae, naturally resented this, and took steps to abolish the nuisance. Helen's face was not the only thing which

launched a thousand ships
And burnt the topless towers of Ilium;

there were more mundane motives: the hope of putting money in the pockets of the lords of the great strongholds in Argos and elsewhere in Greece.

Who were these lords, and the people over whom they ruled? How did Greece ever come to know herself as Hellas and to include in the Hellenic name settlements as far removed from one another as Miletus and Marseilles, as if they were all one nation? There is no simple answer to this question. Herodotus asked it, and looked for answers to the inherited memories of his race. At some time in remote antiquity, perhaps a couple of thousand years before he was born, Attica, he thought, and parts of the Peloponnese, were inhabited by a barbarian (that is, a non-Greek) people, the Pelasgians. There were Pelasgians still surviving in his own day at Creston, in Thessaliotis, and in two settlements, Placia and Scylace, on the Hellespont, and they spoke not Greek but a foreign tongue. The Ionian Greeks Herodotus supposed to be Pelasgian by descent, and therefore the original, anthocthonous inhabitants of Attica, and he says that they changed their language when they 'passed into the Hellenic body.' These are vaguer words than Herodotus is accustomed to use, but they suggest what is certainly true, namely that the Greek race was built up over the course of many centuries by the gradual mixing and fusion of Greek-speaking invaders from the north—or rather immigrants, for in the earliest times their coming was nothing so definite as an invasion—with a native population of different race and different speech. The Greek language prevailed and the Pelasgians (or whoever they were) gradually adopted it and, except for the surviving pockets mentioned by Herodotus, forgot their own. Greek is a vigorous language, just as the Greeks were a vigorous people; it has lasted until today with remarkably little change. Plato and his friends would have less difficulty in reading today's Greek newspapers than most of us without previous study have in reading Chaucer—and much less than Caesar or Livy would have in trying to understand what their countrymen have made of Latin.

That two distinct cultures, that of the original inhabitants of Greece, strongly influenced by Crete, and that of incoming and more barbarous northern tribes, were blended over the course of many generations to form what we know of the classical culture of the Hellenic world, is further suggested by other considerations: the existence, for instance, of place names which are not Greek at all. Athens is not a Greek name; nor is Corinth; nor (surprisingly), as H. D. F. Kitto pointed out in one of his recent books, is the Greek word for 'sea'—*thalassa*. Again, there are curious confusions in Greek religion which suggest a double origin: the existence, namely, of the Olympian hierarchy—gods, predominantly male, who were felt to preside over a man's activities as a member of a group, whether of the family, the tribe, or the nation—side by side with nature goddesses (Athene herself was originally a nature goddess) and the mystery cults in which a man looked for some sort of personal comfort or enlightenment from doctrine, such as the doctrine of purification or of immortality. It was the immigrants and invaders who brought the Olympians into Greece; and the Olympian religion became in time the public and official religion, and succeeded by the sort of ingenuity which all races have displayed in similar matters in finding a place for some, at any rate, of the native goddesses; but the old worships remained, personal and private.

If Herodotus was right in supposing the Ionians to be a Pelasgian people, then the first 'Greeks' to penetrate into Greece would be the Achaeans. The Mycenaeans were Achaean Greeks; the name is the one most generally used by Homer—when he does not call them 'Argives', an obvious name derived from the power and predominance of Argos. But their power was destined to be broken by another Greek-speaking people, the Dorians, who about the year 1100 B.C., nearly a century after the traditional date of the siege of Troy, came with their iron weapons down from the north in hordes and carried all before them. This was not a peaceful infiltration like that of their predecessors, but an invasion and a conquest. Unlike the Achaeans who adopted as their own much of what they found in their new home, the Dorians were destroyers. Their coming brought a period of great confusion; as they poured southward over central Greece and into the Peloponnese, tribes and communities were reduced to serfdom, or swept away. Over a course of two centuries and more there was a continuous movement of peoples before the pressure of the invaders. The Dorians were a barbarous and virile race, and it took them a long time to learn civilised ways: some of them, one is tempted to think, never did; for in the years to come the greatest of the Dorian towns was Sparta, and it is not easy to associate the idea of civilised ways with that profoundly interesting but hateful place.

An important result of the Dorian invasion and the spreading of the Dorian tribes over a large part of the mainland of Greece, and of the shifting of peoples consequent upon it, was the colonisation by Greeks of the coast of Asia Minor and of Cyprus and the Aegean islands. The movement of colonisation had begun before the Dorian invasion, but it was now greatly accelerated. The Achaeans, with their kinsmen the Aeolian Greeks, were the first to seek new homes in the kindlier land of Asia, and in the off-shore island of Lesbos; their settlements were mainly on the Mysian coast, extending as far south as Old Smyrna, and they were followed by Ionian venturers, who settled to the southward, as far as Miletus. Lastly the Dorians themselves joined in the search for new lands, built settlements in the islands of Cos, Cnidus and Rhodes, and continued the line of Greek coastal towns to the borders of Lycia. These successive waves of emigration were rendered possible by the fall, about 1200 B.C. of the Hittite power in the west, and the rise of the Phrygians, who, with the Lydians, were to become during the following centuries important neighbours of the Asiatic Greeks and intimately concerned in their history.

When these first great movements of colonisation were complete and Greeks were settled on both sides of the Aegean; when, by about 700 B.C., Assyria had finally defeated the Hittites, and the ancient trade routes from the east to the Aegean cost were in the control of Phrygia and Lydia, with the Greek towns well placed for commerce with Egypt and the west on all the best harbours; when rumours of a far West in Italy and beyond, even perhaps beyond the Pillars of Heracles at the gate of the Mediterranean, had begun to reach Greek ears through the fabulous voyagings of Phoenician seamen; when commercial contacts between the Asiatic Greeks and their kinsmen on the Greek mainland were becoming more frequent, and, not many years later, Greeks were permitted by the Pharaoh Psammeticus to establish a port at Naucratis on the Nile Delta: by that time, it might be said, the world of Herodotus had taken shape. Greeks now knew themselves to be Greeks, and the rest of mankind to be barbarians. In Homer's poetry there are no barbarians; Homer tells of Achaeans, or Argives, or Trojans, or whoever it may be, courteously using the names that belong to them. But the world has now changed. The Greeks—though any two neighbouring communities may still at any moment and on any pretext hate one another and fight like Kilkenny cats—are conscious of themselves as a people, bound together not, indeed, by territorial bonds, but by something less tangible but stronger, something strong enough to survive mutual treachery and continuous internecine strife. The Greeks had looked at the great civilisations of Egypt and the East—and they had not liked them. They knew that they were fit only for slaves. For themselves, they wanted something different; they wanted what the peoples of the East, poor sheep under an all-powerful shepherd who cared nothing for their lives, had never either had or dreamed of having. They wanted liberty—liberty to save themselves or to destroy themselves in their own way, without subservience to a master. What bound the Greeks together and set them sharply apart from all the other nations of their world, was a new conception which had grown up within them of *how to live*.

CHAPTER 8

Early Society

THE HOMERIC GREEKS, IN THEIR LITTLE SEPARATE COMMUNITIES, were governed by kings, though 'king', with its modern associations, is too big a word to describe them. Even Agamemnon King of Men, to use Homer's phrase, the lord of golden Mycenae, though his influence was apparently great enough over other Greek communities to enable him to organise, and lead, the expedition against Troy—the first concerted effort of Greek peoples—was little more than a petty princeling and tribal ruler, one amongst many, though the richest and most powerful.

This smallness and separateness of the Greek communities is of fundamental importance, for it remained as a primary characteristic of their civilisation throughout their history. Their political institutions were to change; they were to put more of their passion and energy into political thought and political practice than any people the world has known; they were to show themselves masters of political improvisation, and political theorists of a high order—within their limitations, which seem, to a modern student of politics, extraordinarily, almost absurdly, narrow. The population of Attica, in the period of its greatest power and influence at the beginning of the Peloponnesian war (431 B.C.) has been estimated at between 60,000 and 70,000 adult males, with perhaps 50,000 slaves; and there were hundreds of Greek towns of no historical importance whose population was hardly a tenth part of that, but whose people lived the same life of intense local patriotism, fighting their neighbour on the other side of the hill, and gaily slitting each other's throats in the struggle for internal political power. Various communities at various times did, indeed, attempt for some particular end to form leagues under a recognised leader, but such leagues were, in general, ephemeral. The Athenians did it, and called their league by the grand name of empire; but the result was only to awaken the fear and envy of their rivals in the Peloponnese who, in the course of a war more

savage in its brutality than any other till modern times, destroyed
not only the League but Athens herself too. Nationalism meant
for the Greeks not a united nation but the keeping of one small
town master of its own destiny, independent not only of the
foreigner but of the next small town perhaps twenty miles away.
Of nationalism in our modern sense they understood nothing.
Yet, as I have said, they were a nation, and conscious of their
nationhood, for they knew that they shared a secret which the
others, the barbarians, would never be able to discover. The secret
was a spiritual secret; it was their conviction that they, alone of
the nations of the world, knew how life should be lived by a man
who was indeed a man, and not a slave. They called their secret
by many names, the most obvious of which were autonomy and
liberty; they demanded a life in which each member of the community could realise and develop to the full his potentialities as a
man. They would choose, at all costs, their own road—to heaven
or hell. It is significant that the only institutions which the separate
Greek communities shared were religious institutions—the Games
at Olympia in honour of Zeus, a truly national ceremony in which
all Greece expressed its spiritual unity; the acceptance of Homer
as the national poet and teacher; the Great Dionysia at Athens,
which, though an Athenian ceremony, was thrown open to all
others who wished to attend; the Panionium at Mycale in Asia
Minor, where the twelve Ionian cities could meet for common
worship and feel, at least momentarily, their brotherhood; the
Amphictyons—*dwellers-around* certain shrines—who felt themselves united by the shared influence of the sacred place. But of
political unity there was none—or where at any time it happened
to exist, it had been imposed by force, and the weaker members
would seize any chance to break it and resume their independence.

The smallness of the Greek political unit gave rise to a kind of
patriotism which has no parallel in the modern world. A Greek
belonged to his community in a way no one nowadays can
understand without an effort of the imagination. In it and through
it he found, or failed to find, all the satisfactions that his life
demanded. We get a hint of how much he loved it by the sort of
epithets which Greek poets applied to towns or places: *violet-
crowned* Athens; *lovely* Salamis—the word has nothing to do with
scenery: it means 'inspiring *himeros*' which is properly the longing

of a man for a woman—the *holy* citadel of Troy. I do not know exactly what Pindar had in mind when he called Athens violet-crowned; but at least it is not the sort of epithet a man nowadays would think of applying to Birmingham. The word was often used of the Graces and the Muses; so perhaps when Pindar thought of Athens he connected her in his mind with those fair creatures. And everyone remembers how Pericles, in his funeral speech at the end of the first year of the Peloponnesian war, urged his fellow-Athenians to be the 'lovers' of their city; and the Greek word he used was no vague or general one, but precisely that which means a man who loves a woman—like Solon's word when he wrote of lovely Salamis. The intensity of this local patriotism also, I think, explains its opposite—the (to us) almost incredible treachery of which any Greek was potentially capable. Greek history is full of instances of distinguished men who, having fallen from power in their native town, promptly went over to its bitterest enemies and did their utmost to ruin it. It suggests a relationship primarily of passion, however much reason may have also entered into it: it was a love-hate relationship—an *odi et amo*—like that of a man betrayed by his mistress who goes to any lengths to wreck her happiness.

This local patriotism, so profoundly characteristic of the Greeks, was the result not only of temperament but also of geography. Greece is, so to speak, all islands. There are the actual islands of the Aegean and Ionian seas; and there are also, in effect, the islands of the mainland. Much of the mainland consists of rugged and impassable ranges of limestone mountains, and between their peaks and spurs lie small tracts of level and cultivable land, many of them on the coastal strip. These tracts are almost as effectively isolated from each other by the mountains as the islands are isolated from each other by the sea. In classical times there were few roads, and those few were only mule-tracks; and in Greece proper there are no navigable rivers. In circumstances like these intercommunication was not easy. There remained, of course, the sea, and the sound and smell of the sea run through all Greek literature and history, for it did indeed come to dominate their lives; yet the Greeks were timid sailors, and it took even Athens three or four centuries of comparatively prosperous life to realise the use that could be made of it—now that old Minos and his maritime empire were forgotten. The Greeks sailed only in the summer season, first taking to the water when 'the new leaves on the fig-tree', as Hesiod said, 'are as long as the print of a crow's foot on the sand', and laying-up their ships well before the rainy Hyades vexed the dim sea. Odysseus had many adventures afloat; but he much preferred dry land. It was the Phoenicians, not the Greeks, who were the sea-farers of the ancient world; and if ever a Greek sailor found himself far from home and the familiar islands, as Colaeus of Samos did, when once, to his great surprise, he landed up somewhere near Cadiz, it was by accident rather than by design.

In such circumstances it is not surprising that the men of the little, isolated Greek communities should come to guard them jealously and to identify themselves with the walled town and its few square miles of ground which, in the early days at least, had to provide all the grain, the rare joint of meat (for special occasions only), the cheese, milk, olives, figs and garlic which made up their meagre and abstemious diet. The town and its bit of land, watched over by its own gods and the guardian spirits of dead heroes, was an extension of themselves; it was an entity with a life of its own; it was 'holy', it was 'lovely'; it was 'violet-crowned' or 'far-seen' like the white cliffs of Ithaca shining on the horizon of the sea.

A beautiful touch in what is, for me, the finest of Sophocles' plays, the *Oedipus at Colonus*, is the evocation of this spirit of place—Colonus, just outside Athens, was Sophocles' native village, and in a famous chorus of his solemn and awful drama he brings all the resources of his art to sing its praise. The place was only a patch of laurel and shrubs and ivy on a stony hillside, but to the poet it was holy, and haunted by divine presences:

> Earth's loveliest, where the nightingale's
> Liquid notes most haunt
> The darkness of green glades,
> In her home amongst ivy dark as wine
> And laurels thick with berries,
> Holy with the presence of God, unpierced
> By the sun and windless from the storms,
>   Where Dionysus, the wild one, walks continually
>   With the nymphs who nursed him.

Few people, I imagine, in days when the whole world is open to them for the price of a visa and a steamship ticket, feel quite like this about their homes.

Exile was for a Greek worse than death: a Greek who had lost his home had lost most of what made life worth living for him. He had become a nothing, as is poignantly illustrated by the taunt of the Corinthian admiral, Adeimantus, against Themistocles before the battle of Salamis. Themistocles, against the judgement of the other captains, had urged that they should remain at Salamis and engage the Persian fleet in the straits. Athens had been already burnt and sacked by the Persian armies, and Adeimantus, who was in favour of withdrawing the allied fleet to the Isthmus, bitterly attacked Themistocles, telling him to hold his tongue, as he was *a man without a city*.

In all this I am anticipating, what I have said being most relevant to classical Greece, the age of the *polis*, or city-state. Nevertheless the general principle holds good even for the more primitive Homeric society, with its attachment to place, its small independent economic units—the 'household' of the chieftain, or king—the assumed hostility of neighbours, the reliance upon the ties of kinship and blood.* Throughout Greek history the passion for local independence was the driving force; the inability of the Greeks to achieve any sort of real political combination was what in the end destroyed them; but at the same time it was precisely those qualities in the Greek character which have made them immortal. Assyria, Babylon, Persia, Egypt are, for us, the mighty dead; but Greece is as much alive as she ever was. Her influence has remained vital, and the modern Western world is connected with her by a thousand subtle and invisible strands of feeling and thought. Not in spite of, but because of what must seem to us her political incompetence—so different from the ruthless competence of Rome—she was able to evolve certain seminal ideas which are at the root of all subsequent European history. Shelley idealised the Greeks and invested them with a halo of nineteenth century romanticism; but he spoke no less than the truth when he wrote that

---

* The case for the Homeric poems representing not the closing years of the Mycenaean age, to which the 'heroes' by name belong, but the period of gradual recovery (say the 8th century B.C.) after the chaos caused by the Dorian invasions and the destruction of the great Mycenaean centres, has been ably argued by M. I. Finley in his book *The World of Odysseus*.

Greece and its foundations are
Built below the tide of war,
Based on the crystalline sea
Of thought and its eternity.

No modern man could endure to live for ten minutes in ancient Athens (to choose the most advanced of the Greek city-states); the danger, the discomfort, and the dirt would be too much for him; but he knows, or ought to know, that to Athens and hundreds of lesser towns scattered about the Greek world from the far west of the Mediterranean to the eastern shores of the Black Sea he owes much of what he most prizes in the civilisation of today and the whole of the impulse towards what are still, I suppose, two of the chief characteristics of Western society: the liberty of the individual, and a climate of opinion in which the saying of Socrates that a man is, or should be, a being capable of giving a rational answer to a rational question, remains valid.

Homer's world was a simple world. It had no problems and—to judge by his poems, which are our only evidence— no psychological conflicts. Of the mass of the 'people' Homer tells us almost nothing; he is concerned only with the 'heroes', the men, that is, who were princelings in their own right, masters of their own households and estates, leaders in raids and any sort of fighting which offered. To Homer they were all 'kings': Odysseus was King of Ithaca, Achilles King of his Myrmidons, Menelaus King of Sparta. The word may as well stand. Take it that they were a warrior caste, with the warrior's mentality and the warrior's code. The chief article in that code was Honour; and honour was to be won by Prowess, which itself included qualities that a later and more self-conscious age would hardly admit. Prowess for the Homeric hero meant all the powers of the dominant male; it included adequacy in battle and adequacy in bed; it meant keeping one's own, and increasing it not only by the power of the arm but also by the power of the tongue, by cunning and trickery as much as by bold robbery and deeds of arms. And the Homeric gods on Olympus precisely matched the Homeric princes on earth, surpassing them only in degree and by the gift of immortality. The society which Homer described was an aristocratic society, a society of adventurers and swashbucklers not without nobility of spirit, proud, hungry for glory, always preferring death to dishonour, fiercely in love with life. Better, said the ghost of Achilles, to be thrall to the meanest man on earth than to be a king amongst the dead. In that society the common people counted for nothing, and the idea of justice had not been born. The first hint of the idea of social justice, or rather of injustice, is to be found in the poems of Hesiod, the sour old Boeotian farmer whom the later Greeks, including Herodotus, supposed to be a contemporary of Homer, but who wrote in fact at least a century later.

It is a curious and interesting fact that Homer's poems remained as the basis of a Greek boy's education for centuries. He learned them by heart, or as much of them as his memory would hold. Far into the more sophisticated days of the Greek city-states it was still felt, apparently, that all life's most valuable lessons could be learned from these unburdened songs of dawn. That all the attributes of manhood were enshrined in the persons of those half-barbaric heroes and their familiar, almost brotherly, dealings with their gods. For later Greece, Homer was not a poet merely; he was The Poet, and by inference The Teacher too—as it is only the modern world which has separated the spheres of artist and teacher. Voices, indeed, were raised in protest against the Homeric morality, especially against the Homeric conception of the gods. 'Homer and Hesiod', complained Xenophanes, a native of Colophon, who wrote in the sixth century B.C., 'credited the gods with every disgraceful action—theft, adultery, deceit, and all evil deeds.' And in another surviving fragment he said that if oxen or lions had hands and could paint, they would paint the gods in the form of lions or oxen; while Plato, coming later, made the sweeping and ill-considered proposal to banish not Homer only, but all the poets, as corrupters of the truth, from his ideal society. Yet in spite of protests the near-worship of Homer remained an integral part of the Greek consciousness throughout the classical period. The Greeks never quite lost their admiration for Homeric prowess, for the ideal of the dominant male. Alexander the half-barbarian fillibuster who wished so much to be a cultivated Greek, slept during his campaigns with Homer's poems under his pillow.

By the eighth century before Christ the rule of the Kings, except in a few backward and outlying districts, had vanished from Greece, and the classical age had begun. The chief service of the Kings seems to have been their attempt to amalgamate the scattered hamlets in which their people lived into towns. It was Theseus, Herodotus tells us, the legendary King of Athens, who made a single community out of the villages of Attica, making the villagers, or demesmen, all citizens of Athens where, though they continued to live in their demes and on their farms, they could seek shelter and protection in times of danger or stress. These concentrations of the people, though originally convenient for the Kings and tending to increase their power, obviously contained also the seeds of change which would in the end abolish their power altogether. Exactly how the change occurred we do not know, but it is not difficult to guess. There is a hint of it in the *Iliad*, in the episode of Thersites. Agamemnon the King had summoned an Assembly—the Council of Elders (heroes or chieftains), and the mob, or common soldiery, whose function was to hear the King's decision and to give their assent. Thersites, however, though a man of the people, was not content with the time-honoured role of signifying dutiful assent to the opinion of his betters. Indeed he did not agree with it at all, and said so in no uncertain terms. Why should the likes of him and his friends spend ten years far from home, fighting the Trojans with whom they had no quarrel, simply to fill the coffers and increase the glory of the King? It is an amusing touch that Homer the aristocratic poet, is careful to inform us that Thersites was the ugliest man in the Greek army, a misshapen hunchback with bandy legs, always ready with a scurrilous jibe against authority, to make the troops laugh, and that, when he had said his say, Odysseus beat him into silence with his staff and reduced him to tears. Discipline must be maintained; mob rule is a bad thing; 'let there be one leader, one King.'

Grant the institution of an Assembly, and its subservience, however much hallowed by tradition, to the will of its master, is bound sooner or later to disappear. And disappear it did. The royal authority was broken, and its place was taken not, indeed, by the authority of the people as a whole—not yet—but by that of the aristocrats, of the great families like that of the Bacchiads at Corinth, or the Alcmaeonidae at Athens, or the Aleuadae at Larisa in Thessaly. Demos had not yet lifted his head to any purpose; or, if he had tried to do so, he had been beaten, like Thersites, into silence and tears. But his day was to come.

CHAPTER 9

Lydia

HERODOTUS BEGINS HIS BOOK WITH AN ACCOUNT OF LYDIA; IT was the last Lydian king, Croesus, who 'was the first foreigner so far as we know to come into direct contact with the Greeks, both in the way of conquest and alliance.'

The Lydian people, naturally enough, always interested the Greeks. In their obscure beginnings they with other tribes akin to the Greek—Lycians, Carians, Phrygians and others—had come down from the north some time in the second millennium before Christ to find new homes in western Asia Minor and on the coast of the Aegean.

Their early history, like that of all the peoples in this corner of the continent, so full of shifts and changes of population, dim struggles and migrations long lost, or nearly lost, in the mist of time, is legendary and obscure. One would like to believe the tale, preserved by a Greek from the queer chronicle of a native Lydian, that there was once a king of Lydia who had an appetite so insatiable that one night in his sleep he accidentally ate his wife; but I fear it is difficult to do so. It is not till near the end of the eighth century B.C. that Lydia emerges clearly into history. For some—perhaps five—centuries before that, kings of a Phrygian dynasty had been on the throne, and the Greek sense of some kind of kinship with these peoples is evident in the legend that the Phrygian royal house traced its ancestry back to Heracles that philoprogenitive and much-travelled hero with children in many lands. The Greek settlements on the coast, already prosperous by the end of the eighth or the beginning of the seventh century, lived mainly by commerce and seem to have preserved friendly relations with the peoples of the interior, to the mutual benefit of both; but a change was to come.

Herodotus relates how Candaules, the last king of the Phrygian line, was murdered by his Captain of the Guard, Gyges, a native Lydian, who usurped his throne and married his queen. The

Greeks had many tales about 'golden Gyges', as the poet Archilo-chus called him; the familiar one told by Plato about the magic ring which could make him invisible is not in Herodotus, but the one which Herodotus does tell—how he was led to see the king's wife naked, and how she, in shame and anger, gave him the choice of either killing himself or killing the king and becoming her husband—is in his best Arabian Nights manner.

Gyges extended the power of Lydia northward to the Bos-phorus and over the Troad, and had designs upon the Greek settlements of the coast. The empire of the Hittites had been finally broken by Assyria some fifty years before; their great military highroad from east to west had been organised for commercial purposes by Phrygia and Lydia, and Gyges needed the ports on the Aegean, to give him an outlet to the sea. But death cut short his enterprise, for he was killed in battle with the barbarous Cimmerians (their name still survives in the Crimea), who, driven from their homes by marauding Scythian tribes, swarmed southward and westward in search of new lands. Gyges' successors continued his policy of seeking an outlet to the sea, and it was Croesus, the last of his line, who brought it to fruition, but did not live long to enjoy his conquest.

The story of Croesus, upon which Herodotus lavished all the resources of his art, profoundly impressed the imagination of the Greeks. It is so important both as an illustration of Herodotus' power when he has a theme which fully engages his sympathy, and also in its bearing upon certain qualities of Greek feeling that I must dwell upon it at some length. For the Greeks, the fate of Croesus was the supreme instance of the Envy of the Gods, who would never allow human prosperity to rise too high or last too long. The great King and mighty warrior; the kindly ruler, rich beyond the dreams of the little, hard-living communi-ties of Greece, continually extending his dominion by a series of unbroken successes; dreaming of the conquest of the vast empires of the East, suddenly, in a single day, tumbled from his throne and made another's slave: all this perfectly expressed the sense which lay deep in the Greek consciousness—and derived naturally enough from the circumstances of the world they lived in—of the instability of human things. *Phthonos theon*—the Envy of the Gods: it is a recurrent and characteristic theme in Herodotus' book, but nowhere more poignantly illustrated than in the story of Croesus.

Croesus succeeded his father Alyattes when he was thirty-five years old, in 560 B.C. He at once set about the subjugation of the Greek cities of the coast, beginning with Ephesus. All his campaigns were successful, and all the Asiatic Greeks were compelled to pay him tribute, together with all the peoples westward of the River Halys, except only the Cilicians and the Lycians. He further proposed, according to Herodotus, an attempt on the Greek islands, but was dissuaded by the sensible advice of a certain Greek from the town of Priene, who pointed out to him that the islanders could use the sea as familiarly as fish, while the Lydians knew nothing about it whatever and would most certainly, if they rised such an enterprise, come to grief. The Lydian empire was now at the height of its wealth and prosperity, and it became the custom for distinguished Greeks from the mainland, especially the teachers and thinkers, to visit its capital city, Sardis, to see its wonders, and perhaps to learn a thing or two from a civilisation so different from their own. For in spite of the subjection of the Greek Asiatic settlements Lydia was not looked upon as a necessarily dangerous or hostile power; nor was she, when all is said, for though she exacted tribute from the conquered cities, she never destroyed them as going concerns, but allowed them, to her own advantage as well as theirs, to continue to play their important part in commerce. This was true, though to a lesser degree, even of Persia in the coming years, after the defeat of Croesus by Cyrus the Great. The Greek mainland, for obvious reasons, was to look upon Persia as the great enemy; but not the Greek settlements on the Asiatic coast. Most of them were to be under the control of an autocratic native ruler friendly to Persia, and by no means disapproved of at least by the aristocratic party within the various communities.

The Greek passion for dramatic stories led them to associate the Athenian statesman Solon with the tale of Croesus. As a matter of sober history Solon died just about the year in which Croesus ascended the throne; nevertheless Herodotus adopted the familiar legend and turned it to magnificent account. Solon, we read, was hospitably received by Croesus, and a few days after his arrival was taken on a tour of the royal treasuries and shown all the splendid sights of the king's palace and of the capital. When he had seen everything, the king sent for him again, and in the self-satisfaction of superlative wealth and acknowledged power, said: 'Well, my Athenian friend, I have heard a great deal about your wisdom and how widely you have travelled in the pursuit of knowledge. I cannot resist my desire to ask you a question: who is the happiest man you have ever seen?'

'An Athenian,' Solon replied, 'called Tellus.'

Croesus was taken aback. 'And what,' he asked sharply, 'is your reason for this choice?'

'He had fine sons and grandsons,' said Solon. 'He fought for his country, routed the enemy and died like a soldier.'

Croesus, already somewhat piqued, hoped at least that Solon would award him the second prize in the competition for happiness. But no: the next two happiest men were, in Solon's judgment, the brothers Cleobis and Biton, who, having proved in a spectacular manner their filial piety, fell asleep for ever in the temple of Hera in Argos.

'That's all very well,' said Croesus, now thoroughly angry; 'but what of my own happiness? Is it so utterly contemptible that you will not even compare me with common folk like those you mentioned?'

'My lord,' Solon answered, 'I know God is envious of human prosperity. Take seventy years as the span of a man's life; then the total for your seventy years will be 26,250 days, and not a single one of them is like the next in what it brings. You can see from that, Croesus, how chancy a thing is mortal life. You are very rich and you rule a numerous people, but the question you asked me I will not answer until I know you have died happily. Till a man is dead, keep the word 'happy' in reserve; before that he is not to be called happy, but only lucky. Look to the end, no matter what it is you are considering. Often enough God gives a man a glimpse of happiness, and then utterly ruins him.'

Croesus, unconvinced by Solon's wisdom, let him go with cold indifference; but before many days had passed God, in anger at his belief that he was the happiest of men, sent him a dreadful punishment in the death of his son Atys at the hands of a fugitive and suppliant whom Croesus himself had succoured and befriended. For two years Croesus mourned for the death of Atys, until news from Persia dragged him back into the world of affairs. Cyrus, son of Cambyses, had destroyed the empire of the Medes, and the power of Persia was steadily increasing. Would it be possible to check it, before it became irresistible, and swallowed Lydia too? Only the Oracles could tell him.

Having satisfied himself in the way I have related of the reliability and omniscience of the Delphic Apollo, Croesus, to get the god on his side, sent treasures of fabulous worth to his temple in Delphi, and, through the mouth of his messengers, asked his question: should he march against Persia, and would it be wise to seek the alliance of any of the Greek states? As to the first part of the question, the reader knows the oracle's answer; for the second, Croesus was advised to find out which of the Greek states at that time was the most powerful, and to come to an understanding with it.

With all this Croesus was delighted, and, eager for yet another flattering prophecy, asked the oracle if his reign would be a long one. The Priestess answered:

'When comes the day that a mule shall sit on the Median throne,
Then, tender-footed Lydian, by pebbly Hermus
Run and abide not, nor think it shame to be a coward.'

This gave the King more pleasure than anything he had yet heard; for he did not suppose that a mule was likely to become King of the Medes, and that meant that he and his line would remain in power for ever.

Accordingly, filled with vain hopes, Croesus, having concluded an alliance with Sparta, began his campaign against Cyrus and the Persians. There was an indecisive engagement near a place called Pteria in Cappadocia, after which Croesus withdrew to his capital, intending to build up his forces to greater strength for a final campaign the following spring. He already had treaties of alliance with Babylon and with Amasis, King of Egypt, as well as with Sparta, and he had called upon all of these to send contingents to his support within four months. Cyrus, however, was too quick for him: he was, Herodotus says, 'his own messenger', and marched straight upon Sardis before news of his intention could reach the city. Sardis was besieged. Croesus sent a second, and desperate, appeal to his allies for immediate assistance, but within fourteen days the city was in Cyrus' hands. Lydia had fallen; the oracle was fulfilled; Croesus had destroyed a mighty empire—his own.

With the highest art of the myth-maker and teller of tales Herodotus ends this crucial episode in his history thus: 'The

Persians brought their prisoner into the presence of the King, and Cyrus chained Croesus and placed him with fourteen Lydian boys on a great pyre that he had built. Perhaps he intended them as a choice offering to some god of his, or perhaps he had made a vow and wished to fulfil it; or it may be that he had learned that Croesus was a god-fearing man, and set him on the pyre to see if any divine power would save him from being burnt alive. But whatever the reason, that was what he did; and Croesus, for all his misery, as he stood on the pyre, remembered how Solon had declared that no man could be called happy until he was dead. It was as true as if God had spoken it. Till then Croesus had not uttered a sound; but when he remembered, he sighed bitterly and three times, in anguish of spirit, pronounced Solon's name.

'Cyrus heard the name and told his interpreters to ask who Solon was; but for a while Croesus refused to answer the question and kept silent; at last, however, he was forced to speak. "He was a man," he said, "who ought to have talked with every King in the world. I would give a fortune to have had it so." Not understanding what he meant, they renewed their questions and pressed him so urgently to explain that he could no longer refuse. He then related how Solon the Athenian once came to Sardis and made light of the splendour which he saw there, and how everything he said, though it applied to all men and especially to those who imagine themselves fortunate, had in his own case proved all too true.

'While Croesus was speaking, the fire had been lit and was already burning round the edges. The interpreters told Cyrus what Croesus had said, and the story touched him. He himself was a mortal man, and was burning alive another who had once been as prosperous as he. The thought of that, and the fear of retribution, and the realisation of the instability of human things, made him change his mind and give orders that the flames should at once be put out, and Croesus and the boys brought down from the pyre. But the fire had got a hold, and the attempt to extinguish it failed. The Lydians say that when Croesus understood that Cyrus had changed his mind, and saw everyone vainly trying to master the fire, he called loudly upon Apollo with tears to come and save him from his misery, if any of his gifts had been pleasant to him. It was a clear and windless day; but suddenly in answer to Croesus' prayer clouds gathered and a storm broke with such violent rain that the flames were put out.

'This was proof enough for Cyrus that Croesus was a good man whom the gods loved; so he brought him down from the pyre.'

Herodotus adds a curious little pendant to this story. Cyrus asked Croesus, whom he now regarded with a kind of awe, if there was any particular favour he could do him. Croesus pointed to the chains he was bound with. 'Let me,' he said, 'send these chains to the god of the Greeks whom I most honoured, and ask him if he is accustomed to cheat his benefactors.' Messengers were accordingly sent to Delphi with the chains, which they laid on the threshold of the temple; then, pointing to them with accusing fingers, they asked the God if, when such things were the fruits of war, he was not ashamed to have encouraged Croesus by his oracles to take the course which he had taken. The God's answer, through the mouth of his Priestess, is both odd and interesting: Croesus, he said, had expiated in the fifth generation the crime of his ancestor Gyges; the God of Prophecy, grateful for Croesus' gifts, had been eager that the fall of Sardis might occur in the time of Croesus' sons rather than in his own, but he had been unable to divert the course of destiny. Nevertheless, what little the Fates allowed, that he had done; he had postponed the evil day for three years, and he had saved Croesus from being burnt alive. As to the oracle which prophesied that he would destroy a great empire, the sensible thing would have been to send again to inquire which empire was meant. This Croesus failed to do, so the fault was his own. Furthermore, he failed to understand the meaning of the last oracle about the mule. The mule was Cyrus, who was the child of parents of different races, for his mother was a Mede and his father a Persian. All these explanations Croesus accepted: he admitted that the God was innocent and he had only himself to blame.

In this, nothing could be clearer than the Greek sense of a power beyond the gods; but the most interesting thing about it is the attempt it embodies to reconcile free will with Destiny—the overruling power of Fate, which not even the gods can escape. Croesus was fated to fall; but at the same time, in some way, it was his own fault. He *ought* to have sent again to the oracle; he *ought* to have been a more intelligent interpreter. Nevertheless (we cannot but ask) what would have happened if he had? Herodotus, as the whole tenor of his work reveals, believed in human responsibility. A history without such a belief would be nothing better than either the baldest chronicle or a set of fairy stories. But he also believed—being a Greek—in Fate.

Herodotus, clearly expressing the feeling of his day, considered that Lydia, in a very real sense, was the protectress of the Greek settlements. Other Greek states, too, beyond the Aegean, had agreed to support Croesus should the need arise. But Croesus, by his defeat at the hands of Cyrus, failed to give the protection which the Greek states looked for, and it was this failure which in the view of Herodotus made him the principle cause of the great conflict between east and west.

Yet Croesus remained in the Greek imagination a benevolent, and in some ways a romantic, figure, unlike any other Eastern despot. Pindar, writing about 470 B.C., took him as an example of the great who enjoy a fair after-fame in the hearts of men: 'the generous kindliness of Croesus passes not away.'

Greece was not without her debts to Lydia: the chief of them was the invention of coinage. Till the early iron age, trade was conducted by means of barter, and it is said to have been Gyges (687-652 B.C.) who was the first to issue coins. This revolutionary invention was at once adopted by Miletus and Ephesus, two Greek coastal cities in close contact with Lydia; they issued coins of electrum—an alloy of gold and silver—stamped with the emblems of the state. The off-shore islands, notably Chios and Samos, soon followed with a silver coinage of their own, and it was Croesus who issued the first bimetallic currency, consisting of *staters*—i.e. coins of a standard or specific weight—of pure gold and pure silver. The Greek mainland was slower to introduce a coinage; Pheidon of Argos was the first ruler to do so. The previous means of exchange had been iron in the form of spits (*obeloi*) or bars; and after the introduction of coins the old word was retained—the 'obol'. The drachma too, the most familiar Greek coin to modern readers, took its name from the same source: the word means 'a handful (of spits)'. It used to puzzle me why Rhodopis, the highly successful Thracian prostitute who went to Naucratis in Egypt and made a fortune there, presented as a thank offering to the Delphic oracle a large number of iron spits—'fit', says Herodotus, 'for roasting oxen whole.' It seemed an unlikely sort of present; but the fact that such things were once the common means of exchange throws a little light on her odd choice. Characteristically, the Greeks never developed a uniform national coinage, different commercial centres continuing for centuries to produce their own.

In obvious connection with a coinage, which alone rendered it possible, retail trade, too, passed into Greece from Lydia, or so the Greeks themselves believed. The Lydians, according to Herodotus, were also the inventors of dice, knuckle-bones and ball games—which they originally devised to alleviate the misery of eighteen years of national famine, playing and eating on alternate days. Another Lydian custom, the prostitution of all working-class girls with the object of collecting for themselves a dowry, remained, one is pleased to know, within the country of its origin. For all Greeks Lydia was long the type of luxury and wealth. They adopted her music too: the 'Lydian mode' became familiar in Greece, and was deprecated by Plato and other austere philosophers as relaxing and effeminate. Above all, Lydia, before the coming of Cyrus, was for Greece the great imperial power, dividing Asia with the Medes, and keeping the East at bay. God himself had prevented a clash between the two, when in the reign of Alyattes, the father of Croesus, an eclipse of the sun had separated the hostile armies. Thales the Milesian had foretold the eclipse, and his prediction had been fulfilled. It took place on May 28, 585 B.C.

The whole story of Croesus, standing as it does at the beginning of Herodotus' book, is, even apart from its literary excellence, highly important as an illustration of his historical method. Right at the outset we learn from it what sort of history to expect. It is very different from the kind of history which historians give us today. In the first place, one must recognise that in its broad outline Herodotus' account is true. He makes no mistakes about the essential nature of the relationship of the Lydian kingdom either with its neighbouring kingdoms or with Greece, and especially with the Greek cities of the Asiatic coast. He is perfectly right in saying that the defeat of Croesus by Cyrus of Persia led by a connected and inevitable chain of events to the great conflict between East and West. But within that framework of valid history Herodotus has, with deliberate intention, both moral and artistic, constructed from his own imagination working upon all sorts of popular traditions and received material a drama, containing—as Aristotle said all good dramas must—a beginning, a middle and an end. The course of actual history seldom has such well-proportioned and convenient parts; it pounds along, defying the chronicler to detect too shapely a pattern in its movement. Herodotus, on the contrary, always saw a pattern in history; or, if he did not, he invented one. It was the best method he knew of imparting to the reader his own sense of the nature of human destiny. The drama of Croesus, as Herodotus tells it, would have made an admirable plot for a tragedy by Sophocles. In its structure it does, in fact, closely resemble a Greek tragedy, and it is almost as closely knit: first the prologue, with the treachery of Gyges, to be expiated in the fifth generation; then the coming of Croesus to the throne, and his unexampled prosperity; then the premonitions of doom—Solon's warning, and the death of Atys; then the misconstruing of the oracles, and the swift and utter defeat by Cyrus. Finally, if one cares to pursue it, the *deus ex machina*—the rescue of Croesus from the flames by the god Apollo.

At one point the drama is broken by an interlude, when Herodotus, having told how Croesus was advised by the oracle to find out which of the Greek mainland communities was the most powerful, takes the opportunity to sketch in brief the contemporary condition of Athens and the rise to power of Sparta. Some writers have tried to see this passage not as a digression but as integral to the drama, forming a sort of dramatic 'chorus' to the main development of the plot. But this is to seek a perfection of shapeliness which is foreign to Herodotus; moreover, the chorus in a Greek drama consists always of songs or descants on a theme intimately connected with, or suggested by, the leading idea which the play as a whole embodies; they are like musical variations on a theme; but this passage, on the contrary, bears no relation at all, either in tone or feeling, to the tragedy of Croesus. It is pure digression; nevertheless it is digression exceedingly skilfully contrived, and characteristic of Herodotus' art. Athens and Sparta are to play together the leading part in the total drama of the book as the two powers jointly responsible, more than any others, for the happy outcome of the impending struggle between oriental despotism and the free world, and, somehow or other, they must be introduced to the reader as soon as may be after the rise of the curtain. Seizing his chance, offered by an incident in Croesus' story, Herodotus performs the introduction with consummate address.

CHAPTER 10

Athens and the Economic Background

THE INQUIRIES OF CROESUS REVEALED THAT ATHENS WAS UNDER the dictatorship—or 'tyranny', a word borrowed by the Greeks from the Lydian language, and signifying 'despotic rule' without overtones of praise or blame—of Pisistratus, the son of Hippocrates. She had a thousand years of history—of a sort—behind her, and was now recognised as sharing with Sparta the most influential position amongst the Greek communities. Yet by modern standards of size and wealth she was still no more than what we should consider a small, isolated country town, and as poor as a church mouse. It is the diminutive scale of things in ancient Greek history, and the tiny material resources of the little, independent communities, which divide them by so wide a gulf from modern civilisation; the same cause produced their distinctive characteristics, both good and bad.

Greece was always a poor country, though in classical times a rather larger area of land was cultivable than today, and there was more forest. Even in the fourth century B.C. Plato wrote that the soil of Attica was by no means what it had been in the past, before the storms of many thousand years had washed it away from the hillsides down into the sea, leaving only the bare rock, like the bones of a skeleton with all the flesh gone. The areas of fertile plain—the coastal, backed by mountains, or the inland, ringed with mountains—were in consequence all the more precious; most communities had their bit of it for grain-growing, chiefly barley, with sheep and goat pasture higher up the hillside, and bee pasture (for honey was an important commodity) amongst the scrub higher still. The olive was indigenous and the most valuable of trees, providing food, and oil for cooking, lighting, and the ancient equivalent of soap. Vines flourished and provided wine almost everywhere. Most Greek communities remained agricultural throughout their history; even the important trading towns, like Corinth and Athens, rested upon their agriculture. The Greeks were a hardy and frugal people; they lived almost entirely in the open air; their houses were unheated, and kept only for their women to work in and for the men to sleep in. A Greek winter can be cold, but through it the open-air life went on; the festival of Lenaea at Athens, at which comedies were performed, was in early February. Men lived on two meals a day: a lunch at noon, after working from sunrise, and a supper in the evening. The staple diet was farinaceous, with fish and cheese for relishes, and meat only upon festive occasions. Persians used to complain that they always got up from a Greek meal hungry: it consisted normally of two courses, the first (as one historian has put it) consisting of a sort of porridge, the second of another sort of porridge. Their wine they drank mixed with water.

Herodotus tells a story of the Spartan general Pausanias, the victor of Plataea: Xerxes, after his withdrawal from Greece, had left his tent with Mardonius, the commander of his army. The tent, together with the rest of the Persian spoils, fell into Pausanias' hands after the battle, and when he saw it, with its embroidered hangings and gorgeous decorations in gold and silver, he sent for the cooks and bakers who had served Mardonius and told them to prepare a meal such as they were used to serve to their former master. His order was obeyed, and when he saw everything prepared with the greatest magnificence and all the good things set out upon tables of silver and gold, he could hardly believe his eyes, and just for a joke ordered his own servants to get ready an ordinary Spartan dinner. The difference, said Herodotus with his customary understatement, was indeed remarkable, and, when both meals were ready, Pausanias laughed and sent for the commanding officers of the various allied Greek contingents. He then invited them to take a look at the two dinners, laid out side by side, and said: 'Well, gentlemen, I asked you here in order to show you the folly of the Persians, who, living in this style, came to Greece to rob us of our poverty.' Even in fifth-century Athens, the richest of the Greek cities and then at the height of her prosperity, it was said that only Alcibiades went to the absurd and unnecessary expense of decorating the interior of his house with paintings.

It was always the desire of the Greek communities to be economically self-sufficient, and in times of stress most of them could, at a pinch, raise enough food to keep themselves going. In early times, when the population outran the food supply, the difficulty would be met by emigration—the Greeks called it sending out a 'colony', but the word for us has quite different associations: a Greek colony was not a commercial venture, or an attempt to penetrate and exploit an alien or savage people; it was simply a group of adventurers sometimes drawn by invitation from various communities and always under the direction of a leader, who sailed away to some previously selected spot, where the climate was known to be favourable to the traditional Greek way of living, and there built a new town, as like as they could make it to what they were familiar with at home. Or, if emigration, for one reason or another, could not make inadequate resources go round, there always remained robbery by violence, sometimes dignified by the name of war. Before the full development of the city state, when there was as yet no maritime power able to control the seas, piracy throve, and was a respected profession. Most Greek towns were built a little away from the coast, to avoid surprise by raiders from the sea. 'Are you pirates, or peaceful traders?' was the customary greeting to strangers unexpectedly coming up from the shore; and the question expressed nothing but genuine curiosity. One did not blame, whatever the answer was to be; but it was as well to know.

War was endemic in the history of the growth of the Greek city states and was waged with cheerful barbarity. Its causes were not complex, as in the modern world, but agreeably simple. Aristotle called it a means of acquisition; a character in Xenophon's *Memoirs of Socrates* suggests to the sage that it is a useful source of wealth to a community which happens to need it, and 'of course,' Socrates replied, 'provided that you are the stronger; should you be the weaker, you will only lose what you've got already.' Nothing could be more practical. The Greek states fought each other with zest and evident enjoyment for land and supplies.

An entertaining example of piracy is the story which Herodotus tells of Miltiades, the victor of Marathon. Miltiades' reputation in Athens, already high, had been greatly increased by that resounding success, so, presuming upon his popularity in the town, he asked for a fleet of seventy ships together with troops and money for a certain enterprise which he had in mind. He did not specify his objective, but merely told his fellow-citizens that he was bound for a place where they could easily get as much money as they wanted. This sounded so good that the Athenians made no objection whatever, but promptly let him have the ships and the men. Full of confidence, Miltiades then sailed for the island of Paros, where he landed and laid siege to the town, sending in a demand for a hundred talents and threatening that, if the Parians refused to pay, he would persist in the blockade until he had starved them into surrender. Unfortunately, the siege operations went wrong, and Miltiades himself somehow or other seriously injured his knee and was forced to sail home to Athens without a penny-piece to show for his adventure. There he was received by no means like a national hero; on the contrary, he was brought before the people to be tried for his life on the charge of defrauding the public. He was acquitted on the capital charge, but fined fifty talents. A footnote on this story is that Miltiades chose Paros as his objective not because the island community was particularly rich or offered a better prize than any other place, but in revenge for a private grudge: a certain Parian called Lysagoras had, he believed, told tales against him to Hydarnes the Persian. There is much of Greek morality in this simple tale.

Nevertheless though economic self-sufficiency, like every other sort of independence, remained attractive in theory to the Greek communities, trade relations existed between them from the earliest times. Within the Greek peninsula there was, and is, much variety in soil, temperature and weather, depending largely, as is natural in so mountainous a country, on altitude; thus the various states had their special products, such as the olives and oil of Attica, the woollen goods of Megara, the perfumes and unguents of Corinth, the wine from the islands of Chios or Peparethus, and this encouraged trade and intercourse within the peninsula, while easy communications by sea led, even in pre-historic times, to commercial contacts with Asia, Egypt and the East.

But the basis of the Greek economy was, and remained, agricultural. 'Most of mankind,' wrote Aristotle, 'get their living from the land and the cultivation of crops.' It was true at any rate of Greece. When one reads of the Greek 'city states', one tends to think primarily of urban communities, and of course it is true that the actual city, especially in later days when there was less buccaneering and greater commercial prosperity, was of enormous importance in the life of its members; but at the same time it must never be forgotten that the majority of its members continued to get their living from their farms. Thucydides tells us that every family in Attica who owned land, lived on it until they were driven to seek protection within the city by the Spartan invasions during the Peloponnesian war. The Greeks, a politically minded people if ever there was one, continued to regard agriculture as, at any rate in theory, the best and most natural occupation for a free man. So it had been in prehistoric days, when the wanderers first settled on some piece of land which they came to look on as their own; and so it remained throughout the history of classical Greece. Conservative in most things, the Greeks were in nothing more conservative than in this; when writers such as Plato and Xenophon praised the farmer's life (even though, by then, times had changed for the worse) they were sincere themselves and said what all would understand, unlike Vergil, for instance, who, though he doubtless remembered with a certain sentimental regret his father's farm at Andes in Cisalpine Gaul, wrote his charming poem in praise of a country life for a cultivated circle of confirmed city-dwellers who cared little or nothing for bees and bullocks and beans. The city was to become in a very real sense the centre of their lives; but the country with its unchanging and immemorial routine of labour was still the indispensable background. From the little family property outside the walls the men would go to the city—though the word 'city' is misleading, suggesting something much bigger than the reality —to attend to their duties as citizens, to take part in the debates in the Assembly, to sit on the huge juries to try cases in the courts, to be present at religious functions or festivals, and to enjoy, as no people ever enjoyed more keenly than the Greeks, social life and gossip. But even in the city they were still under the open sky, and they took their country thoughts with them. Dicaeopolis in Aristophanes' play the *Acharnians* can speak for a thousand others. Driven from his village farm by the Spartan invasions to take refuge in the city, waiting, bored and angry, for the Assembly to begin, 'Here I sit,' he grumbles, 'looking out to the country beyond the walls, longing for peace again, hating the town, and sick at heart for my native village. There at least there has never yet been talk of buying charcoal or vinegar or oil—Buying indeed! I never knew the word; the farm produced all I wanted.'

In modern civilisation there is a gulf between the life of the country and the life of the town, and the ways of thought in each are barely intelligible to the other; in ancient Greece there was no separation at all, but the two lives were aspects the one of the other. One result of this was the sanity and balance which even the most casual acquaintance with Greek life and literature cannot but reveal. Greek life, even in its later and more sophisticated development, never cut a man off from his natural roots. There are plenty of stories of greed and money-grubbing in Greek literature—Herodotus has a number of them, especially about the Spartans; but no Greek of the classical or pre-classical age would have thought of spending his life in the making of a fortune. He preferred to live. In a trading venture overseas, the adventure itself was, to him, as important as the prospect of gain. He liked a windfall as much as any man, but he could never have brought himself to keep office hours. Moreover, the normal Greek enjoyed his leisure more than we are inclined to do; and he had plenty of it—not because he was lazy, but because he was content to do without innumerable luxuries and comforts which the modern world has let itself be persuaded are necessary to its well-being. No doubt the Greek climate had something to do with this, for it is on the whole a kindly one; but climate was not the only cause; temperament came into it too, that unimpaired zest for the physical realities of living which is possible, I suppose, only in a young civilisation.

But though agriculture remained paramount in the economy of the city state, the craftsman, too, had his place, and that an increasingly important one. Solon writing at the end of the seventh or early in the sixth century mentions in one of his poems, in addition to the fisherman's craft, the 'works of Athene and Hephaestus', that is, weaving and metal-work, divining (a dubious craft) and medicine. There were of course innumerable others, the leather-workers, the stone-masons, and the potters, all with their shops in a special quarter of the town. Plato's dialogues are full of references to them, and he builds many a philosophical speculation on the consideration of the humble skills of shoemakers or ship-wrights. At least in the earlier days before the catastrophic increase in slavery had upset the balance of Greek society, craftsmen were honoured in an ancient Greek city, and the true democracy of Greece consisted less, perhaps, in democratic institutions—where such obtained—than in the fact that there were no class distinctions based upon a man's profession or trade. The only kind of work which seems to have been looked upon askance was retail shopkeeping; 'no one,' said Plato, 'will earn his living in this way if he can help it.' It is not unlikely that the distrust of the retailer arose in the early days from the fact that his primary object was to make money. This sounds odd to our way of thinking; but it is indisputable that the object of the old Greek craftsmen, like that of the farmers and small landowners, was not to make money but to make a living, which is a quite different thing. A man's farm fed him, and so enabled him to live; if he had no land, but possessed some special skill, he used that skill to get a livelihood. The exercise of the skill was in itself a satisfaction. The retailer on the other hand, having no special skill, dealt in goods which he had not himself been concerned in producing. He was interested only in what they would fetch in the open market. Such men, said Plato, in a well-ordered community tend to be those who are physically weak and therefore not much good for any other sort of occupation.

Herodotus tells a story which may or may not be apocryphal: the Asiatic Greeks had failed to enlist the active support of Sparta against Cyrus and the Persians; the Spartans, however, though they refused direct interference, sent a galley to the Asiatic coast by way of a general reconnaissance. 'The vessel,' wrote Herodotus, 'put in at Phocaea, and a certain Lacrines was sent to Sardis to forbid Cyrus, on behalf of the Lacedaemonians, to harm any Greek city upon pain of their displeasure. The story goes that when Cyrus heard what the herald said he asked some Greeks who happened to be with him who the Lacedaemonians were, and what were their numbers that they dared to send him such a command. On being informed he gave the following answer to the Spartan herald: 'I have never yet been afraid of men who have a special meeting place in the centre of their city, where they swear this and that and cheat each other. Such people, if *I* have anything to do with it, will not merely have the troubles of Ionia to chatter about, but their own.' This was intended by Cyrus as a criticism of the Greeks generally, because they had

markets for buying and selling, unlike the Persians who never
bought in open market. Herodotus' usual gusto in telling this
anecdote seems to suggest that up to a point, at any rate, he saw
eye to eye with Cyrus in the matter of retail trade. And no doubt
he spoke for a majority of his countrymen. Swearing in the
market-place that a stinking fish was straight from the sea that
morning, or that the loaves at the bottom of the basket were
just as big and brown as the ones on top, was no doubt necessary
in an up-to-date community, but—it was not the work for a
decent man. Making boots, on the contrary, emphatically was:
the retailer made money (if he could) out of other men's labour
and skill; the bootmaker made a living out of his own. The
Greeks always respected the 'maker', whatever the object he
made, whether it was a pot, a pair of shoes or a poem, and they
felt no need to arrange the various skills which men possess in
an order of dignity. Their word for a skilled craftsman (*technites*)
was applied not only to shoemakers, shipbuilders, weavers,
potters and so on, but equally to the sculptor and the doctor. They
had, too, another word for a craftsman, which is most revealing;
Herodotus himself uses it on several occasions: it was *cheironax*—
'king of the hands'. Socrates himself was a craftsman, a stone-
cutter; Socrates was certainly not a typical Greek, but he was
typical at any rate in the amount of time he was willing (and
able) to take off from his working hours. The fact that the object
of Greek craftsmanship was to supply needs and not, as today,
to create needs for subsequent satisfaction, to make a living rather
than a fortune for the craftsman, is no doubt one reason for the
sustained excellence of its products—or of such of them as have
survived for us to see. Something similar might be said of Greek
literature, but of that it is not yet time to speak.

I do not at all mean in what I have said to imply that the
Greeks as a race were careless of material success or prosperity,
or that they had a lofty indifference towards money. The opposite would be nearer the truth. Greek commercial morality
was low—as indeed one might expect in a people, one of whose
gods (Hermes) was said to have taught Odysseus' grandfather and
no doubt many another fine fellow to be a pre-eminent trickster
and thief. Demosthenes' speeches are full of references to dis-
honest guardians and trustees; and Herodotus is by no means the
only writer to tell, without any apparent condemnation, of the

readiness even of his most distinguished countrymen to take
bribes: the great Themistocles, for instance, the victor of Salamis,
and the Spartan King Leotychides. No: the Greeks were as
materially-minded as any other people; they possessed from
immemorial antiquity their strict notions of 'justice'—their *dike*—
or 'way': the right way of doing things—but that 'way' included
no prohibition of the natural human desire to overreach one's
neighbour. What I have intended to suggest is something quite
different: it is to point to a fundamental difference between the
Greek sense of values and that, in general, of the modern world.
The Greeks were an acute and perceptive people, but they never
saw fit to make a necessary connection—as we presumably do—
between a man's activity and his pecuniary profit. The connection
would not have been beyond their intelligence, but they did not
choose to make it. No doubt every Greek would have been
pleased, had his income been doubled, provided that the means
to doubling it did not interfere with the sort of life he liked to
live. Nevertheless, even if he quadrupled it, his neighbours would
not have regarded him with any greater respect.

Money, in fact, was never in the Greek view an end in itself,
and a life devoted to the acquisition of it would have been to a
Greek an inconceivable stupidity and waste of time. This was
partly due to the simplicity of the economic foundations of a
Greek community, where there was little credit and no unem-
ployment and existence was of a much more hand-to-mouth
nature than it is in the modern world; but it was due also to the
Greek temperament, which always sought direct satisfactions. A
common phrase in Greek poetry for 'to be alive' is 'to see the
sunlight', and the phrase is not without significance, for it
suggests an active and actual pleasure in a purely physical condition, a pleasure which modern complexities tend to overlay.
Most Greeks in the developed city state had either a farm or a
trade; but the evidence of literature all tends to the conclusion
that no Greek would have thought of identifying his 'work'
with his 'life'. His 'life' was in his leisure, of which he had plenty,
partly because, as I have already suggested, he was willing to do
without so many of the luxuries which the modern world
considers necessary and therefore has to work for, and partly
because many menial tasks (though fewer than is often supposed)
were done for him by slaves. That leisure he filled with many

and various activities, of which the chief were politics (the *koinon*, 'that which interests everybody'), fighting, and attendance at the periodical beanfeasts provided by his religion, when he could laugh himself sick at the cheerful obscenities of an Aristophanes or gape in wonderment at the awful grandeurs of a tragedy by Aeschylus. A Greek life was a full life, and it was lived—if the phrase is intelligible—at first hand, including its physical satisfactions which were taken with an animal frankness and gusto. It is, I think, a significant fact that in the great age of Greece there was no literature or art with an aphrodisiac or provocative intention; the cheerful obscenities of Aristophanes we can call obscene only in the light of a change in public manners. Real obscenity, which can be found in some late Greek literature—in Lucian, for instance, as almost everywhere in modern fiction and drama—is always accompanied by a failure in vitality and is totally uncharacteristic of the great age of Greece. Drabness and dirt are an indication that the taste of life has gone flat upon the tongue. The Greek character was equipped with a rich assortment of vices, but the vices were neither complex nor furtive and they were all called by their proper names. The Greeks were not given to self-deception. As a people, they were, for instance, cruel, revengeful and utterly unscrupulous in their dealings with a personal or national enemy; but whatever the atrocity which a man or a state proposed to commit, it would be committed, so to speak, in the daylight: no one would have bothered his head to veil it under an invented moral justification.

Anyone who has the slightest acquaintance with Greek history will remember the case of the Athenian treatment of Melos. The example is perhaps not altogether a fair one, as it occurred when the shadows were already beginning to fall over the great age of Greece; nevertheless it is in essence characteristic. The tiny island of Melos had declared its neutrality in the war between Athens and Sparta. Athens nevertheless assessed it for tribute amongst her subject allies. The tribute was not paid. Nine years later Athenian troops landed on the island and informed the islanders that they must enter the Athenian alliance or take the consequences. The islanders resisted the intolerable demand, fought for their independence and were of course defeated. The Assembly met in Athens to decide their fate, when Alcibiades, one of history's most brilliant cads, proposed, with others, that the entire male adult population should be butchered and the women and children sold into slavery. The proposal was carried out. The incident is related at length by the historian Thucydides who, as his way was, leaves the reader to make his own deductions. The moral background of the tale has its horrible simplicity and clarity: the Greeks did indeed both live and think directly.

A further comment on the characteristic I am trying to describe is provided by the remarkable fact that the Greeks, before their decadence, never invented the art of fiction. They wrote only about what they supposed to be fact: Homer's splendid stories, like all the myths and legends which provided plots for their plays, were *true* stories. The Greeks believed in them as authentic history. Why trouble to invent, when the world is so full of actual wonders?

Athens had had a hard struggle to attain to her comparative prosperity under Pisistratus. At the beginning of the seventh century B.C., which was about the time when Hesiod wrote and when Greek recorded history may be said properly to begin, conditions throughout mainland Greece were still chaotic. The time of the great Lawgivers, of Solon at Athens and of Lycurgus at Sparta, was at hand but had not yet come. In most of the states of Greece, as we have seen, the passing of the Kings had been succeeded by the government of the noble families, more or less oppressive and constantly at feud amongst themselves. The feuds led to the emergence of one or another of the oligarchical leaders as supreme, and thus to the establishment of authoritarian rule—which the Greeks called 'tyranny'. From the rivalries and hatreds within an oligarchy 'factions', Herodotus wrote, 'arise, and out of factions comes bloodshed, and the result of bloodshed is tyranny.' It was an age of rapid growth and change, a scramble for power still without direction and control, when the weakest went to the wall. 'The doer of evil and the rash, proud man,' wrote Hesiod, 'will have the honour. Justice is in the might of the hands, and conscience is nowhere found. The wicked will hurt the good with crooked words, and break the oath which he has sworn.' Wealth was increasing with the growing importance of the towns, and was more and more concentrated in the hands of the few. Some states, notably Corinth and Megara, were already sending colonies overseas. The poor had no means of redress against their masters, and all over the country they were sinking to a state of serfdom. There was no body of law to which to appeal for the settlement of injustices, but only the local lordling, whoever he might be—the 'bribe-devouring prince,' as Hesiod calls him. 'I will tell you a tale,' he goes on, 'for wise princes to hear. A hawk seized a tawny-throated nightingale in his talons and carried her high up into the sky. The nightingale, clutched in the crooked claws, piteously bemoaned her fate, and the hawk, in his lordly way, said: "What is your complaint, my friend? A stronger one than you has got you in his grip, and you must go where I choose to take you, for all your pretty singing. I shall eat you or let you go, just as I please." '

In southern Greece, especially in the territory dominated by Sparta, the masses had been reduced to serfdom and deprived of political rights by a straightforward process of conquest; but in the more advanced communities to the northward, including Athens herself, a subtler and more interesting force had been at work. This was the introduction, probably from Lydia of a metal currency. By about the middle of the seventh century all the leading Greek states, except Sparta who was always slow to move, were coining their own money, and every creditor was expecting to be paid what was owed him in cash. The old system of barter and of payment in kind was gone for ever. The invention of a metal currency, without which no progress in material civilisation would have been possible, nevertheless had a disastrous effect upon the small peasant farmer living on the produce of his land. 'He used,' wrote Zimmern in his *Greek Commonwealth*, 'to take his stuff to market and exchange it for the goods he needed—wool for the wife to spin, children's shoes for the winter, or tiles to mend the roof; or he would pay the smith and the joiner in kind for reparing his plough or his cart. But now most of them will not accept his corn and wine till he has turned it into money. How much is it worth? He has not the least idea: for it depends on factors outside his range and which he has no means of controlling. He takes what the middleman gives him; and the middleman makes a living on his commission. At the end of the first year he is alarmed to find he has not as much margin in hand as usual. When the inevitable lean year comes he has no margin at all. In fact he cannot see his way through the winter without help. His only resource is to borrow.

'So he applies to the Big House (for the day of the professional Shylock is not yet). The Well-born or Eupatrid (as the Athenians called him) is most accommodating. His heroic ancestors used to take their gold with them to the grave, in masks and such like. He is delighted to have found a better use for it. Certainly he will keep him through the winter. But of course he must be repaid punctually next harvest. And he wants a little extra as well to make up for what he might have been doing with his money in the meantime—say twenty per cent for the six months. The old 'garlic-smelling Acharnian' . . . agrees. One more detail before the transaction is concluded. Is he sure he can repay? The Eupatrid has his oath, but he wants some more substantial security. Can he produce a friendly neighbour to go bail for him? He fears not. They have all grown cautious these days—ever since on market-day there was a stranger from Laconia, telling all and sundry about the miserable state of the peasants there. The wisest man in Sparta, he said, summed up the position in five words: 'Go bail and see ruin.' . . . So neighbours are no good. He is thrown back on his own resources. What has he got to offer? Only his land and his labour. He had never really thought of his land as his own: properly speaking it belongs to the family, to his ancestors and descendants as much as to himself. Still, the neighbours keep telling him that this is an old-fashioned idea, and that nowadays land can be bought and sold and sliced and pieced together just like any of the ordinary wares in the market-place. What will the children do if he has no land to leave them when he dies? And what about all the religious associations? Well, necessity knows no religion, and his children must pray for happier times. So he consents, reluctantly, to make a bargain about his land. If he does not repay next spring, let the Eupatrid take it over: he will cultivate it as his tenant, and pay him a sixth of its produce as rent. Done. He goes away with his money, and the Eupatrid sets up an eyesore of a pillar, with letters on it, in full view of the house. He cannot read the letters, but he supposes they are to keep him in mind of his bargain.

'Alas he needs no such reminder! Lean years have a way of running in cycles. Next spring the harvest is as bad as its predecessor. By the end of the year his land is no longer his own, and he has joined the ranks of the 'clients' or 'sixth-parters.' For some time all goes well. Then there comes a bad year, when

expenses are heavy and he cannot pay his sixth . . . What remedy
has the landlord? He could no doubt evict him. But, besides
being impious, this is to neither party's advantage. For the landlord could not easily replace his tenant nor the tenant his home.
What has the peasant left to offer? Like the modern proletarian,
nothing but his labour. So he makes another and still more
humiliating bargain. Unless his rent is paid (of course with
interest) by next spring, the whole produce of his labour shall
henceforward belong to the Eupatrid. In other words he will
become his slave . . .

'Such, roughly speaking, is the history of many of the debt-
slaves whose bitter cry goes up in seventh-century Greece and in
the prophecies of Israel—perhaps the bitterest of all forms of
slavery, because its victims are suffering in the midst of increasing
abundance.'

In Athens, of whose political fortunes we know more, by the
accident of literature, than of the other Greek states, the desperate
situation which had been brought about by the economic revolution was checked, if not remedied, by the political courage and
ability of Solon, the man of whose reputed wisdom Croesus
had expressed such grave doubts. Some time in the first decade
of the sixth century he was given special powers by the ruling
clique in Athens, and began his reforms by a sweeping measure
which came to be known by the picturesque name of the Shaking
off of Burdens. By this measure all the debt-slaves were declared
free, and all mortgages and debts by which the debtor's person
was pledged were annulled. It was a fair start, and the general
relief was celebrated in the ancient characteristic way by a
public feast and thanksgiving. A further blow was struck at the
rich by the introduction of a limit to the amount of land which
could be owned by a single person, and by the prohibition of the
export of grain to foreign markets where higher prices had up
till then been obtainable. 'The land which was enslaved,' Solon
wrote in one of his poems—he was not much of a poet, but
wrote in verse for the simple reason that no one had yet thought
of writing in prose—'I made free. I brought back to their heaven-
built fatherland of Athens many who had been sold as slaves,
justly or unjustly, and many who for their debts had been driven
to exile and had almost forgotten their native speech from
wandering abroad so long. And those who here endured cruel

slavery and trembled at the harsh temper of a master I restored to liberty.'

But Solon was no demagogue, and sensibly refused to go nearly as far in his reform as the oppressed classes hoped and wished. 'In high matters,' he wrote, 'it is hard to please everyone. I threw my strong shield over the high and the low, and suffered neither party to vanquish the other unjustly.' Nor, unlike most Greeks, did he covet either power or wealth for himself. 'No man,' he said, 'can take his superfluous cash with him to Hades nor by repayment of a ransom escape death or disease or the unkindly approach of old age.'

But Solon's true title to fame as a statesman rests not upon these preliminary measures of relief but upon his subsequent reform of the Athenian constitution, a reform which was to lead, in due time, to the establishment in Athens of that democratic régime which was the proper expression of the Greek temperament, though it was never universally achieved, and never either stable or assured. The most radical measures were, first, the admission to the Assembly of the lowest class of citizens, and, secondly, the institution of a court of justice comprising the whole citizen body; the panels of jurors in this court, the Heliaea, were enrolled by lot, so the poorest could take their turn with the richest. Before this court any magistrate, when his annual term of office was concluded, could be arraigned for misconduct, so that control over the administration was in effect given into the hands of the people. This second measure, in spite of the fact that actual office was still reserved for the aristocracy, gives Solon the credit of being the chief originator of European popular government. He did not establish a democracy, but he made its establishment possible—for better or worse. It was Solon, too, who introduced the custom of choosing state officials by lot—reducing, at the same time, the excessive rashness of such a method by having a certain number of candidates previously put up by a general vote, and then allowing the lot to make the final choice amongst them. Solon's laws, once they were established, were inscribed on wooden tablets which were kept thereafter in the Town Hall, and copies were incised upon stone pillars and kept in the building known as the King's Portico. They included the provision that every Athenian should have a trade, and imposed heavy penalties for idleness. The laws once written, everyone knew at least where he stood. Justice was no longer in the 'might of the hands'. The fame of Solon's laws, as readers of the Roman historian Livy will remember, spread westward into Italy, and the infant Rome, whose political and economic troubles had been not unlike those in Greece, sent a deputation to Athens to bring back a copy of them, to form a basis for a Roman code. The result was the Twelve Tables of Roman law—and the unhappy interlude of the *decemvirs*.

Having done his work, Solon left Athens and went on his travels. It was a risky thing to do; but even Solon was Greek enough not to wish to devote his whole life to a single object. He had other irons in the fire, amongst them, if the stories are true, a desire to extend his knowledge coupled with an addiction to good living and the pleasures of wine and love: of these the first is wholly in character, and the second is at least suggested by some of his extant verses. As was to be expected, the smouldering fires of faction broke out again in Athens as soon as his back was turned, and were quenched only in the way which he had himself foretold but had none the less hoped to prevent. 'From the great men', he had written, 'destruction comes to the state, and the people in its folly falls a slave to the tyrant.' This is what happened, and the tyrant was Pisistratus.

One last service had been rendered by Solon to his country, after his return from his travels. Lying just off the coast of Attica is the island of Salamis. It belonged to Megara, then a town of considerable importance with a growing trade. Athens needed to control it, if her own commerce was to expand, and it was Solon who roused the Athenians to act. The days of political oratory had not yet come, and Solon made his appeal in a set of verses, some of which still survive. There was no nonsense in those days about art and its inward mysteries: poetry had a purpose, and everybody could understand it. Athens responded and Salamis became Athenian, and the port of Nisaea on the Megarian mainland was taken at the same time. The two together made a vital addition to Athenian strength.

It was some ten years later that Croesus, on the advice of the Delphic oracle, sent his emissaries to Greece on the mission I have already described. Pisistratus was by then firmly established in power, and under his capable and generally benevolent guidance party faction for a time ceased and the community prospered. The manoeuvres by which he came to power are worth a mention, as they illuminate, not unpleasantly, the political atmosphere of those early days. Two factions, one led by Megacles (who also figures in one of Herodotus' best stories, which I will relate in its proper place) and the other by a certain Lycurgus, were at each other's throats in a struggle for supremacy in Attica. Pisistratus, seeing a chance to outwit both of them, came forward as the professed champion of the 'hillmen', the poorest section of the Athenian people, and succeeded in collecting a number of supporters. One day, to win further sympathy, he cut himself and his mules about the body and drove his cart into the market square of Athens, where he loudly lamented that the wounds had been gratuitously inflicted upon him by his enemies as he was harmlessly driving out of town. Then, trusting in the reputation he had already won in the capture, planned by Solon, of the port of Nisaea, he asked the people to give him a bodyguard for his protection. This was done, and with the help of the men told off for the purpose, he seized the Acropolis and found himself master of Athens.

In these circumstances his two rivals agreed to combine; their joint strength was too much for Pisistratus, but hardly had he been evicted before the old quarrel was resumed, and Megacles, getting the worst of it, approached Pisistratus with an offer to help restore him to power. Pisistratus jumped at the offer, and he and his new friend Megacles devised between them what Herodotus calls the silliest trick which history has to record. 'The Greeks,' Herodotus wrote, 'have never been simpletons; for centuries past they have been distinguished from other nations by superior wits; and of all Greeks the Athenians are allowed to be the most intelligent: yet it was at the Athenians' expense that this ridiculous trick was played. In the village of Paeania there was a handsome woman called Phye, nearly six feet tall, whom they fitted out in a suit of armour and mounted in a chariot; then, after getting her to pose in the most striking attitude, they drove into Athens, where messengers who had preceded them were already, according to their instructions, talking to the people and urging them to welcome Pisistratus back, because the goddess Athene herself had shown him extraordinary honour and was bringing him home to her own Acropolis. They spread this nonsense all over the town, and it was not long before rumour reached the outlying villages that Athene was bringing Pisistratus back, and both villagers and townsfolk, convinced that the woman Phye was indeed the goddess, offered her their prayers and received Pisistratus with open arms.'

But there was still trouble to come. Pisistratus married Megacles' daughter, to seal the friendship between them. Unfortunately, however, the seal was less strong than it might have been; for Pisistratus, having married the girl, refused to go to bed with her, and this so enraged Megacles that he made up his quarrel with his political enemies, and once more succeeded in forcing Pisistratus out of Athens. Pisistratus took refuge at Eretria in the neighbouring island of Euboea, and there laid his plans for a final effort. This time he was wholly successful. He raised money and men from various friendly communities in Greece and the islands, and, when he felt himself sufficiently strong, once again marched on Athens. A characteristic touch at the end of this story is that the Athenians, who had marched out towards Marathon to check his advance, happened, at the critical moment when Pisistratus appeared, to be taking their lunch, or having a nap as the result of it, so that the invading force met with no resistance whatever. Surely the Greeks, for all the reckless daring of which, on occasion, they were capable, could be the most incompetent soldiers the world has yet seen—all the Greeks, that is, with the exception of the Spartans, who made war their business as well as their pleasure.

The autocratic rule of Pisistratus was a blessing to Athens at this troubled period of her early history. Though power was concentrated in his own hands, he did not do away with Solon's constitutional reforms, and freedom from the perpetual threat of anarchy enabled the Athenian people to profit from a period of economic and political development. In his foreign policy Pisistratus worked to maintain friendly relations with the leading Mainland communities, especially with Sparta; and it was he who first, by bringing the Chersonese—the Gallipoli peninsula—under Athenian control and by the recapture of Sigeum, a valuable port in the Troad near the entrance to the Dardanelles, opened the way to Athenian expansion overseas. It was he, too, who asserted the claim of Athens to be the mother and leader of the Ionian Greeks, introduced regular recitations from the

Homeric poems at the Panathenaic festival, and, most important of all, instituted for the worship of Dionysus a new festival called the Great Dionysia of the City, at which choirs dressed in goatskins as satyrs performed their dance and song round the altar of the god. The choirs competed for a prize—the 'goat-song' prize, the prize of 'tragedy'. Within little more than a generation these songs had developed into the Athenian tragic drama, perhaps the noblest, and most austere, expression of the Greek genius.

CHAPTER II

Sparta

IT WAS NOT WITH ATHENS THAT CROESUS SOUGHT AN ALLIANCE, but with Sparta—the second, as the Delphic oracle had declared, of the two chief powers in mainland Greece.

Sparta was the least typically Hellenic of the ancient Greek communities. A modern student of Greek history and literature can fancy himself spiritually at home, despite the physical discomforts, under the democratic régime of fifth-century Athens, or the brilliant authoritarian regime of such men as Periander of Corinth or Thrasybulus of Miletus, or, again, under almost any of the shifting and unstable oligarchies which ruled at various times in almost every Greek city state; but in Sparta he cannot but feel himself an alien. The atmosphere which surrounds Sparta is dark and cold.

It had not always been so. Back in the seventh century the Spartan nobility had cared, like other Greeks, for the graces of life; the individual had been free, as elsewhere, to live as he pleased, or as he could; music and lyric poetry flourished; Laconian potters produced work said to have been second only to that of Corinth; Terpander of Lesbos, who invented the seven-stringed lyre, visited Sparta and instituted the musical contest at the great Spartan festival of the Carneia; the Lydian poet Alcman, some of whose beautiful surviving fragments I have already quoted, made Sparta his home, and the native poet Tyrtaeus wrote rousing lyrics which can still stir the pulses. In those days Sparta, it seems, was Greek; but at some time towards the end of the seventh century, or early in the sixth, something happened to her and she underwent a lamentable change. She enters the full light of Greek history as something not unlike a police state under an iron and ruthless military discipline.

The Spartans were a Dorian people, and the Dorians, far back at the beginning of things, had fought their way down from somewhere in the north-western regions of Greece into the

Peloponnese, where they had wrested the land from the original inhabitants. Probably they had fighting in their blood more than the other branches of the Greek peoples, and certainly the Spartans, once they were settled as masters of the greater part of the Peloponnese, were compelled to maintain their position amongst the conquered population by force, and the threat of force. Sparta itself was a small community, little more, indeed, than a collection of villages; in it lived the true-born Spartan nobility, perhaps eight or nine thousand of them, while everyone else on the scattered farms of the fertile plain of Lacedaemon had lost even their names: they were the 'perioeci'—the 'dwellers-around'; or else the helots, the Spartans' slaves.

No doubt it was partly the sheer difficulty of survival necessarily threatening a small dominant clique in the midst of a conquered and hostile population enormously superior in numbers, which led gradually and in the course of time to the strange institutions, the rigorous and unnatural discipline and the, to us, repulsive mode of living with which we are familiar. I say 'familiar' but that is not strictly true, for even to their contemporaries in other parts of Greece the Spartans and their way of life were always something of a mystery. The Spartans did not like inquisitive strangers. It was difficult for any Greek from another township even to visit Sparta, except by invitation or on official business; and Spartans themselves were discouraged from travelling, even if it were not actually forbidden. What was it really like, this queer secluded community of almost invincible soldiers, hidden away in 'hollow Sparta'—the outwardly unpretentious little township in the plain, surrounded by a barrier of mountains? Many Greeks asked themselves this question, and some of the most intelligent of them, notably Plato and Xenophon, gave answers which cannot but surprise us.

The entire Spartan people—the true Spartans, that is, the 'Spartiates', as distinguished from the 'dwellers-around' and the serfs and helots who worked for them—were a purely military caste, exclusively devoted to the service of the state. Unlike other Greeks, who farmed their land or followed trades and professions, no Spartan ever lifted a finger to earn his living: he was provided for either by his possession of the family domains, or by the state grant of a portion of common land, which was worked for him by the helots who, in their turn, were compelled by law to deliver to him a fixed amount of its produce. He was thus liberated from all the normal human cares of providing for himself and his family, and enabled to devote himself without distraction to his military training. A Spartan's discipline began at birth: male babies were submitted to inspection by the authorities and, if fit to live, they were allowed to do so. If unfit, they were exposed to die on the wild slopes of Mt. Taygetus. At seven years old a boy was taken from his mother and turned over to the state for intensive conditioning, moral and physical, and both as hard as iron. Up to the age of twenty all boys lived in a kind of military school, divided into 'herds' and 'pens' commanded and instructed by young men under thirty—thirty being the age at which a man was admitted into full citizenship and allowed (for what it was worth) to marry. The full citizens—the 'Peers' —continued the barrack life, dining together in tents at public messes to which each was compelled to make a fixed contribution from the produce of his land. The Spartan food from what we hear of it—especially the Spartan 'black broth'—seems to have been peculiarly disagreeable. Spartan girls, as potential mothers, were subjected to a discipline only less severe than that of the boys, its sole object, including the training in athletic exercises, being the production of healthy (male) children. They were said to be chaste; nevertheless Spartan women were liable to receive a sudden government order to breed children for the state, and they were quick, upon receipt of it, to do so with any suitable breeder, whether husband or not. Thus no Spartan, woman or man, had a private life of his own. All were dedicated absolutely to the service of the state, whose sole object was to train a body of citizen soldiers of the highest possible efficiency. To a Spartan the Law—the law of his own community—was all; he must have no thought, no will, no speculation beyond it. 'They are free— yes—' said Demaratus, the exiled Spartan King, to Xerxes, 'but not entirely free; for they have a master, and that master is Law, which they fear much more than your subjects fear you. Whatever this master commands, they do; and his command never varies: it is never to retreat in battle, however great the odds, but always to stand firm, and to conquer or die.' The command is, no doubt, a good one; but a healthy society could do with one or two others besides.

Just how, or when, this state of things in Sparta came into

being—together with the queer Spartan constitution with its
two kings, each jealous of the other and both subject to the
supervision of the Ephors, its Council of Elders (all over sixty)
and its Assembly in which the citizen's sole privilege was to
signify assent to a measure proposed—nobody knows. Herodotus
himself did not know, though he is inclined to attribute it to the
mythical, or half-mythical, lawgiver Lycurgus. To the Spartans
of the sixth century it seemed to have been there from immemorial antiquity, and to be destined to last for ever. Indeed,
it does seem, even to us, as it certainly did to many contemporary
Greeks, to have a sort of cold and static perfection. At least—for
several centuries—it achieved its purpose. Perhaps the general
temper of it may be indicated by that most hateful of all Spartan
institutions, the Crypteia. This was a body of young men whose
duty it was to murder secretly any helots who were suspected of
possible insubordination—or simply, on occasion, to keep down
their rate of increase. The murders were done at night. All
Greeks were cruel; all Greeks butchered their prisoners of war,
taken in fair fight; any Greek was capable of savage vengeance on
a private enemy; but it seems to have been reserved for the Spartans to murder in cold blood, as a matter of policy, their unarmed
and helpless dependants.

The Spartans, as one might guess from their other characteristics, despised trade, and helped to discourage it within their
domain by preserving, down—probably—to as late as the fourth
century, their currency of iron lumps and iron spits, either of
which must have been awkward to go shopping with.

Plato and Xenophon, the former a great philosopher with his
head in the clouds, the latter a man of action and a litterateur
with his feet firmly, or fairly firmly, on the earth, both admired
Sparta. I have said that to us this admiration is surprising, and so
it is; nevertheless I suppose that it is not unintelligible. To the
rest of Greece Sparta represented an ideal—the ideal of order
and stability. All Greeks were conservative by nature, and in all
Greeks the love of order was one element of their genius. It is
best revealed in their art and literature, in which, perhaps more
than in any other art and literature in the world, the passionate
impulse from which it rises is subjected to control. But the
average Greek found it hard to bring a similar order and control
into his personal life or into his politics. Savage political faction

was as natural to him as the air he breathed. For all his conservatism of spirit, based upon the ancient sanctities of place, the countless local shrines where his ancestors had worshipped, and the unchanging life of the fields which furnished his physical needs, he nevertheless lived, and liked to live, at any rate in the later times of the classical era, in an atmosphere of revolution. He was an excitable man; independent by nature and fiercely competitive. 'All things,' said Heracleitus, though with a loftier reference, 'pass away; nothing remains;' and so the Athenian, and the members of many another Greek community, might well have said of his political affairs. But Sparta was stable; Sparta was a rock upon which the winds and waves of political experiment and change beat in vain. That an Athenian (for instance) could not have endured to live for half an hour under Spartan discipline, is neither here nor there. Intellectually, and as—for him—an unrealisable ideal, he found it admirable.

Plato in one of his dialogues even goes so far as to say that the Spartans were the true philosophers of Greece. There are more teachers of philosophy, he says, in Sparta than anywhere else in the world, though the Spartans pretend to have won their supremacy by martial prowess and manly courage. But not at all—they have really won it by their addiction to philosophy. Plato, it is true, was not incapable of a joke; and, in this passage, there is just the hint of a smile. Nevertheless, from what else we know of his genuine admiration for Sparta, we cannot but admit a certain seriousness underlying it. And it makes us stare. What? The Spartans—who never wrote a book, or even (we fancy) read one—*philosophers?* The thing is preposterous. 'Ah but,' Plato goes on, in effect, to say, 'anyone who has talked with a Spartan for a minute or two, though he may, at first, have thought him dull and ill-informed, will surely have been astonished and delighted, before the conversation came to an end, at certain *pithy sayings*, brief yet compact with wisdom, which fell, almost casually, from his lips.' It was, after all, Spartan men who first said, 'Know yourself' and 'Nothing too much', and 'Go bail—and face ruin.' Well, for Plato's sake we must try to believe that he was smiling, at least a little, when he wrote this passage in the *Protagoras*. I for one suspect that it takes no great intelligence to invent a pithy saying or two, the harder test being the ability to talk sense connectedly and at length. Many a man has won a reputation for profundity by saying little, or even nothing at all. That it was a Spartan characteristic to be niggardly in speech—in itself no bad thing—is undoubtedly true, and the best instance of it I can remember comes (of course) from Herodotus. During the rule of Polycrates in Samos, certain exiles from the island, hoping to be able to enforce their return, applied to Sparta for assistance. 'They procured an audience,' wrote Herodotus, 'with the magistrates and made a long speech to emphasise the urgency of their request. The Spartans, however, at this first sitting, answered the speech by saying that they had forgotten the beginning of it, and could not understand the end; so the Samians had to try again. At the second sitting they brought a bag, and merely remarked that the bag needed flour—to which the Spartans replied that the word 'bag' was superfluous. All the same, they decided to grant the request for assistance, and began their preparations at once.'

Modern writers as well as ancient have idealised the Spartans and their way of life; one of the most impressive was Walter Pater, a scholar with great subtlety of perception in spite of the fact that his manner of writing, reminding one of maidenhair fern in a Victorian greenhouse, makes him difficult to read today. In his highly-wrought and in some ways beautiful picture of Lacedaemon—if a false picture can be beautiful—in his *Plato and Platonism*, he almost persuades an unwary reader that the Dorian sense of Order, so perfectly given outward and living form in Spartan institutions, was the most essentially Greek thing in the complex and many-sided genius of the Greeks. That it was indeed a vital and essential element in that genius, no one will dispute who has any knowledge of Greek literature and Greek architecture and Greek plastic art—or even of Greek philosophy, which originated, I suppose, in the intellectual need to find an order in the chaos of appearances, or to impose one upon it. But the virtue of order is surely correspondent to the richness and variety of the elements it contains and controls. The philosophical One would not be very interesting if it did not embrace within itself the Many, and a harmony of, say, two notes only is apt to be thin. Spartan life was indeed a harmony, and the living embodiment of an Order—of a *cosmos*, to use a favourite word of the Greeks; but it reached that harmony, that *cosmos*, by a process of exclusion, and thus drained itself of interest—except

as a curiosity. What is one to make of a people who had no
family life (few Greeks had much, but the Spartans had none
whatever), no literature, and no occupation of any kind except a
military training?

The Spartans were said to sing and dance well—for ritual
purposes, that is; and to take much trouble over their personal
appearance. They devoted more time to religious observances,
always a powerful cement of the corporate consciousness, even
than their cousins elsewhere in Greece.* They were late for the
battle of Marathon, one remembers, because religion obliged
them to wait for the full moon before marching; the fighting
was over when they arrived, and the only satisfaction they
could get was to inspect the dead bodies. It was generally observed in Greece that the Spartan abroad, freed from the restraints
which his national institutions imposed upon him, was avaricious
and ill-behaved. Two Spartan kings, Demaratus and Pausanias—
the latter actually a regent for Pleistarchus, who was a minor—
were traitors to their country and either intrigued with Persia or
entered Persian service. Treachery, it is true, was ubiquitous in the
Greek world, and even the most conspicuous instances of it
seem to have been regarded, though perhaps with disapproval,
certainly without surprise. But one would hardly have looked
for it in Sparta, where the whole object of a severe and ruthless
conditioning, from infancy onward, was single-hearted devotion
to the common weal.

The Spartan constitution was anciently supposed to have been
derived from Crete. The power—and it was very great—which
it conferred upon the Spartan community was of course due to the
fact that, whereas in the Ionian communities generally the influence of the great families was unduly strong and tended in
consequence to internal strife and therefore to instability, in
Sparta the whole emphasis was thrown from the first upon
service to the state as such. This was an additional reason for
the admiration bestowed upon Sparta by political thinkers

* It is a curious comment on Greek religion that the deity pre-
eminently honoured in Sparta was Apollo, the God of the sun, of
poetry and of healing. Because of this particular worship the Spartans
always felt a kind of proprietary interest in Delphi and its oracle—so
much so that Cleomenes, the Spartan King, bribed it on one occasion
to give the answer he wanted.

elsewhere, especially by those whose political theories, like
Plato's, were mixed up with morals and metaphysics. To them,
Sparta presented the appearance of an integrated community, of
which each member devoted his whole energies to the good of the
whole. In point of fact, however, it is possible to argue that the
Spartan state was not a community in the proper sense at all;
it was simply a dominant military clique, living on the forced
labour of its dependents and serfs. No society can properly be
called a community which does not draw within itself, or extend
its influence and protection over, all the multifarious labours and
occupations of men, which are necessary to its existence. All
Greek communities employed slave labour; but they did not
live on slave labour—in Athens, for instance, slaves and free
citizens would be found working side by side at the same tasks,
say at building, or in factories; but Sparta did live on slave labour
—as I have said, no Spartan—no Spartiate—ever did a hand's
turn of work of any kind whatever. So it is only in a very narrow
and unpractical sense that Sparta can be called an integrated
community: integrated, in a way, she was, but there were few
elements to integrate.

Organised though she was exclusively for war, Sparta did not,
during the period with which we are now concerned, follow
an aggressive policy. After her conquest of Messenia, about
620 B.C., she sought no further territorial expansion, but contented herself with securing a series of military alliances with
most of the other Peloponnesian states. The declared aims of this
'Peloponnesian League' were, first, the liberation of the rest of
Greece from the autocratic rule of the tyrants, and, secondly,
protection against the expansionist ambitions of Argos. When,
in 555 B.C., Croesus' messengers arrived in Sparta and the alliance
between Sparta and Lydia was formed, Sparta, though powerful,
was not yet secure in her supremacy. She was still threatened by
the rivalry of Argos. Nine years later the quarrel with Argos
came to a head over the disputed possession of a tract of land at
Thyreae on the borders of Argive territory. By a curious ar-
rangement which I do not profess to understand (could it have
been a thousand-year-old memory of the single combats of the
heroic age?) the two states agreed to settle the dispute by a com-
bat between 300 picked champions a side. The battle took place
and was fought with unexampled fury; two Argives and one

Spartan were left alive, with the result that both towns claimed a victory. Being therefore no further ahead than they were before, they each took the field in force, and in the ensuing struggle Argos was decisively beaten. This was a critical battle in Greek history, as it left Sparta undisputed leader of the Dorian Greeks. Herodotus tells us that it was in the midst of these troubles that Croesus' messenger arrived at Sparta with his request to the Spartans to honour their pact and send a force to assist in raising the siege of Sardis. But by the time their preparations were complete and their ships ready to sail, a second messenger arrived on the heels of the first with the news that Sardis had fallen and that Croesus was a prisoner in Cyrus' hands.

CHAPTER 12

Greek Political Tensions

IN THE COURSE OF THE LAST TWO CHAPTERS I HAVE SAID A CERTAIN
amount about what the Greeks called 'tyranny', or 'tyrannical'
government. It is convenient to keep the word, though the
connotations of it are quite different for us from what they were
to the Greeks. For the Greeks, though on the whole they disapproved of the *thing*—of tyranny as a form of government—the
word itself was indifferent and carried no derogatory meaning.
A tyrant was simply an autocratic ruler; tyranny was simply
one-man government, or dictatorship. There were good tyrants
and bad tyrants; under some of them, as under Pisistratus at
Athens, the state prospered and the people remained more or
less contented, in the enjoyment of comparative, though temporary, stability and in freedom from the internecine feuds of the
great rival families. It was a form of government under which all
the Greek states—except Sparta—at all times, were liable to fall,
not, as some historians have argued, a stage through which the
Greek peoples passed in the course of their political development.
It was the natural outcome of a split in the ruling oligarchy, one
or another member of which, feeling himself strong enough,
bribed or persuaded such malcontents as he could find to support
him, seized power by force, and kept it if he could. Herodotus is
plain enough on the subject; having described the personal
jealousies which are bound to exist within an oligarchy, 'out of
these,' he writes, 'arise factions; from factions comes bloodshed,
and the result of bloodshed is—tyranny.' Solon, it will be remembered, said much the same, nor did it call for exceptional
acumen to do so. A similar pattern is not uncommon in the
modern world.

It is difficult for us fully to grasp in imagination the savagery of
Greek political strife, and the utter lack of moral principle in its
conduct. Settled government in any Greek community at any
time was the exception, not the rule, and if we want to form a

picture of the everyday colour and atmosphere of Greek political life, we must get right away from the lofty speculations of a Plato or from the image of Periclean democracy in its fugitive and transitory glory—even Herodotus can mislead us, so coolly and in so ironical and detached a tone does he speak of the most abhorrent brutalities. This savagery and lack of principle in the struggle for power within the Greek communities was the reverse side of one of the best qualities in the Greek temperament. Greek men cared about politics; for them, politics was not a career or a profession, as it may be with us; it was—to repeat what I have already said—the consideration of *to koinon*: 'the thing which interests everybody.' In their small communities, every man counted, or might count, if he asserted himself; and to assert himself was, if he found the least chance to do so, one of his greatest pleasures and satisfactions. Every aspect of state policy, economic, military or domestic, was within the competence and understanding of any intelligent man. He did not have to depend upon 'experts'; nor would he have considered anyone necessarily more expert than himself, except for the occasional recognised leader who might persuade him for the time being to accept his judgment. The Greek looked upon his city and its patch of land as a 'common wealth' in the proper sense of the word; it belonged to him and his fellows, and he had every intention of playing what part he could in the direction of its affairs. That was the fundamental point of difference between the Greeks, who prided themselves on being 'free men' and the great Asiatic empires whose people they regarded as 'slaves'. It was that concept of 'freedom' which inspired the momentary heroisms of the Persian wars. Even the freedom to cut one's neighbour's throat, should he be a democrat or an oligarch as the case might be, was not to be despised. The poor tame cattle who bowed before Darius enjoyed no such happy privilege.

Thus it will be seen that democracy of a sort, though democratic governments were far, at any period, from being universally established in the Greek world, and were never in any state, not even in Athens, permanently secured, was nevertheless, ideally, the form of government towards which the Greek genius aspired. Indeed, there may well have been small city states in Greece, comparatively unknown and of which no details have come down to us, 'little towns by river or sea shore', in which a democratic government quietly flourished and continued; but I suppose it is doubtful.

The general temper of Greek political rivalries is vividly suggested in the verses written about the middle of the sixth century by Theognis of Megara. Megara during the first half of the century had made rapid commercial progress, her fabrics especially being in request over much of the Greek world. As always in these early days of the city states, the increasing wealth of the community was ill distributed, and there was acute suffering amongst the peasant population. It was the old story, and its course was determined by the very nature of Greek politics: the moment came when one member of the ruling aristocracy, Theagenes by name, saw his chance and came forward in the familiar role of deliverer of the oppressed peasantry. Like Pisistratus of Athens, he succeeded in obtaining a bodyguard; then he proceeded to butcher his rivals and to establish himself as tyrant. A few years later he was thrown out, and the two surviving parties, democrats and oligarchs, faced each other, snarling. Theognis belonged to the aristocratic party, and saw, or professed to see, the end of the world in every concession it was forced to make to the democrats. He appears to have lost his property during the course of the troubles, but even that is hardly sufficient justification for the virulence of his language. With an agreeable simplicity and inclusiveness he refers to the aristocrats as 'the good' and to the democrats as 'the bad'. He prays to 'drink the black blood' of his enemies. 'Grind your heel,' he cries, 'on the empty-headed people; spike them with the sharp goad; put the intolerable strap around their necks.' 'Speak your enemy fair,' he advises; 'then, when you have him in your power, strike—and don't wait to say why.' Again: 'May I die if I can find no rest from my griefs, and oh that I might give pain for pain!' The odd thing is (or *is* it odd?) that Theognis considered himself a moderate man, and says so frequently and emphatically in his verses. 'Do not be over-zealous,' is his advice to his young friend Cyrnus; 'the middle way is always best; only thus will you have virtue, a difficult thing to acquire.' It certainly is. One can but suppose that Theognis, wishing to drink his enemies' blood, wished to drink it in moderate quantities only— much as he says of wine in a more sociable context: 'when you are at a party, get drunk, but not very drunk.'

Theognis' verses were later adopted for study by school boys, together with Homer and Hesiod. They are second-rate verses, but in Greek verse even the second-rate has its charm; they at least have the virtues of vigour, clarity and directness. I suppose they were found useful in schools as a storehouse of political maxims; for after all, one could always have interpreted Theognis' 'the good' and 'the bad' according to one's own political predilections. The spirit, it seems, was all. His work is also liberally sprinkled with gnomic sayings about life and morality in general, such as the Greeks always loved.

> 'Youth's joy is the time for play; for when I am dead
> Long shall I lie under earth, dumb as a stone,
> Far from the darling sunlight. Then, for ever and ever,
> For all my virtue, shall I see—nothing.'

Reading those verses, at any rate, one has a stir of sympathy and affection for the old scallywag. There is not a little in them of the early Greece.

It will be noticed that in the hot and excitable verses of Theognis from which I have quoted, though they are political verses, there is no political speculation, no evident principle whatever; they might, unlike the grave and expository verses of Solon the Athenian, have been written equally well by either of the conflicting parties in the state. Theognis does, it is true, occasionally lament the tendency of newly acquired wealth to blur or obliterate social distinctions and so to corrupt the blood of the old nobility; but the general tone of his utterances is that of a dispossessed man snarling at his dispossessors and longing for the moment, which well might come, when the wheel should turn again, or—which is to put the same thing in other words—when he should once again have the chance to live what for a Greek was the only full and natural life. The Greeks made no distinction in their minds between public life and private life, and a man whom circumstances debarred from taking part in the former was like a man with one eye, or a maimed foot. This is the real reason for the Greek dislike of autocratic government—of 'tyranny'—and one reason amongst many why in the more advanced communities there was a movement, however precarious and interrupted, towards democratic institutions. Under democratic institutions more people could live a full and natural life.

There is an interesting passage in Herodotus in which he analyses the characteristic merits and defects of the three forms of government, democracy, oligarchy and tyranny. For some unexplained reason he puts the defence of each form into the mouths of Otanes, Megabyzus and Darius, respectively, three of the seven Persian grandees who successfully plotted the overthrow of Smerdis, the usurper of the Persian throne. Nothing is less likely than that any Persian grandee would have recommended the institution of an oligarchical régime, still less a democratic one, and Herodotus, well aware of the fact, remarks (with a smile) that certain Greeks refuse to believe that they ever did so. 'All the same,' he adds, 'they did.' Well! I don't suppose it matters very much whether they did or not, and we may take it that the highly intelligent and instructive criticism of the three forms of government is in effect Herodotus' own. Otanes, the champion of democracy, begins by pointing to the appalling excesses of the late King Cambyses, the paranoiac, and proceeds to ask how it can be possible to associate absolute power with any reasonable system of ethics, when it allows a man to do what he pleases without responsibility or control. Absolute power, he says—anticipating the familiar modern dictum—cannot but absolutely corrupt; the best of men must inevitably be changed by it for the worse. No monarch can hope to escape the two vices which are the root cause of all wickedness, envy and pride, and each of them leads to acts of unnatural savagery. Kings are jealous of the best of their subjects and take pleasure in the worst, whom they employ as informers and spies; they break up the structure of tradition and law, force women to serve their pleasure, and put men to death without trial. But the rule of the people—*isonomy*, or equality before the law—does none of these things: under the rule of the people, magistrates are appointed by lot; they must answer to the nation for their conduct of office, and all questions of national interest or policy are put up for open debate.

To this temperate exposition Megabyzus replies by asserting that the people as a whole in any country are a feckless lot, likely, if entrusted with power, to prove every bit as violent and irresponsible as a monarch. A king at least acts deliberately and, presumably, with knowledge; the masses have not a thought in their heads and act, in consequence, solely upon impulse or passion. If, therefore, ruin is to be the obvious result of either monarchy or of democratic institutions, what alternative remains? Clearly the only alternative is government by an intelligent and aristocratic elite. Choose the best, says Megabyzus, and you will get the best results—adding, in a truly Greek spirit, that they themselves, who were debating this important question, would certainly be amongst the candidates chosen.

Lastly Darius, who in fact succeeded to the Persian throne, spoke for monarchy, and in terms even more characteristically Greek than the other two. The criticisms of both oligarchy and democracy which Herodotus puts into his mouth are based firmly upon Greek local politics, and accurately describe the dangers which by the nature of the Greek temperament are inherent in each: under an oligarchical regime there are bound to be personal rivalries, leading through bloodshed back to monarchy as the only solution, while under any sort of popular government inevitable corrupt practices lead to the formation of secret associations within the state, all of which being out for their own advantage, only produce tensions and feuds of a different, but not less destructive, kind. It is the old story, which we have already seen working itself out in Attica to its conclusion—or, rather, to the end of its first chapter—in the tyranny of Pisistratus, and of which vivid incidents are brought to our imagination by the verses of Theognis.

Herodotus wrote his book when Athens was still at the height of her power, and we know that the general tendency of it was in favour of free institutions; yet nothing could be more critically impartial or enlightened than the foregoing sketches. What is chiefly remarkable about them is the tacit recognition they contain of the gap between theory and practice: ideally, each of the three forms of polity is admirable; no one can deny that a state would prosper under the control of a wise and benevolent autocrat, careless of his own advantage; or who can fail to admit that government by 'the best'—the aristocrats— must be the best government? and is there anyone so blind to the ideal as not to be moved by the very word *isonomy* (the most beautiful of all words, Herodotus declares)—*equality before the law?* But—and this is the point—each of the three forms, ideally so excellent—or, to put it better, which might be so excellent in an ideal world—is doomed to corruption by the sheer intracta-ability of human nature. That is why 'tyranny', once a neutral word, has become an opprobrious one—and where is the virtue in equality before the law, if it merely gives scoundrels richer opportunities of pursuing their own ends? The problem is by no means a specifically Greek problem.

Of the great Greek autocratic rulers there are a number of vivid pictures in Herodotus' pages. Perhaps the most entertaining of them is that of Cleisthenes of Sicyon, a member of the distinguished family of the Alcmaeonidae, if only for the well-known story it contains of the wooing of Agarista. Sicyon, neighbour to Corinth, was a Dorian state of great antiquity, originally founded by Dorians from Argos. After following the pattern of development common to most Greek communities she fell, about the middle of the seventh century, under the 'tyranny' of a certain Orthagoras, whose dynasty lasted for nearly a hundred years. The last of the dynasty was Cleisthenes. Cleisthenes was remembered by the later Greeks for the part he played in the Sacred War, by which the independence of Delphi and its oracle was won from the threatened domination of the people of Crisa; by his part in the founding of the Pythian Games, the second of the great panhellenic festivals after the much more ancient Olympian—the two remaining festivals, the Isthmian and the Nemean, were founded at about the same period; and, perhaps, especially, by the brilliance and richness of his court. It is this last that the tale of Agarista, as Herodotus tells it, is designed to illustrate—and to comment upon.

Cleisthenes had a daughter, Agarista, born, as her father's daughter was bound to be, to greatness. Who, of all the proud lords in Greece and beyond, was worthy to be her husband? During the festival of the Olympic Games Cleisthenes had a public proclamation made to the effect that any Greek who thought himself good enough should present himself within sixty days at the court in Sicyon, where Cleisthenes would put him through his paces, and examine him thoroughly in all manly accomplishments, to determine his fitness for the eminent position of his son-in-law. The proclamation was a great success, and Herodotus, gravely and in the true epic manner, chronicles the long and splendid list of competitors for the prize, some of them coming from as far west as the cities of southern Italy. What?—says the reader to himself as the Homeric catalogue of resounding names rolls on—can this tremendous prologue be the prologue to a *wedding*? or is Herodotus about to give a twist to his story, and to show this gathering of Grecian chivalry to be bent, in reality, upon some sterner purpose? The reader has not long to wait: the company once assembled, the Lord of Sicyon informed them that they were to be his guests for a year—for a shorter period would scarcely enable him to test satisfactorily the virtues of each. So the testing began; proficiency in gymnastics and conversation, quality of temper, manners, personal accomplishments, all came under strict and continuous observation; and the most stringent test of all was their behaviour at the dinner table.

At last the day of decision came. Cleisthenes sacrificed a hundred oxen and gave a banquet to which not only the suitors were invited, but every man of any consequence in Sicyon. The banquet over and the wine brought in, the noble competitors were put to the test for the last time—in speaking (like the guests in Plato's *Symposium*) on a set theme to the assembled company.

Now amongst the competitors there was a certain Hippocleides, an Athenian, the richest and best-looking man in that famous city. The Lord of Sicyon regarded him with favour: he had proved himself throughout the long year to be by far the best talker, the wittiest companion, the most excellently-mannered man of them all. In fact, he had a long lead, and the prize was already within his grasp. But—he was an Athenian, and Herodotus has already told us that of all Greeks the Athenians were the most intelligent, and therefore (may we not assume?) the readiest to become aware of the ludicrous. In any case, whatever the reason, something, at this culminating moment, *happened* to Hippocleides: what it was, and the result of it must be told in Herodotus' own words. 'At last, as more and more wine was drunk, Hippocleides asked the flute-player to play him a tune and began to dance to it. Now it may well be that he danced to his own satisfaction; Cleisthenes, however, who was watching the performance, began to have serious doubts about the whole business. Presently, after a brief pause, Hippocleides sent for a table; the table was brought and Hippocleides, climbing on to it, danced first some Laconian dances, next some Attic ones, and ended by standing on his head and beating time with his legs in the air. The Laconian and Attic dances were bad enough; but Cleisthenes, though he already detested the thought of having a son-in-law who could behave so disgracefully in public, never-theless restrained himself and managed to avoid an outburst; but when he saw Hippocleides beating time with his legs, he could bear it no longer: "Son of Tisander," he cried, "you have danced away your wife."

' "I could hardly care less," was the cheerful reply.'

The prize of the beautiful Agarista (one cannot but hope, after all this, that she was beautiful) was given to Megacles, also an Athenian and son of the Alcmaeon who founded the family fortunes by carrying away such an inordinate quantity of gold dust from the treasury of Croesus. Megacles' son was another and more famous Cleisthenes, the real architect—working upon the first sketch made by Solon—of Athenian democracy; and a grand-daughter of Megacles, a second Agarista, became the mother of Pericles. As for Hippocleides one hears no more of him; but I trust that he lived merrily ever after.

The great tyrants on the Greek mainland, Pisistratus, Cleisthenes, Periander of Corinth—not to mention those who ruled in the island communities, on the Asiatic coast and in Southern Italy, of whom something will be said on a later page—exercised, on the whole, a beneficent influence upon the development of Greek civilisation. No doubt they were hated by all except those who directly profited by their friendship or patronage, and their seizure of power was certainly looked upon by the Greek people in general as a retrograde step in their political development, of which the proper and ideal direction was from the ancient monarchies, through the control of the aristocratic families, to a government based upon democratic institutions. But the Greek temperament had its own particular demon, which made any such orderly progress impossible; whatever their goal, the Greeks were bound by their own nature to have a rough passage to its attainment. As I have already suggested, the periods of autocratic government in this or that community usually followed upon a period of commercial expansion and increased prosperity in the cities, which exacerbated, in its turn, the discontent of the farmers and villagers who did not share in it; the establishment of the 'tyranny' gave, at any rate, a respite from internal strife, relieved the artisans and the peasantry from the worst forms of direct oppression to which they were subject under an oligarchical régime, and allowed them, perhaps, some opportunity to win such knowledge and experience as might later fit them for self-government. The tyrants were also patrons of the arts, and that, in a Greek community, was more important than in a modern one, for art in Greece was never the preserve of an intellectual minority.

The aims and methods of the tyrants are well illustrated by the rise and rule of the Cypselids at Corinth, of whom Herodotus gives a full and interesting account. He begins with the popular legend of the birth of Cypselus, the founder of the dynasty, and tells it with a tenderness which is rare in Greek literature. The tale goes that a certain Amphion, a member of the ruling clan in Corinth, had a lame daughter named Labda. Because of her deformity no one of her own status was willing to marry her, and she was given, for want of a better husband, to Eetion, a man of good blood who had come down in the world. For some years Labda had no child, so Eetion determined to consult the oracle about his chance of an heir. No sooner had he entered the shrine than the priestess addressed him in the following words:

> Eetion, worthy of honour, no man honours you.
> Labda is with child, and her child will be a millstone
>   about the neck of the rulers.

This mysterious utterance came to the ears of the nobles in whose hands was the government of the state, and they, interpreting it —all too rightly—as a warning, silently resolved to make away with Labda's child the moment it was born. Ten of their number were accordingly sent to Petra, the village where Eetion lived, to do the deed, it having been arranged between them that whoever first got hold of the child should dash its brains out on the ground. Arrived at the house, they went in and asked to see the baby, and Labda, who had no suspicion of their purpose, gave it to one of them to hold. Providence, however, was on Labda's side, for the baby, when it found itself in the man's arms, smiled at him, and he, seeing the smile, could not bring himself to kill it, but passed it to his neighbour who, in his turn, passed it on again until all ten had had it in their arms. Then they gave it back to its mother and went out of the room. Outside the door they stopped and began to reproach one another for failing to fulfil their mission, until at last they decided to go back into Labda's room and all to take a share in the killing. But fate once more had intervened, and Labda, who had heard everything which the ten men had been saying on the other side of the door, had hidden her child in a chest. The murderers searched the room in vain, and then returned to Corinth, pretending, for their own safety, that they had done the deed.

The child grew up, and was named Cypselus after the *cypsele*, or chest, which had preserved him from death.

Cypselus seized power in the familiar way, and, after thirty years of bloody, oppressive but prosperous rule, was succeeded by his son Periander. The story of Periander is preserved in greater detail than that of his father. Undoubtedly he was a great man, though hardly an agreeable one. The story which Herodotus tells of his crimes must be taken with a grain of salt, as he puts the recital of them, in his dramatic way, into the mouth of a Corinthian nobleman who came, some seventy years after Periander's death, to plead with the Spartans to abandon their project of helping to restore the exiled son of Pisistratus to Athens. The Corinthian nobleman—his name was Sosicles—knew all too well from recent memory what autocratic government could be, and what it could do, especially, to its natural rivals, the nobility, so when he urged the Spartan envoys in the name of all the gods of Greece not to help in saddling the free communities with despotic institutions, he naturally painted the dead tyrant in as dark colours as he dared.

Periander, we read, learned his first lesson in tyranny from Thrasybulus, at that time lord of the wealthy and prosperous city of Miletus on the Asiatic coast, with which Corinth had both political and mercantile ties. To the court of this despot Periander sent a messenger, with instructions to inquire his opinion upon the best and safest form of political constitution. The question was duly asked, and Thrasybulus, instead of replying, led the way into a field of growing corn, through which he walked with the messenger at his side, and, as he walked, kept slashing off with his stick all the ears of wheat which stood up above the rest. Then, having come to the end of the field, and having thoroughly spoiled the best part of the crop, he sent the messenger away without a word spoken.

'Well, and what did he say?' asked Periander when the man was home again.

'Nothing,' was the answer. 'He is undoubtedly mad.'

Then he described Thrasybulus' apparently lunatic behaviour—and Periander immediately understood its purport. Was it not obvious that Thrasybulus was recommending the murder of every man in Corinth of outstanding influence and ability? It was obvious indeed, and Herodotus—or Sosicles—goes on to inform us that Periander was quick to take his friend's advice, and that anything in the way of killing or banishing which his father Cypselus had left undone, he diligently did for him.

'There is nothing in the world,' Sosicles is reported to have said, 'wickeder or bloodier than despotic government.' No doubt he was right; but at the same time we are justified in supposing that it was not the blood he objected to, and that, had he been pressed, he would have admitted that the wickedness consisted solely in the fact that the blood which had flowed was mostly that of the noble Bacchiadae, to which clan he himself belonged. In this, moreover, he would have been fully representative of his time; for no Greek of the classical age had any objection to bloodshed as such, or any shrinking from the stark fact of violence. A tender conscience in these matters is the product of many contributory causes, by no means only of an advance in human kindliness: it is the product also of several generations of an increasingly industrial and technological civilisation, which tends to remove us further and further from the primitive springs both of evil and of good. Nor was death in itself so terrible a thing to a Greek as it is apt to be to ourselves. Perhaps the horror of death is in inverse proportion to the fullness and instancy of life: in the actual heat of battle, for instance, it does not take a hero to accept death's imminence. I stress this point because many writers about ancient Greek life have tried to gloss over and minimise its essential savagery, in the belief, I suppose, that it is difficult to reconcile with what was germinal in Greek civilisation and often, in itself, truly exquisite.

It was in the reign of Periander (627-586 B.C.) that Corinth, already a wealthy city as wealth went in those days, reached the zenith of her prosperity and influence. Tolls levied on ships using the ports of the Isthmus and on traffic passing through the markets raised revenue for the tyrant. The Corinthian fleet was the most powerful in Greece, using both the western and the eastern seas. The rebellious colony of Corcyra (Corfu) was brought to heel, and new colonies were planted at Apollonia Illyrica on the

Adriatic coast and Potidaea in Chalcidice. Trade flourished with Miletus and with Egypt. The poet Arion lived for many years at Periander's court—Arion who, as the pleasant story goes, sailing from Sicily to Greece, and, forced by the ship's blackguardly crew to leap overboard leaving his money behind, was incontinently picked up by a passing dolphin and landed safely at Taenarum, the southernmost promontory of the Peloponnese. Corinthian pottery was the finest in Greece, and it was Corinthian craftsmen who by inventing roof tiles enabled the roofs of public buildings to be constructed with a steeper pitch, thus leaving space for the pediment, which came to be enriched with sculptures in marble.

'It is not every man's luck to visit Corinth,' wrote Horace, some five centuries after Periander's death; and it may well be that in Periander's day, in spite of the hatred of the nobility for the tyrant by whom they had been dispossessed, the humbler people of that most beautiful of all Greek cities lived well and contentedly; had they not, they would doubtless have found an opportunity to cut his throat, despite his bodyguard. But they never seem to have tried, though it might in the end have been better for Periander if they had.

The story of Periander's latter days, beautifully told by Herodotus, reads like a cautionary tale against human pride. Periander was not destined, as Croesus was, to lose his throne; he was destined to lose his delight in the possession of it, a subtler and more grievous loss.

It began with the murder of his wife, Melissa, the Bee. Now Melissa had borne Periander two sons, who were eighteen and seventeen years old respectively when she died. The boys, knowing nothing of the cause of her death, went to stay shortly afterwards at the court of her father Procles, tyrant of Epidaurus, where they were entertained with much kindness. When the time for parting came, Procles said to them: 'Do you now know, my children, who killed your mother?' The older of the two boys, who was a stupid youth, took no notice of this question, but Lycophron, the younger, was deeply troubled by it, and, the conviction growing upon him that his own father was the murderer, he refused when he was home again to speak to him. This went on until Periander, in a rage, turned him out of the house.

Lycophron gone, the guilty father asked the other boy what it was that their grandfather had said to them before they left his house. At first the boy could remember nothing of any consequence, but finally, under continuous pressure, he recalled the ominous words and repeated them, whereupon Periander sent to the people with whom Lycophron was staying and ordered them to turn him out. The boy found another refuge, but the same thing happened again, until at last he became a homeless wanderer in the city, forced to find what shelter he could under the public colonnades or in the porches of houses. Some days later Periander found him in the street, hungry and dirty; moved by unaccustomed pity, he asked him to return home and to remember his duty as a son, but he was met, as before, by silence. Convinced now that the boy's trouble was desperate and incurable, Periander, to ease his conscience, sent him to Corcyra— out of sight, out of mind.

Many years passed and at last, when he was old, Periander found his thoughts returning to his lost son; he needed him as his successor to the throne of Corinth. Longing for a reconciliation, he sent a messenger to Corcyra and asked Lycophron to return, but he did not deign even to answer; then Periander sent the young man's sister to plead with him, but again to no avail. He refused ever to go back to Corinth while his father was alive. Finally in desperation Periander offered to exile himself to Corcyra, if only his son would return to Corinth and take over the direction of affairs. To this Lycophron consented, but before his preparations for the journey were complete, the men of Corcyra, who had got wind of what was happening and of all things in the world most dreaded the presence of Periander in their midst, murdered him.

Periander's successor, his nephew Psammetichus, was killed after a reign of four years; the dynasty of the Cypselids came to an end, and once again an oligarchical régime was set up in Corinth. It appears to have been successful, and less subject to be torn by internal jealousies than was usual elsewhere. 'Fortunate Corinth,' wrote Pindar, some twenty years later, 'gateway to Poseidon's Isthmus, city of splendid youth. In thee dwells Order with her sister Justice, firm foundation of cities, and Peace nursed at her side; these are the stewards of wealth and the golden children of Right, the wise counsellor.' Pindar, no doubt, had his professional poetic axe to grind, and was by nature and nurture partial to the nobility; but his word for 'Order' here (*Eunomia*) is not without significance: it is the word so often applied by Greek writers to the political institutions of Sparta, and expressed that ideal which the turbulent Greek spirit was always seeking, and usually in vain. In the same poem Pindar further praises Corinth for her three notable contributions to art and the techniques: the invention of the dithyramb (the choral song in honour of Dionysus) by the poet Arion, the improvement of the bridle, and the addition, which I have already mentioned, of the sculptured pediment to temples and public buildings. The pediment was called in Greek the 'eagle'. 'Who', says Pindar in his magniloquent way, 'set the twin Kings of the birds upon the temples of the Gods?'

It was during the century which saw the birth of Periander that Greek temples, previously built of wood and brick, first began to be built of stone.

CHAPTER 13

Life in the Islands

I SUPPOSE THERE IS NO POINT ON THE GREEK MAINLAND WHICH IS more than fifty or sixty miles from the sea, and the breath of the sea blows through much of Greek literature, nautical metaphor being as common in it as it is in Shakespeare. Everyone knows the incident in Xenophon's story of the Ten Thousand, when, after their terrible march through the mountains of Armenia, they came at last, almost exhausted and near to despair, to the crest of a hill from which the waters of the Euxine could be glimpsed below them, and with the joyful shout of 'The sea! the sea!' they knew that they were home again. The story is no doubt true, and certainly characteristic: no Greek, though he feared and mistrusted the sea as all seamen do, could live far from it for long. It was in his blood and bones. One feels that all Greeks would have been islanders if they could, and it is easy to fancy, if one can get away for a moment from the literary and historical tradition which forces upon our imagination the dominance of the great cities of the mainland—Athens, Sparta, Corinth, Thebes—that the breath and finer spirit of Greek life and history was in its island communities. The history of almost any one of the Aegean islands would make a tale to hold old men from the chimney corner, if only we possessed it in full and could trace it back through the mists of forgotten centuries and the first days of Mediterranean men. In Herodotus we have glimpses of the story of many islands, and in his masterly, allusive way he gives us a sense of the continuity of the island life stretching back to the darkness of legend and pre-history, and, by some remembered incident, brings to life a portion of the composite picture of the interconnections, rivalries and jealousies of these fiercely independent little communities—communities, now, of Greeks, but of Greeks taught by legend and tradition to remember their predecessors there, Phoenicians, perhaps, or Minoans from Crete, or some still more ancient peoples who lived in the dawn of time.

Thera comes to my mind—perhaps because the island itself is so strange a piece of nature's workmanship. Thera is the modern Santorin, lying south of the Cyclades on the road to Crete. Some four thousand years ago the island blew up—literally exploded, and was changed by the convulsion into a ring of islands about a central lagoon—or crater, rather, for that is what it is, and the water in it is nowhere less than a thousand feet deep. Around the crater the cliffs rise perpendicular and black. On the outer circumference the ring of islands slopes gently to the sea, and their soil is fertile. This island, Herodotus tells us, was once called Callista—the Beautiful. One wonders why: could it have been a propitiatory name, such as the Greeks were fond of using in the hope of blunting the edge of danger in places and powers which they knew all too well to be hostile—like the name Euxine, 'friendly to strangers', which they gave to the far from friendly Black Sea, or the 'Kindly Ones', the name by which they invoked the Furies who pursue a guilty man to his doom? Callista is fair enough on its seaward rim, but its central crater is haunted by demons.

Callista, says Herodotus, was once inhabited by Phoenicians—maybe for the murex-fishing, the shellfish from which was extracted the dye for the Tyrian purple, famous throughout antiquity. It was Cadmus who landed the Phoenicians there: Cadmus, as Herodotus relates in another place, was the man who introduced writing into Greece—the Phoenician alphabet—and it is a curious fact of history that archaeologists have discovered in the island traces of the Greek alphabet in its earliest stage, before the addition of the double consonants.

At some date late in the twelfth century B.C. Callista was settled by men from Lacedaemon under the leadership of Theras, and from him it took its new name of Thera. How Theras and his Lacedaemonians got on with the Phoenicians there is not recorded, but some five centuries later the island again emerges into history. At that time it was ruled by Grinnus, a descendant of Theras, and it so happened that one year there was a serious drought and the islanders were faced with famine. Hoping for the help of Apollo, Grinnus set out for Delphi to consult the oracle and to offer the sacrifice of a hundred victims on behalf of his community. 'What shall I do,' he asked, 'to restore the prosperity of my people?' With apparent irrelevance the Priestess replied that he must found a city in Libya.

'Lord Apollo,' said Grinnus, 'I am too old for such a venture. Can you not tell one of my younger friends to go?'

To this there was no further answer; so the deputation went home and put the matter out of their minds, for neither Grinnus nor any of the rest of them even knew where Libya was. But Apollo's commands cannot be thus ignored, and for the next seven years not a drop of rain fell in Thera: every tree on the island except one withered and died. In these desperate circumstances there was nothing to do but once more to seek the oracle's advice. They did so, and the answer was the same: they must found a city in Libya. This time the Theraeans knew that they must obey, so, though unwillingly, they sent some men to Crete to inquire if any Cretan, or any venturesome stranger who had visited that island, knew where Libya was. Wandering about Crete in their search for information, the men met by chance a dye-merchant named Corobius, who told them that, though he had never actually been to Libya, he had once been forced by stress of weather to seek shelter for his vessel under the island of Platea, just off the Libyan coast. The men from Thera paid Corobius to return with them, and shortly afterwards a reconnoitring party, taking him as their pilot, sailed for the unknown southern sea. The party reached Platea in safety, put Corobius ashore with several months' supplies, and returned to Thera to report their success.

Herodotus does not tell us whether Platea was inhabited or desert; but presumably it was empty of people, for the marooned Corobius, when the agreed time had passed and there was still no sign of a ship from Thera coming to relieve him, began to suffer from lack of supplies and would have starved, had not history repeated itself in the shape of another north-easterly gale which forced a vessel from Samos, bound for Egypt, to run for shelter under the lee of Platea, just as Corobius had himself done long ago when he was out fishing for murex. The Samians took pity on Corobius when they heard his story, left him food for a year, and made sail, as soon as the weather seemed good enough, for Egypt. However, they never got there, for it soon set in to blow hard from the east, and they were compelled to run before it. Day and night they ran, and still it blew hard, until at last they sailed out through the straits of Gibraltar, and, making northward, finally fetched up at Tartessus in Spain. The captain of this Samian vessel was the Colaeus whom I mentioned on an earlier page: as it happened, the gale turned out a lucky gale for him and his men, for they made . fortune in Tartessus and returned to Samos wealthy men—not to mention the splendid story which they were able to tell their friends.

It is pleasant to know that the men of Thera did ultimately find their way to Libya, and succeed in pacifying the anger of Apollo. They settled at a place called Aziris, not far from Platea, where the natives gave them a friendly welcome and later proposed that they should move to a better spot 'where there was a hole in the sky'. They accepted the proposal and founded what was to become the wealthy and important settlement of Cyrene.

The mention of Samos leads me to say something of that island, the history of which in its brilliance and cruelty, in its swift reversals of fortune, and the passions of patriotism and of treachery it aroused in the hearts of its people, holds much which is characteristic of this ancient island world. Herodotus lingers over his account of Samos, as if he were loth to let it go, and excuses his lingering by telling us that he has said so much only because Samos contains three of the greatest wonders of the world: an aqueduct driven through the base of a hill to supply the chief town with water; an artificial harbour formed by a mole running out into twenty fathoms of water and with a total length of over a quarter of a mile; and the temple of Hera, the largest of all the temples in Greece. Whether or not that was Herodotus' real reason for writing so fully about this island, I do not know; it might well have been, for Herodotus was always delighted by the works of men's hands. Perhaps another reason was the fact that he had himself, according to one traditional account, spent a number of years there when he was a young man, and re-membered it with affection. Or, possibly, he found the story of Polycrates too good—and too valuable a lesson in the instability of human greatness—to omit. Of the three 'wonders', one, at least —the aqueduct—was an astonishing achievement. The tunnel was nearly a mile in length, eight feet wide and eight high, with a second cutting, thirty feet deep and three broad, in the bottom of it to carry the pipes. Modern excavation has shown that in the construction of this tunnel borings were begun simultaneously from both ends, and that when the two borings met in the middle of the hill they were only a couple of feet out of true. How did Eupalinus, the architect from Megara hired to undertake this work, manage it? The question is a far from idle one, for it forces upon our notice the fact of ancient Greek technical achievement, which too easily escapes the mere student of literature. Polycrates had his aqueduct made round about 530 B.C., nearly a hundred years before Herodotus finished writing his history; yet even at that early date there must have been enough mathematical knowledge available to render possible the carrying out, with astonishing precision, of a major engineering feat. The story of Greek science, with its brilliant promise and early frustration, is an interesting one; but the discussion of it must be postponed to a later chapter.

Samos lies a mile or two off the Anatolian coast, a little to the northward of Miletus. It is one of the larger of the Greek islands, being about twenty miles long and ten wide. The cult of the goddess Hera—Argive Hera, as she was called—suggests that the island was originally settled by men from Argos. Early in the latter half of the sixth century, when Pisistratus was in power at Athens, the old story was repeated and Polycrates together with his two brothers and helped by a certain Lygdamis, the tyrant of Naxos, by a bold stroke seized the reigns of government. Finding his brothers an unnecessary nuisance, he murdered one of them and banished the other, thus establishing himself as sole ruler. Polycrates was a man of parts, and he had ambitions; he was also, in the true spirit of the age, untroubled by scruples. He had the throne of a rich island, and he meant to keep it; and he meant, too, to make his island richer still. Following the age-long and respected career of piracy, he built up his fleet to a strength unprecedented for the times and succeeded in extending his control to a number of the neighbouring islands and to some of the mainland settlements as well. He came near, says Herodotus, to earning the name of Thalassocrat—Lord of the Sea—and was the first man, certainly the first Greek 'within ordinary human history,' to do so since the legendary Minos of Crete.

Polycrates' piracies and those of his tough and experienced seamen were on a large scale or a small, as occasion offered. One notable instance, which was to have not unimportant consequences, was a venture which took place soon after Croesus had made his alliance with the Spartans. Croesus, generous as always, had a few years previously made a free gift to Sparta of a quantity of gold which the Spartans had offered to buy from him to gild a statue of Apollo, and in gratitude for the gift, and to express their pleasure in being chosen by the Lydian King as the fittest of all Greeks to be his friends, the Spartans decided to make him some return. Accordingly they caused to be made a bronze bowl with a capacity of 2,500 gallons, delicately worked with figures round the rim, and sent it off as a present to Croesus in Sardis. Some Samian vessels, however, always on the look-out for a windfall—Samos lay directly on the sea-route from mainland Greece—got wind of the approach of this valuable cargo, slipped out to sea, and stole it. Of course the Samians subsequently denied the theft—who wouldn't?—and swore that the Spartan crew, having learned that they were already too late and that Sardis had fallen to the Persians, themselves sold the bowl in Samos for a handsome sum and then pretended, when they got home, that it had been stolen. Well, which were the liars?

One thinks of the epigram—typical of many—about the men of another island, this time of Chios: 'The Chians are a bad lot; not one here, one there, but every man-jack of them. Except, of course, Procles—but even Procles is a Chian.'

Polycrates had a pact of friendship with Amasis, the philhellene Pharaoh of Egypt, and, like the mainland tyrants Cleisthenes and Pisistratus, lived in his island court in luxury and splendour. The poet Anacreon, writer of love-lyrics and drinking-songs—of which some survive, together with innumerable imitations by other hands—lived for many years as an inmate of the court, to amuse the tyrant and add a grace to his festivities. So, with his fleet of fifty-oared galleys rigged with a single great squaresail for use when the wind was fair, Polycrates year after year would put to sea from that splendid harbour for his cheerful blood-letting and piratical adventures, never meeting with a reverse, always increasing his dominion, and piling up the wealth in his coffers, until, if we may believe Herodotus, his friend the Pharaoh of Egypt grew alarmed—not, indeed, that the master of a little island might come to rival a potentate like himself, but simply out of pure affection for his guest-friend. For, said Amasis, it is not in nature for a man always to succeed, and success too long continued is assuredly the prologue to disaster. So concerned, indeed, was Amasis at this certain prospect of a reversal of fortune stored up for Polycrates in the womb of time, that he wrote him a letter of advice and warning. If, he wrote, Polycrates was unable ever to encounter misfortune in the ordinary course of his affairs, he must manufacture a bit of bad luck for himself, deliberately. The only thing to be done was, in short, to decide what of all he possessed was most precious to him, and to throw it away . . . 'What nedeth it (if I may quote Chaucer) to sermon of it more?' Everyone knows the old story—how Polycrates took the advice, chose from amongst his treasures a priceless emerald ring cut by the famous Samian jeweller, Theodorus, and threw it into the sea; and how, that very evening, his cook, slitting the belly of a fish brought by a poor fisherman as a present for his master, found the ring inside. Poor Polycrates, the fortunate-unhappy! Amasis, when he learned of his friend's failure to make himself miserable even for an instant, promptly severed the ties between them, 'in order,' says Herodotus, 'that when the destined calamity fell, *he might avoid the distress he would have felt, had Polycrates still been his friend.*' That is surely what Sir Toby Belch might have described as an exquisite reason; and it is one of the engaging qualities of Herodotus that on many an occasion he will give his stories a twist which leaves us wondering if, or how much, he is laughing at us.

One other detail of this story is, I think, worth noticing: when the fisherman brought the fish to Polycrates, declaring that it was too fine a one for his own humble table, Polycrates invited him to dinner. In that refined and luxurious court with its noble buildings and rich appurtenances, where the tyrant drank from his silver goblets and listened to the songs of one of the foremost poets of the age, there was yet, it seems, no artificial barrier between man and man; the tyrant had the power of life and death over all his island subjects, rich or poor, and would use it without a qualm to gain his pleasure or ensure his safety; yet a humble fisherman—so poor, as Theocritus said of another fisherman in a later age, that he needed no watchdog to guard his door, as poverty itself was his best protection—such a man he rewarded for a negligible gift not by money, so easily bestowed, but by an invitation to share his table. It may well be that our modern humanitarianism (a very recent growth) has destroyed in us much of our essential humanity.

Now whether Polycrates double-crossed Amasis, or whether

Amasis had already repudiated Polycrates' friendship because of
the ominous affair of the ring, is not clear; nevertheless it is a
fact that, though Polycrates had promised to help Egypt against
attack by Persia, what he actually did—or, rather, tried to do—
was precisely the opposite. Having heard that Persia was preparing an invasion of Egypt, he sent secretly to Susa and invited
the Persian King Cambyses to apply to Samos for aid. The
reason for this offer is instructive, and very simple: Polycrates,
like all the Greek tyrants, was well aware that there were plenty
of men of noble family in Samos who would have liked, had an
opportunity arisen, to step into his shoes, having previously cut
his throat, or not, according to convenience; so when his offer
of assistance was accepted by Cambyses, he manned forty ships
with island men whom he suspected of disloyalty, and sent them
off to fight against the Egyptians, with an added instruction to
Cambyses that they were on no account to be allowed ever to
return.

One could wish that in the ancient historians there was more
of the intimate gossip of history such as is to be found in our
modern memoirs, for then we might know just how and when
the true object of the voyage became apparent to the crews of
those forty Samian galleys. Being Greeks, no doubt they guessed
pretty soon; for when they had sailed as far south as the island of
Carpathus, they unanimously decided to return to Samos and to
make a bid to oust Polycrates. Back they went, thirsty for revenge,
and were met off the island by Polycrates' fleet. In the ensuing
fight they were victorious, and forced a landing; but then things
went against them and they found themselves no match for the
paid troops under the tyrant's command. They fought hard,
however, and kept Polycrates on the jump with anxiety lest
others of his islanders should play traitor and join them—to
prevent which he had the wives and children of all the leading,
and therefore most suspect, families shut up in the boat-sheds as
hostages, determined to burn them alive, sheds and all, should the
need arise. Luckily the need did not arise, for the rebels, over-
matched, withdrew to their ships and made sail for Sparta in the
hope of persuading the Spartans to lend them troops for a further
attempt. This the Spartans consented to do, not, however, at the
bidding of principle or out of any desire to assist men who had
been hardly used, but simply to get their own back on the

Samians for the theft of that bronze bowl. So the Spartans sailed
for Samos—in its way a historic event, being the first time that a
Spartan force had ever undertaken an expedition to the Asiatic
coast. It was their first step to something more than their merely
local politics.

The expedition was not, however, a success. After a siege of
forty days the Spartans threw up the sponge and withdrew.
There was a silly story (says Herodotus, who none the less takes the
opportunity to tell it) that Polycrates bribed them to abandon the
siege, manufacturing for the purpose a large number of leaden
coins, which he gilded and passed off on the money-hungry
Spartan leaders as pure gold.

The rebels—if that is the proper name to call them by—were
now no better off than they were before; so once again they put to
sea to seek their fortune. It so happened that shortly before this the
men of the little island of Siphnos had discovered rich veins of
both gold and silver, as a result of which they had rebuilt the
council chamber and market-place of their town with Parian
marble, deposited considerable treasure in the temple at Delphi,
and shared out what remained amongst themselves. Siphnos, in
fact, was, for the moment, on top of the world; so what more
natural than that the now homeless Samian exiles should call at
the island to see what they could get? This they did, and demanded immediate payment of ten talents. The Siphnians
refused, whereupon the Samians landed, routed the native force
which tried to oppose them, and refused to go until they had been
paid ten times the amount of their original demand. With this
comfortable sum they bought the island of Hydrea, off the
Peloponnese, which they handed over in trust to the people of
Troezen, while they themselves went on to Crete and founded
the new settlement of Cydonia. Here they lived prosperously for
half a dozen years, after which they were attacked by the men of
Aegina, beaten in a sea-fight, and reduced to slavery. The reader
will not be surprised to hear that the reason for the attack was
revenge—for some time previously, before the reign of Polycrates, a Samian fleet had raided Aegina and had done to that
island considerable damage.

These men, and there were thousands like them, certainly
tasted to the full the changes and chances of this mortal life.
Tough and unscrupulous, hungry for the sunlight, they lived in

fierce enjoyment of the present hour, knowing that death was always near; fighters, corsairs and throat-slitters, they lived, while they had a home, in the constant presence of a beauty which is vanishing from the modern world, tempering the passion of their hearts by the familiar sight of the things made by their hands—gems, coins, temples, pottery—whose purity of line has never been surpassed, and feeding their imagination on the verse of Homer, the music of Phrygia and Lydia, and the many songs of their lyric singers; and, when they lost their home, they were ready to go to any lengths of treachery and violence to recover it.

Greece, in the seventh and sixth centuries, was still young; in many ways this was her finest age. Was she civilised? You may answer how you please. In many ways she was still barbaric, and in some ways she remained barbaric until her final decline. But her men knew how to live, and many things which we, after our long struggle through the centuries, with all our knowledge and wealth and skill, grasp at almost despairingly and often in vain, these men lived with as their natural and familiar possessions. They knew how to live; and it was that knowledge which enabled the best of them to steel their hearts, when the time came, against the threat of being swallowed up in the advancing empire of the East.

But it is time to relate the end of Polycrates, and to show how the forebodings of Amasis came true. A Persian grandee named Oroetes had been appointed by Cyrus governor of Sardis, and the story goes that he found it necessary on one occasion to send a messenger to Polycrates in Samos. Polycrates, at the height of his power and prosperity, and already planning to make himself master of Ionia and the islands, had little regard for Oroetes, or indeed for anyone else, so when the messenger entered his hall, and found him at supper with the poet Anacreon, the lordly tyrant did not bother even to turn his head and look at him. This vexed Oroetes, who thereupon plotted his revenge. Now we read elsewhere that speaking the truth was one of three important accomplishments in which Persian boys were trained; and, if this was indeed so, then Oroetes cannot have learned his lesson well; for he wrote Polycrates a letter, in which he declared that the Persian king was plotting his death, and that if Polycrates would come to Magnesia, where Oroetes was then living and help him to escape from the country, he would give him enough money to enable him to realise all his ambitions.

Polycrates' friends did their best to prevent him from going to Magnesia; all the professional soothsayers declared that it would be madness, and his own daughter, who had dreamed that she saw him hanging in the air 'washed by Zeus and anointed by the Sun-god', added her entreaties. But all to no purpose: Polycrates liked money—and was he not always a lucky man? No luck, however, can endure for ever, and no sooner had the tyrant reached the house of Oroetes, than he was seized by hired assassins, brutally murdered, and his body hung on a cross. 'The precise manner of his death,' Herodotus adds, 'need not be told.'

Not long after this Syloson, the brother whom Polycrates had banished at the beginning of his reign, saw his chance of returning home. He was helped in this by a remarkable stroke of luck. He happened one day to be hanging about the streets of Memphis in Egypt, flaunting a handsome, flame-coloured cloak, when Darius, then a member of the Persian King's bodyguard, noticed the cloak, coveted it, and offered to buy it. Syloson replied that he would not sell it at any price, but that if Darius wanted it so badly that he could not possibly do without it, then he would give it him as a free gift. It was bread cast upon the waters, for not many years later Darius found himself on the Persian throne. Syloson hurried to Susa, obtained an audience with the King, and tactfully reminded him of the incident of the coveted cloak. 'Sir,' said Darius, 'you are the most generous of men. I will give you in return more silver and gold than you can count, that you may never regret that you once did a favour to Darius the son of Hystaspes.' Syloson, in reply, declared that it was not money he wanted, but the isle of Samos. The request would seem to have been a simple one, and Darius was willing enough to grant it; but, Greek life being what it was, things turned out by no means as Syloson had hoped. After Polycrates' death a certain Maeandrius had been in charge of affairs in the island; for a brief moment he seems to have seen himself as a liberator and democrat; but his political convictions were not very firmly founded, as in consequence of an insult flung at him by some noble or other he at once changed his mind and had all the leading men in the island put in irons. He then fell sick, and his brother Lycaretus, thinking he was going to die, had the prisoners butchered, to facilitate his own seizure of the sovereign power. It was at this moment that the Persians arrived with Syloson. No opposition was offered and Maeandrius, who was now feeling better, entered into negotiations with the Persian leaders, professing himself willing to leave the island quietly, upon certain terms. At this juncture Maeandrius' brother, Charilaus, suggested that it would be a sound move to murder the Persian grandees, and Maeandrius agreed—not because he felt any resentment against them, but simply because he disliked the idea of handing the city over to Syloson absolutely intact. So the Persian grandees were set upon and killed. The rest of the Persian force then appeared upon the scene, and took a proper and ruthless revenge: so thoroughly, indeed, did they do their job that they caught the entire population 'like fish in a drag-net', as Herodotus puts it, and presented Syloson with an empty island. This was just what his countryman Maeandrius had wanted.

'Rejoice in good fortune, repine not overmuch in ill. Learn to know how the pendulum swings in human affairs.' So sang the poet Archilochus, looking around with a clear and steady eye upon the life he loved.

CHAPTER 14

Some Island Poets

THE SEVENTH AND SIXTH CENTURIES B.C. SAW THE RISE AND
flowering of Greek lyric verse. Till then, the epic had held sway.
The change arose naturally out of the change in the nature of
Greek society. In the time of the Kings the epic was the appropriate form: when Priam sat on the throne of Troy and Agamemnon lorded it in golden Mycenae, what could the singer do but
sing their praises and recount their deeds? The King—'the
shepherd of the people', as Homer called him—needed his
chronicler and bard to celebrate his prowess and to grace his
board; but the sheep—the nameless thousands—were conscious
as yet of no such need. But with the passing of the kings, other
men came into their own, and had their chance to do and to be;
the nameless thousands, or at least the best and luckiest amongst
them, assumed a name and knew themselves to be men with the
shaping of their lives—under heaven and Fate—in their own
hands. For these men the great epic cycles were not enough:
those poems told of the past, and what men wanted now was the
present, hot and immediate, and felt upon the pulse. They wanted
a poetry which was the direct personal expression of a man in all
his moods. Epic poetry is impersonal poetry; the poetry of
Homer has indeed its own indelible character stamped upon every
line, every phrase, every cadence, and it is unlike anything else
in the literature of the world; nevertheless the character it so
nobly reveals is not that of a man, but of a time and place, of a
way of looking at things, of a certain quality of feeling towards the
great ultimates of life and war and death, shared by the men to
whom it was addressed. We do not know who Homer was, and
our ignorance does not distress us: it is enough to accept him as
the disembodied voice of an age at once remote and familiar,
barbarous and beautiful, which only the imagination can grasp
and dwell in.

But lyric poetry is personal poetry, and the men—and some

of the women too—of these centuries, with the creative genius native to the Greek people, invented it and brought it to perfection.

I like to say that the men of this age 'invented' lyric poetry; but perhaps I should be cautious and qualify that word, for no art was ever brought out of nothing as a wholly new thing. All arts grow from humble beginnings, from the attempts of the unlettered and simple to give some sort of spontaneous expression to their terrors and delights. Folk-song is older than poetry. Greece, like every other country, had its songs of the people, older than its literature. Some of them survive, handed down by oral tradition from generation to generation, until somebody or other thought fit to write them down and preserve them for posterity. What we have are mostly bits and pieces—work-songs, like the

> *Grind, mill, grind:*
> *Pittacus too he grinds,*
> *Lord of great Mitylene . . . ;*

or children's game-songs, like

> *I will chase a fly of brass.*
> *Chase—but you won't catch him;*

and

> *'Where are my violets, where are my roses, where my*
> *beautiful parsley?'*
> *'Here are your violets, here your roses, and here is*
> *your beautiful parsley.'*

or celebrations of ill-remembered national events, like the well-known freedom-song,

> *I will wreath my sword in a myrtle wreath,*
> *Like Harmodius and Aristogeiton*
> *Who slew the tyrant and set Athens free—*

though, in point of fact, those two young men did not slay the tyrant at all, but his brother, and only for personal revenge; or gnomic songs, like

> *Health is first for a mortal man,*
> *Second a handsome body,*

> *Third a fortune got without cheating,*
> *And fourth, to be young with one's fellows.*

Perhaps the most charming of all these artless songs is the Rhodian *Swallow Song*, sung by begging children at the beginning of spring:

> The swallow has come
> With the fine spring weather
> And gift of good years;
> > White-belly,
> > Black-back,
> The swallow has come.
> > Roll out the raisin-cake,
> > Mistress, from the larder,
> With a basket of cheese and a cupful of wine.
> > Wheaten bread, pulse-bread,
> > Swallow will accept them.
> Come, mistress, do we take? or must we go away?
> > Give—and we thank you; give us nothing
> > And we'll steal the door and lintel
> > And the good wife in the kitchen—
> A little thing she is, we'll lift her lightly.
> But give, give, and get your blessing.
> Open the door, let swallow in.
> > Not old men we, but only little children.

Such songs are poetry of a sort, and no better and no worse than countless nursery-rhymes and folk-songs of England. Of course the Harmodius song is not so old, and belongs properly not to folk-song but to what the Greeks called *scolia*, songs, that is, which were sung in turn around the dinner table, in any age. A number of these scolia survive, some of them of a much more consciously poetic quality and of much greater sophistication; for instance:

> *Would I were an ivory lyre,*
> *That pretty boys might carry me to the dance of Dionysus.*

or

> *Would I were a red rose, that she might take me*
> *And give me the gift of her snow-white breast*

or, more cynically,

A mortal man needs not many things—
To eat and to love suffice him.

or, more cynically still,

Look warily at all,
Lest one speaking with a smile
Have a dagger hidden in his heart,
And his words be the double-talk of a black mind.

There is a touch of the national character in such things and they are good enough for the dinner-table; but for us, I suppose, their only value lies in the limpid clarity and directness of the language they employ, a clarity and directness which Greeks of the best age seemed blessedly unable to avoid.

Out of the songs of the people, some time during the period I am speaking of, grew the true Greek lyric poetry, the first personal utterance of Greeks who, long nurtured on the heroic lays of the old epic writers, were now in their changed condition beginning to feel that as individuals they counted for something in the world. Throughout the rest of their history this passion for self-realisation, this fervent individualism, was an essential element in the Greek character; it was the reverse side of their devotion to tradition in religion and the arts, and their equally passionate corporate sense as members of a community. The two elements were always at war in the Greek breast.

The surviving fragments of this lyric poetry are few but precious, and I for one, surveying the general wreck of Greek literature (the library at Alexandria is said to have contained half a million volumes, of which we today have perhaps a thousand) would rather have the lost poems restored than anything else in the rich and varied field which Greek literature covered. This is no doubt a purely personal predilection and might not be shared by others who care for Greece; I can see the raised eyebrow, and hear the pained surprise in the voice that asks me: 'What? You would prefer a lost poem or two by Archilochus to another tragedy of Sophocles?' I can but whisper *yes, I should.* Not that I believe one to be better than the other, for it is always foolish to try to arrange the different kinds of art in an order of merit; moreover I know very well that if I had to choose between the possession of one poem by Archilochus and one play by Sophocles, I should choose the latter because it provides an imaginative world of vaster horizons for the spirit to wander in. But from his seven surviving dramas we can know Sophocles, or fancy that we know him; and perhaps an eighth would not tell us much more. Would a second Parthenon tell us much more about the Greek spirit than we know from the first? But is it not possible that we should indeed learn very much more, if by a miraculous regression in time we were enabled to see the dwelling-houses in some small Greek town, or the rows of shops in the Cerameicus, or one of Polycrates' merchantmen making her landfall, homeward bound to Samos, or a group of peasants paying their respects to Demeter the Hearth-Holder at a wayside altar in Eleusis? These things are the stuff of history, and we can never really know them; we have to imagine them, and, no doubt, usually imagine them wrong.

This is one reason for the charm of the early Greek lyric poetry, and perhaps the chief reason for regretting the disappearance of so much of it: being personal poetry, it helps us to feel the pulse of ancient Greek life more vividly than any other sort of literature—perhaps more vividly even than the sight of the things used by Greek hands.

Many of the island Greeks were poets, and the fragments of their poetry which survive add much to the picture of that intense and reckless island life which I tried to describe in the last chapter. One of the best known in his own day was Archilochus, whom the Greeks themselves put next to Homer. We have only enough of him to make us wish for more and to wonder, incidentally, why his compatriots compared him with Homer at all; for the two are worlds apart. Archilochus was a native of Paros, the island of marble. He was apparently the son of a slave, and early in life set out in search of wealth and adventure on the sea—'the servant of Poseidon, Lord of the Sea, and possessed of the lovely gift of song.' Scattered surviving verses hint at his wild and roving life, how he kneads his bread spear in hand, and leaning on his spear drinks the wine of Ismarus, or how in a scuffle somewhere in Thrace he was forced to leave his 'blameless' shield (the word is used with a smile) under a bush while he fled for his life. 'But be damned to it,' he adds; 'I'll get another just as good.' Archilochus had learned that there was gold in Thasos, that island which looked to him from seaward 'like a donkey's back, all covered with shaggy trees. Nowhere is it beautiful or lovely or beloved, like the country round Siris' stream.' So off he went to seek the gold, but in vain:

> 'Nothing to me is the wealth of golden Gyges;
> I am not covetous; I gape not in wonder
> At wondrous things, or yearn to be a king.
> Such joys are so far off I cannot see them.'

So he shrugs off his failure, and takes to the sea again, learning to know by ever closer acquaintance 'the intolerable gifts of Poseidon', and growing wise to watch for 'the pillar of cloud over Gyrea, sure sign of wind on the way.' Presumably before long he returned to Paros, and there he fell in love with Lycambes' daughter Neobule, 'her hair and breast so sweet with myrrh that even an old heart would be stirred.' He describes how he saw her once 'with a rose and a sprig of myrtle in her hand, her long hair shadowing her shoulders and her back.' Lycambes betrothed her to him, but later for some reason broke the connection, and according to old gossip Archilochus in bitterness and rage wrote verses against them both of such savage scurrility and abuse that they hanged themselves for shame.

The reader at this point may think that I am hard up for subject matter, if I bother to chronicle so commonplace a fact as that a poet and jolly sea-rover, out to snatch enjoyment from his sunlit yet dangerous world, should fall in love. But that fact, or rather Archilochus' expression of it, carries a hint of something of more general interest. The emergence of love poetry at this time (Archilochus wrote at the beginning of the seventh century) not only indicates an important change in the conception of what poetry may, or can, do, but also suggests certain reflections upon the position of women in the ancient world. There is little doubt that the Greeks on the whole treated their women abominably; there is no doubt at all that they treated them abominably in Periclean Athens—the very place and age usually held up to us as representing the finest flower of civilised life. This is not the place to attempt a definition of what a civilised life means, but it is unlikely, one would think, that a society could be civilised in any high sense, if one half of it—or perhaps three-quarters—consisted of slaves, while of the remaining section all the women except the prostitutes were kept in Oriental seclusion and considered (as Aristotle said) to be a lower order of creature than the men: not just different, or less good at politics, fighting and other masculine pursuits, but inferior in quality, as animals were inferior, or slaves.

It is amusing to recall Plato's theory of 'evolution' in the *Timaeus*, where he decides that Nature, always striving to attain perfection, produced men, and that those men who chanced by some unfortunate oversight to be less perfect than she hoped (being cowards or liars or suchlike) were subsequently reincarnated as women; while others, still worse in quality, became animals. The worst of all—the rejects, as one might call them—became fish. All this was pure wantonness on Plato's part, as he could have learned from Anaximander, who wrote 200 years before him not that fish were descended from poor-quality men, but the more probable doctrine that men were descended from perfectly good fish.

Now in these earlier and (as I consider them) sunnier ages slavery was the exception not the rule; and the general attitude towards women much more humane and enlightened than it was later to become. I do not like to call these ages more 'civilised', because the word demands definition; but I believe that they provided, within strict limits, a better chance for any man of the Greek temperament *to live well* (a favourite phrase of the later philosophers) than any age before or after in the long history of the Greek people.

In Homer, in the *Odyssey* at any rate, there is plenty of evidence of respect for women and of the recognition of their place in society. Apart from Penelope herself there is the beautiful picture of Nausicaa, and one remembers how Odysseus was advised, when he reached in his rags the palace of Alcinous, to make straight for Arete, the wife of the King and to throw himself upon her mercy—for Arete, Athene told him, was not only the Queen but a woman too with a wise heart, who would settle even a dispute between men when she cared to do so. In the verse of Hesiod—the next literary evidence we have—the feminine radiance has gone out, at any rate in Boeotia where that grumbling old poetical farmer lived out his harsh life, cursing the weather and the rich and thinking about the gods. But in the Lyric age—for so we should call it—the light comes flooding back. Herodotus, though he wrote in the fifth century and was a member of the Periclean circle in Athens, was concerned almost exclusively with this earlier age, and from the tone of his writing shows clearly enough that he belonged to it in spirit. His attitude to women was always gentle and humane; I would not be misunderstood in this: never at any period in Greek history was there the least whisper of *romanticism* in the Greek attitude towards women; still less was there any sign of what we might call chivalry. Chivalry and romanticism needed an utterly different mental and emotional climate to grow in from that of ancient Greece. In the Greek experience of love there was delight and anguish, but (I think) little mystery. In the romantic experience, love becomes a symbol of all sorts of other things; it becomes a window through which the eye of the spirit looks out upon a new and previously undiscovered world. The word itself is given an immense extension of meaning, till it is allowed to cover almost all the outward-moving and creative impulses of the heart and mind, including worship. But the Greek *eros* is a precise word, and maintains its precision: it means physical passion, and it was by an easy metaphor that Pericles applied it to the feeling of Athenians towards their city. The difference between the ancient and the modern can be illustrated by contrasting two passages: Shelley, steeped in Greek *thought*, but very far from Greek *feeling*, wrote in *The Revolt of Islam*:

Was it one moment that confounded thus
All thought, all sense, all feeling into one
Unutterable power, which shielded us
Even from our own cold looks, when we had gone
Into a wide and wild oblivion
Of tumult and of tenderness? Or how
Had ages, such as make the moon and sun,
The seasons, and mankind their changes know,
Left fear and time unfelt by us alone below?

I knew not. What are kisses whose fire clasps
The failing heart in languishment, or limb
Twin'd within limb? or the quick dying gasps
Of the life meeting, when the faint eyes swim
Through tears of a wide mist boundless and dim
In one caress? What is the strong controul
Which leads the heart that dizzy steep to climb,

Where far over the world those vapours roll
Which blend two restless frames in one reposing soul?

Those questions make beautiful poetry, but a Greek poet
would not have bothered to ask them. Before they could be asked,
a great deal had to intervene: Plato, first, turning away from a
world which the passions of men invested with a growing
darkness and perplexity, had to find refuge in a strange, new,
intellectual universe of Forms which were the only Reality, and
of which the things we touch and see are the shadows; the neo-
Platonists had still further to abstract and refine, in their search for
the mysterious ONE; to be followed by the dichotomy of spirit
and flesh in Christianity, and the aspirations of Christian mysticism in which the body could be laid asleep and become one with
God. This whole movement of the human spirit was at the
same time a flight from the visible and tangible world and an
incalculable enrichment of it, because it gave the imagination a
new dimension to wander in, enabling the poet to see heaven in a
wild flower, like Blake, or the corn, as Traherne saw it, as orient
and immortal wheat.

Now Sappho (and this is the second of my passages) describes,
in what I suppose is the most generally familiar of her few
surviving verses, the emotion aroused not, indeed, by a kiss, but
simply by the proximity of the loved. I translate her molten
words into cool prose, being able to do no better: 'Godlike seems
to me that man who sits by you and hears your sweet voice and
lovely laughter—it makes my heart flutter like a bird in my
breast. For when I but see you, I have no speech, my tongue is
broken, and straightway a subtle flame runs under my skin;
my eyes are blinded, there is a throbbing in my ears, the sweat
pours down and trembling seizes me; I am paler than grass, and
so changed that I seem as dead.' There are no questions here, no
rising on the wings of love to some star 'pinnacled dim in the
intense inane'; there is only the Greek *eros*, naked and triumphant.

Sappho was a native of the Aeolian island of Lesbos, and the
fact that her verse was counted in antiquity as the fine flower of
Greek lyric poetry is at least an indication that women in that
epoch enjoyed a fuller life and a greater respect in society than
later ages were to accord them. The mere existence of love
poetry points in the same direction, because it postulates a

relationship which has become personal. Achilles in the *Iliad* sulks because a girl is refused him; but there is nothing personal in the relationship whatever, and no hint of passion. Women have to be more than cattle before a poet can see one of them as Archilochus saw Neobule with her rose and myrtle, her hair shadowing her shoulders—or perhaps, if the lovely phrase refers to her, 'standing at the meeting-point of wind and wave.' Nor could any poet, in a climate of opinion in which women were despised, have written the lines about Danae and the infant Perseus turned adrift to drown:

> When in the well-wrought chest she lay,
> And the wind blew, driving it
> Over the wild sea,
> Fear stole upon her heart, and with tear-wet cheeks
> She took Perseus in her arms, and said: 'My babe,
> All is grief for me,
> But you are sleeping; so young, so tender,
> You lie at rest in the grim
> Nail-studded chest,
> Though the murk thickens and the night is starless.
> The surge of the passing wave, towering high,
> You heed not, nor the wind's voice, as you lie wrapped
> In your cloak, your face close to mine.
> If to you terror were terrible,
> You might have listened to my words.
>   Sleep on, my baby; and may the sea sleep too,
> And our own distress.

Those lines are a fragment of a poem by Simonides of Ceos, who wrote in the last quarter of the sixth century, and was chosen in his old age to compose the epitaphs for the men killed at Thermopylae. His epitaph on Leonidas and his three hundred Spartans is familiar to most people:

> Go tell the Spartans, you who read:
> We took their orders and are dead.

Herodotus quotes it, with the others, of course without comment but for us who read it today, our sensibility dulled and our minds cluttered with so much rhetoric and verbiage, it is hard to say nothing, even if our comment is as banal and obvious as to point to the stripped economy of the lines, the language (spoiled by translation) so cool and pellucid, the sentiment so true. No language can touch in a word the heart of the matter more surely than Greek, and few poets have equalled the best of the Greeks in the severity of their refusal of adventitious aids to stir a reader's response. All that is noble in the Spartan conception of a soldier's duty is in those two quiet lines.

There was another Simonides, a native of the small island of Amorgos and a near-contemporary of Archilochus. He was a much lesser poet, and seems to have been of a somewhat curmudgeonly nature, and pleased with his own misery. In one poem, if poem it can be called, he observes that mortal hopes are seldom fulfilled and that most men, before their dreams can come true, are either crippled by senility, or die of disease, or are killed in a fight, or drowned, or hang themselves: an observation which may be accurate but is not inspiriting. Yet even this old grumbler, who was surely not grateful enough for the salt and sunshine of the Aegean, has a word to say for women— only a word, it is true, and only for those rarities, the good ones. It occurs at the end of a long and dreary set of verses in which he compares the various feminine types he is acquainted with to animals, the pig, the fox, the dog and so on, adding that some women, having been created out of mud can do nothing except eat and are so lazy that they cannot bring themselves on the coldest day to pull the chair closer to the fire, while yet others are as changeful as the inconstant sea. Then, having run through a few more types, such as the mare, the cat and the monkey, he suddenly at the end surprises and delights us with The Bee. Lucky the man who has the Bee for his wife,

> For she alone is free from all reproach;
> Under her hand comes plenty and all good things;
> Husband and wife grow old together in love,
>> And more than mortal grace
>> Hovers around her face.

That last charming phrase atones for much. One can be sorry for Simonides, for it is surely obvious that his own wife cannot have been a bee, but spent her time, when she wasn't eating, in what he notes, even in those days, as the favourite female occupation—visiting her neighbours and swopping stories about men. 'Live with a woman,' he says, 'and you will never enjoy a whole day of peace.'

A characteristic of the love poems of the Lyric Age is their comparative freedom from the taint of pederasty, which in later Greek life is all but universal. The whole subject of homosexuality in ancient Greece is a tricky one, and I shall try to say something about it when I come to discuss Greek manners and morals; it is a fact however that in what we possess of the work of these early lyrists it is much less in evidence than it was later to become, and it is tempting to guess—though it can be no more than a guess—that its comparative rarity was due in part to the better position in society of women. In a later age, when there was no sort of social equality between men and women, perhaps it was easier for the Greek, with his insatiable erotic impulses, to find 'love', as distinct from mere enjoyment, amongst his constant companions, the young men and boys. Anacreon, indeed, the friend and court-poet of Polycrates, wrote love-songs addressed to boys; but Anacreon, though his touch was exquisitely light, was a lesser poet than many of his contemporaries; he was a *bon-viveur* writing to please his elegant and luxurious masters, and one does not easily detect in his verses what Keats called 'the true voice of feeling', except perhaps in his sighings over the passing of youth.

Sappho is in a very different category, and I hesitate to enter the lists in which scholars have fought for five and twenty centuries over the question of her private morals. For me, the exact quality of her feeling for the girls whom she celebrates in verse is of no importance, the excellence of every art (to quote Keats again) being its intensity, which makes all disagreeables evaporate by being in close contact with beauty and truth. The murky stories which gathered in antiquity about Sappho are undoubtedly nonsense, and to me it seems as silly to censure her love poems as to censure Shakespeare's sonnets. It is an understandable foible of Greek scholars (grinding their axe) to pretend that all Greek literature is unsurpassed and inimitable, which it certainly is not; but none of them, not even Swinburne, has said too much in praise of Sappho. Only two poems of hers survive complete, or almost complete—possibly three, as the lyric I quoted in an earlier chapter at any rate *seems* complete; the rest is scattered fragments—three lines, four lines—sometimes a word or two only—preserved by old grammarians who quoted them to illustrate some vagary of the Aeolic dialect or the origin of some metrical innovation. But these meagre remnants are enough to reveal her supremacy. I called her language molten, and so it is, for words in Sappho's poetry seem to lose their solidity and to dissolve into light. The movement of her verse, though wrought with consummate artistry, seems the very music of thought and as spontaneous as the singing of her own nightingale, 'the sweet-voiced messenger of spring.'

> Cool is the noise of water through the apple orchards,
> And down from shimmering leaves
>   Falls sleep, like rain.

Nothing can annihilate time as poetry can, or so whisper to us of the everlasting.

> Sweet mother, I cannot mind my wheel.
> Aphrodite has put her delicate hand upon me,
> And I am broken with longing.

again, of a bride:

> As the sweet-apple reddens on the bough,
> So high, so high, on the topmost bough of the tree;
> The pickers have forgotten it: no, not forgotten—
> They could not reach so high . . . ;

and of a group of girls, seen in moonlight which invests them with mystery and a sort of ritual significance:

> The moon was full, and they stood there,
> Motionless, as round an altar.

Or of the girl Anactoria:

> Some say the loveliest thing on the black earth
> Is a troop of horsemen, or marching men, or ships sailing—
>   But I say it is what one loves.
> I think again of Anactoria, who is not with me,
> And long to see the grace of her walking
> And the glancing brightness of her face,
> More than the chariots of the Lydians and armed warriors in
>   battle.

One more quotation: Sappho's endearing curse upon some woman she hated not, indeed, for wickedness, but simply for her stupidity:

> Dead will you lie, you who care not for poetry's rose,
> Unloved, unremembered, vanished for ever and ever,
> There in the house of Death, with the blind ghosts
> Flitting, a Nothing, a bodiless shadow . . .

I call it an endearing curse, perhaps foolishly; but at least to me Sappho is endeared by it, because she has not written, as a modern would do in similar circumstances, with any satirical intention, but with perfect gravity, stating the obvious fact that any woman, or man either, who is not moved by beauty is indeed damned.

'Holy Sappho,' as her countryman and fellow-poet Alcaeus calls her, 'with the honey smile and hair dark as violets,' was the queen of the island poets, and she had noble subjects. As for Alcaeus himself, it may be that luck has been against him, for what fragments we have of his verse hardly justify the high reputation he enjoyed in antiquity. He was a true islander and seems to have lived a life no less full of changes and chances than Archilochus did, playing a violent part in politics, on the side of the oligarchs, suffering exile, and winning his return. He enjoys the doubtful privilege of having invented the metaphor of the ship of state, tossed on stormy seas, a figure copied by the Roman poet Horace, and studiously repeated throughout European history in political rhetoric. His verses, so far as we are able to know them, lack variety of subject, being nearly all about drink. The wine-cup is his cure for all ills: it is hot weather, he says, the dog-days when women are most lustful and men most impotent—so let us drink. It is cold; let us pile logs on the fire—and drink; Myrsilus the tyrant has been murdered at last—everyone must be *forced* to drink for joy; it becomes a little tedious. One fragment runs: 'I have something to say, but shame prevents me'; critics have imagined that the poem in which these words occur was addressed to Sappho, for there is a fragment of Sappho's which says: 'Had you desired any good or noble thing, had not your tongue framed any evil speech, shame would not have filled your eyes, but you would have said it honestly.' One cannot but wonder what it was Alcaeus wished

to say—perhaps it was only to ask Sappho to drink with him.
If it was so, no wonder his heart failed.

The poetry of this age, all of it pulsing with life and much of
it supremely beautiful, is not 'literature' as we understand the
word. It is pure song, which is indeed what the word 'lyric'
means. It was made to be sung to the lyre amongst friends, at
table, on shipboard, by the camp fire, or whatever the occasion
might be. It seems for all its artistry to come to the lips of the
singer 'as naturally as the leaves to the tree'. Many of the poets in
addition to their occasional lyrics also wrote hymns for ceremonial
worship: 'I can do a dithyramb myself,' said Archilochus, 'if I am
thunderbolted with wine'; and so could the rest of them, with or
without the thunderbolt. But we know hardly anything of their
hymns; for us, it is the personal lyric which is the glory of these
centuries, reflecting as it does in many mirrors that vivid, ad-
venturous life which, though removed from us by more than
two thousand irremeable years, is yet as real and intelligible as
yesterday. The poets have made it so, because they never sought
for their themes, but wrote—or sang—directly out of the moment
as it flew, making the eternal commonplaces of sorrow and joy,
pleasure and pain, the matter of their songs. Nothing was too
high for them, or too trivial: a couple of lines occur to me—not
by an island poet, for Hipponax, their author, came from
Ephesus:

Come (he says), take my cloak. I will hit Bupalus in the eye.
I am ambidexterous—and I never miss.

CHAPTER 15

The Gods

REFERRING TO THE TRICK BY WHICH PISISTRATUS PERSUADED THE Athenians that the goddess Athene was herself bringing him to the throne of Athens, Herodotus remarks that it was the greatest piece of nonsense ever perpetrated since 'the Hellenic peoples were distinguished from the barbarians as being more intelligent and freer from futile absurdities.' Herodotus is here speaking as an emancipated fifth-century Greek looking back with a tolerant smile upon the blind superstitions of the Grecian past and of the barbarian present. Precisely when that moment of distinction came, or, to put it into other words, when what we know as Classical Greece first took shape, it is not possible to say. It is safe however to say that by the beginning of the seventh century B.C. the shaping was well under way and that it rapidly accelerated during the next two hundred years, until by the time of Herodotus, in the middle of the fifth century, there was an absolute difference in quality of civilisation between Hellas, on the one side, and the 'barbarian' world on the other. Herodotus is evidently amused—even, perhaps, a little shocked—by the survival of primitive credulity in the Athens of Pisistratus; he does not bother, for once, to reflect that strong emotion can produce at any rate a momentary belief in the unlikeliest things even amongst the most enlightened. Much primitive superstition survived in Greek religion (as I suppose it survives in most religions) until the end of the classical epoch, though attempts were continually made to reinterpret it in the light of new ideas. The Greeks never became a nation, but it was religion as expressed in their great, shared religious festivals, of which the festival at Olympia was the earliest, which first gave them the sense of being a people.

Greek religion is peculiar in that it had no dogma, no sacred Book, no Prophet, no revelation, and no permanent, professional priesthood. Thus it might be not wholly nonsensical to say that the Greeks had no religion at all, in spite of the fact that they were a deeply religious people and brought their religious sense to bear upon the smallest details of everyday life to an extent which is difficult for the modern man to appreciate or understand. Their religion was based not upon a theology or any system of organised belief, but upon innumerable local sanctities and innumerable traditional acts. It had little or no philosophical content except what isolated individuals—such as Aeschylus or Plato—chose to give to it, until the emergence in the fourth century of the great philosophical schools of the Stoics, the Cynics and the Epicureans, and by that time it was for all practical purposes dead, having died with the old ideals of the City State. One result of the local conservatism of Greek religious practice, combined with an extreme fluidity in the interpretation of the significance of the acts involved, was the absence throughout Greek history of religious persecution. In modern Europe much blood has been shed, or frizzled, in the name of the Creator, but this particular form of bloody-mindedness, even if no other, was entirely foreign to the Greek character. 'Custom is all,' wrote Pindar, and Herodotus quotes the words with evident approval. To worship the wrong gods, or the right gods in the wrong way, would have seemed to a Greek foolish and possibly dangerous, but to burn a man alive in order to save his soul would have seemed a very odd and barbarous proceeding. Socrates, indeed, was murdered by his fellow Athenians for 'corrupting the youth' and teaching strange doctrines, but the murder of Socrates occurred when the great achievements and splendid hopes of Athens had fallen in ruin, and the Athenians in bewilderment and despair were looking for a scapegoat.

Greek religion had nothing to do with morality, or conduct. It did not preach virtue. Its basis was the ritual act, the thing done, the thing which had always been done from immemorial antiquity, in propitiation of, or in thanksgiving to, the mysterious powers of life, death and growth, the sense of whose existence, vast, menacing and inscrutable, is in primitive man what first distinguishes him from the beasts. The development of Greek religion consisted in the attempt to exalt and purify the conception of the nature of these powers, and, when Greece had inherited and accepted the Olympian hierarchy, to assign their operation to a decreasing number of gods. Ideally the tendency of Greek religious thought was towards monotheism, and something not unlike it is to be found in individual thinkers—in some of the sixth-century Ionian philosophers for instance, and in Aeschylus and Plato; but just as the Greek political ideal of democracy (of a kind) was continually frustrated by internal struggles for power, so the monotheistic religious ideal was frustrated by the weight of ancient custom and local pieties, by the natural resistance of the Greek mind to intellectual dictation, and by the conservatism of Delphi and the other oracles. There was a time, Gilbert Murray has suggested, when, 'if there had been some Hebrew prophets about, and a tyrant or two, progressive and bloody-minded, to agree with them, polytheism might perhaps actually have been stamped out.' Hebrew prophets, however, were not at any time common in the Greek world, and even had one, or his equivalent, existed, it is unlikely that a bloody-minded Greek tyrant would have agreed with him; he would have preferred, like Polycrates, to look after his navy.

There is a passage in Herodotus in which he says that it was only, so to speak, 'the day before yesterday that the Greeks came to know the origin and form of the various gods, and whether or not all of them had always existed; for Homer and Hesiod, the poets who composed our theogonies and described the gods for us, giving them all their appropriate titles, offices and powers, lived, as I believe, not more than four hundred years ago.' Herodotus is speaking, of course, of the Olympian hierarchy; but his words are misleading, and throw too much responsibility upon the poets, almost seeming to suggest that Homer and Hesiod not only described the gods but invented them. But the Olympians had existed for a thousand years before Homer fitted them to preside over a civilised, or fairly civilised, society of gallant chieftains gaily fighting for honour, trade and women; they had come into Greece, presumably, with the Achaeans in the days of the migrations, and had made a home there as best they could amongst the nameless, and mostly horrible, powers which the Pelasgians, or whoever were the original inhabitants of the Greek peninsula, tried blindly to placate. Their struggle for supremacy—if one may so speak of gods—was a long and difficult one, and never fully successful, for they never wholly ousted the old nameless powers, until, with the collapse of classical Greece, philosophy took over the functions of religion and there was no room left for them at all, except as a memory or as decorative figures in an old tale.

Greek religion differed from most religions in that (I do not speak for the moment of the mystery cults) it had no prophet and no revelation; it enforced no belief, and persecuted no heresy. Nor were its gods all-powerful: they had not, for instance, created the world—they only governed it; and above and beyond them there was always another Something—Herodotus calls it Fate, or Necessity—which even they could not escape. The essential thing in the religion of a Greek was duly to perform the immemorial ritual act: how he interpreted the act was largely his own concern, or, rather, how he envisaged the power whom his act was designed to propitiate. In the dark age of Greece that power was some faceless and incomprehensible force of nature, threatening the blighting of crops, or famine, or disease, or death, some living ghost of a dead ancestor, perhaps, or the winged Keres (Spirits) 'in their thousands and thousands,' as Homer says, 'which no mortal man can escape.' These were not gods; they were before the age of gods, which are not within the power of primitive men to conceive. These were terrors, without form or name; and men, ignorant of all natural causes, had by some blind magic to thwart their malevolence and to get them on their side.

Religion in every age is concerned with the vast and fluctuant regions of experience which knowledge cannot penetrate, the regions which a man knows, or feels, to stretch away beyond the narrow, closed circle of what he can *manage* by the use of his wits. How small this circle was, and how great the circumfluent darkness, in primitive Greece, or in any other primitive community, is not easy for us to imagine. Agriculture, for instance, was in primitive Greece a matter not of knowledge—for there was no knowledge—but of religion; if the crops failed, it was because someone had broken a tabu, and something must be done to trace the pollution and to free the conscience from guilt. All this is well known from the findings of anthropology all over the world; but what is less well known, and more interesting, is the extent to which the sense of these vague, haunting presences or powers survived in Greek religion long after the time when what Herodotus called silly nonsense, or 'absurd trivialities', was supposed to have been banished from the minds of cultivated men,

and the Olympian hierarchy was firmly established in the governance of the Greek world. The anthropomorphic Olympian
hierarchy, aided by the imagination of poets and artists, only
took over, and partially absorbed into itself, the functions of those
dark and terrifying forces which primitive men had felt to be
menacing continually their frail chances of survival.

Many scholars, notably J. E. Harrison in her *Prolegomena*,
have helped to make clear to us the presence of these primitive
terrors underlying the worship of the Olympian gods far into
the great age of Greece. In Athens, for instance, there was celebrated twice a year the festival of the Diasia, the chief festival of
Zeus, King of Heaven and Father of Gods and Men—a great
God, if ever there was one; yet in the actual rites of the festival
Zeus had no place. Moreover he was called for the occasion
Zeus Meilichios—the Appeaser—as if he were not the Zeus men
knew at other times, but someone else: Zeus, and not-Zeus. In
reliefs he was often represented as a bearded snake—and snakes
were emblems of the underworld. And why call him the Appeaser, and not the Appeased as a god might reasonably be
thought to be? It seems as if he were not a god at all, but some
sort of shadowy projection of the ritual appeasement of the powers
of the dark. Normal sacrifice to the Olympian gods was a Feast:
the slaughtered animal was shared between the God and his
worshippers. But at the Diasia the sacrifice was a holocaust: the
victim, that is, was burnt to ashes, and there was no feast, no
rejoicing. It was the form of sacrifice always offered to placate
the dead, the ghosts, the powers of darkness. Amongst civilised
men the ancient terror—the 'silly nonsense'—survived; right
back through the dim ages the ghosts and the powers of darkness
had been placated, and they were still being placated, even though
men pretended, or tried to believe, that they were doing service
to Zeus.

Similar elements are found in another Athenian festival, the
Anthesteria, the oldest of the festivals of Dionysus. It was the
great Spring Festival, and in it Dionysus, god of wine and of new
life and growth, did, indeed, appear. But here again, as in the
Diasia, the central mystery was not at all the worship of the
Olympian Dionysus, but simply the appeasement of the dead.
The Funeral Jars were opened, the spirits of the dead were let
loose; then, duly appeased, they were bottled up again in their

proper place and every man swept and cleaned his house, and the streets of the town, from the presence of death.

Thus in both these festivals are seen at work the immemorial terrors of the family or tribe, striving by the propitiation of their ghosts to avert pollution and its attendant calamities of famine or disease or death, and at the same time the attempt to associate the ancient ritual with a God. In the beginning there had been no God: he—or rather they—came later, and somehow or other they had to be made the object of an already accepted and necessary ritual. The process of identifying the nameless, ancient Powers with a named and recognised God with defined attributes and with temples and statues to honour him, was a gradual one and cost centuries of intellectual and imaginative effort. The family or tribal ghosts, with power to save or destroy, had to be granted a wider influence as well as a name, and to become gods of the City, or of all Greece. The process of transformation was never complete; for side by side with the twelve Olympians* the ancient local pieties and terrors lingered on, as can be seen by the fact that many of the Olympian gods continued to be known by many names, or to be given surnames to express some limited and local aspect of their powers.

Further evidence of the survival of primitive rites in the worship of the Olympians is the appearance, somewhere in the ceremonial, of the divine or sacred animal. In the Diasia it was the snake; part of the ritual of the Anthesteria consisted of a sacred marriage, ostensibly of the god (Dionysus) with the daughter of the King; but the marriage was said to be celebrated not in the god's temple, as one might expect, but in the *Bucolion*, or Bull Shed. Pigs—emblems of fertility—figured largely in the Thesmophoria, the festival of Demeter and Persephone. Many gods were habitually associated with animals or reptiles or birds: Athene with the owl, Zeus with the eagle, snake or bull, Hera with the cow, Apollo with the bull or the dolphin, Dionysus with the goat, the lion, or the snake. The creatures came to be known as 'attributes' of the gods with whom they were associated, but Gilbert Murray, following Jane Harrison, expressed the conviction that in all these cases the 'attribute'—that is, the animal—is original and the god is subsequently added. As in most primitive

* Zeus, Hera, Athene, Apollo, Artemis, Aphrodite, Ares, Poseidon, Demeter, Hermes, Hades, Hephaestus.

religions, the animal played a leading part in the ritual because of his strength and fertility, or whatever other power he was felt to possess—because of his *mana*. The bull especially figures in the primitive Aegean religions; he was the beast of beasts; he dominates the religious ritual of Minoan Crete; he is worshipped for his enormous strength and lordliness. His blood was holy; right into classical times it was death to drink bull's blood— the great Themistocles was said to have killed himself by drinking it. In the blood of a divine bull the religion of Mithras sought salvation.

Primitive religion is always practical; it aims to attain a definite object, the survival of the tribe. That is why it pervades every aspect of life. Primitive man could not, as perhaps some moderns can, keep one part of his mind and heart for religion, and another for his affairs. What threatened the survival of the tribe was, first, a failure of the crops, and, secondly, a fall in the birth-rate: starvation, that is, or conquest by the tribe next door. One way to ensure physical strength and healthy sons was to take into oneself the *mana* of the beasts: one ate their flesh to acquire their vitality and power. If, in spite of all, the power was still lacking, and disaster came, it was because something, some time, had been *done wrong*: there was pollution somewhere, an obscure guilt of omission, or commission. If the crops failed, it was the same— some power had been offended, the *right thing* had not been done. In primitive religion the positive side is to acquire the power, the springing life, the negative side is to avoid offence—the *tabu*. This is the reason for the enormous importance, lasting right through the religious practices of classical Greece, of ritual—of ritual properly and exactly performed in accordance with custom. Who was to know in primitive times what was Right—what was *Themis*? Obviously, the old men of the tribe, because their memory went further back; they knew the custom—the *patria*— what their ancestors had once done and what, therefore, they too must do. It was the task, or privilege, of the old to warn the ignorant young against the tabu, the forbidden thing. But some- times a situation might arise in which even the traditional wisdom of the old was insufficient, and then it was that they had to seek a still older authority—the authority of the dead. This was how oracles arose. An oracle might be established at the tomb of a dead ancestor of the tribe; failing this, men might go further afield to some other sacred place, to Dodona or Delphi. There they would ask what it was they had done amiss, to invite calamity; and the oracle—the god, or the spirit of the dead ancestor—would give his answer. The Greek word for the oracular response means simply 'to give advice;' and the giving of advice was the first, and always the principal, function of the oracles. This explains why the influence of the oracles was conservative, and hostile in later days to experiment and the growth of knowledge.

The gods and goddesses in Homer hardly seem to have much religious significance: they are too human for that, being largely employed, as the poet Xenophanes complained, in theft, adultery and mutual deceit. They are savages for all their splendour and strength and beauty, and well enough suited to the buccaneering princes for whose pleasure the old epic lays were originally made. But by the time that, purged of some of their grossness, they had been brought with Homer from Ionia on the eastern shores of the Aegean, into Greece, the old heroic days had become a distant memory, far more distant, even, than they had been to Homer, who had thrown a colouring of romance over the wild doings of that shadowy past. So when, in the course of the sixth century, Pisistratus brought the Homeric poems to Athens and instituted the regular recitation of them at the festival of the Panathenaea, and from thence the knowledge of them spread throughout the Greek mainland, Greeks, looking back, as most of us will, upon the vision of a past which never quite existed were able to see it invested with the splendour of high endeavour, and to find in the radiant forms of the Olympian gods both an emblem of what humanity might be and a conception of the divine far removed from the ghosts and demons and nameless hauntings which the terror of ancient ignorance had called up out of the darkness.

'Since the Hellenic peoples were distinguished from the barbarians as being more intelligent and freer from futile absurdities . . .' I have suggested that the time Herodotus had in mind when he wrote those words might be put somewhere during the seventh century, and no doubt the process of distinction had by then begun; but it may well be that the decisive moment—if there can be such a thing in the growth of a people —came with the coming of the poems of Homer to Athens and

Greece. Without any doubt at all Homer's Olympians wrought a profound change in the religion of Greece, and it was a change very much for the better. They led men to look away from the brute facts of physical growth and decay to an imagined Being, or Beings, behind them, benevolent, on the whole, to mankind —provided they were treated right—and responsible, up to a point at any rate, for the governance of the world and what goes on in it. They were gods made in the image of men—but how else could they be made? If cows and lions, as Xenophanes put it, had hands and could draw, they would draw the gods like cows and lions. It is natural to men, at least to ordinary men who have not Xenophanes' intellectual insight, to imagine gods in their own image. But the image of the Olympians, aided by poets and sculptors, was a not ignoble one. They stood for law, and against the barbarous and bloody rites dictated by ignorance and fear. Again and again they are represented in reliefs as fighting with the Giants, just as men are represented as fighting against the Centaurs, and scholars have reminded us that these battles held for the Greeks a deep symbolical meaning: they were the struggle of human intelligence against mindless strength, the image of awakened Hellas in conflict with the blind forces of nature and of barbarism.

It cannot in fact be too often repeated that the Olympian religion of Greece differed from most religions in that it had nothing in it of revelation: it was the progressive imaginative act of a highly intelligent people—let us leave out for a moment the 'average man'—to find a form which would express its growing consciousness of order and of mind in a universe which had once seemed to consist only of brute forces. In the more advanced communities it did succeed in liberating worship from barbarity and beastliness—from demon-hunting, the rending of live animals, the drinking of blood, even from human sacrifice. It did, too, help to strengthen the bonds between communities, and, thirdly, it never, by trying to force a rigid conformity, barred the way to greater knowledge. I have said that the Olympian religion was founded upon no revelation: one might go further and say that it had no doctrine either, no formal teaching of any kind. It attempted to make no proselytes; it persecuted no heretics: how could it? for one cannot persuade another to an imaginative act, or persecute him for a private vision the quality of which only himself can know. One can be pretty sure that the best minds in classical Greece never for an instant took the Olympians as *existences*: they felt them as symbols; and if one is asked symbols *of what*, one can give no more precise answer than would be implied in one's total conception of the nature and direction of Greek experience, leading, as it did lead, to the confident assurance that to belong to Hellas meant, very definitely, not to be a barbarian, to be free from 'futile absurdities.'

The Olympians took many centuries to grow up; they were savage enough when they first came to Greece, and, with their cheating, adultery and thievishness, all too human. But grow up they did, in the fervid imagination of the great formative age, until it was possible for humble men and women, who had blindly hoped to propitiate with the coming of spring the dark spirit which could curse or bless their own little plot of ploughland, to identify that spirit with the gracious figures of Demeter and Persephone—Persephone

> *who cost Ceres all that pain*
> *To seek her through the world.*

They remained to the Greeks—at least to the better minds among them—allegories, as they have to us. They could inspire worship, and lead the mind beyond the 'ignorant present' towards some sense of the divine; but they were never taken as the truth. For what is a man, as the Greeks might have said, to presume to know the ultimate causes of life and death? But through the Gods and the noble carved images which represented them, they could, if their minds were open, catch glimpses of the divine and imagine a state of being of which the earth showed only an imperfect shadow. Gilbert Murray, in his *Five Stages of Greek Religion*, quotes a beautiful passage in defence of images from Maximus of Tyre, who lived about 200 B.C. 'God Himself,' it runs, 'the father and fashioner of all that is, older than the sun or the sky, greater than time or eternity and all the flow of being, is unnameable by any lawgiver, unutterable by any voice, not to be seen by any eye. But we being unable to apprehend his essence use the help of sounds and names and pictures, of beaten gold and ivory and silver, of plants and rivers, mountain peaks and torrents, yearning for the knowledge of him, and in our weakness naming all that is beautiful in this world after his

nature—just as happens to earthly lovers. To them the most
beautiful sight will be the actual lineaments of the beloved, but
for remembrance' sake they will be happy in the sight of a lyre,
a little spear, a chair, perhaps, or a running-ground, or anything
in the world that awakens the memory of the beloved. Why
should I further examine and pass judgment about Images?
Let men know what is divine, let them know: that is all. If a
Greek is stirred to the remembrance of God by the art of Pheidias,
an Egyptian by paying worship to animals, another man by a
river, another by fire—I have no anger for their divergences;
only let them know, let them love, let them remember.'

To quote that passage is, of course, to leap forward some three
centuries beyond the period I have been considering, and the
writer of it has lived much with the thought of the great philosophical and religious schools which grew up in the fourth century
after the collapse of Athenian supremacy in mainland Greece.
But it is the old Olympian religion still, however broadened by
the realisation that God, to be a true God, must belong not to
Hellas only but to the world. In its charity to human weakness it
is unsurpassed by any of the greater and more durable religions
which were to come after it.

The general tendency throughout the classical age was, as I
have already suggested, to merge the local cults more and more
in the universal. The case of Hermes is an interesting instance: a
Herm, in the dark ages, was a stone post with a phallus, symbol
of procreation. Set on a grave, he (or it) was the power which
generated new lives, or brought back the souls of the dead to
be born again. He was thus the herald between the two worlds.
A herm was also a boundary stone, the mediatory mark between
neighbouring tribes. There were herms in Athens in the fifth
century, and everyone remembers the outcry when, one night,
they were mysteriously mutilated; yet by that time, and indeed
long before, these old stone posts had been merged in imagination
into the single divinity of the god Hermes, the Messenger and
Mediator. The name of Athens may itself be another instance:
an *athena* was possibly (though not certainly) simply the name of
some earth spirit, or of the image which represented it, in that
particular locality; so that 'Athens' originally meant 'the place
where the *athenas* are.' The imagination of men was to fuse them
into the single and radiant figure of Athena, emblem in her

wisdom and purity of all that was best in the aspirations of Athens, and a great goddess throughout the Greek world.

Apart from the many primitive survivals underlying the worship of the Olympians, the Olympian religion may seem from what I have said of it to have about it an air of preternatural calm, and I suppose that in the form in which the most imaginative minds conceived it, it had. But the Greeks were not by any means a preternaturally calm people; on the contrary, they were excessively excitable. It is not surprising, therefore, to find amongst them certain cults of a nature quite different from the Olympian. These were Orphism and the Eleusinian Mysteries. The two cults, which became more or less assimilated, seem to have provided an emotional outlet for those—such as are found in every race—who needed it. The Orphic cult originally came into Greece from barbaric Thrace, and was assimilated to the worship of Dionysus, the god of wild life, of fertility and of wine; it seems to have originated in a wholly abominable frenzy, or 'possession', in which women—the Maenads, or 'mad ones'—tore living animals to pieces and ate the raw and quivering flesh. The God who inspired the frenzy, was himself devoured. The genius of Euripides, in his *Bacchae*, invested with a wild beauty these old, forgotten things, and horrors of long ago. Orpheus, like Dionysus, was believed to have been torn into pieces by Thracian women, when

> *His gory visage down the stream was sent*
> *Down the swift Hebrus to the Lesbian shore.*

The details of Orphism as it was practised in classical times are obscure; but, unlike the Olympian religion, it seems to have had a doctrine. The Titans—so ran the Orphic myth—devoured the god Dionysus and were destroyed by the lightning of Zeus. From the ashes of the Titans sprang mankind, with its double nature—the divine spark derived from Dionysus, and the flesh polluted by the crime of the Titans. It is the familiar dichotomy. The inherited pollution could be purged away only by a life of ritual purity, and death was to be desired as the liberation of the soul from its tomb. The souls of the good lived henceforth in bliss, the souls of the wicked endured the punishment they deserved. Both the mystery cults clung to the doctrine of the immortality of the soul, a doctrine of which the Olympian religion had nothing to say. It was left to the poets, from Homer onwards, to imagine what happened after death—if anything happened at all. Before the philosophical speculations of the fourth century the religious approach outside the mystery cults to the question of a future life was ambivalent and fluctuating, a matter not of belief but of poetic tales of very various content, telling of the Islands of the Blest, or of the Meadows of Asphodel, or of the mystical dream of Er the son of Armenius, or of gibbering ghosts crowding to drink the sacrificial blood, or of Ixion and his wheel. The normal Greek attitude to this insoluble problem was, I think, 'one world at a time', as Thoreau put it: one can hope and dream—and dread; but meanwhile the present life is enough to absorb one's energies and thoughts, and if, when it is over, we do not go down into the dark forever, the life which awaits us will probably be somewhat thin.

I have spoken of the survival of primitivism which underlay the worship of the Olympians, of the imaginative interpretation of those serene figures which certainly existed in the best Greek minds, and of the more emotional secret cults such as seem to be found amongst almost every people at almost every stage of their development. There remains another aspect of Greek religious thought, and that by no means the least important—the philosophical criticism of accepted religious ideas. I am not for the moment thinking of the philosophic and religious schools of the fourth century—of the Porch, the Garden and the Dog-House (if one may call it so)—for the teaching of these schools represented a turning away from the hopes and ideals of the true classical Greece and arose from their final failure; I am thinking of a much earlier period, when the flame of Greek civilisation must have looked to Greeks as if it would burn for ever. The criticism came from Ionia, mother of so much that was best in Greek thought, and it is directed against what was felt to be the vulgar anthropomorphism of current religious ideas and towards a conception not of gods, but of God, and it was bound up with the first stirrings of the scientific spirit and its search for the cause of things.

At the beginning of the sixth century Xenophanes of Colophon from whom I have already quoted, turning away from the gods of Homer, was seeking for 'the one God, the greatest amongst gods and men, like to mortals neither in form nor in thought,' the one God 'who remains for ever in the same place, moved not at all, nor does it befit him to go hither and thither;' the one God who 'sees entire, thinks entire, hears entire.' Rejecting old tales and looking for physical causes for physical phenomena, 'She whom they call Iris, or the Rainbow,' he says, 'is but cloud, purple and violet and saffron to our eyes.' He gropes towards a higher truth than the old mythologies can tell: 'there has never been, nor ever will be, a man who has clear knowledge about God;' and he can be content on occasion, as he shows in a charming elegy, with a simple reverence for godhead which he does not attempt to define. I turn his easy-flowing verse into prose: 'Now the floor is clean, and our hands and our cups; one crowns our heads with garlands of leaves, and another offers fragrant myrrh. There stands the mixing-bowl, filled with gladness; more wine is ready—it will not betray—honey-sweet in the jars, smelling of flowers. Amongst us frankincense breathes its holy fragrance, and there is water, cold and sweet and clean. At hand lie brown loaves, and the lordly table is loaded with cheese and rich honey. An altar in the midst stands flower-wreathed, and song and rejoicing fill the room. Men of goodwill must first praise God with words fair and clean; then having poured a libation and prayed for strength to do right, they will nowise offend if they drink as much as a man can carry home without a servant to help him—if he be not very old. And let us praise him who, having drunk his wine, does nobly in the trial of skill, as his memory serves: let him not tell tales of Titans or Giants or Centaurs, those vain imaginings of days gone by, or of civil strife, for in such things there is nothing profitable. But it is always good to give heed, with reverence, to gods.'

There is a quiet happiness in those lines, which breathe the very spirit of the old Ionia, of a world not yet gone stale. It was still possible to find delight in common things—in brown loaves, in water 'cold and sweet and clean'; it was still possible to feel that honey was rich and that the smell of myrrh and frankincense was holy.

Heraclitus, of Ephesus, said that God 'is day-night, summer-winter, war-peace, satiety-hunger,' finding him behind, and through, the perpetual tension of opposites in the world as we know it. Parmenides, of Elea, said that God *is* the universe, which in its totality is one and immoveable. The later Greeks recognised the existence of a double tradition in the history of their thought about the nature of the universe—what they called the 'atheistic' tradition of Ionia (though it was by no means necessarily atheistic, in spite of the fact that it sprang from a deliberately scientific attitude) and the religious tradition, founded by Pythagoras after he had left his native Ionian island of Samos and settled at Croton in southern Italy. The 'atheistic' thinkers attempted to find a material basis—certain 'first elements' such as earth, fire, air, water—for the building-up of the physical universe, and supposed that life, or the soul, was afterwards formed out of these same elements; the 'religious' tradition taught that mind, or Providence, came first and that the natural world is subject to its direction. All these thinkers, from Thales onwards, whether their approach to the problem of the origin and governance of things was materialistic or not, obviously acted as a disruptive force so far as the somewhat insubstantial allegories of the Olympian religion were concerned.

How far their speculations affected the beliefs of the ordinary man and woman, one cannot know: probably very little. No doubt the ordinary man and woman, even if they heard of these lofty imaginings, continued, like their fathers and grandfathers, to find sufficient satisfaction in giving 'heed, with reverence' to their local divinities, paying their respects to the hero's tomb, and not forgetting the proper libation before they drank their wine. Nevertheless great ideas have a habit of not dying, however thickly they may be overlaid by the normal indifference or stupidity of mankind. They remain as little points of fire in a great mass of hardly combustible matter, until a time comes when they break out into a larger flame, perhaps to be smothered down again, perhaps to start a conflagration. Looking back over what we can recover of the ancient Greek world, one is aware of the seminal thoughts of these old philosophers and speculators—present, even where they are unknown or ignored; little points of fire, or grains of yeast, working. These speculations were indeed, as everyone knows, the first sentences in the long and brilliant story of western scientific thought, and also, I suppose, the basis on which could be built a loftier religion than Greece herself was ever destined to know; and without them much that was finest in the Greece of Herodotus would have been impossible. To them indeed Herodotus himself owes his en-

gaging blend of scepticism and tolerance, not unmixed with a
certain cautious and traditional piety; and without them we
should hardly have had the dark sublimities of Aeschylus feeling
his visionary way towards a God beyond the gods: 'Zeus, whoe'er
he be, if thus it is his will to be named, so I name him. For
weighing all things in the balance, I can grasp at naught but
Zeus, if I am indeed to rid my thought of its vain burden . . .
Zeus who led us along the path to wisdom, who established for
ever the law that by suffering we learn;' or the sense in Sophocles
of a mysterious divinity, antecedent to human law and custom,
enshrined in the consciences of men. The passage I have in mind
is a well-known one: it occurs in the *Antigone*, when Creon,
the King, asks Antigone if she knew of the proclamation he had
issued against the burial of the traitor Polynices. 'Yes,' she answers,

'But you are a man—no more—and no word of yours
Can oversway God's law, unwritten, inalterable—
Not made for time that passes, yesterday and today,
But everliving and timeless, whose beginning no man knows.
Not for fear of human pride would I break this law
And be guilty before God.

Aeschylus and Sophocles would not have written like this in
their stage-plays unless they had known that their audience, not
the educated audience the modern world imagines for high or
difficult themes, but the whole citizen-body, including the riff-
raff and the slaves, would take their meaning. And take their
meaning that motley audience undoubtedly did, in spite of the
fact that most of them would continue, in their deeply ingrained
Greek conservatism, to pay duty to the local shrines and to see
the owl and the snake and the lizard behind the majestic figures
of the Athena, the Zeus or the Apollo, which the genius of their
sculptors had made visible to their eyes.

Greek religion had its origin in the tribe; in the classical period
it was embodied in, and seen through the medium of, the worship,
or near-worship, of the City state. It was after the City State
had finally and irrevocably failed, during the fourth century,
that the Olympian religion lost its power to inspire. I have said
in a previous chapter that the writings of Plato mark the decadence of classical Greece and a turning away from the old
assurances to seek reality in the unseen. His writings were also

the beginning of a new quest of the human spirit. The quest was
carried on, in various ways and with varying emphasis, in the
thought of the Stoics, the Cynics and the Epicureans. An entirely
new intellectual and spiritual world was taking shape. The
effect upon the masses of the crumbling away of the Olympians
was at first disastrous: if Zeus did not rule the world, who did—or
what did? The answer was Fortune, or Chance (*Tyche*), which
all over the ancient world was elevated to the position of a
god, with altars in its honour. But Chance is a poor divinity,
and is not likely to command devotion for long. Nor did it
need to do so; for the seeds of a deeper philosophy, sown long
ago by the thinkers of old Ionia and by the thinkers and writers
of the fourth century—Plato himself, first; then Antisthenes,
founder, with the notorious Diogenes, of the Cynic school, with
its total rejection of this world's values; Zeno of the Porch, with
his recognition of a purpose in the Cosmos and of a man's duty
to accept and obey it whatever the cost in pain; Epicurus, the
refugee from Samos, making it his business to free men from the
terrors of superstition and to teach them that by 'virtue' they
could be happy—all these seeds were beginning to grow. I call
them the seeds of a deeper philosophy; and so, I suppose, they
were. But that philosophy marked the end of classical Greece;
it rejected the world and its ways, shut its eyes deliberately to its
brilliance and glory and shame. It was no longer an attempt to
find how to 'live well' in the world as it was. It was a cry for
salvation. Only Aristotle, in these days, continued quietly and
steadily to pursue his scientific studies and to combine them with
the truths of religion, reaching towards his conception of the
First Cause, unmoved itself, yet moving the universe 'as the
beloved moves the lover.' The influence which the thought of
Plato and the neo-Platonists was to have upon Christian theology,
and the eminent position occupied in it during the middle ages
by Aristotle is known to everybody, but is beyond the scope of
this book to discuss.

CHAPTER 16

Greek Life and Manners

THERE IS A MOVING STORY IN HERODOTUS ABOUT THE PEOPLE OF Phocaea, a little Ionian town on the Anatolian coast some twenty miles north of Smyrna. The Phocaeans are of some interest in history, as they were the first Greeks to venture upon long voyages by sea, showing the way, in their narrow *penteconters*, or fifty-oared galleys, up the Adriatic and westward as far as Tartessus (Tarshish), near the present site of Cadiz. Now it happened that when Cyrus began his conquest of the Ionian coastal towns, the first one to be attacked by his general Harpagus was Phocaea. The siege began, and Harpagus sent word to the defenders that he would be satisfied if they consented to pull down a single tower in the fortifications and set apart one house for the service of the King. Unable to endure the prospect of slavery, the Phocaeans, to gain time, promised to answer Harpagus' request on the following day, and meanwhile made hasty preparations to abandon their home altogether rather than submit. The galleys were launched, the children and the women were put aboard, together with all their moveable property, and, to ensure unity in the venture, fearful curses were laid upon any man who refused to go. Never, they declared, would they return to Phocaea until a lump of iron, which they had dropped into the sea, floated to the surface again. Early next morning they sailed, but hardly had the familiar and beloved coastline faded from their view before more than half of them, 'seized', as Herodotus says, 'with passionate longing to see their city, and their old homes once more, broke their oath and returned.'

There is much of Greek life and feeling in this story, which only Herodotus, of ancient historians, could, I think, have told—and he tells it quietly, passingly, and without emotion. What a vivid picture it brings of the *scale* of things in that ancient world: the little town, isolated by the mountains which run steeply down into the bay of Smyrna where it stood, independent and self-sufficient and all in all to its people—and those so few that in a single day they could reach amongst themselves their tremendous decision, and embark everything they possessed for a new life in a new world. No need for organisation—none of the formal and tedious processes of politics: simply one fiery dispute, and the decision was made. They packed up their traps, and were gone. Nothing, moreover, could more forcibly bring before us the frightful insecurity of life in those days, the perpetual menace of annihilation, the need to live in the constant acceptance of what the morrow might bring; and above all this story—Herodotus had no need to dwell upon its implications which were, to him, a matter of course—helps us who live in circumstances so different, to enter in imagination into one of the primary passions of Greek life—the attachment to home.

Place, and the associations of place, had for a Greek a deeper meaning than they can possibly have in our more diffused and undifferentiated world, where a man can move a hundred, or a thousand, miles and still feel himself at home. But the Greek was rooted in his little community; there it lay, on some lonely hill, perhaps, or in the corner of some deserted inlet of the coast, isolated and alone, the symbol to him of everything he held dear, his only protection, such as it was, against wild nature, and the enemy who might at any moment be at the gates. Every stone of it was sacred, every yard of its surrounding fields and olive-groves and scanty pasture. He knew it all, and loved it all, as he loved his own house; it was his intimate possession, haunted and blessed by its own guardian spirits and gods. And because it was in perpetual peril, he only loved it the more. I have said something in a previous chapter about the *adjectives* which Greek poets found it natural to apply to their towns and islands—adjectives which to us seem more suitable for a lover to apply to his beloved; and perhaps it was this same passionate attachment which made the Greeks lavish so much labour on the adornment of their homes. Even the defence-walls which surrounded a town were works of exquisite craftsmanship, the stones which composed them being cut and squared with ungrudging labour, to endure for ever. It is hard for us to think of Homer's phrase 'the holy citadel of Troy' as anything but a piece of literary grace; but for a Greek, in every age, his citadel was in fact, and not in metaphor, a holy place: his gods lived with him there, the projections of his own love.

This attachment to place helps to explain not only the fervour but also the narrowness of Greek patriotism. By the beginning of the classical age the Greeks were certainly conscious of being a people, but neither then nor at any time later were they conscious of being a nation. The bond which united them was cultural, never political: Greeks in Italy shared the same views on how life should be lived as Greeks on the Black Sea Coast or in Cyrene, and those views, they felt, were very different from the views of 'barbarians'—however civilised those barbarians might be, and frequently were. Hence no Greek cared overmuch what happened to the little community next door: it was his own community that mattered, and it was up to his neighbours to look after themselves. It cannot but seem odd to us to read in Herodotus of the large number of Greek mainland towns which refused to oppose the Persian invasions; Herodotus himself of course chronicles the facts—for they are a part of his story—but he passes no judgment. For him the facts were not odd at all: he certainly admired Athens and Sparta for the parts they played in that tremendous struggle, just as he admired any act of courage, and he did believe that their efforts saved something which was infinitely precious to the world; but it seemed to him perfectly consonant with the Greek way of looking at things that this or that particular community should send 'earth and water' to Darius or Xerxes, in the belief that resistance would mean annihilation, while surrender might enable them to continue to live much as before, despite the probable presence of a Persian satrap in their midst. After all, had not the Greek settlements in Ionia remained Greek enough, and prosperous enough, after their 'enslavement' first by Lydia and then again by Cyrus of Persia? It was easy to think that there was more danger of annihilation from a struggle with one's next-door neighbour than from any threat by the vast, and by no means wholly malevolent, empire of the East.

Any form of altruism or self-sacrifice was wholly foreign to the Greeks, in their personal as well as in their political relationships. Their morality, public and private, was profoundly selfish, and it was selfish not only in fact—for in that they possibly did not differ very greatly from the moderns—but also in theory.

They did not believe, or pretend to believe, in the virtue of altruism, and there is no word for it in their language. If any Greek, at any time down to the end of the fifth century, had been told that it was good to love one's enemy or that spiritual riches might be found in poverty, he would have gasped at the sheer absurdity of such notions. 'Life is short,' he might have answered, 'and exceedingly chancy, and *my* business is to make the best of it while it lasts.' Precisely how to do so admitted, no doubt, some argument; but whatever the conclusion reached, it was a practical one, with no transcendental nonsense about it.

The Greek view of the good life was firmly founded upon a proper appreciation of its physical basis. Wealth, as such, was, as I have already indicated, seldom sought after, because the process of acquiring it got in the way of too many other things which were felt to be indispensable; nevertheless a constant ingredient in all the Greek definitions of a good life was a competence—enough to live on. Another was health; another the possession of sons to look after their father in his old age. Each of these is a practical good, if ever there was one. A man consists of a body, and something else—call it, if you will, a soul: at any rate it is a mysterious entity, distinct from the body, though informing it, and capable of such operations as thought, aspiration, understanding, worship. Both elements, body and soul, must be properly considered in any estimate of the good life; and, if possible, their claims, often conflicting, must be brought into some kind of harmony. The Greeks never believed that the body was in any way intrinsically evil, or ever set its demands in direct opposition to the demands of its partner, the soul. Actually, they went to what seem to us absurd lengths in their admiration of physical qualities, of strength, dexterity and beauty—especially of male beauty. The most obvious instance of this is the Greek attitude towards athletics, fundamentally different from our own: the great festivals—the Olympian, the Pythian, the Nemean—at which men from all parts of the Greek world competed for athletic prizes, were all religious festivals. Not only were they an opportunity for beanfeasts and general enjoyment; they were also, and primarily, an offering to the gods —to Zeus, or Apollo, or Poseidon—of a man's most precious possession, his beauty and strength. The competitors ran, or wrestled, or boxed, or drove their racing chariots, naked. Naked beauty was felt to be a holy offering to the divine. The prize of victory was in itself valueless—a crown of olive leaves; but the glory of winning it was great. An entire *genre* of Greek literature, the victory ode, grew up about these contests. The victory odes of Pindar, famous in antiquity and still read by a few scholars who can cope with their obscurity and have patience to allow their sudden splendours to outweight the tedium of commonplace moralising, are all of them elaborate poems, written to be sung, and accompanied by dancing, in praise of successful athletes. This exaltation of the physical may seem strange—almost childish; but an attempt must be made to understand it, if one is to have any due sense of the moral *colour*, so to speak, of ancient Greece before the years of decadence—of the failure of the old assumptions and ideals.

I suppose the notion which still underlies much modern thinking, in spite of our revolt from the hypocrisies and pruderies of our grandfathers, that in the human trinity of body, soul and spirit the body is something of a poor relation which must be kept well under lest it corrupt the other two, can arise only in a society in which the general climate of opinion, expressed or assumed, finds its true values not in this world, but in a beyond. The Greeks, of course, themselves came to this way of thinking, in time; but they did not think thus in the classical age. To the Greeks of the classical age the world of appearances was substantial and real; they had no sense that the cloud-capped towers and solemn temples were destined to fade, and leave not a wrack behind. They had made the world very much their own, and lived in it familiarly, in spite of the demons which might haunt the dark. They felt no need of faith, as the evidence of things unseen; they looked forward to no crown of happiness in another world beyond the grave. This world was their all, and they made the best of it.

It is against a background such as this that the Greek worship— it is hardly too strong a word—of the body can best be understood. The moral implications of this worship are not far to seek.

I have often met the statement in books about Greece that the Greeks had no sense of sin. But such a statement is difficult to maintain for anyone who has read, say, the plays of Aeschylus or Sophocles, in which the awful power of inherited guilt, hanging over and dominating the lives of men, is so conspicuous a theme.

Yet it is true that the Greek sense of sin was radically different, and sprang from radically different sources, from our own. The nearest approach in Greek feeling to what we mean by 'sin' arose from the old, close tribal loyalties of primitive times, and is expressed in Greek drama by the tales of blood-guiltiness and pollution pursuing the members of a family, until it is somehow purged away. The blood guiltiness came always from some deed of blood within the circle of family or tribe; or perhaps it might be from the murder of a guest by his host, who thus violated another most sacred tie. 'Sin' to a Greek was never, so far as I can understand it, identified with the flouting of divine authority or with disobedience to God, or to gods. To 'think more than mortal thoughts'—the *hubris* of which all Greek literature so often speaks—was not sinful so much as silly: it was a man's quickest way to self-destruction. It was only one, though a very specially dangerous one, amongst the many 'bad shots' (*hamartiae*), which men, in their folly and ignorance, are all too apt to make. Greek morality was self-regarding; it had nothing transcendental about it. It had no sense of a divine 'ought', or of any external obligation whatever; its obligations were inward and concerned the welfare of the individual person. I speak in this of what appears to have been the commonly accepted view, leaving out the visionary flashes of poets, as of Sophocles when he wrote of the 'ever-living and timeless' law of God. The philosophers, moreover, themselves accepted the common view, however much they may have refined upon it. Plato, the most unworldly of the Greek philosophers, finds no mysterious external sanction for virtue; he finds it in a proper balance, or harmony, between soul and body. Neither soul nor body, in Plato's writings, is belittled at the expense of the other. Order and proportion—that, in morality as in everything else, was the constant ideal, the unchanging object of aspiration in this most passionate and disorderly people. Christianity looks to the triumph of the spirit over the flesh; paganism strove for a harmony between the two. The common Greek term of praise for a decent man was *kaloskagathos*—'beautiful and good.' The word is an interesting one: it almost makes it true to say that the Greeks thought of morality in aesthetic terms.

To say that paganism 'strove' for a harmony between spirit and flesh is, of course, to speak like the philosophers. One need not

suppose that the ordinary man strove at all; and the point I want
to make at the moment is not so much the nature of Greek moral
theory as of Greek practice in ordinary life. Now the Greeks were
an exceedingly acute, hot-blooded people, with a capacity for life
far exceeding (I believe) our own in the modern world; for them,
the edge of things had not been blunted. This sheer vigour and
vividness of life, coupled with the fact that except in the immediate
loyalties to family, clan and city there was no external, or transcendental, sanction of 'virtue'—that what a man did was not a
matter between his soul and God, but simply concerned his own
personal well-being—this condition of things, this almost wholly
self-regarding ethic, explains, at any rate up to a point, a number
of conspicuous characteristics in the Greek people: it makes
intelligible, for instance, their habitual cruelty, their unashamed
lasciviousness, their treachery, their common dishonesty, and their
almost total disregard, outside the immediate circle of family and
friends, of anybody else's interest or convenience.

'The Greeks are our masters in civilisation:' so Alfred Zimmern
begins one of his books. Well—one is permitted to wonder.
There are undoubtedly aspects of Greek life in which this statement has some truth: to some extent Greek political theory, to a
greater extent the achievement, in a few Greek states at the peak
of their development, by a small and privileged class, of a manner
of life permeated by a peculiar grace and brilliance, seem to support it; but as a claim for Greek life as a whole the most casual
acquaintance even with the writings of the grave and tolerant
Herodotus, not to mention innumerable touches in the lyric poets
and a flow of facts and anecdotes in the orators, will prove it to be
nonsense. Let us admit that the Greek intellectual and aesthetic
achievement was a miracle; but to idealise their manners is quite
another thing. Writers on ancient Greece have done it constantly,
and they have done it by basing their descriptions upon the
noblest products of the Greek mind and imagination and ignoring
the rest. Now I am aware that all writers and artists are children
of their age and in part dependent upon it; they are less lonely
figures than they seem; they focus rather than invent, drawing
together and moulding into form all sorts of dim and fluctuant
half-perceptions and shadowy imaginings in the emotional and
intellectual atmosphere of their time. If this were not so, nobody
would understand them; if Plato and Aeschylus and their peers

had not expressed something which was indeed essential in the general consciousness of their contemporaries, their contemporaries would have paid no heed to them. The Athenians of the fifth century *did* respond to Aeschylus and Sophocles and Euripides, and that in itself is remarkable enough when one considers the kind of stuff which nominally cultivated people seem to respond to nowadays. As for Plato, I suppose they responded to him too, a few of them; though probably his readers, during his life-time, were to be reckoned in hundreds rather than in thousands. Nevertheless to found one's estimate of Greek civilisation and manners upon the exclusive consideration of these supreme examples of the Greek genius is absurd. The Greeks were not always at the play, or always dying for their country at Thermopylae, and only a tiny minority of them read books.

Perhaps I have said enough about the cruelty of the Greeks already, in my account of the island life and elsewhere; but here is one more example, not, this time, a fact of history, but simply an anecdote which, whether it is true or not, is evidence of an habitual attitude of mind. It occurs in Plato's *Euthyphro*. 'The dead man,' says Euthyphro, 'was a poor dependent of mine who worked for us as a field-labourer, and one day, in a fit of rage caused by drink, he quarrelled with one of our slaves and killed him. My father trussed him up and threw him into a ditch, and then sent to Athens to inquire of a diviner what he should do with him. Meanwhile, as he considered the fellow a murderer, he did not bother his head about him, thinking there would be no harm done even if he died in his ditch. And this is just what happened; for such was the effect upon him of cold and hunger and chains that before the messenger returned from Athens, he was dead.' A small thing, perhaps, in the bloodstained history of Greece, where we can read of the massacre in cold blood of 6000 prisoners of war after the battle of Aegospotami; but it is none the less revealing of a basic callousness towards suffering—and that, too, the suffering of a helpless dependent. Moreover the story is told as a matter of course, without the least disapproval expressed or implied, by the most refined writer of the one Greek community—Athens—whose citizens prided themselves upon their mercifulness and deprecated the barbarity of their neighbours. It may be remembered, too, that the Athenians, like the rest of the Greeks, regularly tortured slaves to extract evidence from them in the law-courts, and exposed unwanted children.

The question of Greek homosexuality, which I touched on in a previous chapter, calls for another word or two here. The over-whelming evidence of literature points to its universality through-out the Greek world. As everyone knows, it is widespread in the modern world too; but the difference between the modern and the ancient attitude towards it is that the moderns look upon it as a deviation from the normal, whereas the ancients did not. The ancients took it as a matter of course; they neither made jokes about it, nor raised a deprecatory eyebrow, nor attempted to conceal its existence. It was not considered to be a vice, but a normal aspect of male sexuality. Nor were homosexuals dif-ferentiated, as a class; a man might be recognised as predominantly homosexual, like Sophocles—if the remark of Athenaeus is worth anything—or predominantly heterosexual, like Euripides (accord-ing to the same authority); but it was generally assumed that both heterosexual and homosexual impulses were common to every-body. Homosexual practices were therefore rampant, there being no check in the form of public opinion to minimise them or to drive them underground, and especially (I believe) in the later age, say from the fifth century onward when the social position of women began to deteriorate.

There was, of course, another side to the business, and most writers on Greece have chosen to concentrate upon it. This was the romantic and ideal side, and even the most cynical student of antiquity will admit that it existed, however hard he may find it to enter into it with sympathy.

There is no doubt that in many instances passionate friendships between men or boys in the ancient world were a genuine source of inspiration and high endeavour. Greek literature constantly suggests it: everyone knows the pairs of friends famous in story—Pylades and Orestes, Damon and Pythias, Epaminondas and Pelopides, Patroclus and Achilles. 'Achilles wept when he remembered his dead comrade, and sleep who subdues all things came not to him, but he turned this way and that in his longing for the lost manfulness and strength of Patroclus; all he had done in his dear company he remembered, all he had suffered, in fights and on the bitter sea, and remember-ing he shed big tears, lying now upon his side, now upon his back, now upon his face. Then he would rise from his bed,

and roam wildly along the salt sea beach.' So wrote Homer,
and, though Homer's verse invests everything it touches with
light and grace, the sentiment is purely Greek and could hardly be
found outside Greek literature. Romantic love is necessary for all
civilised peoples, and the Greeks, when they did not find it in the
love of women, found it in friendship. The love of friends was the
inspiration of noble living—of courage and endeavour and self-
sacrifice. One must always be on guard against taking philosophers
as representatives; nevertheless, as I have already suggested in the
case of poets, they would not write as they do if their words
found no echo at all in more commonplace breasts; and thus it is
impossible in any consideration of this question not to go to
Plato, for Plato of all Greek writers most rarefied and idealised the
idea of friendship. Of course he did not call it friendship: he called
it love—*Eros*; but he did not mean the love of women, which he
despised—or thought of merely as a biological necessity; he
meant the love of men for men, and for the beauty they could see
in men. And this love he described, in a famous passage of the
Symposium, as the first rung of the ladder which leads the soul
upward to the contemplation of eternal truth and eternal beauty.
'He who would proceed aright in this matter (so says Diotima
to Socrates) should begin in youth to visit beautiful forms; and
first, if he be guided by his instructor aright, to love one such form
only—out of that he should create fair thoughts; and soon he will
of himself perceive that the beauty of one form is akin to the
beauty of another, and then if beauty of form in general is his
pursuit, how foolish would he be not to recognise that the beauty
in every form is one and the same! And when he perceives this
he will abate his violent love of the one and will become a lover
of all beautiful forms. In the next stage he will consider that the
beauty of the mind is more honourable than the outward form.
So that, if a virtuous soul have but a little comeliness, he will be
content to love and tend him, and will search out and bring to the
birth thoughts which may improve the young, until he is compelled to contemplate and see the beauty of institutions and laws,
and to understand that the beauty of them all is of one family,
and that personal beauty is a trifle; and after laws and institutions
he will go on to the sciences, that he may see their beauty, being
not like a servant in love with the beauty of one youth or man or
institution, but, drawing towards and contemplating the vast sea

of beauty, he will create many fair and noble thoughts in bound-less love of wisdom. . . .' And thus, Diotima concludes, the true lover will come in the end to the knowledge and love of 'beauty itself, absolute, simple and everlasting, which without diminution or increase or any change is imparted to the ever-growing and perishing beauties of all other things.'

Eros is indeed a strange and magical word on the lips of the passionate Greeks. Pericles, one remembers, applied it to the feeling of Athenians for their city; and Plato uses it to express the passion of the philosophers searching for truth. Perhaps all love is one, whatever its object, and all our passions, as Keats said, in their sublime, are creative of essential beauty. But the qualification is a big one.

Plato, talking of the love of boys, does not always soar into so lofty an empyrean as in that passage from the *Symposium*. Some-times he is lighthearted on the subject, even skittish, at any rate in his introductory remarks, before his philosophical theme begins to unfold. For instance, at the beginning of the *Charmides* he represents Socrates as having just returned to Athens after a pro-tracted period of military service at Potidaea. Socrates is eager for news of the latest 'beauties' in Athenian society, and, entering the palaestra, 'I began,' he says, 'to make inquiries about home affairs—about the state of philosophy, and about the young men. I asked if any of them were intelligent, or outstandingly hand-some, or both.'

'You will soon be able to judge of the beauties for yourself,' replies Critias; 'for those young men who are coming in now are the advanced guard of the great beauty of the moment—and I expect he himself is not far off.'

Charmides then enters the palaestra, and, says Socrates, 'con-fusion reigned. Everyone seemed to be enamoured of him. A troop of lovers followed him.'

Again, in the *Lysis*, Plato describes Lysis as 'standing amongst the other boys and young men, with a wreath on his head, like a lovely vision, and as worthy of praise for his goodness as for his beauty.'

Philosophy apart, all this grates somewhat on our modern sensibilities. It has a mawkish flavour, and it is hard to stomach the constant attribution of 'beauty' by men to men. Reading such passages as these in Plato, one longs for old Archilochus again and his little, bandy-legged captain, 'crouching behind his shield and full of guts'—and one remembers, too, with gratitude, that the noble Socrates was, himself, as ugly as sin.

Taking into consideration, then, the absence of women from any participation in the intellectual and social life of the Greek citizen-class, the odd twist in Greek moral theory which led them almost to identify the beautiful and the good, the familiarity with the naked body at games and festivals, and as represented in art; considering these things and combining with them the innate eroticism of this southern people—an eroticism which could soar or sink according to the individual temper—one can perhaps see the reasons, or some of the reasons, for the existence of an intensely Greek characteristic, about which a great deal of idealistic nonsense has been written. Greek friendship did—like any other friendship—have its ideal and ennobling aspect; but that is no reason for shutting one's eyes to the general acceptance amongst Greeks of the practice of pederasty. The evidence for it in Greek literature is overwhelming. One might be content with a casual remark in the pages of Herodotus, a remark which carries all the more weight because Herodotus makes it without emphasis and wholly as a matter of course. Speaking of Persian customs and character, he notes the readiness of the Persians to adopt the practices of foreign peoples with whom they come into contact; 'from us,' he notes, 'they learnt to go to bed with boys.' How low unillumined sensuality could sink may be illustrated in a later age by a dialogue of Lucian's, in which two cultivated gentlemen of leisure are represented as discussing the amount of pleasure to be derived respectively from homosexual and heterosexual intercourse.

Nothing is easier, and few things more foolish, than to grow hot about unfamiliar sexual practices, and my object in saying what I have said about Greek homosexuality has been to record rather than to condemn. The balance needs to be redressed, so many writers upon Greek life having glozed over this disagreeable aspect of it. There has been a tendency to gloze over other disagreeable aspects too, such as the inveterate Greek habit of lying and general dishonesty. I have suggested that Greek sexual morality deteriorated with the passing of the Lyric Age; the regard for truth, however, seems to have been equally weak throughout Greek history. Even the Homeric gods, one recalls,

were addicted to mutual deceit, as well as to theft and adultery.
Herodotus tells us an amusing story of a certain Cadmus at one
time tyrant of the island of Cos. Gelo of Syracuse, the greatest
prince of western Hellas, shilly-shallying over which side to
support in the Persian wars, sent Cadmus to Delphi with a large
sum of money and instructions to await events: if the Persians
were victorious, he was to hand over the money to Xerxes; if
they were defeated, he was to bring it back again. Now Cadmus
was chosen for this mission because of his reputation for honesty;
and behold—Herodotus tells us—on this occasion 'yet another
honest action, the most remarkable of all, was to be added to the
former ones: having in his hands the large sum of money which
Gelo had entrusted to him, with every opportunity of turning it
to his own use, he remained faithful to his trust and after the
victorious battle at Salamis he returned to Sicily with every
penny intact.' Herodotus is seldom surprised at human behaviour,
never at human wickedness; but that a Greek should return to its
owner a sum of money which he might easily have stolen, was
remarkable indeed. Incidentally, this same Cadmus had abdicated
his power in Cos 'simply,' Herodotus says, 'in consequence of his
sense of what was fair and honourable'; but then, having honour-
ably given his fellow-islanders their chance of free institutions, he
sailed for Sicily, forcibly ejected the Samians from the town of
Messene and lived there himself with his friends. Remarkable
honesty seems to have been characteristic of Cadmus' family, for
Herodotus further informs us that his father, Scythes, was considered by King Darius the most honest of all the Greeks with
whom he had come into contact. And why? Simply because
while he was living in Persia under Darius' protection he had
asked leave to pay a visit to Sicily; leave was granted on condition that he promised to return—*and he kept his promise*.

Herodotus, as the reader will remember, further records, as an
instance of the odd habits of foreigners, that one of the three
things taught to Persian boys as the staple of their education was
telling the truth—the other two were riding and the use of the
bow. The slightest acquaintance with Greek forensic literature
gives a picture of the Greek attitude towards evidence such as
would make a modern jury gasp. Both prosecution and defence in
a court of law were founded upon emotional appeals to the jury—
the enormous jury, approved by Athenian custom, consisting of

hundreds of members with no judge to guide or control them. The common form of prosecution was to declare that the defendant obviously had a bad record (evidence of previous offences being then adduced) and that therefore he must, in the present case, be guilty too. A part, at any rate, of the defence consisted in the production in court of the defendant's children and other relatives, whose howling and tears and general misery would, it was hoped, move the jury to mercy. Cicero had some severe words to say on this subject, and though by his time the Greeks had in most ways degenerated, there is no reason to believe, granted our other evidence, that in this particular characteristic they were ever very different: 'I grant,' Cicero wrote, 'their literary eminence, their skill in many arts, the wit and grace of their conversation, their intelligence, their eloquence, and anything else they may like to claim; but there is one thing the Greek nation has never cultivated—the sanctity of words spoken upon oath. Of this whole question of the importance of evidence, of its weight and authority, they have no notion whatever.' Even in early Roman days commercial swindling was known proverbially as 'Greek honesty' (*Graeca fide mercari*). This volatility of temperament and constitutional inability to honour an agreement was no doubt one reason why the Greeks never became a great commercial nation, as the Romans did; and it was certainly one reason for their political failure ever to unite or to make themselves into a nation at all. It is not easy to make a lasting settlement with habitual opportunists and liars.

This is a melancholy catalogue of shortcomings, and they all stem from the self-regarding nature of Greek moral theory. That theory could rise to great heights in the hands of a master like Plato; and even in practice, amongst the most cultivated Greeks, it could result in a true grace and sobriety of living, turning men away from the innate Greek proclivity to excess towards that harmony of body and spirit at which it aimed. But we can be sure that for the masses it did no such thing: the ordinary Greek was ethically rudderless; religious duties and religious tabus he had in plenty, but he had no sanction or external standard—no 'public opinion', even—to measure the rights and wrongs in his daily intercourse with his fellows. Even his often perfervid patriotism was in a large measure self-regarding, for one of his most crying needs and most intense delights was political activity—and that activity, if his state lost her liberty at some enemy's hands, would be taken from him. He found his *own* fulfilment in the service of his city—and that fulfilment was all the more complete if he could himself play a leading part.

Nothing is more difficult than to enter imaginatively into a civilisation other than one's own, to be aware in any true sense of its colour, its flavour, its living reality. Perhaps it is impossible. The temptation is to take a bundle of qualities and to suppose that they make a character; but character is always more than a bundle of qualities, in individuals or in nations. What is it, then? In literature it is 'style', that mysterious and indefinable essence which permeates and informs the whole, and by virtue of which the earthiest matter is illumined and even the most trivial given a kind of blessing. There is a 'style' in living as well as in writing, and it is no easier to define. I am led into these commonplace reflections by the knowledge that the catalogue of vices which this chapter contains does not really describe ancient Greek life any better than those idealised pictures of which I have complained. 'With the Greek civilisation,' wrote Lowes Dickinson, 'beauty vanished from the world.' That is simply not true; the world has been full of beauty ever since, and still is, though not in cities, save for a few. Nor was the Greek civilisation itself, in many of its aspects, anything but hard and repellent; my list of vices could be extended: to cruelty, lust, lying, treachery and egotism one might add cowardice. The Greeks liked fighting and fought continually; but though they were capable of heroism in battle, they were equally capable of running like rabbits, when the mood took them; and as for discipline, none of them except the Spartans had any conception of the meaning of the word. They had neither pity for weakness nor respect for age: they threw their old men on the scrap-heap, sons prosecuting fathers for incompetence to manage their affairs, and taking over their property if the suit succeeded. They were childishly eager for personal distinction and praise; they bragged like schoolboys; they turned everything into a competition, even the writing of plays; and after a battle they awarded, after much preliminary squabbling, the 'prize of valour' to whoever they fancied best deserved it.

All this is true, and must be taken into consideration if we are properly to appreciate the achievement of this extraordinary people. To face these facts squarely is a better preliminary to

understanding the Greeks than any attempt to judge them
purely from an unavoidable admiration of their art, literature and
philosophy. It may even help us to admire more those very
things, by revealing something of their genesis and helping us to
see *of what* they were the quintessential expression.

Greek life, I repeat, was in many respects hard and repellent,
especially during the period when the City State civilisation
reached its acme during the fifth century and men's minds were
turned to politics to the exclusion of too much else that was good.
Nevertheless no one can amuse himself for long with Greek
studies without discovering that Greek life in all periods, like
Greek literature, had a *style*, permeating and illumining it. I
believe myself that the secret of this style was the fact that the
Greeks, for all their other barbarisms, were never hypocrites.
They did not pretend. They called things by their right names,
plainly. They lived within their own human capacities, knowing
they were not gods. Other nations with more exalted creeds are
forced by those very creeds into a kind of duplicity; we ourselves,
for instance, in our Western half of the world live, or try to live,
simultaneously on two different planes, the worldly and the
spiritual; we profess an ethic of (amongst other things) the
brotherhood of man, and live an ethic diametrically opposed to it.
The Greeks, on the other hand, until the time of the collapse of
the City State, were content to live in one world only, without
distractions from another. They were prepared to accept what they
found, including their own natures, and their religion offered
them no revelation in the light of which they might see themselves
either as miserable sinners or as fallen from grace.

When Matthew Arnold wrote that the Greek 'saw life steadily
and saw it whole,' he uttered a valuable half-truth. The Greek
certainly saw life as *a* whole, though in that whole much that we
now know was omitted. What he saw, fell into place; he was not
troubled, as we are apt to be, by bits of the puzzle which obstin-
ately refuse to fit. The modern experience is in many ways richer
than the Greek, but it is more diffuse and tends to shade off into
the undefined and indefinable; we are aware of mystery, where
the Greeks were aware of none, and we are driven, in consequence, to speak in metaphors, where the Greeks were contented
with a plain statement. They did not love, as did Sir Thomas
Browne, to lose themselves in an O *altitudo*; they preferred facts,

however harsh. Thus they were masters of their intellectual and
spiritual world in a degree unattainable by us, to whom the
continually receding horizon of knowledge (or at least of speculation) brings a continual accession of uncertainty and bewilderment—still more of those awkward bits to be fitted into the
jigsaw. This mastery was the source of what I called their 'style',
and the metaphor expresses at any rate something of my meaning.
The Greeks were never hypocrites, because the nature of their
experience did not compel them to be so.

And there is another thing: any generalisation about Greek life
and manners is invariably ruined by a host of particulars which
refuse to submit to it. I have myself provided in this chapter an
instance of the danger of generalising, in that my purpose in it
had been to take the gilt off what I feel to be the gingerbread of
other people's idealised pictures of Greek life. Hence my catalogue
of disagreeables. But, having compiled that catalogue, I cannot
but remember all that I have left out on the other side. For
instance, these heartless people were fond of their dogs: there are
epitaphs on dogs in the Greek Anthology, and dogs are said to
have swum after the ships which carried their masters across to
Salamis, when Attica was being evacuated at the approach of the
Persians. And they were very fond of their children. I have already
referred to the beautiful story which Herodotus tells of Labda
and her baby, and there are other touches in his book which have
a similar delicacy of sentiment—the reference, for instance, to the
death of over a hundred schoolchildren in Chios, caused by the
collapse of the schoolhouse roof, as one of the worst disasters in
the island's history; or, again, the Spartan legend about the wife
of Agetus. This woman was unrivalled in Sparta for her beauty,
but, says Herodotus, as a child she had been extremely plain. 'She
owed the transformation to her nurse, who, seeing she was not
much to look at, and well aware, moreover, that her parents, who
were people of substance, were distressed at having such an ugly
baby, conceived the idea of carrying her every day to the shrine
of Helen at Therapne, above the temple of Apollo. She would
then take the baby in, lay it down in front of Helen's statue, and
pray the goddess to take away the ugliness. One day as the nurse
left the shrine, a woman appeared and asked her what it was that
she had in her arms. The nurse replied that it was a baby. The
woman asked to see it, but the nurse refused, for the child's

parents had forbidden her to show it to anybody. The woman however persisted, and at last the nurse, seeing how extremely anxious she was to have a look at the baby, showed it to her. Thereupon the stranger stroked the baby's head and declared that it would grow to be the most beautiful woman in Sparta. From that very day there was a change in its appearance.'

Such an anecdote would hardly have found a place in a volume devoted to world history, had not Herodotus known that it would awake an echo of sympathy in his readers. One likes to remember, too, the story which Plutarch tells of Themistocles and his little son: 'This boy,' Themistocles declared, 'is the greatest man in Greece. Why? Because I rule Greece, my wife rules me, and he rules my wife.'

All these tales are of the older Greece—of the happier Greece before Athens started her career of self-aggrandisement.

The two which Herodotus tells, he wrote when that career was already nearing its tragic end; but he trusted that his hearers would still respond to a word out of the past. And no doubt they did, just as they responded to the beautiful portrayal by Euripides of a whole series of young women in his plays—figures like those of Alcestis, Macaria, Iphigenia—though they themselves, in their ever increasing absorption in politics had long since created a hard and masculine world in which there was no room for a woman to play any part at all except within doors, as a child-bearer.

PART THREE

The Persian Wars

CHAPTER 17

The Rise of Persia

IN THE PREVIOUS CHAPTERS I HAVE GIVEN SOME ACCOUNT, DRAWN
partly from Herodotus himself and supplemented from other
sources, of Greek life and history up to the period of the Persian
wars. It is now time to return to Herodotus' main narrative, which
I left at the fall of Sardis and the overthrow by Cyrus of the
Lydian empire. 'Who was this man (so Herodotus makes his
transition) who destroyed the empire of Croesus, and how did the
Persians win their predominant position in Asia?' The answer
which he proceeds to give is, like his presentation of the life and
death of Croesus, full of popular legend and romance and at the
same time of great historical interest, containing as it does a
sketch, rapid and superficial but entirely adequate to Herodotus'
purpose, of the dark struggles of dynasties and peoples which led
to the break up, after five or six centuries, of the Assyrian empire.
As for Cyrus himself, the hero of ancient Persian history, it is
only to be expected that his birth, his deeds and his death should
have attracted tales of wonder as a magnet attracts steel; Herodotus is well aware of this, and informs us at the outset of his
story that he might, following Persian accounts, have told it in
four different ways had he wished to do so, but that he chose the
version which 'seemed to tell the simple truth' without any attempt
to exaggerate the magnitude of his exploits. Fortunately for him
and for his readers, even the Persian account which seemed best
to tell the simple truth about Cyrus' early years, was as rich with
romantic incident as any tale in the Arabian Nights. So he
proceeds, with relish, to tell it.

By some time late in the second millennium before Christ the
Assyrians had extended their power over the whole of upper
Asia, and they continued to hold it until, about the year 700 B.C.,
a certain Deioces, a prince of the Medes, an Iranian people closely
akin to the Persians, led a revolt against his Assyrian masters.
The revolt was successful and was followed by others. Indepen-

dence however led to disorder amongst the scattered Median communities, and their last state would have been worse than their first had not Deioces, an ambitious and able man, seen his chance, and seized it. Herodotus' account of the way in which he established his authority is unhistorical but of great interest, for, just as he put Greek notions of government into the mouths of the Persian grandees when they were represented, in a passage to which I have already referred, as debating the relative merits of democracy, oligarchy and dictatorship, so here he makes his story of Deioces' rise to power a sort of Greek parable of the old days when the Greeks themselves were finding it necessary, or convenient, to submit their insoluble difficulties to the authority of a prince.

Deioces' first concern was, Herodotus tells us, to make for himself a reputation for just dealing within his own small community. To have a man they could trust and to whom they could take their disputes, when there was no law to protect them, was a boon to his neighbours, and little by little the fame of this wise and impartial arbitrator spread beyond the boundaries of his village to other communities, until they, too, began to avail themselves of his services. A just judge in a world of rapine and disorder—it was a wonderful thing. Before long all the Median people were looking to Deioces to settle their disputes: in short, they couldn't do without him. This, of course, was precisely what Deioces had been working for; so, as soon as he was sure that his services were indeed indispensable, he announced his retirement into private life. No more judging, no more arbitrating, no more selfless labour in other people's interest; for, after all, had he not affairs of his own to attend to?

For the unfortunate Medes this was a bombshell. Hurriedly they called a conference of their leading men to discuss what should be done, and in the course of the discussion 'I presume,' says Herodotus, 'that it was Deioces' friends who did most of the talking.' Their proposal (as the reader will guess) was that the only way to save themselves from the intolerable chaos which threatened them was to elect a King. This was done, and the King was Deioces. Once elected to the throne Deioces took all the steps necessary to make his power absolute, including the familiar one of protecting himself with a personal bodyguard. He then, further to concentrate authority in his own hands, ordered the

building of a great capital city: this was Ecbatana, the city on a
hill, fortified by seven concentric walls, each higher than the one
below by the height of the battlements, and all painted in different
colours. No longer was Deioces merely the man of justice, first
amongst his peers, looked to by all as a friend in need; he had
suddenly become the oriental despot, and to mark the change he
introduced the ceremonial of royalty: he withdrew from the
common gaze; no man was allowed to see him; all petitions had
to be sent to him by messengers; laughter within the royal palace
was forbidden; his spies were abroad, watching and listening in
every corner of his dominions.

Media was united, and Deioces' son Phraortes further extended
the Median power by his conquest of Persia, thus forming a great
Aryan Kingdom which stretched from the Caspian Sea to the
Persian Gulf, eastward of Assyria. The Assyrian empire was
breaking up; Egypt had already thrown off the yoke of the Kings
of Nineveh, and Babylonia had won independence under the
leadership of Nabopolassar. In 612 B.C. Nabopolassar and
Cyaxares, successor of Phraortes, joined forces, defeated the
Assyrian army and divided the empire between them. Assyria
itself and the country to the westward into Asia Minor as far as
the river Halys were annexed to Media. It was Cyaxares who
fought the indecisive battle against the Lydians on the occasion of
the eclipse of the sun, which had been predicted by Thales of
Miletus.

These shiftings and meltings in the huge, dark lands of the
East, with the emergence of Media as the third, with Babylonia
and Egypt, of the great powers outside the Greek world, Herodotus sketches in his brief and masterly way as the necessary
preliminary to the story of Cyrus and the rapid rise of Persia.
That story he now proceeds to tell.

Cyaxares was succeeded by his son Astyages, who had a
daughter named Mandane, and one night Astyages dreamed that
she made water in such quantities that it swamped the whole of
Asia. So odd a dream could hardly be without significance, and
the Magi to whom Astyages applied for advice did little to
relieve his anxiety. Consequently when Mandane was old enough
to marry, her father took the precaution of giving her not to a
noble Median, as he would otherwise have done, but to a comparatively humble, though respectable, Persian named Cambyses.

Hardly had the two been married a year before Astyages had a second nightmare: this time he dreamed that a vine grew from his daughter's private parts and continued to grow till it overshadowed the continent. Once again the Magi were prophets of doom, telling the unhappy Astyages that the grandson about to be born would usurp his throne. Hoping to circumvent his fate, Astyages determined to kill the child. As soon as it was born he summoned Harpagus, his most trusty minister, and told him to see that the baby was exposed to die in some desolate spot amongst the hills. Harpagus however, for various reasons, by no means all of them humane, was unwilling to kill the child himself, though if he refused he knew that the King's wrath would fall upon him; so he secretly sent for a certain herdsman named Mitradates, a slave of the King's, and ordered him, under the threat of the most horrible punishments, to do the deed. Mitradates took the baby, carried it home to his hut at the foot of the mountains and showed it to his wife. Now it happened that on that very day, while the herdsman was in the city, his wife Cyno had given birth to a still-born son, and when she saw Mandane's child, so fine and strong, and dressed in beautiful rich clothes, she begged her husband not to destroy it, but to bring it up as their own. The dead baby could easily be exposed in its place, and nobody would know the difference.

Such a tale is after Herodotus' own heart, and he tells it with vivid detail and exquisite art. There is no need, perhaps, to continue it here, except to record the way in which the fraud was revealed to Astyages. 'When (to quote Herodotus' own words) the boy was ten years old, he and some other boys were playing the game of "Kings" in the street of the village where Mitradates kept his oxen, and it so happened that Cyrus—the supposed son of the herdsman—was the one whom the boys picked as their king. In the course of their game, he was giving his subjects their various tasks—some to build houses, others to be his bodyguard, one to be the "king's eye", and another his messenger—when one of the players who happened to be the son of a distinguished Mede called Artembares, refused to do what King Cyrus commanded, and Cyrus ordered his arrest. The other boys accordingly seized him and Cyrus beat him savagely with a whip. Furious at this undeserved treatment the boy, as soon as he was released, ran home to his father's house in the city and bitterly complained of his rough handling—saying, of course, that it was the son of Astyages' herdsman who had beaten him. He did not say it was Cyrus, because that was not yet his name. Artembares was very angry. He took the boy to Astyages, and reported the monstrous treatment he had received, showing the weals on his shoulders and complaining of the insult offered them both by a cowman's brat, a mere slave of the King. Seeing his raw shoulders Astyages, when he had heard the story, was willing for the sake of the father's rank to give the boy his due; so he sent for the herdsman and his son. They came, and Astyages, fixing his eyes upon Cyrus, said: "Had you—the son of a slave—the impudence to handle in this outrageous manner a boy whose father is my most distinguished subject?"

'"Master," Cyrus replied, "there was nothing wrong in what I did to him. We boys in the village—and he was with us—were playing our game, and they made me King, because they thought I was the best man to hold the office. The others obeyed my orders, but *he* did not; he took no notice of me—until he was punished. That is what happened; and if I deserve to suffer for it, I am ready."

'Almost before he finished speaking, Astyages had guessed who he was, for that was not the answer of a slave; moreover the cast of the boy's features seemed to resemble his own, and he was just of an age to fit the date of the exposure. . . .'

So the cat was out of the bag. Cyrus, on the advice of the Magi (who were subsequently impaled for giving it), was sent into Persia to the house of his true parents, and on his coming of age he was induced by Harpagus, who had been disgustingly punished by Astyages for his failure to carry out his orders, to lead a Persian revolt against the Medes. The revolt succeeded. The Median army, led by Harpagus, was easily persuaded to surrender without a struggle, and Astyages was taken prisoner. The dreams had been fulfilled, and Cyrus found himself master of a great kingdom.

Modern historians seek for impersonal causes, economic, social, or whatever they may be, to account for the growth and decay of people's and civilisations; ancient historians almost without exception found the driving force in individuals. Herodotus was no exception: in his narrative, Media fell not only because Cyrus was destined to conquer it, but also because

Astyages was a bloody tyrant and deserved to fall; moreover, he must have been mad when he gave the command of his armies to Harpagus, the man who of all others had reason to hate him and was most likely to betray him. In one way at any rate we can be grateful to Herodotus for tracing historical events almost exclusively to the actions of individuals, because it provided matter for all his finest stories. Amongst those stories that of Cyrus' boyhood takes a high place, almost on a level with the story of Croesus, though it has less of essential humanity in it and reverberates less deeply.

After his defeat of Croesus, Cyrus left the reduction of the Greek settlements on the Anatolian coast to Harpagus, and himself marched eastward in pursuit of bigger game. Nevertheless, the conquest of Asiatic Greece, though an easier task, was hardly less important to him than the extension of his power eastward; for Cyrus had two main objectives, to gain possession in the West of the Mediterranean coast and the seaports which were the terminals of the great Asiatic trade routes, and, in the East, to secure his empire from attack by the peoples of 'Outer Iran', who were still on the move. The Greek towns, with the exception of Miletus which had made a separate treaty with the Persian conqueror, were an easy prey. Making no attempt to combine for mutual protection, they fell singly one after another, beginning with Phocaea, whose story I have already told. Following their subjection the off-shore islands surrendered too. It should be observed, moreover, that the merchant community in most of these coastal towns was in general favourable to Persia, seeing in the existence of a strong and settled imperial government commercial advantages for itself. It was always lack of unity which made the Greeks most vulnerable; the whole impulse of their lives seems to have been hostile to political combination, though often enough they saw, intellectually, the need of it. They saw it now—or at least two men did; for we read in Herodotus that a man of Priene, named Bias, proposed at a meeting of the Ionians at the Panionium, after the defeat by Persia, that all the Ionic peoples should unite and sail away together to Sardinia and settle there in a single community, where they 'would escape subjection, rule over their neighbours and be rich and happy.' Herodotus calls this a most admirable suggestion, though doubtless he knew as well as anybody that, Greeks being Greeks, it was utterly chimerical. Some time previously, before the Persian conquest, Thales of Miletus had made another, and much more practicable, proposal: this was that all the Ionian Asiatic communities should set up a common centre of government at Teos; local independence in minor matters should be retained, but in major questions of policy and defence the various towns should be subject to the central government, in the relationship of outlying districts to the mother city. Thales has been much maligned by the legend of his tumbling into a well because he was interested only in the stars; he was a practical man as well as a speculative philosopher. As a further proof of it, he is said to have made a fortune in olive oil, by buying up all the oil-presses in a bad year, just to show his friends that a philosopher did not necessarily have his head always in the clouds. But of course his proposal for a central government at Teos was as fruitless as the proposal of Bias. The Ionian communities preferred to stick to their absolute independence and to hope for the best.

Herodotus in his narrative skips over the lesser conquests of Cyrus' first campaigns in the East and hurries on to the capture of Babylon, which Nebuchadnezzar had made the greatest city in the world. At the time of the Persian attack Nabonidus (whom Herodotus calls Labynetus) was King of Babylon, but he had apparently withdrawn from active control of affairs and left the defence of the city to the Crown Prince, Belshazzar. The defence was ill-conducted—nothing, in fact, whatever was done, it being supposed that the city walls would be in themselves sufficient protection. One engagement was fought on the plain, and the worsted Babylonian troops retired within their walls, cheerfully and confidently prepared to withstand a siege. The confidence was by no means wholly unjustified, for the walls which Nebuchadnezzar had built at such cost in human life and misery were indeed a wonder. Herodotus, who had visited the city, describes them with the delight which he always manifests in the notable works of men's hands. Built of brick, they were some 300 feet high, with a circuit of 56 miles, and their thickness was such that on the top, along each edge, a row of buildings was erected with sufficient space between for a four-horse chariot to drive and turn. They were surrounded by a moat and pierced by a hundred bronze gates with bronze uprights and lintels. Within the great wall was a second one, 'not so thick,' says Herodotus, 'but hardly less strong.' To capture such a place would seem to be a problem; but unluckily for the Babylonians Cyrus was a man of ideas and Belshazzar a young prince fonder of amusing himself than of paying attention to the safety of his people.

Now as everyone knows the river Euphrates ran through the centre of Babylon, and it was this fact which Cyrus determined to use for his advantage. In the course of some two and a half or three years he succeeded, by digging channels and canals, to divert enough of the water to reduce the depth of the river in mid-stream to about three feet, and then, when all was ready, on the night when 'Belshazzar the King made a great feast to a thousand of his lords and drank wine before the thousand'* the Persian army entered unopposed along the river-bed. The city was surprised and fell almost without a blow. If this account is true the (to us) incredible thing is that so immense a feat of engineering taking so long to complete, was apparently unobserved by any single person in authority in the city. I have already had occasion to comment upon the casualness of Greek warfare; but this—as Herodotus remarked elsewhere on the ingenuity of a certain Egyptian thief—'beats the lot.'

Herodotus in his description of Babylon is interested more than anything else in the size and wealth of the city—after the Indians, Babylon and Assyria paid twice as much into the royal treasury of Darius than any other of the twenty provinces of his empire; nevertheless certain customs of the Babylonians did not escape Herodotus' humane and discriminating eye. The custom which pleased him most was the Babylonian marriage-market: once a year the girls of the surrounding villages used to be assembled for inspection, under an auctioneer. The auctioneer began by offering the prettiest, and the rich men in need of a wife would bid for her; then, when all the pretty ones were sold, the ugly ones were told to stand up and the process of auction was put into reverse, the poor men present being asked which of them would take the smallest sum to accept them as wives. 'The money,' Herodotus adds, 'came from the sale of the beauties, who in this way provided dowries for their ugly or misshapen sisters.' Another practice which took Herodotus' fancy was the treatment of disease: there were no doctors in Babylon; invalids were carried

* It is difficult, though attempts have been made, to reconcile this account with the account in the Book of Daniel.

out into the street, and anyone who chanced to come by would offer advice upon their complaints, drawn either from personal experience or from observation of similar complaints in others. No one was allowed to pass a sick person in silence; duty required that he should ask what ailed him. The tedium of such conversations can well be imagined, but the Babylonians apparently enjoyed them. Herodotus found this peculiar practice next in ingenuity to the marriage-market—an opinion which is surprising, in anyone of the same race as Hippocrates. Possibly, however, he thought it was funny—for one can never be quite sure of the precise tone of Herodotus' voice—as when he goes on immediately afterwards to describe Babylonian husbands and wives cautiously sitting over incense to fumigate themselves after intercourse. They must have used a lot of incense. Always as interested in practical matters as in the oddities of human behaviour, Herodotus further gives a fascinating description of the coracles, some of them with a carrying capacity of fourteen tons, which used to carry wine from Armenia down the Euphrates to Babylon.

Human labour was cheap and inexhaustible in the great empires of the ancient east, and doubtless no eastern potentate cared how many lives were sacrificed to his ambitions or his pleasure; nevertheless, to me at any rate, the sheer magnitude of some of the works these men achieved, in building or in engineering, is a perpetual wonder. I have mentioned the walls of Babylon and Cyrus' feat of diverting the water of the Euphrates, but even more astonishing was the undertaking of Queen Nitocris, the predecessor of Nabonidus on the throne of Babylon. This monarch, seeing the danger of attack from the north by the Medes or others who, sailing down the straight and swiftly-flowing river, might well take her city by surprise, altered the course of the stream, making it (in Herodotus' words) 'wind about with so many twists and turns that now it actually passes a certain Assyrian village called Ardericca three separate times, so that anyone today who travels from the Mediterranean to Babylon and comes down the Euphrates finds himself three times over at Ardericca, on three different days.'

After the capture of Babylon Cyrus marched to try to secure his north-eastern frontier. His objective was the Kingdom of the Massagetae, a people akin to the Scythians, whose domain stretched from the river Araxes far over the Russian steppes to the eastward of the Caspian Sea. It was in this campaign that he met his death. As to the manner of his death, Herodotus once again chooses from the various accounts which he had heard the one which 'seemed most likely to be true.' That he fell in battle there is no doubt; but after the battle we are told that Tomyris, the queen of the Massagetae, sought and found his body, and in revenge for the capture of her son who had killed himself for shame, severed the head and flung it into a skin filled with human blood.

Cyrus deserved his title of The Great, for he was something more than an adventurer. He was not only the founder of the Persian empire, but a prince with ideals of government hitherto unknown in the world, and not to be found again before Alexander of Macedon. He was organizer as well as conqueror, and he had the wisdom and tolerance to allow the conquered peoples to keep their own way of life and their own religions. He won the lasting gratitude of the Jews—as the reader will remember from the tribute to him in the book of Ezra in the Old Testament—by allowing them to return home from their captivity, taking with them the sacred objects stolen by Nebuchadnezzar from the Temple.

The Persian empire, which within a generation was extended over the greater part of the known world, from the borders of India almost to the Aegean and from the Black Sea to the Persian Gulf, was the first in history to have an organised system of provincial administration, which it owed to the administrative genius of Darius, the successor of Cyrus' son Cambyses. Cyrus, like Alexander the Great, envisaged an empire subject, indeed, to his own control, but consisting of peoples and nations all of whom should keep their national way of life, their religion and customs, intact. Because of its efficient organisation under the provincial governors, or satraps, its system of roads, radiating from the capital at Susa, by which the King's Messengers could reach every part of the dominions and merchants and traders move their wares, and the comparative mildness of its rule, the Persian empire was able to last for two hundred years, whereas the empire of Alexander fell to pieces immediately after his death. Alexander had his splendid vision of East and West living in harmony under Hellenic leadership, but whether or not he had the qualities to make such a dream come true nobody can know, for he died too soon and had no time to consolidate his conquests. We are inescapably ignorant of the true motives which drove the men of the ancient world. We admire Alexander, perhaps rightly, for his vision; yet Hitler, too, had his dream of a world united for a thousand years under the control of the German Reich. Was Alexander any better? As to the Persian empire, we at least know that it was efficient and enlightened, and on the whole kindly in its treatment of subject peoples, in marked contrast to the older and more savage rule of the Assyrians.

Herodotus' admiration of the Persians was deep and genuine, and one could wish that he had told us more about the details of their way of living and thinking. What he does tell us is interesting and attractive enough: originally a hardy, mountain people of warlike and frugal habits they were always quick to assimilate the ways of others with whom they came into contact, so that the spread of their power across the ancient empires soon habituated them to luxury. Yet a basic simplicity of manners seems to have remained amongst them, at least down to Herodotus' day. Boys were brought up entirely by women until they were five years old, when their formal education began. As to this, I have already had occasion to mention the three subjects which it comprised— riding, shooting and telling the truth—and I suppose it would be hard to think of three better ones for the training of boys in an age when mere knowledge was not yet at a premium. The Persians celebrated family birthdays, as we do; men greeted one another in the street with a kiss; their meals, unlike Greek meals, were enlivened with many sorts of dessert, and they drank wine liberally. They thought that there was truth in wine, but not the whole truth; for any decision taken when they were sober they would reconsider when they were drunk, and any decision taken when they were drunk they would reconsider when they were sober. They honoured a man most for prowess in war, and next for being father of a large family of sons. They considered lying more disgraceful than any other vice, and, after lying, debt, as they felt that a man who owed money was bound also to tell lies. No Persian, not even the King, ever punished an inferior for a first offence. They could punish, on occasion, with hideous cruelty, but in this differed little from any other ancient nation, including the Greek. There was much in the Persian civilisation which was gay and graceful and kindly, as is born out by the evidence of its plastic and graphic arts. Except for the official annals of the Court, there seems, in Achaemenian times, to have been no literature. Herodotus, as always, has a word or two to say of Persian religious practices: the Persians, he tells us, did not conceive of the gods in anthropomorphic terms, as the Greeks did, and hence neither statues nor temples were to be found in their country. They worshipped the forces of nature, sun, moon, stars, winds and rivers. 'Zeus', in their system, was 'the whole circle of the heavens', and they sacrificed to him from the tops of mountains, without an altar. Herodotus does not tell us, as he presumably did not know it, that Darius of Persia adopted Zoroastrianism as the official religion of the country, with its monotheistic worship of Ahura-Mazdah—though doubtless even then, and for long afterwards, the old polytheism and nature-worship continued side by side with the new cult.

Cyrus was succeeded by his son Cambyses, whose first task was the subjugation of Egypt. Preparations for the campaign were already well in hand before he ascended the throne.

The beautiful simplicity of the broad outline of Herodotus' book will by now be apparent: the double object which he stated in his opening paragraph—to record everything of interest in the known world, and to trace the steps by which East and West first came into conflict—is achieved with perfect naturalness and apparent ease by the description of the countries which fell successively under Persian dominion in the rapid process of expansion set on foot by Cyrus, while at the same time the description of the wealth and resources of these countries, added one after another to the Persian power, dramatically heightens for the reader the impact of the crisis, when it comes—how the forces of this vast wealthy and seemingly invincible world-empire were defeated and flung back by a handful of comparatively impoverished Greek city states, armed only by their courage and their love of liberty.

CHAPTER 18

Egypt

HERODOTUS ENJOYED HIMSELF IN EGYPT. IT WAS FULL OF WONDERS, and Herodotus liked wonders. It contained, as he tells us, more monuments which beggar description than any other country in the world. It had its mystery of an untellable and enormous past, with a life stranger even than the life of Assyria and Babylon. It had its present and abiding mystery of the Nile. It had mummies and crocodiles and—to Herodotus' evident delight—the people of the country did everything, as it were, *backwards*: they wrote from right to left, instead of from left to right; they kneaded dough with their feet, and clay with their hands; women were employed in trade, while men stayed at home and did the weaving; they worked the threads of the weft downwards, unlike normal people who work them upwards; they went indoors to ease themselves, but ate outside in the streets; women passed water standing up, men sitting down—and so the catalogue goes on. It was a fascinating country—even the cats were no ordinary cats, and were treated with a reverent consideration such as would make a practical Greek stretch his eyes in astonishment.

Herodotus probably spent a couple of years over his tour of the Nile valley, and his account is a valuable one. Until the beginnings of modern Egyptology in the nineteenth century, his description of the country was the chief source of our knowledge. Manetho's *History of Egypt* the only other ancient work on the subject written in Greek about 250 B.C., has not survived intact, but has come down to us only in fragmentary summaries preserved in the writings of other classical authors, notably Josephus; and even if it had survived in its complete form, it is doubtful if we should have learned from it very much, as it was written, like so much of ancient history, with a strong bias and was concerned rather to prove a theory than to tell the truth. Manetho was involved in the dispute between Ptolemy of Egypt and Antiochus of Syria, each of whom wanted to prove the greater antiquity of his country. Herodotus, on the contrary, much as he enjoyed theorising when occasion called for it, was principally concerned with facts in so far as he was able to collect them. Travelling over the country he used his eyes, and, as his custom was, asked questions. The result is that the second Book of his *History* all of which is given over to Egyptian affairs, is one of the richest and most entertaining of the whole work.

As to the reliability of Herodotus' information about Egypt, one can safely say that he is accurate and trustworthy when he describes what he saw with his own eyes; a good deal of his historical matter is, on the other hand, obviously suspect; much of it was founded upon hearsay; he was dependent upon interpreters; and it is more than probable that a great deal of the information he passes on to us came from petty officials and local guides, who would not be averse from telling tall stories to capture the interest of a credulous foreigner. Thus we have in Herodotus' account, mixed up with first-hand reporting of the greatest value and interest, a number of contemporary folk-tales and local legends—such, for instance, as the truly admirable story of the Treasury of Rhampsinitus*—which, though not history in the strict sense, are yet assuredly a part of history, as representing what the common man believed about his past.

This tale for liveliness, humour and perfection of form, is amongst the best in the whole of Herodotus' work. It is a true *conte*—a 'Milesian story' rivalled, so far as my reading goes, only by the story of the Widow of Ephesus in the *Satiricon* of Petronius Arbiter.

It must be remembered that long before Herodotus' day the true greatness of Egyptian civilisation had departed and the various upheavals of the Late Period with its dynastic squabbles, unsuccessful foreign ventures and the subjection of the Pharaohs by foreign conquerors had destroyed much not only of the actual prosperity of the country but of the old way of life and of the old forms of thought and belief which had found expression in the serene but awful creations of Egyptian builders and sculptors. By the time of the Pharaoh Psammetichus, in the middle of the seventh century B.C., when Greek mercenary troops were beginning to be employed in Egyptian service, and the Greek trading post at Naucratis was built near the mouth of the Nile

* See Appendix II.

and commercial intercourse between the two countries was becoming a familiar element in Greek life, the old Egyptian culture was dead and the once severe but not ignoble Egyptian religion had degenerated into a complex of superstition and magic. Herodotus says that the Egyptians were more 'religious' than any other people, and the word may stand: what he meant was that they were more concerned than most with rites of purification and preventive magic, all of which Herodotus found of great interest as illustrating the odd ways of human kind. 'I am not anxious,' he says, 'to repeat what I was told about the Egyptian religion, for I do not think that any one nation knows much more about such things than any other;' nevertheless, he does repeat a good deal, being unable, as always, to turn a blind eye to the vagaries of men. What Herodotus was not, and could not be, aware of—for his Egyptian guides had themselves half forgotten it through the long centuries of change and decline—was the true splendour of the Egyptian past and the quality of feeling which had made its most tremendous monuments possible.

No doubt it was his guides who told Herodotus of the thirty years of slave-labour brutally exacted by the Pharaoh Cheops to build his Great Pyramid at Giza, and of his other monstrous crimes and acts of oppression which made his name and that of his successor Chephren so bitterly hated that the Egyptians could not bring themselves to pronounce them. But such stories were a mere fable of the latter and more degenerate days; Egypt in its great period was not a country of down-trodden serfs labouring under cruel task-masters, as is suggested by so much of what Herodotus wrote and by the accounts in our own Bible of Israel in bondage. The researches of modern Egyptologists have painted a very different picture, of a life regulated, indeed, by an iron traditionalism, but not without gaiety and a certain kindliness and charm. Cyril Aldred in his recently published book *The Egyptians*, an admirable short study of Egyptian history as illuminated by the most recent research, has pointed out that in a country whose basic wealth was in its agriculture, the rural life with its dignity and inward peace was recognised as the ideal. 'If a poor cultivator,' wrote one of the sages, 'is in arrears with his taxes, remit two-thirds of them'; and the general tenor of such teaching was that masters should act considerately towards the defenceless and the weak. The Egyptian, according to the same authority, differed from most western peoples in his freedom from a sense of guilt; he believed that it was in the nature of a man to err, and of a God to forgive—'the wrath of the Gods is finished in a moment.' Thus his aim in life was not the uneasy one of atoning before an angry God for his sins, but rather to accept, and to find his place in, the system of *ma'at*—the Order, the divinely ordered Cosmos— which had been created by God. His duty and his delight was to accept the world as it was, created by the Gods perfect, and 'alive from end to end'. It was easier for the Egyptian to feel thus than it is for most peoples, for he was free from many of the anxieties which commonly afflict mankind: the natural conditions of his country were not subject to change; the unchanging climate, the annual rising of the Nile, the protection, at any rate in the early period of his history, afforded by the desert margins against invaders, all helped to strengthen his sense of stability and security. Egypt was the fortunate land where things seemed to remain for ever the same. The Egyptian accepted them, not without gratitude, as he accepted the rule of a Pharaoh who was believed to be God incarnate. The belief in the actual divinity of the Pharaoh rendered intelligible the building of the pyramids: the pyramids were not the tombs of men, raised by slaves to flatter the pride of a tyrant; they were the tombs of gods, who had died to be born again, and they were raised by their worshippers. The technical processes of raising these tremendous monuments fascinated Herodotus, as did all evidences of human ingenuity and skill, and he gives a graphic—and surely an accurate—account of the method of building them, just as he does of the Nile cargo- boats, with their very unusual construction, and of the method employed by the boatmen—almost exactly like what the Thames bargees in the old days of sail used to call 'dredging'—to give them steerage way in a calm by making use of the current and a drag.

The Egyptians of Herodotus' day liked to laugh at the Greeks, who, they used to say, were always children. I suppose this was in part a judgement of character, based on what they saw, or thought they saw, of Greek restlessness and inquisitiveness and love of speculation and adventure and change, and in part a mere judgement of history in view of their own incalculable antiquity. Age brings wisdom, or so it is said, and no doubt the Egyptians of the fifth century, changed though they were from their ancestors, still not only remembered with pride their country's real contributions to knowledge in mathematics and astronomy—it was the Egyptians who invented geometry, to serve a practical necessity in *measuring the ground* for purposes of taxation and so on, and who discovered, as Herodotus tells us, the solar year and were the first to divide it into twelve parts—but were also aware of an inherited wisdom of another kind, very foreign to the mercurial Greeks, drawn from the sense that their people in the ancient days had made their peace with the gods and had built a civilisation which was in their own eyes perfect and destined to endure for three thousand years.

One small piece of Egyptian mockery is recorded by Herodotus, directed not against the Greek character but against the circumstances of their lives: 'What?' they said, when they were told that no rivers in Greece overflowed to irrigate the fields, 'your country then is watered by *rain*? Poor souls! the day will come when the gods take it into their heads to afflict you with a drought, and you will starve.' Herodotus, however, faced with this dismal prophecy, is ready with his repartee, based upon his very shrewd observations of the geological formation of the Egyptian Delta. The priests at Heliopolis had informed him that in the time of Min (Menes) the first Pharaoh, all Egypt except the district around Thebes was marsh, and none of the land below Lake Moeris was yet showing above water, and in commenting upon this Herodotus remarks that the story was obviously true, because any intelligent observer could see for himself that the Egypt of the present day was 'the gift of the Nile'. It was alluvial land, built up by the silt brought down by the river. Take a cast of the lead, he says, a day's sail off the coast, and you will find eleven fathoms, muddy bottom—which will show you how far the silt from the river extends. With a sense of geological time unparalleled (in my knowledge) by any other ancient author, he goes on to argue that the whole Nile valley was once an arm of the sea, like the Red Sea, and what was to prevent it 'in the vast stretch of time before I was born' from being turned into dry land by the accumulated silt of the Nile—'for the Nile is a great river and does, in fact, work great changes?' And by way of illustrating great things by small, he points out that the river Achelous, which flows through Acarnania in Greece, has already joined to the mainland half the islands of the Echinades group. Thus, then, it will be seen that the Nile delta, having risen above the water to become dry land in the course of ages, is still rising; in the reign of Moeris the area below Memphis used to be flooded when the river rose only twelve feet—today the river never floods unless it rises twenty-four. What then is the answer to the Egyptian gibe about Greece starving for lack of rain? If, says Herodotus, the land below Memphis continues to increase in height at the same rate as in the past, is it not obvious that when the river can no longer flood the fields—and there is no chance of rain either, in that rainless land—the people who live there will have to go hungry?

The mysterious Nile itself that

Child of the old moon-mountains African, as Keats called it,

is, of course, the cause of much interest and speculation to Herodotus. Discussing the reason for its annual flooding, he rejects the theory that it is caused by the melting of snow on distant mountains, and produces a very absurd theory of his own which includes the blowing of the sun out of his course by winter storms. For once one blushes for Herodotus. As to the source of the great river, which did in fact remain hidden for so many centuries after his time, he is more interesting and rational, rejecting the pleasing but ridiculous tale of the bottomless whirl-pool between the twin, non-existent mountains Crophi and Mophi, and going on to collect whatever factual information he can. Reckoning the town of Elephantine, which he says he visited, as situated at the southern limit of Egypt proper, he declares that the river continues southward into Ethiopia for as far as one can travel by land or water in four months, and then turns westward through a region uninhabitable because of the heat. On a later visit to the Greek colony of Cyrene in North Africa Herodotus pursued his enquiries, and was told by the people there a wild but by no means impossible story: this was that some men from their city, on a visit to the oracle of Ammon in the Libyan Desert, had got into talk with a certain Etearchus, the Ammonian King, who, in his turn, had spun them the follow-ing yarn. A group of young men from the country to the eastward of Cyrene, out for adventure, set off to explore the desert, work-ing across it in a westerly direction. Struggling for days over the burning sand, they came to an oasis, where, as they were picking the fruit and refreshing themselves, they were attacked and carried off by a party of black dwarfs of unintelligible speech. The pigmies took them over a vast tract of country till they came to a town, where all the people were pigmies, all black, and all wizards. Past the town flowed a great river, with crocodiles in it, from West to East. That river, said Etearchus, was assuredly the Nile (could it have been the Niger?) and Herodotus agrees with him, ending his account with the supposition, based on his own peculiar theory of geographical 'balance'—he illustrates it elsewhere in the view that because there are people called Hyperboreans living 'beyond the north wind', there must also be people called Hypernotians living beyond the south wind—that the river still continued to the westward just so far as would make it equal in its length to the Danube, the whole course of which was known.

On the whole, then, Herodotus' observations on the nature and geography of the country are impressive, when one considers the difficulties of travel and communications in his day and the absence of maps—the first map was the map of 'the world' made by the Ionian philosopher Anaximander early in the sixth century: perhaps it was that, or a copy of it, which Aristagoras of Miletus, according to Herodotus' account, brought to show King Cleomenes of Sparta, when he was trying, unsuccessfully, to persuade him to undertake the invasion of Asia, and the stay-at-home Spartan, having learned that Susa was three months' journey from the coast, indignantly ordered his visitor out of the house.

Hardly less impressive, and more entertaining, are Herodotus' remarks on Egyptian life and manners and on the fauna of the country. He notes with a shrewd traveller's eye their clothes, their food, their ways of greeting; he comments on the condition of medicine in the country—a specialist for every disease, very different from the method in use at Babylon—and on the effects of the climate upon the national health; he describes with immense gusto and in rich detail the three processes (graded according to price) of embalming corpses, and he has much to say upon the highly idiosyncratic attitude of Egyptians towards animals. In his descriptions of the beasts and birds he professes to speak from direct observation, and no doubt does so in some cases, notably in his vivid description of the crocodile and of the bird who picks its teeth; in other cases, however, such as that of the hippopotamus, one ventures to doubt; for it is unlikely that the hippopotamus, even in the fifth century before Christ, had a horse's mane and cloven hooves. The phoenix is another matter, and Herodotus admits that he has no direct experience of it; for this curious but sacred bird visited Egypt only at intervals of 500 years, and only for the purpose of burying its father, whose body it enclosed in a lump of myrrh and carried in its beak all the way from Arabia to the Temple of the Sun in Heliopolis. 'I give the story,' writes Herodotus, 'as it was told me, but I don't believe it.'

The rest of his account Herodotus devotes to a sketch of Egyptian history from the accession of the first Pharaoh, Menes, taking his facts from what was told him by the various guides and priests with whom he talked during his tour of the country. As I have already said, the 'facts' are not historically trustworthy, but rather in the nature of historical folk-tales and legends. Many of the tales can be read with as much pleasure as was obviously taken by Herodotus in writing them; he himself had a touching faith in their truth, telling us that the Egyptians by their praise-worthy habit of keeping records were the best historians in the world. On one occasion he asked the priests at Heliopolis if the Greek story of the Trojan War as told in Homer was fact or fiction, and received in reply certain information which they claimed to have had direct from Menelaus, Helen's husband—a most reliable authority. This information was in accordance with a version of the story already current in Greece, in spite of Homer, to the effect that Helen was never in Troy at all, but was detained throughout the war by the Pharaoh Proteus in Egypt, whither she and Paris, during their flight from Lacedaemon, had been driven by stress of weather. Euripides, incidentally, used this version of the legend in his delightful romance *Helen*. The existence of the variant is interesting in itself, but perhaps less interesting than Herodotus' comments upon it, both critical and moral: he accepts it as the more likely version on the grounds that if Helen had been taken by Paris to Troy, Priam the King, once he was threatened with a long and destructive war for her return to Greece, would undoubtedly have given her up; her abduction was a lawless act, and the Trojans would have had too much sense to want to defend it at the cost of much blood and treasure. Herodotus believes that Homer knew this version of the story, and quotes some lines both from the *Iliad* and the *Odyssey* in support of his belief; but he shrewdly adds that Homer knew his business well enough not to adopt it for his poem, as it would have made a less rich and suitable theme for epic poetry. As to the moral comment, the Trojans, Herodotus says, did not give Helen up because they had not got her; this they told the Greeks, but the Greeks refused to believe them, and their refusal as I have already mentioned in a previous chapter was inspired by providence in order that their subsequent suffering might prove that sin is always punished.

I have included this digression because it so well illustrates the attitude of the Greeks to their national poetry, and indeed to their art in general. The Greeks judged the creations of their poets and artists—with the one exception, I suppose, of the personal lyric—on moral and practical, not on aesthetic, grounds. The objection of a man like Xenophanes, for instance, as I have already suggested, to the Homeric poems was that they represented the gods unworthily and attributed to them human vices; a similar criticism was made by Plato, but neither Plato nor Xenophanes nor any other Greek, so far as I know, ever said that the poems were not beautiful, or that their beauty had any sort of transforming effect upon their doctrine. That a work of art by its own perfection and inner coherence may suggest, like a sort of extended metaphor, some truth of experience which is otherwise inexpressible, is a modern notion, and foreign to Greek thought. A Greek statue of a god was not intended to be a beautiful object to delight the eye of the beholder; it was intended solely to be a worthy representation of its divine original.

The priests at Heliopolis, says Herodotus, told him that the Pharaoh Menes was succeeded by a line of three hundred and thirty kings, one for each generation (representing a period of some 10,000 years), not one of whom was in any way distinguished or interesting. We may take this statement with a pinch of salt, for what Herodotus really meant was almost certainly that no good story could be attached to any of them; so he hurries on to the reign of Sesostris (about 1950 B.C.) and his career of foreign conquest extending as far as Scythia and Thrace, and his exploration by sea of the coast of the Indian Ocean. Then follow anecdotes, bolstered up with bits of history, of the Pharaoh Pheron and his mysterious blindness, of Proteus, of Rhampsinitus, of the tyrannical Cheops and his son Chephren, of Mycerinus and his mild and kindly rule, down to Sethos and the tale of how the Assyrians under Sennacherib came down like a wolf on the fold, only to be defeated by the army of mice which ate their bow-strings while they slept.

At this point Herodotus abandons the authority of the Egyptian priests who had hitherto been his instructors, and bases his account on various sources, which he does not specify, one of them being probably the writings of Hecataeus. Moreover, he is now in comparatively modern times, having reached the period of the first Psammetichus (mid-seventh century B.C.), the ruler who established his power over his rival aspirants to the throne by the help of the 'bronze men from the sea'—the Ionian and Carian adventurers, in their bronze armour, who had been driven by stress of weather to seek shelter on the Egyptian coast. Egyptian history had emerged from its dim and legendary past and with the foundation of the Greek trading-post at Naucratis on the Nile had linked itself with the world which Herodotus knew by more than hearsay. Barely a hundred years later Egypt would be ruled by Amasis, the friend of Polycrates and a phil-Hellene, a King, as Herodotus tells us, who shocked the Egyptian nobles and grandees by spending the latter part of each day, after business was completed, in frivolous amusements, laughing and joking with his friends, and defended such unkingly conduct by observing that 'anyone who was always serious would undoubtedly go off his head, or get a stroke—for do not archers unstring their bows after use?' The ancient Egypt, ruled by its incarnate gods, was indeed a thing of the past.

Interspersed with his tales of the Pharaohs, Herodotus also gives accounts, or eye-witness descriptions, of their building and engineering works, whenever they seem to him worthy of mention—such as the marvellous Labyrinth near the City of Crocodiles, raised by the Twelve Kings as a common memorial of their reign, with its twelve covered courts and three thousand rooms, or the room hollowed by the order of Amasis from a single block of stone, or the canal, begun in the reign of Neco and completed by Darius the Persian, from the Nile to the Arabian Gulf, a distance of four days' journey by boat. Another achievement of Neco, more interesting than Herodotus himself suspected, was the expedition which he sent out to circumnavigate Africa. Herodotus records that the expedition, starting from somewhere in the Persian Gulf, did, after some three years, pass through the Straits of Gibraltar and so find its way back to Egypt through the Mediterranean; but he implies a doubt of the truth of this story by repeating what was, to him, the incredible statement of the Phoenician navigators that, as they sailed westward off the southern coast of Africa, they had the midday sun on their right hand. We can be grateful to Herodotus for his habit of repeating tales, however wild they appeared to him to be; for this particular story, does, of course, conclusively prove to us, with our greater geographical knowledge, that the account of those old Phoenician seamen, was not fiction but fact.

Amasis was nearing the end of his long reign of forty-four years when Cambyses, son of Cyrus, began to plan his invasion of Egypt. That the invasion was an essential part of the Persian aim of world dominion is of course obvious, but Herodotus characteristically looks for, and finds, personal reasons for its inception. One of the current stories he repeats is that Cyrus had asked Amasis for the services of the best oculist in Egypt—Egypt, it will be remembered, was the land of medical specialists—and the man he chose to send, in resentment at being taken from his family and forced to serve the Persians, suggested to Cambyses that he should ask for Amasis's daughter in marriage, knowing that such a request was bound to stir up trouble; for Amasis could hardly consent without personal distress, and he could not refuse without bringing down upon himself the anger of the Persian royal family. He was therefore in a quandary, especially as he knew that his daughter was really wanted by Cambyses not as a wife but as a mistress. Accordingly he resorted to deception and sent the beautiful Nitetis, daughter of his predecessor Apries, pretending that she was his own. The secret soon came out, and Cambyses sought his revenge in the destruction of the King who had deceived him. So much for old tales—which at least add colour to the working of those blind impersonal forces which, as we now believe, control the destinies of nations. There was, however, another circumstance which undoubtedly acted as a contributory cause, not of the invasion itself, but of its timing. This was the desertion from the Egyptian army of a distinguished Greek mercenary soldier named Phanes. This man, dissatisfied with his conditions of service under Amasis, escaped from Egypt by sea and succeeded in reaching Persia, where he obtained an interview with Cambyses.

He was able, through the position he had held in the Egyptian forces, to give information about Amasis's military strength, and, in addition, advised Cambyses to get over the difficulty of the march through the desert between the towns of Ienysus and Lake Serbonis by asking the Arabian King, to whom the country belonged, for a safe-conduct. This was obtained, and the hour for Persia to strike seemed to have come. Meanwhile Amasis had died and it was left to his successor Psammenitus to face the invasion.

A battle was fought near the Pelusian mouth of the Nile and the Egyptians were defeated. Herodotus nearly a hundred years later visited the battlefield, where the skeletons of the dead still lay unburied. With characteristic curiosity he examined a number of them, and discovered that the skulls of the Egyptians were thick and unbreakable, those of the Persians paper-thin: this he explains on the theory that the Egyptians were accustomed to shave their heads from childhood, so that the action of the sun indurated the bone of their skulls, while the Persians, on the other hand, always wore felt caps. After the engagement Cambyses marched up the Nile, laid siege to Memphis and captured it. No further resistance was offered.

Herodotus' account of Cambyses' proceedings in Egypt is so full of revolting atrocities that he must have taken it mainly from Egyptian sources, for the Egyptians hated Cambyses not only as their conqueror but also because he openly mocked their religious sensibilities; it is possible, too, that Herodotus exaggerated the bestialities of Cambyses, because he wished, though he never actually says so, to find in his actions another illustration of his views on divine vengeance, so that just as Croesus was doomed to fall through the action of Gyges five generations before him, so Darius and Xerxes had to pay in defeat for the hideous excesses of their predecessor. This would be quite consonant with Herodotus' general view of history and the way of the world. Further evidence that he was dependent in this part of his book upon obviously prejudiced Egyptian sources is the account of Cambyses' expedition into Ethiopia. What was almost certainly a successful effort to secure his southern frontier the Egyptians represented as a disastrous attempt to conquer Ethiopia as a whole, frustrated by inadequate planning and lack of supplies (Herodotus says the Persian troops were reduced by hunger to cannibalism). Fortunately for us, however, by adopting this view Herodotus is enabled to give us some of his inimitable sketches (albeit founded upon fables) of strange and remote peoples—this time of the 'long-lived' Ethiopians, tallest and most beautiful of men, who manacled their prisoners with gold chains, lived to be a hundred and twenty, drank water from a spring which smelt like violets, used bows which no-one but themselves could bend, and called a cloak which had been dyed scarlet a liar and cheat, like the men who dyed it, for pretending to be what it was not. Herodotus also mentions another disastrous attempt, this time against Ammon Suiva, about 400 miles west of Cairo, in which Cambyses' entire army of a quarter of a million men was swallowed up by a sandstorm in the desert and never seen again. This like the Ethiopian venture is probably another Egyptian fabrication.

If only half of the crimes which Herodotus chronicles were actually committed by Cambyses, it would be only charitable to accept his opinion that he was mad. The Egyptians themselves were convinced that he was so, and attributed the cause to his violation of the sacred bull, Apis; Herodotus, though admitting the fact, seeks a more rational explanation of the cause, and it is interesting to note that what persuaded Herodotus that the man was indeed deranged was not merely his savagery and bloodlust, but the fact that he directly assaulted and made a mockery of everything which law and custom had made sacred in Egypt. 'Everyone,' he writes, 'believes the religion he was brought up in to be the best; and it is unlikely that anyone but a madman would mock at such things.' This recognition of the force and value of custom is one measure of Herodotus' sanity and tolerance; he further illustrates it by an anecdote about Darius, who, when he was on the Persian throne, asked some Greeks what they would take to eat the dead bodies of their fathers. The answer may be imagined. Darius then asked some Indians who belonged to a tribe which did in fact eat the bodies of dead parents, what they would take to burn them. They cried out in horror, and forbade him even to mention a thing so dreadful.

Cambyses met a miserable end on his way home from Egypt, accidentally wounding himself in the thigh as he jumped on to his horse's back, and subsequently dying of gangrene. He had heard before his death that two Medes belonging to the caste of the Magi, named Patizeithes and Smerdis, had plotted to seize the Persian throne, the latter—Smerdis—presenting himself to the people as Cambyses' brother, whom Cambyses had in fact murdered. The murder was not generally known, and it so happened that Smerdis the usurper physically resembled Cambyses' brother, whose name was Smerdis too. Cambyses on his death-bed laid a final injunction upon the Persian noblemen who attended him to punish the rebels and never to allow the Persian throne to revert to the Medes. Herodotus' account of the killing of the Magi and the subsequent accession of Darius to the throne makes one of his most vivid and swiftly moving stories. I propose to trace the outline of it in the next chapter.

CHAPTER 19

The Accession of Darius

THE PERSIAN NOBLEMEN WHO WERE WITH CAMBYSES WHEN HE died were by no means convinced of the truth of what the King had told them. It might well be, they thought, that the Smerdis who had seized the throne was actually Cambyses' brother, for Prexaspes, who had been commissioned to do the murder, now vehemently denied his death. It was not till seven months had passed that the usurper was exposed.

The first man to suspect that the King was indeed the Magus was a certain Otanes, a wealthy Persian in the very highest rank of the nobility, one of whose daughters had been married to Cambyses and had now been taken over, with the other wives, by his successor. It was through this daughter, whose name was Phaidime, that Otanes decided to prove the truth or falsehood of his suspicions. Now it happened that Smerdis the Magus had had his ears cut off by Cyrus as punishment for some crime or other which he had committed, and it occurred to Otanes that here might be the proof he needed. Accordingly he sought out his daughter and asked her, when her turn should come to sleep with the King (Persian Kings slept with their wives in strict rotation), to feel for his ears after he had gone to sleep. Phaidime consented, not without risk to herself—for had her husband not been asleep when she cautiously extended her hand, she would certainly have been killed.

Once it was known for certain that the King was the false Smerdis, the ursurping Magus, events moved quickly. Otanes' first act was to take two trustworthy friends, Aspathines and Gobryas, into his confidence; at their suggestion three more were added as accomplices, and on the arrival at Susa of Darius, whose father Hystaspes was governor of Persia, it was decided to add him to their number. The seven conspirators swore loyalty to one another, and in the discussion which followed Otanes was for caution and delay; Darius, however, was so passionately convinced that the blow must be struck immediately that he vowed that if his friends let a single day slip by he would betray them to the Magus. The urgency of Darius proved irresistible and the seven conspirators made their way to the palace without further delay. Admitted by the guards who knew their rank and suspected nothing of their intentions, and striking down with their daggers the Eunuchs who tried to stop them and to ask their business, they burst into the great hall. Both the Magi—the false Smerdis and his brother—were indoors, and, hearing the cries of the eunuchs and realising their danger, snatched up their weapons and boldly met the conspirators, determined to fight it out. One was soon killed; the other ran into a bedroom and tried to slam the door on his pursuers, but Darius and Gobryas forced their way in with him. Gobryas got his arms round the Magus, and both men fell to the floor. It was dark in the room, and Darius, standing over the two struggling bodies was afraid to strike, lest he should kill the wrong man; but 'Fear nothing,' cried Gobryas; 'spit both of us at once, if need be.' So Darius struck home—by good luck into the body of the Magus.

Five days later the seven conspirators met again to decide which of them should succeed to the throne—for Cambyses had had no son. Otanes having waived his claim, the remaining six agreed to mount their horses on the following day on the outskirts of the city, and that he whose horse neighed first after the rising of the sun should be King. The decision made, Darius called his groom, Oebares, and put the matter before him. 'Master,' said Oebares, 'if your winning the throne depends upon nothing but that, you may rest easy. I know a charm which will suit our purpose.' As soon as it was dark the groom took from the stables the mare of which Darius' horse was particularly fond and tied |her up on the outskirts of the city. Then he brought the stallion and led him round and round the mare in diminishing circles, and finally allowed him to mount her. Next morning the six competitors for the throne came riding, according to their agreement, through the city suburbs, and when they reached the spot where the mare had been tethered, Darius' horse plunged forward and neighed. At the same instant there was a flash of lightning from the clear sky and a clap of thunder. It was a sign from heaven, and all but Darius leapt from their saddles and bowed to the ground at his feet.

This tale, which reads so like a fairy story, had (unless Herodotus is lying) the corroboration of a monument, erected by Darius in Persia, and bearing the image of a man on horseback, with the inscription: *Darius, son of Hystaspes, by the virtue of his horse and of his groom Oebares, won the throne of Persia.* One would like, at any rate, to believe that the destiny of a great nation could, even once in the course of its history, be settled in a manner so innocent and romantic. The other five noblemen with one exception stuck to their word and gave Darius their loyalty.

As it was Cyrus who created the Persian empire, so it was Darius who put it upon a sound financial and administrative basis, dividing the vast extent of territory into twenty satrapies each under a provincial governor and each assessed for annual tribute. It is some indication of the universality of Herodotus' interests that he went to the trouble to collect and record the information not only as to which peoples were grouped together for administrative purposes into each satrapy, but also to what amount, and in what kind, each province paid tribute. Such a list of facts and figures may not have much interest for the general reader today, but few would withhold admiration for the sheer sweep and inclusiveness of intellectual curiosity which it indicates in the old historian. De Quincey, an acute though not always reliable writer, was moved by this particular record to an eloquent passage, which is worth quoting. Herodotus, he wrote, 'is a traveller of discovery, like Captain Cook or Park. He is a naturalist, the earliest that existed. He is a mythologist, and a speculator on the origin, as well as the value, of religious rites. He is a political economist by instinct of genius, before the science of economy had a name or a conscious function; and, by two great records, he has put us up to the level of *all* that can excite our curiosity at that great era of moving civilisation: first, as respects Persia, by the elaborate review of the various satrapies or great lieutenancies of the empire—that vast empire which had absorbed the Assyrian, Median, Babylonian, Little Syrian and Egyptian kingdoms—registering against each separate viceroyalty, from Algiers to Lahore beyond the Indus, what was the amount of its annual tribute to the gorgeous exchequer of Susa; and, secondly, as respects Greece, by his review of the numerous little Grecian states, and their several contingents in ships, or in soldiers, or in both (according as their position happened to be inland or maritime), towards the universal armament against the second and greatest of the Persian invasions. Two such documents, two such archives of political economy, two monuments of corresponding value, do not exist elsewhere in history.'

The catalogue of the satrapies leads Herodotus to relate what he knows, or guesses, or has heard, about various peoples living on the remote fringes of the Persian empire, and about the products of those lands and the birds and beasts which haunt them. All the most precious substances, he remarks (voicing a sentiment by no means yet dead), seem to come from countries the most remote—the perfumes of Arabia, for instance, the frankincense, myrrh, cassia, and the gum called ledanon which is found sticking in the beards of goats, the gold dust of India, where animals and birds, too, are bigger and finer than those near home, and tin and amber from the unknown West—perhaps, as some relate, from the Cassiterides, or Tin Islands (the Scillies). De Quincey in the passage I quoted called Herodotus, amongst other things, a naturalist; and so, I suppose, he was, in so far as he had a chance to see with his own eyes the creatures he writes of, such as the Egyptian ibis and the crocodile; nevertheless not a few of the animals described in his pages come straight from the *Bad Child's Book of Beasts:* the Indian ants, for instance, which are as big as foxes and kick up the gold dust with their hind feet and run faster than camels, the flying snakes of Arabia, which, like adders, have so curious a method of breeding—for when, we are told, they couple, the female seizes the male by the neck at the moment of the release of the sperm and hangs on till she has bitten it through. That finishes the male; and the female, too, has to pay for her behaviour, for the young in her belly avenge their father by gnawing at her insides, until they end by eating their way out. Absurd stories, if you will; but much in the mysterious realm of animal life and behaviour remained hidden until very recent years, and one recalls that even the excellent Gilbert White supposed that swallows in winter conglobulated at the bottom of ponds. Herodotus' anecdotes about the men who lived on these far fringes of the world are hardly less strange, but may, for all I know, be true: there were the Padaei, for instance, a tribe of Indians, amongst whom, when a man fell sick, his closest friends killed him because, as they put it, their meat would be spoilt if he were allowed to waste away with disease. The invalid would protest that there was nothing the matter with him, but to no purpose. His friends killed and ate him just the same. These tales of the men and beasts who lived on the remote boundaries of the Persian empire Herodotus took from Persian sources. They are very entertaining, but it is hard not to wonder if those Persians from whom they came had not failed to profit from the third of the great lessons which made up their education. Nevertheless, entertainment apart, there is a serious side to these fables, if fables they are: they enlarge the world in the imagination of the reader, and teach that there are more things on earth than are dreamt of in the philosophy of the predominantly home-keeping Greek.

The first two years of Darius' reign had been occupied with quelling revolts which broke out all over the empire. During them Darius in nineteen battles defeated nine kings; his military success was due partly to his own ability and partly to the loyalty of his personal troops, a comparatively small force which had never faltered in its devotion. As a young officer Darius had commanded the Immortals, the royal bodyguard of 10,000 men, in the Egyptian campaign of Cambyses, and it was these troops who, when he was proclaimed King, continued to give him their unwavering service. By their help and his own military genius he was able to reunite the vast empire and to set about the administrative reforms which were his truest title to greatness. Herodotus says little or nothing of these campaigns except of the capture of Babylon, which gives him the opportunity to relate the heroic but horrible story of Zopyrus.* This time the great city did not come off so lightly as when it was first taken by Cyrus; Darius, determined to make sure that no future revolt should occur, destroyed the defences, pulled down the gates and impaled three thousand of the leading citizens.

The Persian empire, as it was left by Cyrus and Cambyses, was now once again reduced to order; but the trouble about a career of conquest is, that it never knows when or where to stop. While Darius' eastern campaigns were still going on, he had already become involved in European affairs with his intervention in Samos after the murder of Polycrates. I have already pointed out how important to Persia, as previously to Lydia, was the control of the Greek settlements on the Anatolian coast. Darius possessed this control, but there was always the risk of trouble so long as

* See Appendix II for full story.

their kinsmen on the Greek mainland remained independent. It was therefore inevitable that the thoughts of Darius should turn towards Greece. Herodotus, in his usual way, finds the immediate cause of the Persian attempt to extend its power towards the west in the action of an individual. There was a Greek doctor named Democedes, a native of Crotona in southern Italy, who after a distinguished career as a state-paid practitioner in Aegina and Athens had been employed at a high salary by Polycrates in Samos. After Polycrates' death, he had been dragged to the mainland and lived in great misery until Darius, who had heard of his skill, sent for him to treat his ankle which had been badly sprained and was being made daily worse by the attentions of his Egyptian doctors. Democedes quickly effected a cure and was richly rewarded by the King, given a large house in Susa and invited to dine regularly at the royal table. But, being a Greek, he was not satisfied: there was one thing he desired more than riches—to return to his native town. A little later Atossa, Darius' wife, developed an abscess on her breast, and Democedes promised to cure it if she, in her turn, promised to give him whatever he asked for. The queen consented, the cure was effected, and Democedes demanded his reward: this was that Atossa should inflame Darius' ambition for further conquest, and that the first objective should be Greece—for she had heard about Greece (so she was instructed to say) and coveted the girls of Sparta and Athens and Corinth for her attendants. He—Democedes—could obviously be of the greatest use in this new venture, because knowing the country he could act as guide to the Persian forces. The ruse succeeded, at least so far as Democedes was concerned; for two ships were fitted out, manned with a number of Persian officers, and, with Democedes as guide and pilot, sailed for the west. Having coasted the Greek mainland, the reconnaissance vessels continued westward until they reached Tarentum in Italy, where a friend of Democedes removed the ships' steering-gear as they lay in harbour, arrested the Persians as spies and enabled the doctor to get safely away to Crotona. The Persian officers were then permitted to sail away, but there were still adventures awaiting them: they were wrecked on the coast of Iapygia and sold as slaves, but later ransomed and allowed to return to Susa, where they certainly had a story to tell the King.

Darius did not act immediately upon the information, such as it was, which this preliminary reconnaissance—the first ever made by Persia of the Grecian coasts—afforded him. He had another plan in mind, larger in scope, but almost certainly directed to the same ultimate purpose, namely the subjugation of Greece. This was the invasion and conquest of Scythia. Herodotus represents this undertaking as a mere interlude—though on a great scale—and as something of an aberration on the part of the otherwise extremely competent Darius; actually, however, the attempt was based upon sound and far-seeing strategy, though doomed to fail by the nature of the country and of the people, about which Darius had insufficient information. The Greeks were a maritime people, and nearly all their grain was imported by sea from abroad, and they possessed no native-grown timber suitable for shipbuilding. If, therefore, Darius could take from the rear the thickly wooded Balkan countries from which Greece drew her timber, he would thereby deal her a crippling blow. Moreover, control of the Hellespont (the Dardanelles) would enable him to stop the Greek wheat convoys sailing from the Black Sea, and, finally, the subjugation of Scythia (southern Russia) would give him control of the routes by which gold passed in transit from the mines in Siberia and the Urals. And so it was that about the year 515 B.C., he bridged the Hellespont and marched his army off on this hazardous adventure.

CHAPTER 20

Scythia

ANCIENT SCYTHIA WAS AN ENORMOUS TERRITORY STRETCHING IN the form of a crescent from the Podolia district of the Ukraine, north-west of the Black Sea, to the borders of China, a distance of some 3000 miles. To the east it was broken by mountains—the Altai range, the Pamirs, the Tien Shan; the Urals divided the Asiatic section from the European. The whole vast area, except the actual mountains, was natural grassland, or steppe, interrupted in the east by patches of desert not extensive enough to prevent intercommunication between the various tribes. These tribes, Indo-Europeans probably of Iranian stock, were pastoral nomads, brave, warlike, independent, knowing nothing of urban civilisation, and unlettered. For a brief period in their history—twenty-eight years, according to Herodotus—in the latter part of the seventh century B.C., they looked like changing their ways, for after a victory in war over the Cimmerians they swarmed southward in pursuit of the enemy, established themselves in northern Iran, occupied Urartu, and controlled territory as far west as the river Halys, the eastern boundary of the old Lydian kingdom. They then allied themselves with the Assyrians, broke the Median siege of Nineveh (626 B.C.) and pressed on southward across Syria and Judaea, finally reaching the outposts of Egypt, until a fresh alliance between the Medes and the Babylonians checked their advance and gradually drove them back to their original domain. Thereafter they resumed their nomad life and made no further adventures in foreign conquest, though certain independent groups, separating from the main clan, penetrated from time to time further west, as has been shown by the discovery of Scythian burials in the Balkans, in Prussia, and, of a later period, in Rumania and Bulgaria.

In spite of the fact that the Scythians were a typically nomad race, some of their tribes in the neighbourhood of the Black Sea were agricultural, and a large part of the Greek supply of grain was imported from those regions. There was also a body of trade between the Scythians and the Greek Black Sea settlements in other commodities, such as honey, milk, meat, furs, hides and salt. Slaves, too, were brought into the Greek communities from Scythia—presumably enemies whom the Scythians had captured in war. This trade, of very considerable bulk, together with Scythian prowess in war and the memory of their brief but spectacular domination of Asia—and also, no doubt, the strangeness of many Scythian customs—led Herodotus to devote nearly three quarters of the fourth book of his history to his account of the country, very nearly as much as he devoted to Egypt. To equip himself for writing of this people, he went to Olbia, a Greek settlement on the mouths of the Bug and Dniester. The town was friendly with the Scythians and depended for its survival on trade with the Scythian world, and Herodotus, from this base, made his journeys, and asked his questions. There are scattered references to the Scythians in other classical authors, but the account of Herodotus is by far the richest and most detailed, and in the absence of any native Scythian literature, it remained the chief source of our knowledge until it was amplified, and in most cases confirmed, by modern archaeology and excavation.

Herodotus was careful, as always, to distinguish in his account between what he observed with his own eyes, what he was told by reliable witnesses, and what was purely hearsay or local legend.

It is, as we have seen, essential to Herodotus' method to record, amongst sober facts, any sort of odd tale that chanced to come his way, such as the belief of the Issedones that somewhere in the distant north lived the one-eyed Arimaspians and the griffins that guard the gold, or the report of the Bald Men beyond the Argippaei that the mountains which shut them in were inhabited by a goat-footed race beyond which, still further to the northward, were men who slept for six months in the year. But such tales are tales, and Herodotus never offers them to the reader as anything else. As to his account of the way of life of the Scythians themselves, there is every reason to believe that it is substantially accurate; his careful and elaborate description of Scythian burials has been confirmed in almost every point by recent excavation, and, that being so, it is difficult not to believe in the general truth of the rest.

By the fourth century of our era the Scythians, being no longer a military menace and having no more political importance, were entirely forgotten. Indeed there was nothing to remember them by, as they had left no cities, no monuments and no literature. It was the spade of the archaeologists which rediscovered them, and showed us (what Herodotus does not mention) that though they were an unlettered race and in most ways savage, they did have a not negligible art. Countless objects in bronze or gold have been recovered from Scythian tombs throughout the length of their vast territory, which are not without beauty and show an often admirable craftsmanship: plaques, belt buckles, weapons, necklets, horse-trappings, decorated shield-centres, constantly representing, in a somewhat stylised manner but with a vivid sense of life, the forms of birds and animals.

A good deal of Herodotus' account is concerned with the geography of the country; indeed, he devotes more space to geographical description, and speculation, here than in any other part of his history. He was fascinated by mere size—as in Egypt by the size of the temples and pyramids, as in Babylon by the mighty walls, so here in Scythia by the limitless expanse of plain, the vast unexplored mountain ranges in the east, and the great rivers, so far surpassing in majesty the Anatolian streams he had known in his boyhood. With an accuracy surprising in view of the resources at his disposal, he describes the rivers, with the courses they follow as far to the northward as his own travels or the reports of other men can trace them: the Ister (Danube) 'mightiest river in the known world,' which never varies, summer or winter, in the volume of its waters; the Borysthenes (Dnieper), second largest of Scythian rivers, providing the finest pasture, the best fish and the most excellent water, clear and bright, for drinking; the Hypanis (Bug) with its source in a lake about the margins of which wild white horses graze; the Tanais (Don), flowing from a lake far up-country into the Sea of Azov; all these together with their tributaries, he writes of with a delighted recognition of the wonder and richness of a world which to most of his contemporary Greeks was nothing but a darkness or a legend. Moreover it is in connection with his discussion of Scythia that Herodotus puts forward certain speculations about world geography, which are not without interest and certainly in advance of his time. He cannot help laughing, he says, about the absurdity of the map-makers, all of whom show 'Ocean'

running like a river round a circular earth, with Asia and Europe
of the same size. The idea of the 'stream of Ocean' he rejects outright, for the excellent reason that there is no evidence for it;
Darius, by sending the Greek seaman Scylax down the Indus with
orders to sail westward and explore the coast of the southern
ocean as far as the Persian Gulf, had proved all Asia to be surrounded by sea with the exception of its easterly part—as to that,
nothing was known. The land of the Hyperboreans in the distant
north, 'came' according to a certain Aristeas of Marmora, 'down
to the sea'. Similarly with Europe; never, says Herodotus, has he
been able to meet anybody who could give him firsthand information of sea to the west and north of it—it might, indeed, be there,
but there was no proof of it. He is also much better aware of the
relative size of the continents of Asia, Europe and Libya than the
map-makers apparently were; none the less he quite obviously
enormously underrates the size of Libya (Africa) though his discussion of it is of great interest as it is here that he tells the story
of its circumnavigation by Phoenician seamen during the reign
of the Pharaoh Necho.

As for the Scythians themselves, Herodotus admits at the outset
that he has little admiration for them, as is natural in a cultivated
Greek for whom the life of a nomad would be not far removed
from savagery. There was, however, one thing about the Scythians which Herodotus tells us that he did indeed admire—their
management of the most important problem in human affairs,
their own preservation. This problem, he says, the Scythians
solved better than anyone else on the face of the earth. No invader
of Scythia could escape destruction; no hostile force could, unless
the Scythians wished it, ever even come to grips with them. Without towns or settled dwellings, living in tents and waggons, dependent for food not upon agriculture but upon their cattle, these
people, unless they wished to fight—and why should they?—
could for ever give an invader the slip, luring him on deep into
the heart of a strange country where, sooner or later, he would
starve. And this, of course, was precisely what happened to Darius
and his army of—reputedly—700,000 men. No battle was fought;
the Scythians, retreating before the advancing Persians, scorched
the earth behind them, and Darius was compelled ignominiously
to return home with nothing accomplished.

Herodotus' *sense* of history—a different thing from the collec-

tion of historical facts by observation or report—is well illustrated
in his account of the origins of Scythia. Here, as his custom was,
he recorded the legends: first the native legend of Targitaus, who
lived a thousand years before the coming of Darius, and of his
three sons who disputed the sovereignty between them, until certain golden objects fell from heaven and blazed with fire until the
youngest of the brothers stepped forward to lift them, and thus
was recognised as King of the Royal Scythians, the other brothers
going off to rule their separate tribes; then the Greek legend which
made Scythes, son of Heracles and a viper maiden, the founder of
the line of Scythian Kings; and, finally, another, and much more
prosaic, account, which he declared to be the best. According to
this, which is consonant with the general movement of peoples
in prehistoric times, the Scythians came into the steppe as a result
of the pressure of various migrating tribes (all of which Herodotus
names) moving, one on the heels of another, from the east and
north in search of territory. It is observations of this kind—passages in which the legends are duly quoted as matters of human
interest and curiosity, and then relegated to their proper place—
which perhaps as much as any others indicate the sheer historical
ability and grasp of Herodotus, and incidentally invite the reader's
confidence in the details which he records of the lives and manners
of strange peoples.

Those details are, in the case of the Scythians, many and curious.
The picture they compose is a barbaric and horrible one: the dedi-
cation to war, the scalping of enemies killed in battle, the drinking
from cups made from their skulls, the sacrifice of prisoners to the
War God, represented by an ancient iron sword set upon the top
of an immense pile of brushwood and faggots a mile in circumference, the punishments by burning alive, the sealing of oaths
by a draught of blood and wine, the hatred and suspicion of all
foreigners, the savage self-mutilation of the mourners at the
funeral of the King. Most gruesome of all is Herodotus' description of the ceremony which used to take place a year after a royal
burial: fifty of the dead king's servants were strangled and their
bodies gutted and stuffed, and fifty horses served in the same
manner; the horses were then set up around the tomb on half-
wheels fixed by stakes to the ground, bitted and bridled as in life,
and the men by means of a stake driven upward through the neck
were mounted upon the horses, and there the grisly circus was

left until it crumbled away into dust. There is good reason to believe that this description is a true one, for everything else which Herodotus records about the royal burials (in which, too, other members of the King's household, concubines, butlers, cooks, grooms and so on, were strangled and buried with their master) is amply confirmed by recent excavation. There was, however, one kind of Scythian burial, and that not the least fruitful for modern archaeology, of which Herodotus does not seem to have heard: this was the ice-tomb, as found in recent years in considerable numbers in the Altai. The tomb was dug deep, the ground above it froze iron-hard, and a layer of boulders placed on the top prevented the earth from thawing out.

Darius' broad strategy in undertaking the invasion of Scythia was, as I have suggested, far-seeing and imaginative, but we can hardly suppose that he would have risked the venture had he been better informed of the nature of the country and of the Scythians themselves. The attempt was frustrated from the very beginning, as soon as he had crossed the Danube on the bridge of boats which had been constructed for him by his Ionian mercenaries. The Scythian horsemen led him on and on in an interminable and fruitless chase, until once, in desperation, Darius sent a message to the Scythian King. 'Why on earth, my good sir,' he said, 'do you keep on running away? If you are strong enough, fight; if not, submit.' 'My lord of Persia,' the King replied, 'what I have been doing is precisely the kind of life I always lead, in peace as in war. Why should I fight, having nothing to defend—neither towns nor crops? But we acknowledge no master, so be damned to you.' A few days later he sent Darius a present, not the gift of earth and water, sign of submission, which Darius had hoped for, but a bird, a mouse, a frog and five arrows. Darius, the wish being father to the thought, tried to interpret this puzzling present in a sense favourable to himself, but Gobryas, one of the seven lords who had conspired to kill the usurping Magus, was wiser. 'My friends,' he said, 'unless you turn into birds and fly, or into mice and burrow in holes, or into frogs and jump into the lakes, you will never get home again and escape the Scythian arrows.' So the weary march back to the Danube began.

The Scythians seeing that the Persians had decided to abandon the enterprise, ordered a section of their forces to ride with all speed to the bridge on the Danube and to persuade the Greeks

who were guarding it against Darius' return to break it up, and
so trap the Persian army in enemy country. In this way, it was
urged, Ionia could regain its freedom. With the party at the
bridge were a number of the leading men of the Asiatic Ionian
towns, amongst them Miltiades the Athenian, then ruler of the
Chersonese, and Histiaeus, the tyrant of Miletus. Miltiades urged
his companions to fall in with the Scythian plan, but Histiaeus
violently opposed him, pointing out that all of them owed their
position of authority to the Persian control of Ionia. If the Greek
cities of the coast should regain their independence from Persia,
they—the 'tyrants'—would assuredly be thrown out and democratic regimes established. 'And what,' he said, 'would be the good
of that?' It is a comment on Greek personal and political attitudes
that Histiaeus carried the others with him, and the chance, obviously a good one, of destroying a large Persian army, and
probably Darius himself, was deliberately given up. Darius and
his forces, though not without difficulty, succeeded in evading
the pursuit of the Scythians, and reached the bridge in safety. They
then crossed into Thrace, marched to Sestos in the Chersonese and
were ferried over the straits into Asia. 'The Scythians,' Herodotus
remarks, 'have a low opinion of the men of Ionia in consequence
of all this: to consider them as a free people, they are, they say,
the most despicable and craven in the world; and, considered as
slaves, the most subservient to their masters and the least likely to
run away.' In human judgements quite a lot depends, it seems,
upon the point of view.

Herodotus greatly magnifies the importance of the failure of
Darius' Scythian adventure, for, all things considered, it was only
a minor setback in the expansion and consolidation of the Persian
empire. Possibly it was not even a setback, for the actual conquest
of Scythia may never have been in Darius' mind at all. It was the
control of Thrace that he really needed, and of the Aegean coastline as much further westward as he could reach. In this object he
was successful, for Megabazus, the officer he left in charge of his
forces in Europe after his own return to Susa, completed the conquest of Thrace and extended Persian dominion as far as Macedonia and the river Strymon. If this is the true interpretation of
Darius' policy, then his crossing of the Danube may have been
merely a diversion with the object of laying hands on the gold
mines of Dacia. It was Greek imagination, believing what it

wished to believe, which attributed to Darius the impossible attempt to incorporate the three thousand miles of Scythian steppe into the Persian empire. Simultaneously another Persian venture had been under way in North Africa, as a result of which the Greek settlements at Cyrene and Euesperides were incorporated in a Persian satrapy. The story of this gives Herodotus an opportunity to record facts and legends, whichever they may be, about the innumerable native tribes living along the African coastal fringe from Egypt as far westward as the Straits of Gibraltar. Much of what he has to tell is amusing, some of anthropological interest; one tale, at least—which one hopes is a true one— is worth repeating here. The Carthaginians, Herodotus writes, told that they used to trade with a race of men who lived westward of the Pillars of Heracles. On reaching this territory, they would unload their goods, spread them out on the beach and then, returning to their ships, raise a smoke. Seeing the signal, the natives would come to the beach, place on the ground gold in exchange for the goods, and go off. The Carthaginian merchants would, after a suitable interval, return to see how much gold had been left, and, if they thought it a fair price, they would collect it and go home; should it appear insufficient, they would return on shipboard and wait for the natives to come back and add to it. There was perfect honesty on both sides. The Carthaginians, Herodotus assures us, never touched the gold until it equalled in value the merchandise offered for sale, and the natives never touched the merchandise until the gold had been taken away. Had these admirable savages traded with Greeks instead of with Carthaginians, one fears that they would have had to change their methods.

CHAPTER 21

The Ionian Revolt

WITH THE END OF DARIUS' SCYTHIAN EXPEDITION AND HIS conquest of Thrace, involving, as it did, a firm foothold in Europe, the story of Herodotus begins to move towards its climax. The Persian empire had now (about 512 B.C.) reached the limit of its expansion to the east and south. Asia from the Aegean to the Indus was in Persian hands, together with Egypt and the north-African coast as far west as Euesperides; and mainland Greece was already threatened by the successful campaigns of Megabazus. But it was still to be eleven or twelve years before the curtain rose upon what might be called the first act of the drama which is the central theme of Herodotus' book. This was the revolt of the Ionian cities of Asia Minor against Persian dominion.

Herodotus' account of the origin and progress of the revolt is as full of colour and incident as any romance. There is no reason to suppose that it is anything but broadly true though here, as always, he tends to obscure the deeper causes by dwelling on the personal and proximate. It must always be remembered that the Persian control over the Greek cities of the coast was not in general oppressive, any more than the Lydian control had been before it; and it was by no means universally resented. For one thing, it was good for trade; and anything which is good for trade is bound to be welcome to a section, at any rate, of the community. The Persians were tolerant and kindly masters, and did not interfere in the internal affairs of the Greek settlements, except in one respect—it was an essential part of their system that those settlements should not be allowed to follow the example of so many of their cousins on the mainland of Greece, who had got rid of their despotic rulers and established democratic institutions. All the Asiatic cities were governed by despots ('tyrants'), and the despots, of course, owed their position to Persian protection. The Ionian cities, like many of the cities on the mainland, had come to hate their 'tyrants'. The fire was there, smouldering; and it was ready to burst into flame. It was that, far more than any hatred of Persia, which was the real cause of the revolt. The first step, therefore, was the expulsion of the tyrants; the second, to obtain help from mainland Greece against Persian reprisals.

The immediate occasion of the revolt, on the other hand, was no doubt, as Herodotus describes it, certain selfish and personal ambitions.

When Darius returned to Susa after his Scythian campaign, he was anxious to reward Histiaeus for the service he had rendered at the Danube bridge. Accordingly he asked him what it was that he would most like to receive, and Histiaeus replied that his chief desire was to found a new settlement at a place called Myrcinus, near the river Strymon. The request was granted; but when the building of the new town was already in progress, it occurred to Megabazus, who was still occupied with his campaign in Thrace, that a Greek settlement in that neighbourhood, rich as it was in silver and excellent timber for ship-building, might prove a grave hindrance to Persian control. He expressed his fears to Darius, who was quick to take his point and wrote a letter to Histiaeus, recalling him to Susa—ostensibly because he loved him so dearly, owed him so much, and could not do without his constant companionship and advice. Histiaeus was forced to obey the summons, and found himself, like Democedes before him, a petted captive at Darius' court and an exile from his country.

Now Miletus, in the absence of Histiaeus, was governed by his son-in-law Aristagoras, a man, it seems, of weak character but insatiable ambition, caring not a brass button for the freedom or subservience of Ionian Greece, but determined to play any cards he might hold to his greatest personal advantage. Just about this time luck dealt him what he thought might prove a trump. The island of Naxos in the Cyclades had been enjoying the sort of political squabbles without which no Greek community could be happy for long, and a popular rising there had resulted in the expulsion of the oligarchs; a number of these men, members of the leading families in the island, made their way to Miletus and begged Aristagoras to help them engineer their return to power.

Aristagoras agreed—not out of love for the Naxian aristocrats,

or even out of dislike of the Naxian democrats, but simply because he saw in the venture a possibility of his own aggrandise-
ment. Might there not, he thought with true Grecian perspicacity,
be a chance, when all was done, of becoming master of Naxos
himself? It was the wealthiest island of the Cyclades, and well
worth a risk or two. The subjugation of Naxos could not, however, be achieved without Persian help, so Aristagoras went to
Artaphernes, the Persian satrap for the whole district of the Anatolian coast, and made his proposal: if, he said, Persia would provide a hundred ships—a small matter—he would guarantee for
her not only the possession of Naxos, but of all the Cyclades, and
probably of Euboea as well, that rich and splendid island just off
the coast of Greece. The offer seemed an attractive one; Artaphernes eagerly doubled the size of the flotilla which the wily
Greek had asked for, sought the permission of Darius, got it, and
the expedition sailed. But there was trouble to come: the fleet
made ostensibly, and to cloak its purpose, for the Hellespont, and
on the way thither brought up off Chios, where Megabates, the
Persian officer in charge, on making his inspection one evening
found that a ship of the Greek contingent had neglected to set a
watch. Very properly he arrested the captain, put him in irons,
and left him with his head sticking out of an oar-port. When
Aristagoras discovered the offender in this undignified situation,
he was very angry, promptly released him and told Megabates
that he had no right whatever to treat Greek seamen in such a way
without first consulting *him*—Aristagoras—who by Artaphernes'
orders was commander-in-chief of the expedition. I suppose the
priority of rank cannot have been made clear before the ships
sailed, for Megabates considered Aristagoras' behaviour to be pre-
sumptuous and insulting—as no doubt it was—and at once determined to have his revenge. That very night, therefore, he sent off
a party of Persians in a boat to Naxos to warn the islanders of their
peril; the islanders, in their turn, made every preparation to repel
an attack and to withstand a siege, with the result that the Persian
force, after a fruitless blockade of four months' duration, gave up
the enterprise and sailed home.

Aristagoras was now in an awkward position; he had spent
more than he could afford on the pay of his Greek seamen; he
had thrown away Persian money; and, worst of all, he had quarrelled with Megabates and failed to keep his promise to the satrap.

It was more than likely, he felt, that he would, in consequence, also lose his position in Miletus. Somehow or other it was necessary to retrieve his fortunes.

Thinking over his chances, he had almost decided that his best hope was to start a rebellion against Persia amongst the Ionian cities, when something happened which definitely turned the scale. This was the arrival in Miletus of a secret message from the exiled Histiaeus, urging him to organize the revolt. All the roads from Susa were watched, and it was not easy for Histiaeus to get his message through; but he had solved the problem by the ingenious device of shaving a slave's head, writing the message on his scalp, and then waiting for the hair to grow again before he was dispatched.

Aristagoras now delayed no longer. To win the support of the Milesians he abdicated his position as 'tyrant' in favour of a democratic constitution, and then proceeded to get rid of the tyrants in the other Ionian states—precisely how, Herodotus does not say; but presumably, as hatred of despotic government was the real driving force behind the revolt, it was not difficult—and went on to undermine Persian influence in every way he could think of. His next need was military support from mainland Greece, so off he went in a warship to Sparta, taking with him a map of Asia, engraved on bronze. Cleomenes the Spartan King gave him a somewhat tepid welcome, but Aristagoras, nothing daunted, launched into a fervid and patriotic speech about the glory of freedom and the shame of slavery. Then, knowing that the Spartans were practical men, he produced his map and gave a glowing account of the exceeding richness of each successive country—tracing them with his finger as he spoke—and assuring Cleomenes that all the wealth they contained would fall into his lap like a ripe plum, while the miserable Persian soldiery—who fought in *breeches*, if you please!—would flee in terror at the mere sight of the heavy armoured infantry of Sparta. Cleomenes, however, looked at the map dubiously, for he didn't understand it; then he asked how far, in fact, it was from the coast to Susa, and Aristogaras, forgetting, in his eagerness, to lie, said it was a three months' journey. Cleomenes promptly ordered him out of the house.

Aristagoras then went to Athens, where he had better success. Athens was already to some extent embroiled with Persia, having

revoked the act of submission made by her envoys some ten years
previously when she was soliciting Persian assistance against Sparta, and also because of her successful opposition to the Persian
attempt to restore Hippias, the son of Pisistratus, as tyrant; so the
Athenians were readier to listen to Aristagoras' request, and to
his rosy promises, than Cleomenes had been. Athens being now a
democracy, Aristagoras made his speech before the Assembly, and
'apparently', Herodotus shrewdly remarks, 'it is easier to impose
upon a crowd than upon an individual, for Aristagoras, who had
failed to impose upon Cleomenes, had no difficulty with thirty
thousand Athenians.' He was promised support, and a squadron
of twenty ships was despatched from Athens to the Ionian coast.
Five ships were also sent by the small town of Eretria in Euboea—
not, as Herodotus is careful to add, out of love for Athens, but as
a debt of honour to Miletus, who had helped her during previous
troubles of her own. 'The sailing of this fleet,' Herodotus writes,
with proper solemnity, 'was the beginning of troubles not only
for Greece, but for the rest of the world as well.'

The fleet brought up at Ephesus where the ships were left, and
the troops marched up-country to Sardis, the old capital of the
Lydian empire. The fortified centre of the town, including the
acropolis, was strongly defended, but the outlying parts, which
consisted mostly of poor houses built of wattle and thatched with
reed, were quickly overrun by the Ionians, until some soldier or
other accidentally started a fire, which spread rapidly amongst all
that combustible material. Persian forces soon began to assemble,
and the Ionians discreetly withdrew under cover of darkness to
rejoin their ships; but they were overtaken at Ephesus before they
could get aboard, and severely beaten in the ensuing fight. The
Athenians had now had enough of it; they went home and, in
spite of constant appeals from Aristagoras, refused to lift a finger
to help him further. The Ionians of the coast, on the contrary,
had gone too far to retract. They continued hostilities with all the
vigour they could command, and succeeded in wresting Byzan-
tium and other towns on the Hellespont from the Persians. Cyprus also joined the rebel cause.

None the less, the success of the rebels was short-lived, and the
Persians with their immensely superior forces retook one by one
the towns they had lost. Aristogoras, seeing his own hopes gone,
lost all interest in the cause and thought only of saving his own

neck. He made his escape to Thrace, where, in some petty adventure or other, he was killed. The fate of Histiaeus was no less sordid. Darius, when he heard of the burning of Sardis, sent for him and accused him of complicity in the revolt. Feigning the most utter astonishment, 'What? *Me?*' Histiaeus replied. 'My lord, had I been there, not a single city would have stirred. You are my benefactor; I your loyal friend. Let me but return to Ionia and I will put everything right for you and surrender the traitor Aristagoras into your hands. Nay more: I will not take off my clothes till I have forced Sardinia, the biggest island in the world, to pay you tribute.' Unaccountably Darius who was a shrewd man, let him go; but things worked out by no means as he had hoped. Miletus, having got rid of one tyrant did not wish for another and refused to admit him, so he decided to turn pirate, borrowing a few warships from the Lesbians and holding up the food convoys outward bound from the Black Sea. Finally, in an adventure ashore somewhere in Mysia, he was captured by the Persian general Harpagus, and crucified. His head was cut off and sent, pickled, to Darius in Susa.

Herodotus adds an interesting detail to this characteristic but unsavoury tale. A moment before his capture Histiaeus was about to be speared by a Persian soldier, when, believing that Darius would spare his life if he were taken to him alive, he called out: 'I am Histiaeus, the Milesian.' Herodotus shares that belief— Darius, he declares, would certainly have pardoned him, his gratitude, I suppose, for the old scoundrel's service at the bridge still persisting despite his subsequent, and most blatant, treachery. There were not a few things, it appears, which the Greeks might have profitably learned from their Persian enemies. That Herodotus was himself aware of those things makes another bright strand in his beautiful tapestry. Elsewhere he relates another incident of a similar kind: Miltiades the Athenian, a bitter enemy of Persia and the man who had urged the Ionians to break the Danube bridge and so trap Darius' army in Scythia, had been forced to escape from the Chersonese with a few ships, one of which was commanded by his son. He was chased by Phoenician galleys in the Persian service, and, though he himself got away, his son was captured. The Phoenicians, delighted with what they naturally supposed to be an important prize, took the young man to Darius, and Darius, instead of impaling him for being the son of his father, gave him a free pardon, together with a house and land in Persia and a Persian wife.

The Ionian revolt finally petered out with the capture of Miletus, preceded by a naval engagement off the island of Lade (now joined to the mainland). The conduct of the sea battle illustrates so much of the Greek temperament that a word must be said about it here. At a meeting of Ionian leaders at the Panionium it was decided, in view of the threat to Miletus, not to attempt to resist the superior Persian forces by land, but to get together from all their allied communities as powerful a naval force as they could and to concentrate it at Lade. This was sound strategy, for if they could destroy the Persian fleet and win command of the sea they would have—as Hecataeus the historian had frequently urged—an immensely powerful weapon against Persian domination. The fleet accordingly assembled—353 triremes strong, opposed to the 600 which the Persians had at their disposal. The largest contingent, 100 ships, came from Chios, the smallest from little Phocaea, which sent three. For some days the Persians held off and nothing happened, while the Greek crews took their ease ashore on the island; but the commander of the Phocaean contingent, Dionysius, very sensibly realised that this would not do, and proposed that, as there appeared to be no central authority in control of the fleet, it would be a good thing to have one. Accordingly he suggested that all the local commanders should put themselves under his orders and submit to discipline. The proposal was—surprisingly—accepted, and Dionysius at once proceeded to train and exercise the entire fleet, keeping them on the go all day and every day, and insisting that the ships when not on duty, should lie to their anchors instead of being hauled ashore. After a week of this the crews began to grumble—they were not accustomed, says Herodotus, to such hard work. 'What have we done,' they asked each other, 'to deserve this punishment? We must be crazy to have put ourselves into the hands of this swollen-headed fellow—from Phocaea, of all places, which couldn't provide more than three ships! If it's a choice between two sorts of slavery, the one we are threatened with couldn't possibly be worse than this.' So every Ionian in the fleet refused duty, pitched his tent ashore—'like soldiers' as Herodotus puts it—and lounged about all day in the shade, doing nothing whatever. The crews of the Samian contingent—60 strong—observing all this, quietly sailed home.

At last the Phoenician fleet (most of Persia's navy consisted of Phoenician ships) attacked. There was some sort of brief resistance, and then the Lesbian contingent followed the lead of the Samians and fled, as did most of the Ionians. 'The reports,' Herodotus adds, 'are confused, everybody blaming everybody else.' Some few stayed to fight it out—eleven Samian ships whose officers had refused to obey the orders of their superiors, and the whole of the contingent from Chios which fought a brilliantly courageous, though hopeless, action. As for Dionysius, he, too, abandoned the fight when he saw that it was inevitably lost; but rather than return to Phocaea, which he knew would be enslaved by Persia with the other Ionian towns, he took to patriotic piracy in distant seas, establishing himself in Sicily and raiding Carthaginian and Tyrrhenian shipping. Greek ships he never molested.

Immediately after this Miletus was taken; and so ends the sorry but characteristic story of the Ionian revolt. The other Ionian towns were treated on the whole with great leniency by the Persians. Artaphernes is said to have sent for representatives from all of them and to have forced them to swear on oath to settle their differences in future by arbitration instead of being continually at one another's throats. Each community was re-assessed for taxation, at much the same figure as before the rebellion. Persia also ejected the tyrants from the Ionian cities and replaced them by democratic régimes, presumably because she was aware of the direction political thought was taking, and hoped, by falling in with what the Ionians wanted, to preserve the friendly relations which in many ways had been a benefit to both Ionia and to themselves. Darius, indeed, probably thought of the whole rebellion as a comparatively trivial interlude. However, there had been one incident in it which rankled bitterly—the burning of Sardis by the Athenians. The story of Darius' anger may well have been dressed up by the Athenians themselves, to magnify their future exploits and to represent themselves as the chief object of the Great King's revenge; but, such as it is, it has gone down in history. Each day, when Darius sat down to dinner, a slave was instructed to say to him: *Master, remember the Athenians.*

CHAPTER 22

The First Attempts on Greece

DARIUS, WHETHER BECAUSE OF HIS DAILY REMINDER OR NOT, DID remember the Athenians, and we are told again by Herodotus that the primary object of his expeditions against Greece was to punish them, together with the people of Eretria who had assisted in the unlucky attack upon Sardis. None the less it is hard not to believe that he intended, if not immediately, at any rate on a subsequent occasion to attempt the subjugation of Greece as a whole; for he was a far-sighted man, and only on that supposition can one explain his previous campaigns in Scythia and Thrace.

In the year 492 B.C. the King's son-in-law Mardonius was sent to reassert the rule of Persia in Thrace and Macedonia, with further orders to march down through Macedonia into Greece and to destroy the two guilty cities. The army, as was usual in expeditions on a large scale, was accompanied by a powerful fleet, whose duty was to keep in touch as it sailed along the coast. The fleet captured Thasos—that island with the rich gold mines which the poet Archilochus had once looked for in vain; but in trying to round the promontory of Athos it met heavy weather, and some three hundred ships are said to have been driven ashore and broken up. Twenty thousand men, Herodotus tells us, lost their lives—dashed to pieces, or drowned, or swallowed by the man-eating monsters which swarmed thereabouts in the sea. It was a major disaster, and Mardonius had to abandon the whole enterprise.

Two years later Darius tried again. The slave's reminder had by now sounded many times in his ears, and Hippias, Pisistratus' son, exiled from democratic Athens and living at the court in Susa, never ceased to urge the assault on the city which had ejected him. Feelers were put out to test the attitude of Greece and to find out how much of it, or how little, would be likely to oppose an invasion; representatives were sent to various townships demanding submission. Many towns complied, and most of the islands

which the Persians visited, including the wealthy and powerful
Aegina, for years past a bitter enemy of Athens. At home, Persian
preparations went swiftly forward, Mardonius was relieved of his
command and Datis, a Mede, with Artaphernes, a nephew of
Darius, appointed in his place. This time no risk was taken of
disaster off Athos, but the fleet with the exiled tyrant Hippias
aboard sailed from Samos directly westward across the Aegean.
A number of islands which had not already submitted were taken,
including Naxos. Delos, Apollo's sacred home, was spared—for
'Apollo,' Darius once said, 'has always told Persians the truth.'
From Delos the fleet sailed on to the southern tip of Euboea,
forced supplies and men from the town of Carystus, and proceeded up the Euripus, the narrow channel between Euboea and
the mainland, to Eretria. On the approach of the enemy, characteristically in a Greek town faced with a crisis, counsels were divided. An appeal was sent to Athens for help, but Athens did nothing
except to instruct her colonists who had been settled in the neighbouring territory of Chalcis to do what they could to assist. One
party in Eretria was for resistance, another was preparing to sell
the town for Persian pay; but the patriots prevailed, and the walls
were put hurriedly into a state of defence. But there was too much
weight in the Persian assault for the little place to withstand for
long and there were traitors at work within; after a week's fighting
the enemy was within the gates; they stripped and burned the
temples, carried off as prisoners the whole male population, and
then, elated by their easy success, sailed for Attica, confident that
the punitive mission would soon be accomplished.* On the advice
of Hippias the Persians chose as their landing-place the bay of
Marathon, where below the foothills of Pentelicus there was a
stretch of level country on which the cavalry—Persia's strongest
arm—would be able to operate freely. One battle, it seemed, and
the 9,000 men of the little Athenian army would be overwhelmed,
and the city itself follow the fate of Eretria.

* One reads, with admiration, that Darius, when the Eretrian
prisoners were brought into his presence, forgot his anger and pardoned
them. They were settled on land not far from Susa, and in their new
home preserved their old institutions and their native speech. Curiously
—for the ancients were not much interested in such things—Herodotus
mentions an oil well near the village of Ardericca (about 100 miles
north of Abadan), where the dispossessed Eretrians were settled.

But the Persian command was not aware of the change which had come over the spirit of Athens in the course of the past few years. After the death of Pisistratus, the tyranny had passed to his son, the brutal Hippias, who, when his brother Hipparchus was murdered, began in fear for his own skin to court the support of Persia. He soon came to be bitterly hated, and in 510 B.C., with the help of Sparta who had been called in by the exiled family of the Alcmaeonidae, he was blockaded in the Acropolis. He tried to smuggle his children out of the country to safety, but they were caught, and he agreed, on condition of their being returned to him, to leave Athens for ever. So Athens was free, and the genius of Cleisthenes, working on the foundation which had been laid by Solon, was able to devise and to institute a sound system of democratic government, largely freed from the old menace of perpetual strife between the great rival families, and destined to endure, for better or worse, for a hundred years.* It was this newly won political freedom which Herodotus says provided the inspiration and courage of Athenian arms, and enabled them to face what was hitherto the most terrible menace in their history. The soldiers of an oriental despot fight under the lash; a free people fights gladly for what is, indeed, its own.

In command of the Athenian army was Callimachus, the War Archon, assisted by ten generals, one from each tribe; but the course of events before the battle led to the effective command falling to Miltiades—or so the Athenian legend, repeated by Herodotus, always maintains. Immediately the news of the approach of the enemy was known, the runner Pheidippides had been sent off to Sparta to ask for assistance, but (the story is almost too familiar to repeat) he returned with the message that the Spartans, though entirely willing to help a member of their alliance in her peril, could not manage to do so until after the full moon, as they were engaged upon certain religious celebrations which it would be impious to interrupt. So the Athenians, except for their courageous and consistently loyal friends from the diminutive town of Plataea, were alone. The Persian army landed unopposed and established itself along the shore of the bay, their fleet anchored just off the beach; the Athenians encamped in the hills, in a strong position and out of reach of the Persian cavalry. Several days passed. As usual, the Greek command failed to agree:

* Athenian democracy is described in full in a later chapter.

five of the ten generals urged caution, and the hopelessness of an attack against numbers so superior; five, led by Miltiades, were for rapid action. The votes being equal (democracy is not always efficient in a crisis), Miltiades appealed to Callimachus to give the casting vote in favour of a swift stroke. The Athenian army moved from the hills and took up a position on the plain, a mile inland of the enemy. Then, when the moment was judged to have come, the Greeks launched their attack. Their centre was quickly driven in, but the two wings, which by sound tactics had been widely extended to prevent outflanking, wheeled inwards and took the victorious Persian centre in the rear. The struggle was violent but not protracted; the Persians were outfought by the Greek hoplites and suffered heavily as they tried to regain their ships. They left 6,000 dead on the field; the Greek losses, says Herodotus (always bad at figures), amounted to no more than 192.

There are two puzzles about this famous engagement. What happened to the Persian cavalry? Herodotus does not mention them at all, once he begins to describe the fighting; yet the choice made by Hippias of the unobstructed plain of Marathon for the Persian landing was dictated chiefly by the supposition that the cavalry would decide the day. Some ancient writers, but not Herodotus, say that certain Ionian soldiers serving with the Persians informed the Athenians one night that 'the cavalry had gone away', and that the Greek attack was made at dawn next day in consequence; but there is no explanation of why the cavalry had gone away. The other puzzle, which Herodotus does mention but admits he cannot solve, is the *flashing of the shield*. When the defeated Persian troops, or what was left of them, had re-embarked, the Greeks saw a signal flashed by the sun on a polished shield from ten miles away, presumably from the Acropolis in Athens. The Persian fleet, which had been awaiting this signal, then sailed round Cape Sunium for Athens, intending, one imagines, to attempt a second landing in the bay of Phalerum, then the only harbour which the city possessed. Who raised the signal? Who were the traitors? The tale spread in Athens that they were members of the Alcmaeonid clan, but Herodotus passes this off as absurd, as the Alcmaeonids (of whom Cleisthenes was one) had always shown themselves fierce opponents of tyranny and would hardly be likely to play for a Persian victory and the consequent reinstatement of Hippias. But Herodotus makes no alternative guess, and leaves the mystery unsolved. The Athenian army, having seen the signal and the departure of the Persian fleet towards Sunium, hurried back with all speed and succeeded in reaching Athens before the Persians arrived at Phalerum. When the fleet did appear and came to anchor in the bay, the commanders, finding the Athenians ready to receive them, and also, perhaps, expecting the arrival of the belated reinforcement from Sparta, abandoned the enterprise and set sail for Asia.

Three days after the full moon the pious Spartans, 2,000 strong, arrived in Athens. They are said to have hurried on the way; but they might just as well have dawdled, for all was over. They marched on from Athens to the battlefield, admired the dead bodies, congratulated the Athenians on a good piece of work, and went home again.

The battle of Marathon, though in itself a comparatively small affair, has always been looked on as one of the decisive battles of the world. Perhaps it was, for it almost certainly saved Greece from being immediately subjugated; but it is worth remembering that for Persia herself with her immense resources in men and money the defeat was only a pinprick. None the less it must have given Darius cause for thought, when he was forced to realise that the Greeks, or some of them, unstable, venal, treacherous and self-seeking though they were, were capable on occasion of fighting with great skill and superb courage. Ten years later Xerxes was to learn the same lesson.

CHAPTER 23

Athens and Aegina: an Interlude

FOR THE MODERN READER UNFAMILIAR WITH THE INS AND OUTS OF
Greek literature, and perhaps accustomed to think of ancient
Greece as a single country amongst many others, to read Herodotus' book, with its countless digressions and asides, is as revealing as to look for the first time at a drop of water under a micro-
scope.

I mentioned in the last chapter that Aegina offered her submission to Darius, and Herodotus, recording the fact (as always
without prejudice), takes the opportunity for a long and entertaining digression about the relationship between that island and
Athens. What he has to say is so characteristic of the general tone
and colour of Greek life and politics that it is worth spending a
few pages on it here, before resuming the main course of Herodotus' narrative, now rapidly approaching its climax.

Aegina was a near neighbour of Athens—the island lies only
some twenty miles off the coast of Attica southward from Pei-
raeus. For a long time the Aeginetans, a Dorian people, had been
a prosperous mercantile community; they were amongst the first
of the Greeks to issue a coinage, early in the seventh century B.C.
and the Aeginetan silver 'turtles' remained the standard coinage
of the Peloponnese for two hundred years. The island traded
freely with Egypt, and in the reign of Amasis (569-526) built its
own shrine at Naucratis, the trading-post at the mouth of the Nile.
It was only natural that commercial rivalry, which in the Greek
temperament carried with it personal hatred, should exist between
Aegina and Athens. By the end of the sixth century Aegina was
the strongest naval power in the Aegean, Athens having not yet
embarked upon the naval policy which afterwards made her great,
and some eight years before Darius' attempt upon Greece, war was
declared between the two communities. It was to be no ordinary
war—not a fight and a settlement, however temporary, without
which few Greek states could be happy for long: it was to be a

state of permanent hostility, what the Greeks called 'war without herald.' When, therefore, Aegina submitted to Darius it was no surprise to the Athenians, who knew she desired their humiliation and fully expected that the Aeginetan navy would be used against her in conjunction with the Persians. Accordingly the Athenians appealed to Sparta, the leading state of the Peloponnesian League, of which Athens was then a member, accusing Aegina of betraying Greece for the sake of a private quarrel. Of the two Spartan kings one, Cleomenes, was in favour of intervention, the other, Demaratus, was not; so Cleomenes went to Aegina on his own initiative and attempted the arrest of the men whom he supposed to be responsible for her treachery. But Demaratus had been too quick for him and had got a message to the island reminding the islanders that by the Spartan constitution no hostile act could be properly undertaken unless both kings were present. So Cleomenes' demand for the surrender of the guilty men was refused, as not having the backing of the Spartan government—worse than that, Cleomenes was accused by a certain Crius of having been bribed by Athens. Cleomenes then withdrew, so much enraged against Demaratus that, by bribing the Delphic oracle to declare that he was not the son of his father, he successfully impugned his legitimacy and brought about his banishment—and consequent entry into Persian service.

Demaratus' successor, Leotychides, was more amenable. The two kings—together, this time—returned to Aegina, Cleomenes burning for revenge; they arrested ten of the leading Aeginetans and transported them to Athens for safe-keeping. Cleomenes then became involved in domestic trouble of his own, which so seriously affected him—he had been, in his way, a man of some genius, with a gloomy and highly-strung temperament: Herodotus says that he was always, from the first, a little queer in the head—that (to use Herodotus' phrase) he chopped his belly into mincemeat with a borrowed knife, and died. Various explanations were current for his mental breakdown: Herodotus was convinced that it was God's punishment for his treatment of Demaratus; the Spartans thought it was caused by his bad habit of drinking wine neat, like the Scythians. The Aeginetans when they learned of Cleomenes' death sent a deputation to Leotychides in Sparta to complain about their ten friends who were being held as hostages in Athens; the complaint was brought into the courts, and the verdict was given against the King—the Spartan constitution was, as I have explained elsewhere, a peculiar one—the sentence being that he should be carried away to Aegina in exchange for the hostages in Athens. This, however, seemed somewhat severe, and the Aeginetan envoys, fearing future reprisals if they took a King of Sparta as their prisoner, persuaded him instead to accompany them to Athens and to use his influence to get the hostages released. Unfortunately the Athenians refused to surrender them, on the excellent excuse that, as two kings had put the men in their keeping, it would be illegal to give them up at the request of only one. This was a poser for Leotychides, and all he could think of in reply was to tell the Athenians a moral story.

'There lived in Sparta three generations ago a man named Glaucus; he was in every respect an admirable person, and had, in particular, a reputation for honest dealing beyond any other Spartan of his day. Time, however, had something in store for him which he did not expect. . . . One day a man from Miletus came to Sparta and expressed a wish to talk to Glaucus. "I am a Milesian," he said, "and I have come to you because I should like to profit by your honesty. People all over Greece—yes, and in Ionia too—are always talking of your honesty, and that set me thinking. Ionia, I told myself, is never safe from sudden change and property never stays long in the same hands; but the Peloponnese, on the contrary, is as steady as a rock. This led me to make a decision, namely, to realise one-half of my property and to put the money in your hands, in full confidence that it will be safe there. I ask you therefore to take the money and with it these tallies, which you must please keep carefully. Then you can return the money to whoever brings you the corresponding halves."

'Glaucus accepted the trust on the terms the stranger proposed. Years went by, and one day there came to Sparta the sons of the Milesian who had made Glaucus his trustee. They sought an interview with him, producing their halves of the tallies and asked for the money. "But," said Glaucus, trying to put them off, "I don't remember this transaction, and nothing you say has any effect in awakening my memory. Of course, when I *do* recollect it, I will act as an honest man should: I will pay back the money properly, if I received it, and, if I did not, I will prosecute you according to the law of my country. I promise to settle the matter, one way or the other, in three months' time."

'When the Milesians, supposing their money lost to them, had gone home in great disappointment, Glaucus visited Delphi to ask the oracle's advice; and his question, whether or not he should perjure himself and so rob the Milesians of their property, was met by the Priestess with a rebuke, in the following words:

Today, indeed, Glaucus, it is more profitable
To prevail by false-swearing and rob them of their money.
Swear if you will; for death awaits even the true-swearer.
Yet an oath has a son, nameless, without hands or feet,
But swift to pursue until he has seized and destroyed
Utterly the race and house of the perjured one.
The children of him who keeps his oath are happier hereafter.

'Glaucus, on hearing this answer begged the god to forgive him for his question; but the Priestess told him that to seek God's approval of a sin came to the same thing as committing it. So Glaucus sent for the Milesians and gave them back their money.

'And now, gentlemen (Leotychides ended) I come to the real point of my story. Today Glaucus has not a single living descendant; not a family in Sparta bears his name; all that belonged to him has vanished without trace. That will show you how wise a thing it is, where covenants are concerned, not to hesitate, even in thought, to make proper restitution.'

Such was the story. 'Unfortunately however,' Herodotus adds, 'the Athenians paid not the smallest attention to it; so Leotychides went home.' Later, Leotychides was condemned by his fellow-countrymen on a charge of taking bribes, and exiled: he—the King of the most powerful military state in Greece—was found in his tent during the course of a campaign, *sitting on a glove* stuffed with coins.

The people of Aegina now prepared for action; waiting for the day of a certain festival which the Athenians celebrated at Sunium, they laid a trap for the Athenian state vessel and captured her with a number of distinguished citizens on board, whom they took home and flung into prison. The Athenians countered by planning to invade Aegina, bolstering up their plans by securing the help of an Aeginetan traitor—a fellow who had been banished and now wished, by way of revenge, to do his compatriots down in any way he could. Concerted action was arranged: the traitor with his friends was to seize the town, and the Athenians were to force a simultaneous landing. The Athenians, however, failed to turn up—they had bargained with Corinth to borrow some ships to strengthen their own inadequate navy, but the ships were late in coming, so the Athenians, feeling themselves too weak to risk unaided an engagement with the Aeginetan fleet, did nothing whatever. The Aeginetan oligarchs were now, for the moment, on top of the world, and made short work of the traitor Nicodromus and his revolutionary party. Unhappily, however, in the process of executing them they committed an act of sacrilege, by cutting off the hands of one of the fugitives as he clung for sanctuary to the door-handle of Demeter's shrine. This, Herodotus tells us, led to their own defeat not long afterwards.

When the Corinthian ships did arrive in Athens, the Athenians launched their attack. The Aeginetans got the worst of it in the ensuing fight; and hurriedly sent for help to their old ally Argos; but the help was refused because, as the Argives maintained, some ships from Aegina had landed their crews on Argive territory in support of Cleomenes during a recent raid. Shortly afterwards another naval engagement took place, and four Athenian ships were captured. And so the struggle went on until the very eve of the coming of the Persians; indeed, it continued until the coming of Xerxes in 480 B.C., when at last the two states agreed to bury the hatchet in the face of a common danger. To Athens, at least, it had had its uses, for it turned the attention of the Athenians to the value of sea power and was amongst the chief causes which induced them to increase their navy until it was the most powerful in Greece. At the battle of Salamis the Aeginetans, fighting by the side of their old enemies, did magnificent service.

Apart from the vigorous, and I suppose natural, hatred between neighbours and rivals, it will be noticed that in this story there is not a single move made by either party, or by the other states called in to help them, in which there does not occur either treachery, or treaty-breaking, or defalcation of some kind—or sheer incompetence. Similar local struggles were going on continuously throughout the Greek world. They were the raw stuff of life, out of which Greek intellect and Greek imagination created forms of literature and art which were to endure for two thousand years.

CHAPTER 24

Greece in Peril

HERODOTUS' ACCOUNT OF THE BATTLE OF MARATHON IS COM-
paratively brief, even bald. This is artistically satisfying, as the
invasion of Greece by Darius was only a prelude to the second,
and far more dangerous, attempt of Xerxes. The repulse of this
second invasion, launched by an empire of which the enormous
resources in men and materials have been progressively impressed
upon the reader's imagination by the long preceding narrative of
the conquests of Cyrus, Cambyses and Darius, is the true centre
of Herodotus' book, to which everything else, in its inexhaustible
variety, is peripheral or of which it is illustrative. From now till
the end Herodotus concentrates his strength; there is a mounting
tension as the drama unfolds; there is a wealth of detail of both
human and historical interest, and underlying it all the sense,
characteristic of Herodotus, of an undefined and indefinable
power, which inspires the heroism of men and punishes their pride.

Darius, when the news of his defeat at Marathon reached him,
was more than ever determined to have his revenge upon Athens,
now answerable for a double insult to his greatness. He proceeded
at once to make his preparations, this time on a scale far bigger
than before. For three years, says Herodotus, the whole continent
was in uproar. Further efforts were required because a rebellion
had broken out in Egypt, so that the King had the prospect of
two campaigns on his hands. But Darius died (485 B.C.) before
his preparations were complete, and his throne passed to Xerxes,
who, though a weak man in comparison with his able father, yet
had every intention of carrying out his designs. The Egyptian revolt was crushed, and the way to Greece seemed to be open.

Having given us these facts, Herodotus proceeds to a splendid
piece of historical fiction, purporting to describe in a highly
dramatic form, the conflict of interests behind the Persian throne
on the eve of the great adventure. The drama takes the form of a
conference called by Xerxes, who, being still young and with his

judgement unformed, vacillates between hope and fear as Mardonius—out of mischief and adventure, and seeing himself the future governor of vanquished Greece—urges the campaign, and old Artabanus, the wise counsellor and uncle of the King, pleads for caution and delay, and a dream in the night finally tips the scale. It is a wonderful piece of writing, vivid and subtle and moving, shot through with compassion for the human lot, and—for the reader who knows what the end is to be—casting its shadow forward on the triumph and the tragedy to come. For four more years the marshalling of the Persian armies went on, until at last all was ready. 'The army,' Herodotus writes, in that allusive way which by a backward glance over history and legend he so skilfully employs to inflame the imagination of the reader, 'was indeed immense. It dwarfed the army Darius commanded on his Scythian campaign, and the great host of Scythians who burst into Media; it was incomparably larger than the armies which the stories tell us Agamemnon and Menelaus led to Troy. . . . All these armies together, with others like them, would not have equalled the army of Xerxes. Save for the great rivers there was not a stream his army drank from that was not drunk dry.'

Xerxes was determined that the disaster suffered by the fleet on Darius' first expedition should not be repeated; so he undertook the fantastic labour of digging a canal through the promontory of Athos, a work which occupied thousands of men for two years. The canal—traces of which can, I am told, still be detected to-day—was wide enough for two warships to be rowed abreast of one another. Herodotus, having described in detail the method of cutting it comments shrewdly that the whole undertaking was probably only a piece of ostentation on Xerxes' part, as it would have been perfectly feasible, if he wished to avoid the passage round that stormy headland, to drag his ships across the narrow neck on rollers. Another major feat of engineering was the construction of a bridge of boats across the Hellespont, which Herodotus describes in even greater, and—for anyone who cares for nautical matters—fascinating technical detail. These two operations being completed, and provision-dumps established at various points along the northern coast of the Aegean, the army began its march from its point of assembly in Cappadocia, across the river Halys, through Phrygia to Sardis, and thence to Abydos on the Hellespont.

The reader who has followed me thus far will not be surprised to hear that Herodotus in his account of this march is not content, as a modern historian might be, with the military aspect alone. The military and factual details he gives us are pretty clear, and, on the whole—except where numbers are concerned—reliable; but Herodotus is not writing scientific history (such a thing having not yet been heard of): his theme is the Life of Man, and his book, crammed though it is with *facts*, which he loved both for themselves and for their implications, is concerned to present the life of men, the human condition, with all the resources of the imagination. Hence the presence in this crucial portion of the *History* of much unhistorical matter, more, perhaps, than Herodotus has incorporated in his treatment of any other single enterprise; the purpose of it is obvious, and entirely satisfying: it is, quite simply, to increase the emotional impact of the climax of the story—the defeat of Xerxes. So, interspersed in the narrative of events we get asides, apocryphal tales, dramatic and half-imaginary interludes of varying tone, colour and content, but all contributing to the total imaginative effect. There is the story of Pythius, the Lydian, who—taking a sporting chance in the hope of gain— offered Xerxes as a free gift his enormous fortune of 2,000 talents of silver and 3,093,000 gold darics; The offer was refused, and Xerxes in return for it gave Pythius 7,000 darics to make up his fortune to the round four million. So far, so good. Unfortunately, however, Pythius presumed upon his success to ask as a favour that of his five sons one might be excused service and allowed to stay at home. The Great King was enraged: What? When he, in person, was marching to the war, could a mere subject hope to stay behind? The miserable man must be punished as he—and as his father—deserved. The punishment was not delayed: the young man was chopped in half, and between the halves of his body, one on each side of the road, the army and the King proceeded on their march to the Hellespont. It is a story amusing and satirical in tone, until its unexpected and horrible end. Then there is the account (absurd to us, but not to an ancient Greek who would see in it the certainty of coming punishment) of how Xerxes beat and branded the Hellespont for daring to destroy his bridge, and the beautifully told incident of Xerxes at Abydos, when, reviewing his forces and seeing with pride and delight the whole Hellespont hidden by ships and all the beaches and all the open ground filled with men, he suddenly burst into tears at the thought of the brevity of human life. Above all, there are the two wonderful dramatic interludes of the conversation of the King first with Artabanus, then with Demaratus the exiled Spartan. Both conversations are of course imaginary, but their imaginative truth is a quality which lies at the heart of Herodotus' work, and both are full of compassion for the fate of all men who have not the wit to 'think saving thoughts', but in the pride of power challenge the jealousy of God. The conversation with Demaratus introduces, moreover, the famous eulogy of Spartan courage—prophetic words which Xerxes turns off with a laugh. And in the middle of all this, brought in without any sense of incongruity or strain, Herodotus the industrious researcher, the indefatigable collector of facts, catalogues the contingents of the Persian forces, military and naval, with their respective arms, accoutrements and dress—a catalogue, incidentally, which, like the list of peoples who paid tribute to Darius, is a most valuable indication of the resources of the various states and countries concerned, both Greek and 'barbarian.'

Meanwhile Greece, torn as always by domestic quarrels, was doing what she could to meet the danger. A number of states, of which the most important were Thessaly, Boeotia (with the exception of Plataea and Thespiae), Malis, Locris and the Achaeans of Phthiotis, submitted to Xerxes' demand for surrender. Argos followed suit, when her request to Sparta to surrender the military command was refused. Even in Athens there were perturbation and divided counsels. The Delphic oracle had begun by urging the Athenians to make no resistance, and then, thinking again, had given them the ambiguous advice to trust only in their 'wooden wall.' Had it not been for the determination and foresight of Themistocles, the war might well have been lost; for it was Themistocles who, when a rich vein of silver had been found in the mines at Laurium, prevailed upon his countrymen to use the money for ship-building—for the immediate object of strengthening Athens in her war with Argina—instead of following the foolish but agreeable custom, common in Greek towns after an unexpected windfall, of sharing it out amongst individuals. Thus Athens became a sea-power, and without the Athenian naval strength the Persians, as Herodotus points out, could have landed at any point at any time on the Greek coast, and the Spartan sacrifice at Thermopylae would have been in vain. It was Themistocles, too, who persuaded his fellow-Athenians that the 'wooden wall' of the oracle was the Athenian fleet.

As soon as news came that Xerxes had reached Sardis, the confederate Greeks met for a conference. Their first decision was to patch up their own personal quarrels in the face of the common danger, their second to send envoys to Crete, Corcyra (then a powerful maritime state) and Sicily, to solicit aid. The result of the appeal to Argos I have already mentioned; the appeal to Sicily fared no better. The court of Gelo, lord of Syracuse, was the richest and most magnificent in the Greek-speaking world; the Syracusan fleet greatly outnumbered the Athenian, and Gelo's troops were a well-trained and powerful force. Gelo, however, met the request of the Athenian and Spartan envoys by declaring that he would be delighted to fight for the freedom of Greece, on one condition: that the supreme command of the Greek confederate forces should be his. Sparta, of course, indignantly refused—Agamemnon, declared the Spartan envoy, would turn in his grave at the mere suggestion of Lacedaemonians going to war under the orders of a Sicilian tyrant; whereupon Gelo, half relenting, said he would be satisfied with the command of the fleet only. But at this the Athenian envoy was as indignant as the Spartan had been. So 'My friend,' said Gelo, 'it looks as if you have the commanders, but will not have any men for them to command—go home again and tell Greece that the spring has gone out of the year.' Such squabbling for the privilege of command was characteristically Greek; nevertheless in Gelo's case it was probably only a bit of policy, for he had little faith in the ability of Greece to withstand the Persian onslaught and had already decided to temporise, and to see which way the cat would jump, perfectly prepared to submit to Xerxes if he should succeed in overrunning Greece. In Corcyra the envoys were gratified by a promise of immediate support; but the Corcyraeans subsequently changed their minds, and pretended that the gallant fleet of sixty sail which they had dispatched to the aid of their brothers-in-arms had been prevented by north-easterly winds from getting round Cape Malea in time to be of service. Crete refused assistance outright, on the advice of the Delphic oracle. Asiatic Greece, many of the islands, and the Greek towns along the northern coast of the Aegean were already under Persian control; the loyal states on the mainland were not numerous and most of them comparatively weak, so that Athens and Sparta with her Lacedaemonian dependents, were, to all intents and purposes, left to face the national peril alone—though the naval support of Aegina and Corinth was not to be despised.

At a conference of the allies at the Isthmus it was decided to try to check the Persian advance by holding the pass of Thermopylae. The men of Thessaly, who valued the survival of a free Greece, though not quite so much as their own personal safety, had asked the allies to defend the pass of Tempe, themselves promising assistance. A force was actually sent—10,000 men, all that could be spared; but the discovery that there were two other passes which the Persians were equally likely to use, and the realisation that there were insufficient troops to hold all three, determined them to withdraw. So Thessaly was abandoned. At the same time the fleet was stationed at Artemisium on the north coast of Euboea. Communications between fleet and army could thus be easily maintained. The Persian army, marching down through northern Greece, took up its position just short of Thermopylae at Trachis, and the Persian fleet sailed from its rendezvous at Therma (Thessalonica) to Cape Sepias in Magnesia ten miles north of Artemisium where as many ships as there was room for were beached while the remainder lay to their anchors off shore. It was the month of July, 480 B.C. and the struggle was about to begin.

The Persian fleet greatly outnumbered the Greek, but the balance was redressed by a heavy easterly gale which drove ashore and smashed up some four hundred enemy vessels. Even so—if Herodotus is telling the truth—the Greek naval commanders, with one notable exception, were in favour of retreat. The exception was Themistocles, and the story is that the people of Euboea, who naturally wanted the continued protection of the Greek navy gave him a large sum of money, thirty talents, eight of which he used to bribe his fellow officers to maintain their station. The rest he kept for himself. Meanwhile the Persian ships moved to Aphetae, where they would have better shelter, and sent a squadron to round Euboea and by entering the strait of Euripus to cut off the Greek retreat, should such be attempted. The squadron met more bad weather in the strait, and most of the vessels were wrecked. There was some scrappy fighting off Artemisium, in which the Persians probably had some slight advantage, but the

news of the wreck of the Persian squadron off the Hollows of
Euboea heartened the Greeks enough to prevent any further
prospect of their retreating. At least the Winds had fought on
their side—and Athenians, on their return home, built a shrine
to Boreas on the banks of the Ilissus.

Just about the same time the assault on Thermopylae began.
The story of this famous fight is known in broad outline by every-
one; but the details of it, as told by Herodotus, are not clear. The
Greek confederate army, under the command of Leonidas, who
had brought with him only 300 Spartan soldiers, consisted in all
of about 7,000 men. Why was the Spartan contingent so small?
The Spartans themselves alleged that it was only an advanced
guard, the main army being unable to move until the festival of
Apollo of Carneia was over—just as at Marathon ten years before.
It is more likely, however, that Sparta was really unwilling to
defend the pass at all and would have preferred to concentrate
her strength on the defence of the Isthmus, hoping to stop the
Persians from entering her own territory of Lacedaemon and
caring little about the fate of northern Greece. This would have
been consonant with Spartan mentality. What prevented this
mean policy was Sparta's need of the Athenian fleet. Nevertheless, however mean Sparta's general policy might be, her troops,
if they fought at all, could never fail to fight with selfless courage.

The Pass of Thermopylae, between mountains and the sea, was
—for the sea has now receded—only some fifty feet wide, and in
places no more than a single waggon-track. On the face of it, it
was an easy place to hold even against enormously superior numbers; but there was a rough track over the mountains, leading
down on to the road beyond the village of Alpeni at the eastern
end of the pass. The track was guarded by the Phocian contingent,
posted in the hills, but its existence was betrayed to the Persians
by a Malian Greek, who offered to act as guide. It was this act of
treachery that decided the battle. Only on the third day of the
fighting did the Persians use the opportunity offered them; hitherto all their efforts to force the pass had been frustrated by Leonidas
and his men. But then, early in the evening, the Immortals, flower
of the Persian army, under their commander Hydarnes, were
ordered round. It was dark when they reached the Phocian position, and the Phocians, hearing the rustle of marching feet in the
fallen leaves of the oak woods, fled to the heights, and Hydarnes

passed on. Before he had reached the road at the bottom of the track, deserters had informed Leonidas of the new peril; precisely what his orders then were, we do not know, nor does Herodotus; but it is clear that only the Spartan contingent supported by the Thebans and Thespians remained in the pass, and that the remainder of the confederate army retired southward. Did they disperse to save their skins? Or did Leonidas order them off to spare their lives, or because (as Herodotus guesses) he knew they had no heart for the fight? Anyway, they went, and by their going increased the legendary glory of the Spartans and the Thespians who remained. As for the Theban contingent, we can only guess. Herodotus repeats the story that they were kept by Leonidas as hostages, because he distrusted their loyalty, but that may be only a piece of characteristic Greek malice invented later after Thebes had surrendered to Persia. The story adds that the Theban contingent gave themselves up as soon as Hydarnes and his Immortals appeared in their rear. In any case it was only Leonidas and his Three Hundred, supported by the devoted band from Thespiae, who fought to the last and were finally overwhelmed.

A very interesting new light has been thrown by a recent discovery upon Athenian strategy at this time, and especially upon the quality of Themistocles as a war leader. This is the finding in the summer of 1960 by Professor Jameson of Pennsylvania university of a copy, engraved on stone perhaps 150 years after the event, of a resolution passed by the Athenian Council and Assembly, on the recommendation of Themistocles, two months before the battle of Thermopylae. The text of the resolution, though much damaged, was deciphered by Professor Jameson with the help of Professor Meritt of Princeton, and is a most important corrective to certain parts of Herodotus' narrative. It makes it quite clear that, in Athenian eyes at any rate, the action at Thermopylae was a delaying action only; Themistocles was well aware that the Persians could not possibly be stopped on land, and had made careful plans, months in advance, for the swift and orderly evacuation of Athens as soon as it should be necessary, and for the organisation of naval defence. Herodotus tends to give the impression that the evacuation, when it took place, was the result of panic after the defeat at Thermopylae, and also that the whole Athenian fleet had been sent to Artemisium. The new document, however, shows that only half the fleet was engaged at Artemisium, while

the other half remained at Salamis, and that Themistocles had organised two distinct lines of naval defence, almost certainly intending to fight the decisive action—as in fact he did—at Salamis.
At the same time the resolution made careful and elaborate arrangements for the evacuation of the City, leaving behind only
the priestesses and temple stewards. The City itself was entrusted
to its patron, the goddess Athena.

If the Spartans accepted Themistocles' strategy, then all the
more credit is due to Leonidas and his Three Hundred and to the
Thespians who refused to abandon them; but it is hard to believe
that Spartan policy was so accommodating, especially in view of
their subsequent unwillingness to engage the Persian fleet at Salamis and their selfish and pigheaded determination to defend the
Isthmus and let all northern Greece go. That they were thwarted
in this was again due to Themistocles.

Athens was duly evacuated—and burnt. The men of military
age together with the old men and all moveable property crossed
to Salamis; the women and children were invited to take refuge
at Troezen in the Peloponnese, where they were received with
every kindness, the children (according to Plutarch) being allowed
to take produce at will from private gardens, and being given a
free education.

The Greek fleet, reinforced by small contingents from the islands which had not submitted to Persia, amounted in all to 378
ships, more than half of them Athenian. It was commanded—
oddly, to our way of thinking; but few Greek states would have
been willing to serve under Athenian leadership—by Eurybiades
the Spartan. At a conference of officers after the fall of the Acropolis the resolution was passed to withdraw the fleet southward
and engage the Persians off the Isthmus, thus leaving Aegina,
Salamis and Megara to their fate. Themistocles was determined to
thwart the decision, and succeeded in persuading Eurybiades that
a battle in the open water off the Isthmus would favour the nu-
merically superior Persian fleet, and that their own hope of success
depended upon engaging the enemy in the narrow strait between
Salamis and the mainland. Positions were taken up, but when it
was seen that the Persian fleet was blocking the whole eastern entrance of the strait—the two channels on either side of the islet of
Psyttaleia—the Peloponnesian commanders once again brought
pressure to bear upon Eurybiades to withdraw—for the western

entrance to the bay of Eleusis, on the other side of the island, was still open. Without hesitation Themistocles decided upon a bold stroke: he sent a slave to the Persian commander with a message from himself, purporting to be a friend of Xerxes, that the Greeks intended to sail away through the western entrance under cover of darkness, and that they must at all costs be prevented from doing so. The Greek commanders, he added, were at loggerheads, and a battle in the straits would certainly result in a Persian victory. The innocent Persian took this communication at its face value—which is perhaps less foolish than it sounds; for, Greeks being Greeks, Themistocles *might* have been a traitor, like Demaratus, or Hippias, or a hundred others. But, happily for Athens in this crisis of her history, he was not. The ruse was successful: two hundred Egyptian galleys (the best in the fleet, after the Phoenician) were hurriedly sent round the island and stationed themselves across the channel leading from the bay of Eleusis to the open sea. The Greek fleet was boxed up in the narrow waters without any chance of escape—precisely what Themistocles desired.

I give the bare outline of these famous events, making no attempt to follow the noble sweep of Herodotus' narrative, packed with dramatic incident and personal anecdote—the impassioned disputes at the commanders' conference, the bringing by Aristides, the returned exile and Themistocles' bitter rival, of the great news that the Egyptian squadron had blocked the straits, the battle itself and the exploits of Artemisia the Carian Queen, and the anguish of Xerxes watching from his throne on the slopes of Mt. Aegaleos. The fight began at dawn and lasted all day, a furious confused mêlée in the narrow waters. A large part of the Persian fleet was either destroyed or crippled.

> Divine Salamis, you will bring death to women's sons
> When the corn is scattered, or the harvest gathered in.

Thus had the Delphic oracle spoken. The month was September, and the prophecy was fulfilled.

Salamis was a very serious blow to Persian sea power; but the Persian army remained intact, and the danger to Greece was by no means over. Xerxes himself and the remains of the fleet returned to Asia, and Mardonius was left in Greece in command of the army, wintering in Thessaly in preparation for a fresh attempt the following spring. Themistocles urged the obviously sound policy of following up the victory by pursuing the Persian ships across the Aegean, thus perhaps completing their destruction and almost certainly inducing the Asiatic Greeks to revolt. But once again his advice was turned down: the Peloponnesians refused to sail while there was still the threat of a Persian advance through the Isthmus. Herodotus says that Themistocles, who always had an eye for the main chance, when his proposal was rejected, sent another secret message to Xerxes to the effect that he really was, in spite of appearances, a true friend to Persia in that it was he who had prevented the Greek fleet from following up its advantage by sailing in pursuit of the Persians. Thus he hoped, should he ever get into trouble with his fellow-countrymen at home (as indeed he did), he would be sure of a friendly welcome on the other side of the Aegean. After all, there is nothing like providing for every contingency, well in advance. I do not know if this story is true; but there is no reason why it should not be. The Greeks themselves hardly blamed this sort of conduct. One thinks of Aristides, when the votes of ostracism were being cast: an illiterate peasant asked Aristides whom he did not know by sight to write for him the name of his choice on the potsherd. 'Which name?' said Aristides, 'Aristides,' said the peasant. Aristides duly wrote it, and then asked the peasant why he wished him banished. 'Because,' the man replied, 'I'm sick of hearing him called "The Just." '

One more small anecdote I am tempted to add as a tailpiece to this splendid victory for Greek arms. After the battle the commanders met in order to decide the important question of which of them should receive the Prize of Valour. Votes were cast for first and second place, and, says Herodotus—I think without a smile—'as they all thought they had fought more bravely than anyone else, every one of them put his own name at the top, though the majority agreed in putting Themistocles second. Consequently nobody got more than one vote for first place, while Themistocles easily headed the poll for the second. Mutual jealousy thus prevented a decision, and the various commanders sailed home without making an award.'

In the spring of 479 B.C. Mardonius had been joined in Thessaly by the troops which had protected Xerxes on his retreat to the Hellespont. The Persian navy, still in spite of its losses a strong force, was concentrated at Samos. The Greeks were as sharply divided, in the pursuit of their separate interests, as they had been

before Salamis the previous year. It was as difficult as ever to in-
duce the Lacedaemonians to leave the defence of their own country and fight in northern Greece; an attempt was made by the
islanders of Chios to persuade the Spartan admiral Leotychides to
bring over the fleet and to work for the liberation of Ionia, but
the attempt failed, partly because no Spartan ever much liked distant campaigns, and partly, perhaps, because the Athenians had
changed their minds since the previous autumn and now feared
that if the Persian fleet were put entirely out of action, and the
Lacedaemonians continued to guard the Isthmus, southern Greece
would be safe from invasion and would, in consequence, refuse to
give any further help in the defence of the north. Athens would
once again be open to Mardonius. Mardonius took advantage of
this state of things to offer the Athenians generous peace terms: in
return for the alliance of Athens as an equal and independent power
he offered reparations for all the damage she had received together
with Persian help in acquiring new territory. Had the Athenians
accepted this offer, which only a very gallant people, in their
position, could have refused, Sparta and southern Greece would
have been inevitably overwhelmed. The Spartans, well aware of
this, hastily but unhappily themselves offered to help Athens on
to her feet again, and the Athenians, to their eternal honour, instructed the Persian envoy to tell Mardonius that 'never, so long
as the sun moves in his course, would they come to terms with
Xerxes.' The Spartans promised military assistance to Athens and
the north; they then by working furiously completed their own
defensive wall across the Isthmus—and forgot their promise. Meanwhile Mardonuis was on the march southward from Thessaly. Once
again he occupied Attica, but did no material damage as he still
hoped to detach the Athenians from the Grecian alliance. But again
he failed: the Athenian Council—sitting in Salamis, as Athens had
been once more evacuated—rejected his offer to leave the city un-
harmed, though the temptation to accept must have been almost
irresistible. Then in conjunction with Megara and Plataea the
Athenians sent their representatives to Sparta with their final word:
this was that, unless the Spartans sent a force to support their resistance to Mardonius at once, they would have no choice but to
come to terms with Persia. For ten days the Spartans gave no answer; and then at last, when a man from Tegea pointed out that
an alliance between the Athenian and Persian fleets would render

the fortifications of the Isthmus absolutely useless, as landings could be made at any point on the coast the enemy cared to choose, they changed their minds, rapidly mobilised and sent an army northward. It must be admitted that once the Spartans had been shaken out of their selfish (and idiotic) isolationism, the measures they took were not half-measures; the force they sent was a big one, consisting in all, with their allies in the Peloponnese, of something like 60,000 men, and bringing the total Greek allied strength to not much short of 100,000. The Spartan King Pausanias was in supreme command.

The battle of Plataea, fought in the August of 479 B.C., was a Spartan victory just as Salamis had been an Athenian victory. It was the valour and discipline of the Spartan hoplites, and the determination and tactical skill of Pausanias which decided the issue. Characteristic Greek jealousy led the Athenians afterwards to magnify their own contribution, which was in fact negligible, to the victory, and to spread derogatory tales about the generalship of Pausanias and the bearing of the Spartan infantry. The account which Herodotus gives, full, as always, of life and colour and movement, nevertheless tends to follow the false Athenian legend, and is not to be trusted in detail. Presumably he took his facts from Athenian sources, and for once he allows his pro-Athenian bias to twist his story. But of the significance of the battle, which was the crown of the long campaign, there is, in his brilliant pages, no doubt at all. It was the victory of—to use a modern but not inappropriate phrase—the free world over the threat of enslavement by the East, of men who held their destiny in their own hands over the nameless millions who bowed the knee to a tyrannical master, of civilisation, as the Greeks understood it, over barbarism. There are no final decisions in history, which is a story without beginning or end; but Marathon, Salamis and Plataea can be numbered amongst the decisive battles of the world, if only because they gave to the subsequent course of western civilisation a direction which in spite of many hesitancies and deviations we are still trying to follow. In a number of ways, as perhaps what I have written has already indicated, the finest and most characteristic period of Greek civilisation was the century, or century and a half, before the Persian wars, but it was only when they were over and the threat of absorption into the Eastern empire had passed that the elements of Greek civilisation became, as it were, crystallised—that Greece became fully articulate, and able, in consequence, to transmit her experience to posterity. The Persian wars were not only a crisis in Greek affairs; they were also an inspiration, and a justification of Greek ideals. They proved to the Greeks what a handful of free men, fighting for what they loved, could achieve against a horde of invaders advancing to battle 'under the lash'; they inspired much of their subsequent art, and some of their literature; above all, they gave to Athens the self-confidence which enabled her in the course of the next fifty years to develop, for better or worse, that brilliant, though fugitive civilisation which to many scholars and historians has appeared—not altogether rightly, I think—as the quintessence of the Greek spirit.

If Darius or Xerxes had succeeded in overrunning Greece, the subsequent history of the West would have been very different. To ask if it would have been worse or better is an idle question; for in the long struggle of man it is not results which matter, or at any rate not primarily: it is the struggle itself which is significant. The outcome even of the struggle between East and West at the present time, considered *sub specie aeternitatis*, I presume is indifferent; what is not indifferent at all, but of vital import, is the quality of spirit displayed by the antagonists. It is the quality of spirit displayed by men and nations in the crisis of their lives—and, could we know it, in the humdrum living of those lives from day to day—that the most inward truth of history consists. A fact —or an act—is only as it were the end of an argument or the denoument in the last scene of a play, and of little interest out of its context. That is why there is an art as well as a science of history, and why the great historians have possessed the gift of imagination in the true—and Coleridgean—sense of that much abused word. They have been able to 'see into the life of things'. In reading Herodotus' narrative of the Persian wars we have no sense of listening only to a chronicle of

> old, unhappy, far-off things
> And battles long ago;

we are in the midst of the passions of the men who fought them—and of the men, too, who refused to fight them, and temporised, or shilly-shallied, pursued their private advantage, or sat on the fence, or merely hoped for the best. All the life of Greece is there: all the complex of motives and emotions which go to make up the character of a people. What those who fought were fighting for, is clear enough: they called it liberty, and the word (*eleutheria*) is a good one on Greek lips, as it had not yet lost its original brightness. To the Greeks, though they believed so profoundly in Fate, the word had nevertheless no ambiguity; what it meant to them, much of this book has been intended to suggest, but by way of further comment here are two small anecdotes from Herodotus' pages. When Xerxes after his defeat at Salamis took ship for Asia, a northerly gale struck his fleet and his own vessel, the deck of which was packed tight with Persian grandees, his personal attendants, was in danger. In alarm, he asked the master what the chances were of coming through alive, and 'None whatever,' the master replied, 'so long as we have this crowd on deck'. Thereupon Xerxes turned to his courtiers and said: 'This, gentlemen, is your opportunity to serve your King.' The courtiers bowed low, and jumped overboard, and the ship, lightened of her load, came safely into harbour. Xerxes landed, and then sent for the ship's master. The man came, and the King gave him a gold chain for saving his life; then, to punish him for causing the death of so many Persian noblemen, he cut off his head. I do not know if this story is more funny than horrible, or more horrible than funny; but—and this is my reason for quoting it—it is a tale of Persia, not a tale of Greece. To the Greeks men were men (if they were not foreigners or slaves) to be loved if they were friends and hated—and if possible butchered—if they were enemies, but both upon fair and equal terms; they were not cattle to be herded and forced to obey. Herodotus, as he tells this story, is not particularly sorry either for the Persian noblemen or for the ship's captain. On the contrary, he thinks the whole thing rather silly, and remarks that the obvious course for Xerxes to have taken was to send the Persians below and throw overboard an equivalent number of rowers, who were not Persians at all, but mere Phoenician galley-slaves.

The second anecdote concerns two Spartans, Sperchias and Bulis. Darius had sent envoys to Sparta to demand submission before his invasion of Greece and the Spartans, contrary to diplomatic practice, had pushed the envoys into a well and drowned them. Dire consequences had followed. Talthybius, Agamemnon's herald, now raised to the eminence of a Hero and honoured with a shrine, was angry. Sacrifices offered at his shrine went wrong, one after another. Something had to be done. 'Who,' said the Spartans, 'is willing to die for his country?' Sperchias and Bulis without hesitation stepped forward and undertook to travel to Susa, present themselves to Xerxes, and offer their lives in exchange for the murdered envoys. On the way to Susa they met and dined with Hydarnes (later to command the troops who took the mountain track at Thermopylae) and Hydarnes asked them why they had not the sense to serve the King, when by doing so they might easily become as rich and powerful as himself. 'You understand,' came the answer, 'well enough what slavery is, but freedom you have never experienced, so you do not know if it tastes sweet or bitter. If you ever did experience it, you would advise us to fight for it not with spears only, but with axes too.'

Perhaps I have quoted enough; but let me add, if only for the pleasure of it, the end of this tale. When these two brave men came into the presence of the King and were ordered by his officers to prostrate themselves in the Persian manner, they refused. They would not do it, they said, even if their heads were pushed to the ground by force, as it was not the custom in Sparta to worship a mere man like themselves, and it was not for that purpose they had come to Persia. What the purpose was, they then in frank and simple words declared—and Xerxes who, like his father Darius, could be generous, freely pardoned them and sent them home.

PART FOUR

Greek Literature

CHAPTER 25

Literature: Epic

My OBJECT IN THIS CHAPTER IS (LIKE HERODOTUS' OWN) TWOFOLD: first, to try to show how the Greek temperament resolved in art the fierce tensions which rendered Greek life so disorderly and violent; and, secondly, to suggest where in Greek literature the 'ordinary reader' (that convenient but possibly meaningless abstraction) though not knowing Greek, may expect to find in translations the pleasure, which, as Coleridge reminded us, it is the primary object of poetry in particular, and of imaginative literature in general, to give. Greek is a difficult language, and Greek literature, like any other literature, is of varied quality, but the best of it in both prose and verse has not been surpassed for depth, liveliness and sanity by the work of any single subsequent writer except Shakespeare.

Traduttore, traditore, as some Italian or other once said, not without a measure of truth; and I suppose one cannot deny that style, that mysterious essence which can be felt but not explained, is inevitably betrayed—or at least changed—by translation, simply because it lives within the actual words a writer uses, with their overtones and undertones, their associations and intimate resonances, and the emotive power even of their sounds and shapes, not to mention their own peculiar rhythm and music. Nevertheless there are degrees of betrayal in the art of translation—in Pope's *Homer,* for instance, it was capital and complete; but then Pope knew little Greek, and the verse he so exquisitely perfected moved more happily amongst bag-wigs and buckled shoes,

'and the nice conduct of a clouded cane'

than on the unharvested sea or in company with the half-barbaric innocence of the old heroes and their gods.

All this must be granted, but it remains true that Greek literature probably survives the treachery of a reasonably sensitive translator better than most—or, to put it in other words, there are more qualities in the Greek than in most literatures which cannot be betrayed, or cannot be disguised by an unfamiliar dress. To risk an analogy, the face which photographs most satisfactorily is the face with a good bony structure, not the face which depends entirely for its charm (or its repulsiveness) upon the play of life behind the eyes and lips. Greek literature, both verse and prose, has a good bony structure, which survives translation much as the face survives the photograph—though in each case the play of life is largely lost.

There are certain broad differences between Greek and modern literature. First: Greek literature of the classical and pre-classical period is graphic rather than analytical, and it deals with fact, or what is believed to be fact, and never with fiction. It is not concerned with hidden motives in human action, as is nearly all modern psychology and much modern fiction. The reason for this is that the Greeks frankly recognised and accepted their instincts and did not feel them to be at war with a pattern of behaviour imposed by social conventions on the one hand and by a transcendental religion on the other. One of the prime concerns of modern literature is to reveal what a man 'really' is underneath his façade of normality and conventional behaviour; the Greeks on the contrary knew perfectly well what they 'really' were without the aid of analytical psychology, and never felt the need to assume a facade at all. When they wanted a mystery, they found it not in the involutions of human character, with its intricate complex of conditionings and inhibitions, but in the relationship between man and Fate, or Destiny, or God—which is perhaps unintelligible anyhow. They saw man in time with all his splendour and pathos; and they saw him in eternity, where he cut on the whole a rather poor figure.

Secondly, Greek literature is rigidly traditional. It obeys the rules. Once the appropriate form was discovered, it was preserved and followed. This may suggest a certain stiffness and lack of variety, but nothing could be further from the truth. All art is, up to a point, based upon the acceptance of a convention—I say up to a point, because some of us nowadays are in danger of forgetting that important fact, so that one of the most serious restrictions imposed (or self-imposed) upon contemporary writers and artists is the terror of being thought imitative. The terror, of course, comes from a misconception of the meaning of originality. Nothing is more liberating to the individual genius of an artist than the necessity of working within an accepted convention—

'as those walk easiest who have learned to dance';

the convention, moreover, facilitates communication, as the reader, or spectator, has the comfort of believing that he knows the country he is about to explore, even though he subsequently makes the exciting and delightful discovery that none of the features in it are quite what he expected.

Thirdly (and this is connected with the preceding), the *purpose* of Greek literature was quite different from the purpose of our own today. A writer today writes (like Dr Johnson) to make a living, and he hopes to make it by addressing himself to a selected audience—to the intellectual elite, to the masses, to the ordinary man tired by his day's work, as the case may be. In every case his primary object is to entertain, and his living depends upon his success. Today, if all imaginative literature were suddenly withdrawn, our lives might be duller, but the pattern and functioning of society would remain unchanged. This would not have been so in Greece: in Greece literature—the Homeric poems, the ceremonial lyrics, above all the drama—was an integral part of the social pattern. It was presented on public occasions, to a homogeneous audience, and its object was not primarily entertainment at all, however much (and that was a lot) it happened to provide by the way; its object was either instruction, as in the public recitations of Homer, or worship, as in the performance of the ceremonial odes, or both together, as in the drama. Even the boisterous comedies of Aristophanes and his rivals were offered as an act or worship to Dionysus, a statue of whom was planted in the orchestra during the performance, to make sure that he would hear the jokes. Greek literature, then, even the most ribald, was, until the decline of the City State, a deeply serious thing, and a vital element in public life. It was a matter of course, a well as a matter of importance. The fact that it was so helped to maintain its quality, for the Greeks were a lively and intelligent people who did not readily tolerate slip-slop; it also helps to explain its traditionalism, which, in its turn, discouraged mere idiosyncrasy and the temptation for a new writer to draw attention to himself by odd tricks. It is not without relevance to observe, as I personally believe, that the most original poet writing today, and the poet with the most individual voice, is Mr Robert Frost, whose characteristic verse-form is the unrhymed pentameter, which has been in common use for four hundred years.

Fourth—and last: the arts in Greece were less specialised, or departmentalised, than they are nowadays. In the modern world poetry, music and ballet are autonomous arts; in Greece this was not so, or not quite so: lyric poetry in Greece was made to be sung, not spoken or read; singing and dancing were integral parts of the drama, with tragedy and comedy, as they were of the ceremonial odes; the epic lays of Homer were almost certainly chanted, to some sort of musical accompaniment—Homer calls a poet *aoidos* (singer), and the Greeks usually meant what they said, unlike us who, when we say that a poet sings, are either lying or talking in metaphor. Moreover the tone and spirit of poetry was carried over into much of Greek prose literature: Herodotus' language (like his mind) was steeped in poetry, and it might be said without much exaggeration that the soul of Plato's philosophical writing—in spite of the fact that Plato banished the poets from his ideal republic—is the poetic imagination. This fusion and interdependence of the arts renders inevitable the loss, to us, of the full impact of Greek poetry, because we cannot hear the tunes or see the dancing which inseparably belonged to it. The miracle is that so much remains.

When Herodotus died (if we take the date of his death as 425 B.C.) most of the greatest Greek imaginative literature had already been written, though Sophocles and Euripides still had some of their best work to do. Aristophanes had only just begun to write for the stage; the historian Thucydides was a boy in his 'teens, and Plato was a baby. These three were indeed to prove themselves giants, but their work was done when the glory was already beginning to depart from the Grecian world. Perhaps Herodotus was fortunate in that he never saw the first falling of the shadow.

Literary criticism is always a late growth in the development of a civilisation: there was none in Greece before Aristotle, and Plato, speaking of the poets, confines himself chiefly to complaining that they told lies about the gods. References in the older Greek writers to the poets almost always take the form of quoting some aphorism, or scrap of wisdom, to illustrate a point or drive home an argument. 'As Pindar says,' Herodotus writes, 'custom is all.' Well—no doubt it is; but that is not the kind of wisdom which you or I would look for, and perhaps find, in a great poet. Even Aristotle, in his brilliant but difficult essay the *Poetics*, though he tells us that poetry is the most philosophic of the arts and has much to say about the nature and construction of the tragic drama, never even hints that high poetry is *beautiful*. I suppose that this is not as odd as it sounds, and that the explanation of the apparent reticence of the Greeks about those aspects of poetry which to us are the most important—which are, indeed, the very life of poetry —is that they took them for granted. They felt no need to discuss them, or to draw each other's attention to them, because they were, in their eyes, so obvious. One does not ask a man to write an 'appreciation' of the sunlight—unless he lives for half the year in a cave.

We ourselves are in a different case: to us, poetry and the other arts are not natural and necessary as they were to the Greeks; they are something extraneous to the common run of things—an embellishment, sometimes a comfort, not seldom an escape, though an escape, it may be, into a world of experience we like to call more 'real' than the common one. To vast numbers in a modern state the arts are nothing; to the Greeks, educated or uneducated, clever or stupid, imaginative or dull, the arts—poetry, sculpture, painting, architecture, drama, not to mention the beautiful craftsmanship of things in daily use—were, quite simply, *there*. There was no escaping the sight of them. They were the public possessions of all—of the City herself, and so familiar that they did not seem to call for all the talk and all the effort of interpretation bestowed upon the arts by the critics (and by ourselves) today.

Herodotus, then, might have disappointed us if we had been able to ask him why he thought Homer the greatest of the poets. '*Why?*' he might have answered, with his customary amused acceptance of human stupidity. 'Because, surely, he has a tale to tell of men and gods, of the delight of battle and of its tragic futility, of the brief sunshine and the endless dark. Who would not listen to such a tale well told?' But what the Greeks took for granted in their poetry, we do not, so it will be worth while here to try to find some reasons why Homer's poetry is still, for us, noble and moving and untarnished by the passage of time.

I do not wish to burden the reader with the arguments of

scholars about the origin and authorship of the Homeric poems. For myself, I am content to believe, from the beautiful coherence of the *Iliad* and the *Odyssey*, that each was the work of one man, and probably of the same man. Not that Homer did not draw his material from previous lays: he most certainly did. There must have been an immense body of poetic legend—of oral poetry, floating in the Ionian air and treasured on the lips of nameless *rhapsodes*, or weavers of song, constantly added to, or altered by the inspiration of the singer, who, at the festal board, would begin and end his tale as the spirit moved him, working into the texture of it phrases, lines, whole passages made familiar by use, and inventing where he pleased. That was the ancient storehouse from which Homer drew; the material in it was common to all singers, but Homer made it his own. He imposed upon what he took a form of great perfection; each of his two long poems is a consistent and finely constructed story—the *Iliad* tragic, with touches of laughter, the *Odyssey* romantic, not without a colouring of pain (being concerned with the life of men), and with a happy ending. The excellence of the poems simply as stories is proved by the success of the various prose translations of them which have appeared recently. They can be read with delight simply as tales. One does not fancy that, say, a German prose version of *Paradise Lost* would be an entertaining work, or even a French prose version of *Troilus and Criseyde*, or the *Faerie Queene;* but a prose version of the *Iliad* or the *Odyssey* is very entertaining indeed. And that suggests the first, and most obvious, quality of Homer: he could tell a story. To illustrate this properly would take more space that I can spare, but here are two examples (both a little shortened). The first is a passage from the *Iliad*, describing how Hector, champion fighter of the Trojans, bids goodbye to his wife and child before he takes the field for the battle which is to prove his last:

"So Hector of the glittering helmet went on his way and quickly came to his well-built house. But white-armed Andromache was not there, for she had gone with her child and a waiting-woman up on to the city battlements, where she stood weeping in distress. Not finding his good wife within doors, Hector went to the threshold and questioned the servants. 'Tell me,' he said, 'the truth; where has white-armed Andromache gone? To the house of one of my sisters, or of my brothers' wives? To Athene's temple, where the other women of Troy are praying favour of that dread goddess?'

" 'Hector,' answered one of the busy maids, 'since you bid us tell you truly, she has gone to the Great Tower of Troy, for she heard that our Trojans were hard pressed by the might of the Greeks; so she ran thither, like a woman distraught and a nurse followed with her child.'

"Hector hastened from the house, back along the well-layed streets by the way he had come, and when he reached the Scaean Gate, through which he meant to pass to the plain beyond, Andromache herself, his richly-dowered wife, came running to meet him. With her was the nurse, the child in her arms—a baby, Hector's own beloved, beautiful as a star, whom Hector called Scamandrius, but the other Trojans Astyanax, Lord of the City, in honour of his father, Troy's sole protector.

"Hector smiled and looked at his son without a word; but Andromache came to his side, weeping, and took his hand, and said: 'Good my lord, your valour will be your death; you have no pity for your infant son or for me, your unhappy wife who soon will be your widow. Hector, to me you are father and mother now, and brother too, as well as the husband I love. Pity me then; stay here on the battlements, and do not make your wife a widow and your son an orphan.'

" 'I too,' answered great Hector of the glittering helmet, 'have all these things at my heart; but I should be shamed before the Trojans and before the women in their trailing robes, if I skulked like a coward and refused to fight. Not such is the bidding of my soul; for I have learned to be a good fighter, always in the van of battle, winning honour for my father and myself. Truly I know the day will come when holy Ilium will perish, and Priam too and the people of Priam of the good ashen spear; yet I grieve not so much for the Trojans, nor for Hecuba herself, nor for Priam the King, nor for my brothers so many and so brave who then will be laid in the dust by their enemies, as for the thought of you, led captive and in tears by some bronze-clad Greek, your days of freedom gone. Far away in Argos would you be, working at the loom for a stranger or carrying water from the well, sorely oppressed by harsh necessity. 'Look', they will say when they see you weeping, 'that is the wife of Hector, the greatest fighter of the horse-taming Trojans when they fought in defence of Troy.'

That is what they will say, and a new pang of grief will pierce you, for the loss of the husband who alone could keep at bay the day of slavery. But may the heaped earth cover me before ever I hear your cries as you are dragged away.'

"Then glorious Hector held out his arms for the child, but the child shrank back into the bosom of the nurse crying out in sudden fear at his father's aspect, the bronze of the helmet and its horse-hair plume dreadfully nodding; both father and mother laughed to see him, and Hector took off the helmet and laid it, all shining, on the ground, and kissed his dear son, dandling him in his arms. Then praying to Zeus and the other gods, 'O Zeus,' he cried, 'grant that this boy of mine may grow to be famous amongst the Trojans, even as I am, and as strong, lording it over Troy. May they say when he comes from the field, "This man is much better than his father was." Grant, Zeus, that he may kill his enemy and bring away the bloody spoils, and make his mother glad.'

"He put the child in its mother's arms, and she took it to her fragrant breast, laughing through her tears. Hector was moved at the sight, and touching her gently with his hand, 'Dear,' he said, 'do not grieve too much. No one will send me down to Hades before my time; yet Destiny is not to be escaped by any mortal man, cowardly or brave. Go home now, and do what you have to do, weaving or spinning, and tell the servants to mind their tasks. War is the business of men; all Trojan men must fight, myself especially.'

"As he spoke Hector picked up his helmet with its horsehair plume, and his dear wife set out for home, weeping and often turning for one last look. Soon she was in the well-built house of Hector the killer of men, and finding many of the servants there she roused them to lament. They mourned for Hector, though he was still alive, for they did not believe he would come home again."

Narrative power of that order is rare in literature; it is especially rare in a tale of which the end is known, for then the teller cannot rely for his effects upon the devices of suspense or surprise, but only on his ability fully to realise in imagination his scenes and characters, and to re-create the familiar by the vision which alone can see it as a new thing. Of the poetic power, which is lost in a prose translation, it is more difficult to speak. It is lost, too, in all the extent verse translations with which I am familiar, because no

English poet has ever been master of a style comparable to
Homer's. Many, indeed, have been master of a style much richer
and more subtle, capable of a music far beyond Homer's reach;
but the inimitable essence of Homer's style has nothing to do with
richness or subtlety or the intricate harmonies we have come to
delight in from our knowledge of the long and splendid development of English verse; it consists rather in a kind of primal innocence of speech and rhythm, as pure as spring-water and as
translucent. Only early poetry can speak with Homer's voice—
poetry written (or sung) before men felt the 'burden of the
mystery' and sought to lighten it. In Homer the mystery is there,
but it is borne easily, with courage and resignation: it is the inescapable mystery of the two faces of human life, the glory and
the grief. Of all English poets Chaucer, the earliest, perhaps comes
nearest, in certain passages, to the pure Homeric music, the apparently effortless Homeric song:

> 'What is this world? What asken men to have?
> Now with his love, now in the colde grave,
> Allone, withouten any compaignye. . . .'

A modern reader, running through the passage which I have
translated from the *Iliad*, might well miss the epithets, or feel them
as merely conventional. In fact they *were* conventional, part of the
stock-in-trade of the old rhapsodes, together with whole lines and
even paragraphs which they kept ready in mind to fill a gap or
describe some recurrent act—like eating a dinner. None the less
these repeated epithets suggest something in Homer's poetry,
which is essential to it and cannot be recovered today: I mean
the constant awareness it shows of the qualities in things which
use has caused a later age to take for granted. This awareness is
evident in nearly all Greek poetry, but especially in Homer. The
warrior-prince Hector is 'glorious'—as all men indeed are, if they
are brave and noble-hearted; he has a 'glittering helmet'—a thing
in itself splendid to look at and a cunning work of the craftsman's
hands. Moreover the glittering lights in the bronze match the
'glory'—the Greek word is of the same root as the word for
'bright' or 'shining'—in the wearer. Hector's house is 'well-built'
—'How obvious!' the modern reader might say, not expecting
a prince to live in a hovel. But to Homer it was not obvious at all:
it was natural, to be sure, and familiar, that a house should be

built well, but it was none the less delightful, none the less an agreeable reminder of the skills of men. And so one might go on down the list, to the 'white arms' of Andromache and her 'fragrant' breast, the 'busy' servants, and Hector, again, 'the killer of men'. The epithets are true, not merely decorative; they mean what they say, and the poet assumes that the hearer will share his delighted recognition of the qualities they reveal. It is the same with the beautiful 'conventional' epithets which Homer applies to natural phenomena, to sea, earth and sky: 'the unharvested' sea, the 'wine-dark' sea, the 'life-giving' earth, the 'rose-fingered' dawn; all of them are, so to speak, an invitation to the modern reader to look again at familiar things which he fancied had grown stale. In Homer nothing is stale; there is no satiety, no weariness, no dulling of the senses, no sickness of the spirit. Light lies upon the world, wonderful as on the day of its creation; yet the *Iliad* is a tragic poem and bears its full burden of human sorrow. Therein lies its greatness. Homer does not blame the folly of men; he does not try to *argue them different* any more than Herodotus does. He sees what they are in all their weakness and all their splendour, and would not have them otherwise. It is right that they should be thus, as well as inevitable, and he knows that because they are made in that mould they are therefore born to grief.

Is the *Iliad* the tragedy of Hector, who is killed, or of Achilles, who loses his friend—and is himself doomed, as we know, to early death? The question is idle, because the burden of the poem is the universal tragedy of Man; none the less, the fact that one can ask it indicates another profound and beautiful trait in Homer—the breadth of his imaginative sympathy. It is no part of Homer's purpose to exalt the Greeks at the expense of the Trojans or the Trojans at the expense of the Greeks. He does not take sides. If Mycenae is 'golden', Troy is 'holy'; if Achilles is 'splendid as a god,' Hector is 'glorious', and Priam as well as Agamemnon is shepherd of his people. We are moved by the grief of Achilles when his friend is killed, but we are moved as deeply by the noble scene in which the King of Troy humbles himself to come to Achilles' tent and beg for the body of his son. Greeks and Trojans—all are men, splendid in manhood, and the poet looks upon them with benign and indifferent love. They fight to the death, for it is the nature of men to do so—of men proud of their strength and skill, hungry for honour and fame, glorying in the sunlight and the world of sense, but doomed so soon to fall like the leaves of a tree and to go down into the eternal darkness. It is a view of life stripped of complexity, bare of speculation, unburdened by any mystery but the ultimate mysteries of beauty and of death. Why did the Greeks lay siege to Troy? Homer of course knew the answer, but it was of little moment in the course of his poem, except in one famous passage which describes how the elders of Troy, counsellors of the people but too old to fight, sitting near the Scaean Gates saw Helen on the battlements, and whispered to each other: 'No shame indeed that for such a woman Trojans and Greeks should suffer so much and so long!'

If it was in fact the same Homer, as I think it was, who composed the *Odyssey*, he composed it in a very different mood. In the *Odyssey* there is less power but perhaps more pure delight; it lacks the tragic overtones of the *Iliad*, and in it from beginning to end the tale's the thing. It is told with inimitable verve and brilliancy and vigour, and for narrative skill there is nothing in the *Iliad* comparable with the close construction, mounting suspense (in spite of the fact that the end is known) and dramatic effectiveness of Odysseus' homecoming and recognition, and final triumph over the wicked lords who were wasting his substance and competing for the hand of the wife they thought to be a widow. The previous scenes in the long romance are detached tales of adventure, or magic, or dream (like the descent of Odysseus into the underworld), held together by the character of the hero— that 'talkative, bald-headed seaman', as Flecker called him, the brave old scoundrel always in a scrape and getting out of it by audacity or cunning usually at someone else's expense, and unshakeably confident (but goodness knows why) that if ever he reached home again he would find his wife Penelope still faithful after twenty years. Odysseus was one type of the Greek ideal, as Achilles was another. Neither was exactly what we should describe as a gentleman; but what matter? Both had a healthy appetite for life, and both lived familiarly with death. On the whole Greek boys were lucky to be brought up on Homer: he was more wholesome fare than much which is provided nowadays.

The second passage I want to transcribe tells how Odysseus after leaving Calypso's island sets sail in the boat he had himself built for the land of the Phaeacians, those more than mortal mariners who were destined to carry him home to Ithaca at last. It was to be no easy passage, for Poseidon, Lord of the Sea, was angry with Odysseus who had blinded Polyphemus his monstrous son, and was determined to do all he could, within the bounds of Fate and the will of the other gods, to bring the culprit to misery and ruin.

'Odysseus, full of joy, spread his sail to the breeze and sitting at the helm used all his seaman's cunning to hold the vessel to her course. He never closed his eyes in sleep but kept them on the Pleiads, or watched the slow setting of Boötes, or the Bear, called by some men the Wain, which wheels round in the sky and alone never bathes in the Streams of Ocean but keeps constant watch upon Orion the Hunter. The Bear it was that the goddess Calypso had bidden him keep on his left hand as he sailed over the sea.

'For seventeen days he held his course, and on the eighteenth he made out some shadowy hills, which were the nearest point of the Phaeacians isle. The land lay like a shield on the misty sea. But now the Lord Poseidon saw Odysseus and his ship from the distant mountains of the Solymi and was angry at the sight. He shook his head and murmured, "So the gods changed their minds about this man, once I was out of the way amongst the Ethiops. And now he is near Phaeacia where he is destined to escape at last from all his troubles. But I mean to give him plenty yet before he gets there!" So he gathered the clouds together and with his trident stirred the sea. He roused the blast of all winds that blow; in lowering cloud he hid both land and sea and darkness rushed down from the sky. East wind and South fell upon Odysseus, and the wild West wind too, and the sky-born Norther rolling a great wave before it. Odysseus' knees were loosened, his heart quailed and for all his gallantry he cried out in anguish and fear: "What will become of me now, unhappy man that I am? I fear the goddess spoke all too truly when she said that before I reached my home I should have my fill of misery upon the sea. The prophecy is being fulfilled—for see how Zeus has covered the wide sky with murk and roused up the breaking seas, while fierce squalls from every quarter rush down upon me. My utter destruction is now sure. Thrice and four times lucky were the Greeks who died on the broad plains of Troy, and would that I too had fallen there, when the Trojan armies hurled their brazen spears at me over the corpse of Achilles. Then should I have been buried with honour and the Greeks would have spread my fame; but now it is my fate to die a dishonourable death."

'At that very instant a great comber curled and broke, rushing down upon him with dreadful speed and weight, and his vessel broached-to. The steering oar was torn from his grasp; the warring winds snapped the mast in two and flung both sail and yard far out into the sea. Swept overboard, Odysseus for a long time was kept under and could not struggle to the surface beneath the downrush of that wave, weighted as he was by the clothes Calypso had given him. At last he rose again, spitting out the bitter brine as the water streamed down his face; but for all the punishment he had taken he did not forget his boat, but made after her through the seas, caught her, scrambled in and sat amidships—safe for the moment. . . .

'Now Odysseus was not utterly alone, for Cadmus' daughter saw him—Ino of the slender ankles, who was once a woman speaking human words but now dwells in the sea-depths and is honoured by the gods under the name of Leucothoe. She took pity on his misery and rising from the waves like a gull settled on the boat. "Poor man," she said, "why is Poseidon so angry with you that he plants nothing but trouble wherever you go? But he shall not kill you, however hard he tries. Come now, do as I bid you: strip off those clothes, leave the boat for the winds to work their will with, and swim for your life to the coast of Phaeacia where it is your destiny to be saved. Take this scarf and twist it round your body, and you need fear neither death nor hurt; and when you touch dry land, unwind it again and fling it far out upon the wine-dark sea, turning your eyes away."

'Then the sea-nymph gave Odysseus the scarf and plunged back like a seabird into the turbulent waves, vanishing into their dark depths. Odysseus was left wondering and in his distress took counsel thus with his own brave heart: "Can it be my luck that some god, in urging me to abandon my boat, is but making a fresh net to trap me in? I shall not yet obey, for indeed the land is in sight where she promised me safety. No—this rather is my wisest course: so long as the planks hold together I shall stay aboard and endure what I must; and when a wave breaks her up, then will I swim for it. I can think of no better plan."

'Even as Odysseus was making up his mind, the Lord of the Sea sent another wave, steep and terrible, with a hollow crest which hung above him. Down it came, and smashed and scattered the planks of the boat as a sudden gust will scatter a heap of chaff. Odysseus seized a floating timber and bestrode it as a rider his horse, and stripped off the clothes Calypso had given him; then he wound the scarf around him under his breast, and spreading out his arms plunged headlong into the sea and with eager strokes struck out for land. Poseidon saw him and with a shake of his immortal head, "Thus then," he murmured, "make your way, poor wretch, across the sea till you come to a people whom the gods respect. Even then you will hardly, I fancy, make light of your sufferings." With this Poseidon touched his fair-maned horses with the whip and drove to his place at Aegae.

'And now Athene, daughter of Zeus, had another thought; she checked the other winds and bade them fall into the calm of sleep, and called up a brisk breeze from the north to flatten the seas in Odysseus' path and help him to reach in safety the country of the Phaeacians, those far-famed mariners.

'For two days and nights he was all but lost in the wild sea, and again and again he felt death upon him. But when Dawn, that goddess with the beautiful tresses, brought in the third day, the wind fell and there was calm. Eagerly straining his eyes as a great roller lifted him, Odysseus saw land close ahead. His joy was like the joy of children who see life returning to their father who has long been wasting with disease—no less glad was he at that glimpse of land and trees, and with all his strength he swam, longing to set foot on solid ground again. But as soon as he was within call of the shore, he heard the roar of surf on rocks, for on that inhospitable coast the rollers were breaking in thunder and all was veiled in a mist of spume. Harbours or landing-beaches there were none, but only jagged headlands and cruel reefs. Odysseus' knees were loosened; his brave heart quailed and he cried out in misery: "Against all hope Zeus let me see land—and I have swum to it across all these miles of sea; but now there is no way to get out of the water, and the grey sea must hold me yet. Offshore are reefs, sharp as knives, and a surge of breakers; behind them a cliff sheer and smooth, with deep water at its base, and no chance to get a foothold and escape. If I try, a wave will get me and dash me against the rocks—a sorry end to my struggle. If I swim further along the coast in the hope of finding some sheltered beach or cove, it is odds but another squall of wind will sweep me out again to the fish-haunted deeps, or else ill luck will send a sea-monster to snap me up—one of the many fearsome creatures in Amphitrite's flock—and well I know how bitterly Poseidon hates me."

'But poor Odysseus had no more time to think what was best to do, for a huge roller picked him up and swept him on to the jagged shore, where his skin might have been stripped off and all his bones broken had not grey-eyed Athene made him with a mighty effort lay hold with both hands on a rock, to which he clung gasping till the roller had passed. For an instant he was safe; but then the backwash caught him and flung him into deep water again, while fragments of skin torn from his hands stuck to the rock, like pebbles on the suckers of an octopus which has been dragged from its lair. Submerged by the wave, he would indeed have met a miserable end, had not Athene once again put a thought into his mind. Coming to the surface, he struggled clear of the broken water and swam coastwise in the smooth, keeping an eye on the shore in the hope of finding an inlet where the force of the seas would be broken. At last he reached the mouth of a fair-flowing river, free from rocks and sheltered from the wind, and "This," he cried, "is the place for me!"

'Then he spoke a silent prayer to the god of that river: "Hear me, though I know not thy name. I come to thee as to the answer to all my prayers for deliverance from the sea and Poseidon's anger. Even the immortal gods will hearken to a poor wanderer like me, who turn now to thee for help and seek sanctuary within thy stream after all my sufferings. Lord, pity me and receive me as thy suppliant."

'At once the river checked its current, calmed the waves and smoothed the windless waters in Odysseus' path, bringing him safe to land at its mouth. Worn out with his struggles he could hardly stand; his sturdy arms were weak, his flesh swollen, and salt water streamed from his mouth and nostrils. Speechless and breathless he lay, half dead and overwhelmed with a dreadful exhaustion. But soon his breath returned and his spirit revived; he unwound the goddess' scarf from his body and flung it into the sea-ward moving stream. Down it went on the tide and soon Ino had it in her hands again, while Odysseus turned away from the river, threw himself down amongst the reeds and kissed the life-giving Earth. "And what," he thought, "will become of me now?

How will these things end? If I stay here by the river all through the night, frost and dew together may well make an end of me exhausted as I am, for the river winds blow cold at dawn; but should I climb the hill yonder and find a bed in the undergrowth of the woods, I might indeed sleep sweetly and be warm and rested—but wild beasts might find and devour me, even as I slept."

'At last he decided to make for the woods. Quite near the river he came to a copse with clear ground all round it, and crawled under a pair of bushes growing from a single stem. Their branches were so thick that no breath of the moist wind could penetrate them, nor yet the sun's heat nor the rain. In to this shelter Odysseus crept, and scraped together a broad bed of leaves to lie on— for they lay there thick enough to keep two or three men warm and snug through the hardest winter weather, a pleasant sight for the weary wanderer. So down he lay, piling the leaves on top of him, covering himself as carefully as a lonely cottager hides his burning brand in black ashes, lest he lose the seed of fire. And Athene poured sleep upon his eyes and closed their lids—the best medicine for a weary man.'

Readers who have any acquaintance with the *Odyssey* will happily recall that all was now well; it was not wild beasts that found Odysseus, but the King's daughter, the charming Nausicaa, who with her maidservants chanced on the following morning to come down to the fair-flowing river with the Palace washing. I cannot comment on the beautiful passage I have quoted: it would be like trying to comment on the dawn. None the less it is hard not to point out with what exquisite precision Homer had observed the sea and its wicked ways—I am told by modern travellers that in a Mediterranean or Aegean squall the wind constantly chops round through all the points of the compass, which would make sense even of Homer's statement that all the winds blew at once. And I like, too, Homer's lightly borne sense of the mystery both in nature and in the human heart: *why* did the bad weather come, just then? *Why* did the shipwrecked Odysseus get ideas, or find courage, to help him persevere? In both cases it was the gods who did it. Meteorology and psychology are useful sciences, but even they are forced in the end to confront the mystery—the unanswerable *Why?*

The ancients were in the habit of referring as it were in one breath to Homer and Hesiod—much as we (or the duller witted amongst us) refer to Keats and Shelley. In point of fact no two poets could differ more widely. Alexander the Great is supposed to have said that Homer was reading for Kings, Hesiod for peasants, and the criticism is no bad one.

In most Greek poetry the didactic element was more or less strong, for the obvious reason that in the Greek mind, in the earlier centuries of its development, the departments of knowledge had not been separated and subjected to specialised enquiry in the way which is familiar to us of the modern world. This made more work for the poet, who in addition to his primary duty which was to delight, to exalt and to inspire, had also to teach: he had to combine the function of entertainer (if one may use the word without a derogatory implication) with the functions of the philosopher, the scientist and the theologian. Hence in Greek poetry, even of the loftiest kind and even in the personal poetry of the lyric and elegiac poets, one constantly finds *wise saws*, gnomic utterances, moral apophthegms. In the mind of the ancient Greek knowledge was still one, and still the shared possession of intelligent men, not the personal property of the expert —a fact which also helps to explain—what I hope this book has already indicated—the immense range and variety of non-historical matter in Herodotus' *Histories*. But while in most Greek poetry the didactic *element* was strong, in Hesiod's poetry instruction is everything. He was a purely didactic poet.

To be a purely didactic poet is no recommendation to a modern reader, least of all, perhaps, when the subjects taught are, first, the rules for successful farming in the neighbourhood of the Boeotian village of Ascra, 'a wretched hamlet near Helicon, with bad winters, intolerable summers and no decent weather at all,' and, secondly, the complicated family relationship of the Olympian gods. Hesiod's *Theogony* ('the Gods' Family Tree') has historical interest as an attempt to reduce to order a mass of vague and conflicting popular and local superstitions, and his *Works and Days* as throwing some light upon certain tensions in the social development of early Greece, and as a curious collection of country tabus relating to agriculture; but as my object in this chapter is to suggest to the general reader where in ancient Greek literature he is likely to find pleasure and profit, I should not mention Hesiod at all, were it not for the fact that he illustrates the extraordinary poetic *instinct* of the Greeks. No poet of Greece before its decline could write many lines without some touch of grace or beauty, some phrase of bright, imaginative truth. Hesiod's verses are in the main crabbed enough, and their subject pedestrian; but the poetic feeling is there, constantly struggling to get through. 'I know nothing,' he says, 'of voyaging or of ships; never yet have I sailed the wide sea—save only to Euboea from Aulis, *where the Achaeans waited with the great host they had gathered to pass from holy Hellas to Troy, the city of fair women.*' Poor Hesiod hated the sea almost as much as he hated the Boeotian weather; yet he has advice to give about the conduct and timing of trading voyages, and I cannot but remind the reader once again of the phrase he used to describe the season when it first becomes safe, or fairly safe, to put to sea—'that time,' it runs, 'when leaves have grown as long as a crow's footprint on the ground', a phrase which only a poet, with the poet's dwelling eye, could have fashioned. 'Look after Sharptooth, your dog,' he writes; 'don't spare his victuals, lest *the man who sleeps by day* break in and rob you.' The time when it is already too late to dig round the roots of the vines he describes as 'when snails are beginning to crawl up growing things'—and the word for snail is the charming word *phereoikos,* 'house-carrier.' Such touches of essential poetry continually occur, throwing their gleam upon Hesiod's workaday world and investing with a kind of innocent beauty his sound practical counsel to work hard if one wishes to live well—and to rise with the dawn: 'for dawn does a third of the work for you; dawn brings the traveller on his way, the labourer forward with his task.'

I do not fancy many modern readers except for the purpose of study would make much of Hesiod's other poem, the *Theogony* (I say his other poem, though certain bits and pieces, in addition to the *Theogony* and the *Works and Days,* are attributed to him and may or may not, be his); yet here too in spite of the queer, dry subject the irrepressible poetry flashes. Of night and day, issuing in turn from the underworld, 'the one,' he writes, 'comes with light in her hands for mortal men, the other with *sleep, the brother of death*' (did Shelley remember this when he wrote *Queen Mab?*); and again, of the same two brothers, death and sleep: 'the one, honey-sweet for men, roams the earth and the broad back of the sea in quietness, but the heart of the other is of iron and pitiless bronze. *Whom he catches, him he keeps,* and even the gods hate him.' Hesiod's poetry may have been 'reading for peasants', but they were assuredly *Greek* peasants and therefore not to be satisfied by playing in their pleasures a passive role but both willing and able to let their own sensibilities co-operate with those of the poet, as they listened to his poetry.

CHAPTER 26

Literature: Lyric and Dramatic

PERHAPS I HAVE SAID ENOUGH, IN MY CHAPTER ABOUT THE ISLAND poets, of Greek personal lyric poetry. There is much more of this poetry, not from the islands, which would give me pleasure to talk of, but I do not think that to do so would further serve the purpose of this book. If I were myself a poet, I should attempt a translation of the slight but beautiful surviving verses of Mimnermus of Colophon, but I know that a prose rendering would convey nothing of their charm—less even than my prose renderings of the far more impassioned and profound fragments of Sappho. In Sappho's poetry the image is itself always significant, even apart from the words which embody it; but there is other poetry in which both image and idea are commonplace, and the emotional effect depends wholly upon the particular words and music by which they are presented. I can, for instance, imagine a not wholly ineffective prose translation of Shakespeare's lines:

> Come, seeling night,
> Scarf up the tender eye of pitiful day,
> And with thy bloody and invisible hand
> Cancel and tear to pieces that great bond
> Which keeps me pale;

simply because the pressure of thought contained in them, together with the particular images of the scarf, the bloody hand, and the bond could be expressed—in a measure—in any language. But no translation could, on the other hand, make anything at all of the line:

> *After life's fitful fever he sleeps well,*

because there the image and the thought are both commonplace, and the entire emotional and aesthetic impact is in the expression —the unalterable rhythm and words.

I will therefore attempt no further discussion of the Greek personal lyric. Of the ceremonial lyric a word must, however, be said.

The Greek ceremonial lyric means in effect the poetry of Pindar, for the work of other poets in the same *genre* survives only in a fragmentary state. Of Pindar's *Odes* enough are preserved to make a considerable volume. Pindar's reputation in antiquity stood very high and that is no doubt one reason why so much of his work survives. I suppose his reputation is still very high, though there is little doubt that he is more praised than read. Whereas the Greek personal lyrics are, in their effect, dateless, Pindar is undeniably an Antique. His Greek is very difficult. He writes in the grand manner—whereas Homer attains grandeur through simple speech. He never appears but in his singing robes, elaborately draped. He utters platitudes with the air of an oracle. He is the Theban Eagle and will have no truck with other poets, those lesser birds, whom he calls ravens and jackdaws. His deep-toned speech, said the Roman poet Horace, is like a mountain torrent swollen with rains; he soars, and if any fool of a modern tried to follow him, he would find his wings stuck on with wax, like those of Icarus, and soon tumble down into the glassy sea. In short, a somewhat awesome figure: not a poet, but a Bard. Moreover, Pindar was a professional Bard; he composed his tremendous odes often in praise of some Tom, Dick or Harry who had won the pentathlon, or the foot-race, or the pancratium (no holds barred, not even kicks and bites) at Olympia or elsewhere, but about whom otherwise he knew nothing and cared less, exalting him, family and ancestors included, to the skies—and was, we presume, well paid for it.

These considerations, I admit, prejudice me against Pindar. None the less I am ready to believe that if I had had the good fortune to hear his poems delivered as they were intended to be delivered, I should have bowed the knee to him as willingly as the rest. For it is now for ever impossible to recover the original effect of poems like these, for the simple reason, as I have already said, that they were not only poems, but the verbal element in a complex and elaborate art-form which combined poetry with music and the dance. In its context, with its proper accompaniments, in the setting it was designed for—the ceremonial occasion, the spectators, in their holiday garb and holiday spirits (for the Greeks did not take their pleasures sadly)—with the sheer beauty of the natural background which Greece so amply provides, this poetry must have been a noble thing. But all that is irrevocably gone, and the modern reader struggling through the poems is more or less in the position of someone who, with only an elementary knowledge of music, does his best to read a score.

I should not attempt to read Pindar at all were it not for the sudden flashes of splendour, the evocative word, which lighten the labour. No poet, I fancy, tries harder for his effects than Pindar; his poetry is a notable example of what Keats called the poetry of art, and one looks in vain for the 'true voice of feeling'. Nevertheless, Pindar's was a powerful and sumptuous art, and the persevering reader is not seldom rewarded. I will quote one brief passage; it is free of Pindar's most conspicuous faults, and it describes how the ship *Argo* set out with Jason in command upon the quest of the Golden Fleece:

And when her crew, flower of seamen, came down to Iolcos,
Jason numbered them, praising each one, and the Seer
Foretelling success through God's omens and the flight of birds
With willing heart bade them embark. Then they hung the
   anchors at the prow,
And Lord Jason on the poop took in his hands a golden cup,
And called in prayer upon Zeus the Thunderer, father of the
   Heavenly Ones,
And on the swinging winds and waves to give them swift
   passage,
The nights, and the sea-ways, and days of calm, and the happiness of safe return.
In answer to his prayer came a voice from the clouds in thunder,
Lightning burst from them brilliant, and the heroic company
Accepted the sign and were eased at heart.
   Then the Seer bade them pull at the oars, giving them sweet
   hopes,
And stroke followed stroke under the strong, swift hands.
The south wind blew, and they came to the entrance of the
   Unfriendly Sea,
Where they made a shrine for Poseidon the Sea-god,
Having ready to their hands the dark Thracian bulls for sacrifice
And an altar of stone, new-built.
But peril lay ahead, and they prayed Poseidon, the Lord of
   Ships,
To escape the dreadful inrush of the Clashing Rocks—

Twin rocks they were, alive, and would rush over the waters
Swifter than the marching ranks of winds; but now their
  days of life were over,
For the passage of Argo was to root them for ever.
So they came to Phasis. . . .

That passage has the untarnished brightness of the best Greek
poetry. The reader will notice the imaginative power, characteristically Greek, by which in the seventh and eighth lines the winds
and waves, nights and the days of calm, and even 'the happiness of
safe return' are included in the prayer to Zeus, as if they too were
living and divine.

But what, a reader might ask, is the story of the Argonauts
doing in an Ode, composed (as this one was) to celebrate the victory of Arcesilas, King of Cyrene, in a chariot race? Greeks loved
to trace their descent back to some legendary hero, or god—and
Herodotus tells us that the ease and confidence with which they
did so greatly amused the Egyptians. Grant, then, this trait in the
Greek character, and it will not be difficult to see that an important element in laudatory poems like Pindar's was to do precisely
this—to connect, namely, the subject of praise with as much of
the legendary and glorious past as was felt to be appropriate. At
the risk of tedium, let me very briefly indicate how this particular
poem from which I have quoted is built up. After an invocation
to the Muse, Pindar relates how the priestess of Apollo told Battus
to leave his home in Thera and found a new city in Libya, in order
to fulfil the prophecy of the enchantress Medea. The prophecy is
then related—how a magical Clod of Clay followed the Argo-
naut Euphamus from the Libyan Lake over the sea to Thera, from
which island his descendants were destined to sail away on their
venture and to build Cyrene. It was Battus who fulfilled the
prophecy, and to Arcesilas the descendant of Battus in the eighth
generation, Apollo had given the glory of winning the chariot
race. The Argonauts having thus been introduced, the story of
the Quest of the Golden Fleece follows. Nor is this quite all—for
the poem has another purpose in addition to exalting the fame of
Arcesilas. It was written at the request of a certain Damophilus, a
nobleman who had been banished from the court of Cyrene, and
who now, through the poet's mouth, offers it as a peace-offering
to the King. So Pindar ends by praising Damophilus, and urging

Arcesilas to forgive his fault and allow him to return to his country. The whole poem, then, together with the music to which it was sung and the dancing which accompanied it, was a highly elaborate work of art—and postulates, surely, an exceedingly quick and lively audience. The metre of the poem is as delicate as the verbal texture is rich, but it is not easy for an English ear, accustomed to the simpler iambic or trochaic rhythms, to appreciate.*

A pleasant story is told of Pindar and his excursions into myth. Such excursions were a recognised element in the Victory Odes of his predecessors and contemporaries, but it so happened that the young Pindar, trying his hand for the first time, left the mythology out. Reproved for this by a certain poetess of Thebes, named Corinna, who must have been a brave woman, Pindar in his next poem made up for his omission by cramming in so much mythology that the theme of his ode was buried out of sight. Once again Corinna came forward, and sternly observed: 'Pindar, one should sow with the hand, not with the whole sack.'

It is natural, though often fallacious, for the historian to simplify the past by imposing a pattern upon it, breaking it into epochs each with a salient character. Thus we speak of the Lyric Age of Greece—and it is indeed a fact that at some time during the first half of the fifth century B.C. the springs of Greek lyric poetry appear to have dried up. I say 'appear', because all that we have to go upon is the accident of survival and much may have been written which is now lost. Survival, moreover, is due not entirely to accident, but also in some measure to the taste of later Greek scholars and literary men, who saw that copies were made of the works they thought most worthy to endure. The Greeks like the Romans after them—and like ourselves until comparatively recent times—looked upon the poet as the Teacher, and one reason why so little of the lyric poetry even of the great Lyric Age has been preserved may well be that the later scholars found in it too slight a moral and philosophical content to be worthy of preservation.

* The metre is the dactylo-epitrite, a measure made up of a combination of the foot -◡—with the dactyl (-◡◡) and its variations. I do not think it could be represented in English, though one line of my translation happens, by accident, to come somewhere near it:

   'Níghts and séa-wáys, dáys of cálm ánd—háppiness of sáfe
     retúrn.

But whatever the reasons, the fact remains that Greek poetry in the second half of the fifth century is confined, so far as the modern reader can know it, to the drama: and Greek tragic drama, while it possesses imaginative and poetic excellence in the highest degree, was at the same time designed to elevate and instruct. One might say of it—adapting a famous critical judgement of Keats—that its excellence lies in its intensity, making all platitudinous moralising evaporate by being in close contact with beauty and truth.

It is a notable fact that Greek tragic drama was exclusively Athenian. Athens had produced no lyric poets of distinction; throughout the long period when lyric poetry seemed to come spontaneously to the lips of men all over the Greek world—in the cities of Ionia, in the islands, on the Greek mainland even in Sparta with Alcman and Tyrtaeus, even in Thebes with Corinna and Pindar—the Athenians were dumb. They contributed nothing. Then (quite suddenly, as it seems to us) the lyric voice, formerly so wide-spread and so delightful, was stilled. It was never to be heard again. Athens replaced it with a most noble poetry of her own; but something precious had gone; something of the very essence of the old Greek spirit had vanished for ever. Henceforward, until Hellenistic times, Greek poetry was Athenian poetry, Greek literature Athenian literature. Nobody elsewhere seems to have had anything to say, or to sing.

This is a remarkable phenomenon and has been too little noticed. The rise of Athens to eminence in literature coincided with a general decline throughout the rest of Greece, and the excellence of Athenian literature, first in the drama, then in history with Thucydides and Xenophon, then in philosophy with Plato and Aristotle, has obscured the fact that the moment this great body of literature began to appear marked the drying of the springs of creative art in the rest of Greece. The age of Pericles in Athens, usually regarded as the crowning glory of Greek civilisation, was in fact, it seems, the beginning of the end. The spirit of the old Greece was already in decline. It is possible only to guess why this should have been so: Greeks, as we know, had politics in their blood, and it may well be that in many of the Greek states full participation in the political game turned men away from poetry and the other arts. The tyrants, men like Polycrates of Samos, Periander of Corinth, Cleisthenes of Sicyon,

Hiero of Syracuse, had all been patrons of the arts; they had attracted poets, sculptors, architects and painters to their courts, and their rule, while it lasted, had enforced a leisure in which the arts might grow. But with the passing of the tyrants and the rise of democracies conditions were changed: the patron had vanished, life (though more amusing for most Greeks) became sterner and harder, the political battle more engrossing and insistent. For whom could an Anacreon sing his love-songs, if there were no Polycrates?

As for Athens herself, the very type of advanced democracy in the ancient world, how was it that she, alone of the Greek communities, moved in precisely the opposite direction, and rapidly achieved artistic preeminence? No simple answer can be given, but much of the credit must be given to Pericles, that remarkable man who, though nominally only *primus inter pares* in the political life of Athens, did in effect control her destiny for some thirty-odd years, and succeeded in combining the instincts and ideals of the old 'tyrants' with a democratic policy. Pericles was as fervent and effective a patron of the arts in Athens as any of the old tyrants elsewhere had been; he spent public money with reckless extravagance on the adornment of the city, and did everything in his power to foster in his fellow-Athenians their adoration of their native city and their pride in her leadership, both material and intellectual, of democratic Greece. Athens became, in the words which Thucydides put into Pericles' mouth, 'the school of Hellas'; she also became, or attempted to become, under Pericles' inspiration and guidance the tyrant of Hellas; and it was this melancholy fact which led to her undoing and thence, by an inevitable progression, to the collapse of the whole characteristic structure of the ancient life of Greece. The common view that the Greek achievement is to be identified with the achievement of Athens in her brief period of splendour—barely eighty years, or perhaps a hundred if we include her major contributions to philosophy and science—is wholly erroneous, as the general tenor of this book is designed to show. Even of those eighty years, beginning after the defeat of Xerxes, thirty were occupied in war with Sparta and characterised by the moral degeneration which a long and desperate war inevitably brings. Nevertheless the intellectual achievement of Athens was a marvellous thing, unsurpassed in quality and range by any other people within a comparable period. Such was its influence in antiquity that for centuries after Athens had lost her creative genius and ceased to count in politics she continued to be regarded by the rest of Greece and later by the Romans as the intellectual centre of the Mediterranean world. Of that rich and varied creative genius the noblest product was the tragic drama.

Ought a reasonably intelligent person to be able when confronted with an acknowledged masterpiece of art, to understand it without previous knowledge of the circumstances in which it was produced? In other words, is beauty—or whatever else one takes to be the informing spirit of a work of art—autonomous, so that to see it is to recognise it, or is it, on the contrary, a mysterious end-product of a thousand other things subtly combined and each modifying all the rest? I would suggest that the latter is more nearly the truth, and to back my view I would point to the obvious fact that all art is, and must be, built upon certain conventions. It is a way of communicating, and nobody can communicate with another person without some common ground. We tend in the arts, as in most other matters, to like what we are used to and to be irked by the unfamiliar. Writers and artists draw into a focus, like a lens, the diffused light of thought and feeling characteristic of their time, making their contemporaries know clearly what they half-knew already, or dimly guessed, or caught fugitive glimpses of. They see what others see, but they see it better. Often they are a jump ahead, and in times of change catch and draw into their focus ideas which are only faintly beginning to stir on the outermost edge of the general consciousness, so that what they say seems difficult and strange, till the gap has been narrowed; but the ideas are there, however nebulous.

For these reasons it is not possible, I think, to understand and therefore to enjoy the literature of the past unless one has some knowledge of the conventions within which it was produced. Clearly this is more true of some forms of literature than of others: little previous knowledge is required, for instance, to enjoy the poems of Homer, or Greek personal lyric poetry, narrative and song having a direct appeal to anyone in any age; but this is not the case when we come to the Athenian tragic drama, for of all forms of Greek art the conventions which controlled it and the quality of feeling out of which it arose are most strange to a modern reader. In what follows, having no space to discuss at all adequately the whole body of Greek drama, I shall confine myself principally to the work of Sophocles, not because Sophocles was necessarily the best writer of the three dramatists whose work survives, but because he seems to me to represent in a way which the modern reader can most readily appreciate the essential quality of the developed drama. Aeschylus who preceded him—the mighty poet whose

> giant shapes (in Browning's words) silently flitting
> Pile the dim outline of the coming doom,

with his almost oriental elaboration of diction and metaphor and what Professor Finley has called his 'murky piety', is—as I said of Pindar—an antique; the plays of Euripides, youngest of the three and called by Aristotle the 'most tragic of the poets' though full of beauty and wisdom and human kindliness, and perhaps nearer to modern sentiment than those of either of his rivals, were in many ways ahead of their age: they were experimental and icono-clastic, and represented a break with the old tradition. But right in the centre of that tradition stands Sophocles, and he brought the form he found to a perfection of finish unrivalled by the other two.

In approaching Greek plays most of the ideas we associate with 'the theatre' are irrelevant. Athenian drama had its origin in religion and the production of plays was a part of the ritual worship of Dionysus, god of vegetation, fertility and wine. Both tragedy and comedy, according to Aristotle, 'were originally mere improvisation, the former arising from the dithyramb (the Dionysus-hymn), the latter from the phallic songs which are still to be heard in many Greek towns.' Plays were exhibited only at the annual festivals of Dionysus, of which the most important was the City Dionysia in early spring, when Athens was full of visitors from other states, bent on business or pleasure. The festival was a public holiday; shops were closed, the courts were emptied, no business of any kind was transacted—even prisoners were released from gaol—and for four days, perhaps for five, the whole population of Athens flocked to the great open-air theatre (it held from 17,000 to 20,000 people) at the foot of the Acropolis and sat there from dawn to dusk to watch a succession of plays, tragedy and comedy, and to listen to the choral singing of hymns in honour of Dionysus. The first day was devoted to a grand

Procession; an ancient statue of the God was taken from its shrine and carried along the road to Eleutherae, a town on the Boeotian border from which it was supposed to have been originally brought; and then in the evening it was brought back by torch-light and set up, not in its shrine, but in the theatre, to preside over the spectacles to come. All the City, men, women and children turned out in holiday dress for the procession—solemn in import, but a gay and brilliant spectacle with the companies of young citizen soldiers escorting in full armour the sacred image, the long lines of garlanded animals, victims for the sacrifice, following behind, the girls carrying on their heads the baskets containing the sacrificial instruments, and the City magistrates robed in purple or crowned with gold. The theatre itself was a sacred building, and misbehaviour of any sort within it was looked upon as sacrilege: merely to turn a man out of a seat which did not belong to him was an offence punishable with death.

It sounds a solemn business—and so it was, in so far as the whole Festival was an act of worship; but at the same time it was an occasion for pleasure beyond any other that the course of the year provided. The Greeks felt no hard dividing line between the secular and the sacred; except for festivals such as this they were starved of anything that could be called public entertainment; an exceedingly quick-witted people, with few books, no newspapers or concerts, no theatres as we know them, an unspoiled taste and the keenest of appetites for any sort of spectacle, they looked forward to their annual shows with passionate expectancy and ignorant and educated alike, packed tight on the comfortless wooden benches (the stone theatre in Athens was not built until after Sophocles' time) they sat happily through the long daylight hours watching plays which have hardly been surpassed for subtlety of thought and language, grandeur of feeling and lyrical magnificence. Is it surprising that a lot of garlic-smelling, illiterate or semi-illiterate country bumpkins (as the majority of Athenians were) should find pleasure and nourishment in what seems to us such exalted fare? Not, I think, upon the whole; for people tend in general to like, in the way of entertainment, what they are given, and the Greeks were fortunate in that they had not made the lamentable distinction between entertainment for the masses and entertainment for the elect. Not having been fed upon claptrap, their natural intelligence was still unspoiled. If they wanted plays, they wanted good plays—and that was all there was to it. They had, moreover, at all their dramatic festivals, the further interest and excitement of competition: the plays were staged competitively, judged by a selected board of judges, and the winning author was awarded a prize. The prize, not of much intrinsic value, was nevertheless one of the highest civic honours, the poet being looked upon not only as the provider of entertainment but as the teacher of wisdom. It is a simple view of the function of high poetry, in some ways almost naïve; we could not recover it today even if we wished to do so, for it belongs only to a society which still lives close to life's most elemental springs.

The ancient choral hymn in honour of Dionysus was performed, to the accompaniment of appropriate movement and gesture, on a circular enclosure called an 'orchestra', or dancing-place. This simple and primitive rite was in the course of time elaborated by the introduction of a single actor—the Greeks called him an 'answerer'—whose function was to punctuate, or comment upon, or 'answer' the phases of the choral hymn. In this the germ of dramatic representation can already be seen. How ancient this ritual was, nobody knows, but early in the fifth century before Christ the poet Aeschylus first introduced a second actor and thus made dialogue possible. It was the decisive step forward to the creation of drama. At the same time the ritual nature of the performance remained; the choral hymns were still the centre of it. Even in Aeschylus' three most elaborate and magnificent plays, the trilogy or connected series which tell the story of the curse on the house of Atreus, though in the wild prophesying of Cassandra and the maniac and devoted rage of Clytemnestra the murderess there is indeed drama as we understand the word, the essence of the whole is still in the choral hymns, those dark, intense, brooding poems on the mystery of evil and the helplessness of man before a power, malignant and inexorable, which he can guess at but never understand.

It is the chorus, I think, which to a modern reader gives the greatest sense of strangeness in a Greek play and is most likely to spoil his enjoyment of it; but the difficulty can be overcome if one realises why the chorus was originally there and holds fast to the fact that Greek drama, in origin a religious ritual, kept the ritual form throughout its history. Always essential to the play, the chorus nevertheless passed through certain modifications in the hands of Aeschylus' two successors: in the plays of Aeschylus himself the choral songs contain the fullest expression of the central theme of the drama; even in the *Agamemnon*, the most 'dramatic' (in the modern sense) of his plays, the actors are still 'answerers', answering the difficult and searching poetry of the odes; in Sophocles the position is reversed, and it is the choric songs which 'answer'; they are no longer the embodiment of the theme, but an echo, rather, or elaboration of it. In Euripides the choric odes are still further loosened from the structure of the drama, and not seldom become something like musical interludes.

From the technical point of view the work of Sophocles was so to modify the Aeschylean form of the drama as to bring it nearer—though still not near—to what we understand by the drama today. This he did, first by the shift in emphasis of the part played by the chorus and secondly by the introduction of a third actor, thus making possible, by the interplay of dialogue, dramatic situations more numerous and varied, and a subtler presentation of character and motive. He continued to write until the end of his long life—in all over a hundred plays, of which seven survive. There is a pleasant story told by various ancient writers of the poet in extreme old age; Lucian's version is as follows: 'Having been brought into the courts by his son Iophon on a charge of mental incompetence due to senility, he read to the jury some passages from the *Oedipus at Colonus* (his last play); this proved the continued vigour of his intellect to such effect that the jury were filled with admiration of the old man, and condemned Iophon, instead, as a lunatic.'

Apart from the ritual form of which I have spoken, Greek tragic drama differed from much of the modern in another important particular: the subjects of the plays were always, with only one extant exception, the *Persians* of Aeschylus, taken from ancient heroic legend or myth. These old stories were accepted by most Greeks as historical fact, whether they were stories about gods or about 'heroes'—those shadowy, primeval figures, larger than life, whose exploits were celebrated in the poems of Homer and elsewhere in the great mass of saga and song which was as familiar to an Athenian of the fifth century as the Bible is to us. But the point is that these stories were *known;* and a Greek audience at a play would not, therefore, have had the pleasure and excitement of wondering what was going to happen as the plot unfolded, for that was decided already; their pleasure and excitement came from another cause—from the particular handling, namely, of the familiar theme and from the playwright's ability to bring it home to them as an image (which all good stories are) of human struggle and human destiny. In the work of all three playwrights the principal means to achieving this is the sheer power and magic of poetry: in Aeschylus the poetry is all; in Sophocles there is some attempt to delineate character, as we understand the phrase; in Euripides there is much subtler characterisation, combined with a tendency to *épater le bourgeois* by giving a new twist, sometimes a shocking one, to the ancient and honoured tales which supplied his themes. But all three were, like Shakespeare, primarily poets.

Now the fact that it is the poetry which makes a play of Sophocles or of any other Greek tragic playwright what it is presents two difficulties to a modern reader unacquainted with Greek: first, poetry must always suffer in translation. The bones of it can be translated; but poetry does not consist only of bones. Secondly, the present day is, I think, in the main antipathetic to poetic drama, which requires broad themes and a certain boldness of treatment rather than the burrowing, minute psychological analysis of the novel, which is the characteristic literary form of the modern world. Poetic drama takes the greatest commonplaces of human experience and transfigures them. Shakespeare's tragic themes were ambition, pride, infatuation, jealousy, and it was his poetry which subtilised and illuminated them: Othello without his poetry would be nothing less trite than a jealous husband, but the poetry reveals his glory as well as his shame. Sophocles' tragic themes were the Great Man Fallen, the conflict between private affection and public duty, inescapable destiny, submission to divine law, the darkness which lies in wait for the passion and splendour of man's brief life—and again it is his poetry which brings them home to us. Without the poetry they would be little more than dramatised homilies.

Of Sophocles' extant plays probably the *Ajax* was the earliest, and as it is comparatively simple both in construction and in purpose, some account of it will serve well as an introduction. Ajax was the great Fighter, second amongst the Greeks who fought at Troy only to Achilles. According to the legend, when Achilles died and the question arose to whom his armour should be given, the Greek captains, led by Agamemnon and Menelaus, awarded it not to Ajax but to Odysseus. Ajax in the rage of wounded pride swore to murder them all, but the goddess Athene, always Odysseus' friend, turned the wits of Ajax so that in the darkness of hallucination he killed the army's cattle, supposing them to be his enemies. The deed done, he came to his senses again, and in shame killed himself.

Looked at with detachment, the cattle-killing comes very near to the ludicrous, and for English readers the inability of a brave man to accept the hurt to his pride with any sort of dignity is not easy to tolerate. However, poets have a way with unpromising material; they bewitch us more surely even than Athene bewitched Ajax; they suspend our disbelief, make us see what isn't there, like Macbeth's air-drawn dagger, and involve us in their fantasies. The result is that, reading this play, we do not look at the improbable story with detachment but are drawn within it and forced to realise, against the evidence of the facts, that the insufferable Ajax has a demonic power and a sort of awful grandeur; and that realisation casts, in its turn, a lurid light—or call it perhaps a 'darkness visible' like the flames in Milton's hell —upon certain places of the human heart. Man, we feel, when the last page is turned, even though the gods drive him mad, is greater than we know. Sophocles achieves his effect in this play chiefly by two fine scenes: the first is where Ajax, having returned to his right mind, sees before him the one inevitable thing he must do. He had made a fool of himself, and ridicule was worse to a Greek than pain. Honour must be saved, and it can be saved only by death. To find that death, he must be alone, so he tells the seamen who have followed him to the war from his home in the island of Salamis and his slave-wife Tecmessa that he is going to the sea-shore to some lonely spot where he may wash himself clean of the stain of his offence:

> I will go now to the seaward grasslands and the waters
> To wash the stain and be free at last of Athene's anger;
> I will find some place where no foot has trod
> And there I will hide this sword of mine, this hated sword,
> Burying it in the ground where no man may see it—
> Deep down there night and Hell shall keep it for me;
> For since I took it as a gift from Hector who hated me

Never have the Greeks honoured me as I deserved.
Ah! it is a true word which says an enemy's gift
Is no gift and brings with it only sorrow.
Therefore I will learn henceforward to be humble towards God,
And obedient to Atreus' sons. For they are
My captains, so how should I gainsay them?
Wild things, the mightiest things, yield to authority—
The snows and gales of winter give place to summer's fruits,
The dismal eye of night to the white horses of the dawn,
The tempest's terrible breath lulls at last the sighing sea,
And invincible sleep looses whom he has bound.
How then shall I too not learn to curb my pride?
For nothing remains in a fixed stay, and even friendship
Is a treacherous harbour for most men. . . .Wife, go you within
And pray God that what my heart longs for may be done.
And you, friends, honour her even as you honour me,
And bid my brother, if he comes, be kind to you, and tend me
According to my need; for I go whither I must go.
Only obey me, and perhaps, though I suffer now,
You will soon find me safe enough.

Ajax' friends are unaware of the many ironies in these words: they do not guess *how* he will bury his sword, how he will curb his pride, what it is his heart longs for. With joy for their master's fancied recovery and repentance they let him go. A messenger enters with the news of a prophecy that Ajax is in deadly danger, but that if he is guarded today he will henceforward be safe. Tecmessa and the sailors scatter to search for him, but they are too late. The scene changes to the 'seaward grasslands', and Ajax is alone. He has buried the hilt of Hector's great sword in the ground, and the blade is upward.

There stands the Slayer, where most aptly he can cut
The victim's throat. . . . Fixed he is in the earth of Troy,
My enemy; the whetstone has ground his iron to a bright,
   new edge.
And I have stamped the earth hard, to make him kind to me
With a swift death. It is well done.
And now, O Zeus, do not turn from me, but grant
One boon, a little boon—that some messenger may bear
The ill word to my brother Teucer, to bring him quickly

That he may be the first to lift me and draw out the bloody
  blade,
Before an enemy sees my body and throws it out
To be eaten by birds and dogs. . . . And you, O ghost-guide
  Hermes,
Put me to sleep without a struggle—with one swift leap
Upon the sword-point bursting my side. And I call the
    Avengers,
The Maiden ones, the hastening Furies, whose eye no mortal
  pain escapes,
To witness that it is Atreus' sons who kill me now,
And to sweep them to as bitter a death as mine. . . .

      Sun, who drive your chariot up the steep sky,
When you see my home, check your golden reins and tell
My father and her who nursed me to sorrow of my miserable
  end.

      Death, death, draw near and look at me—
Yet there, whither I go, we shall be close and I shall talk with you.
Daylight and sun—O bright one, O charioteer—
Once more I call your names, for the last time, never again.
Sky-brightness, and you, O holy earth of Salamis,
My home; famous Athens, and all springs and streams
Which here in Troy's plains have fed my life, hail and farewell!
This is the last word I speak to you; the rest I shall tell
Only to the dead in the dark world below.

  Teucer comes; and Ajax is indeed 'safe enough'; he has gone
'whither he had to go.' If a brave man must kill himself for shame,
that, I suppose, is how he should do it; if he must humble himself
before God, he could not do so with more fitting pride. Ajax dies
as he has lived, proud, unyielding, still full of revengeful thoughts.
Do we grieve for him? I think not; rather we are brought
face to face with the tragic fact of human destiny, of the closeness
of death and the impotence of human strength, which make the
'sky-brightness and all springs and streams' the dearer for the
brief time that they are ours. At the end of the play Teucer tells
Ajax' son, the boy Eurysaces, to help him lift his father's body, 'for
still,' he says, 'the hot veins are pouring the black strength up
from his heart.' What an image of the invincible fighter, of the
fierce physical life not yet wholly subdued! And reading the

words one remembers Odysseus, in the first scene of the play,
when Athene has allowed him to see the madman in his tent:

> I weep for his distress
> Though he is my enemy. Seeing his lot, surely I see my own;
> For now I know that we men are indeed nothing
> But phantoms, or a shadow bodiless as air.

It is easy to recognise in this play, though it is far from being
the best that Sophocles wrote, the poetic and imaginative power
which turns the old, dark legend into an image of the human
condition—of Man who in the pride of his blazing physical life
forgets the eternal law and makes his very zest for living the
means of his destruction. 'Seeing these things,' says the goddess
Athene to Odysseus.

> Speak no proud word against God
> Or think yourself big because you are rich or strong;
> There is nothing a man has but a day can bring it down
> And lift it up again. Those who know their place and are
>   humble
> Are the loved of God.

In *Ajax* there is no character-drawing in our sense of the term.
The figures are ideal figures. Up to a point this is true of all
Sophocles' plays; no character in Sophocles (or in Aeschylus
either) speaks with an individual accent; there is no equivalent
in him to—say—Falstaff or Hamlet or Hotspur or Rosalind or
Iago, whose *voices* we know. Such character-drawing is foreign
to the spirit of ancient drama, partly because of its ritual form and
partly, no doubt, because of the physical conditions under which
it was presented. The size of the theatre and the fact that the actors
wore masks and increased their height by thick-soled shoes would
preclude much of the subtle by-play of dialogue and expression
by which a sense of individual character is built up. Greek
playwrights worked in masses; their lines, one guesses, were
declaimed rather than spoken, and under their sculptured forms
beat the hearts not of men, but of Man. Nevertheless Sophocles
in his later plays did take a step towards what one might call a
more modern feeling for characterisation, or at least opened a
gate on to a new path which subsequent playwrights were to
follow. Some people have put it much more strongly and have

claimed Antigone, for instance (in the play of that name) as a piece of consummate characterisation; but though in devotion to the dictates of her heart she weeps for the loss of life and love, to try to see her as something other than a symbolic figure is to misread the intention of the play and of Sophocles' art as a whole.

The *Antigone* is probably the best loved today of Sophocles' plays. It is more obviously 'human' than the others; superficially anyone could enjoy it, as—superficially—anyone could enjoy *Hamlet;* nevertheless its total significance as a work of art, and the resonances of its poetry, call for not less but for more awareness than the simpler *Ajax.* Most readers will already know the story: how Antigone in defiance of the King's proclamation sprinkles the ritual dust upon the dead body of her traitor brother, and is buried alive in a vault by way of punishment; how Haemon, the King's son and Antigone's lover, pleads for her in vain, until a prophecy of doom breaks the King's will and sends him to release her; how he comes too late and finds her hanged by her own hand, and how Haemon kills himself on his beloved's body. It is a plot full of melodrama, and Sophocles, like Shakespeare, manages his melodramatics with great skill.

But, again like Shakespeare, Sophocles was a poet, and it is the office of high poetry to start in us thoughts beyond the reaches of our souls. Like the *Ajax,* though much subtler and ampler in treatment, the *Antigone* is a complex image of human destiny, conceived on a high religious—which to a Greek would not differ from a high poetic or philosophical—plane. It is instinct with the dark fatalism characteristic of Sophocles, and perhaps of most Greeks of his time: a kind of unresentful pessimism which in no way takes the colour and glory from life—while it lasts—and is therefore different from the pessimism widely current in the modern world, which seeks to turn life itself to ashes. For Sophocles Man is indeed born to sorrow: the inscrutable gods have ordained it, though, being what he is—passionate, ignorant, proud—he moves towards it of his own act and by his own will. Is there a contradiction here? Perhaps there is, though it did not appear so to Sophocles, who, in any case, was not a metaphysician but a poet. Much of the power and *weight* of the *Antigone* comes from the fact that the story is part of one of the many Greek legends which concern the curse on a particular family. The family of Oedipus was one such, and it is not hard to see the imaginative use which can be made of such a story of hereditary disaster—the suggestion, for instance, that no human act is ever an isolated thing, that evil inevitably breeds evil, that—in the words of Shelley paraphrasing a passage in Aeschylus—

> Revenge and wrong bring forth their kind,
>   The foul cubs like their parents are:
> Their den is in the guilty mind
>   And conscience feeds them with despair.

This fact of the hereditary curse on the house of Oedipus is brought home to the audience right at the beginning of the play, when Ismene is trying to dissuade Antigone from her enterprise; and it casts its shadow upon what is to come. 'Remember,' she says, 'how our father and mother died—and our brothers' . . .

> Now we two alone are left, and think what our doom will be
> If we flout the law and refuse to obey our king. . . .

But Antigone knows where her duty lies. 'Leave me my madness,' she answers; 'and let me suffer—a worse suffering would be to die ignobly'. That her determination is 'madness' she is well aware; for we misunderstand the play if we read it as some moderns do, as presenting a conflict between right and wrong, good and evil—the good being Antigone's love, the evil Creon's tyranny. It presents no such thing, but a much more deeply tragic conflict; the conflict, namely, not between right and wrong but between two rights. Antigone does not complain that her punishment is unjust; she knows, as a Greek audience would have known, that the law of the State, represented by Creon, must be upheld. Her punishment is cruel, but she recognises it as inevitable. At the same time her rebellion is inevitable too, for had she not rebelled she would not have been Antigone. Creon's fault is not his punishing of Antigone, but the excessive and barbarous severity of his decree against the traitor Polynices—and it is that, which the prophet Teiresias tells him will bring him, too, to ruin. Antigone knows she must die, and she also knows that, though she is flouting the law of the State, she is obeying, as she cannot but obey, a higher law, the unwritten law of the human heart, derived mysteriously from God. When Creon asks her if she knew of his proclamation, 'Yes', she answers,

But you are a man—no more—and no word of yours
Can oversway God's law, unwritten, inalterable—
Not made for time that passes, yesterday and today,
But everliving and timeless, whose beginning no man knows.
Not for fear of human pride would I break this law
And be guilty before God.

I have said that the play presents the conflict between two
rights; and so it does. But that is an inadequate way of describing
its total effect. This cannot, indeed, be described at all; it can
only be felt through submission to its poetry. It is the poetry
which makes the reader, or spectator, aware that he—like the
fabled persons of the old tale—is *in touch* with a mystery which
thought cannot fathom, and linked with a destiny which is
grander than he knew. Why do the passions of man inevitably
destroy him, when at the same time they are what constitutes his
glory? How is it that we know—as the chorus sings at the end of
this play—that the 'crown of happiness is wisdom', yet find it so
hard to be wise?

O love invincible, O conqueror,
You divide the spoils,
You set your night-watch in a girl's cheeks,
Over the sea you come against us, you shun not the shepherd's
    huts.
Neither god nor man can escape you, and your touch is madness.
You turn the heart of the just man to ill thoughts, to his ruin;
You have kindled the strife of son against sire;
The light of desire in a girl's eyes
Triumphs; established law yields to your rivalry
When you sit enthroned,
And Aphrodite laughs in joy of victory.

'Nothing too much'—everyone knows that old Greek proverb.
To us, may be, it tastes a little flat; but then we live cooler
lives than Sophocles and his contemporaries, and therefore have
less need of such warning.

I cannot discuss all the plays, but two more must be mentioned,
Oedipus the King and *Oedipus at Colonus*.

Oedipus the King is the only play of Sophocles, or of any other
Greek playwright, in which, apart from the poetry, the actual

plot is a gripping one; or perhaps I should say the way the development of the plot is handled; for the final issue of the story, like that of all Greek plays, is of course foreknown. The legend, of which the play is concerned with a crucial incident, is as follows. Laius, King of Thebes, was told by an oracle of Apollo that he would have a son whose life would be accursed: it was his destiny to kill his father and marry his mother. The child was born. Was there any way to avert his appalling doom? Laius and his wife Jocasta thought that there was—the baby should be destroyed. Accordingly they gave it to a shepherd with orders that it should be exposed, with an iron pin through its ankles, in a lonely glen on Mt. Cithaeron, and left to die. But the shepherd's heart failed him, and he gave the child to another shepherd, a Corinthian, begging him to take it far away from Thebes and bring it up as his own. In time it was brought to Polybus, King of Corinth, who having no children adopted it, and gave it the name of Oedipus—Swollen-foot.

In the court of Polybus, Oedipus grew to manhood, believing himself the true son of his kind foster-parents. But one day, by chance or destiny, he came to hear of the fate which Apollo had foretold; so seeking, as Laius had sought, to escape from it, he ran away from Corinth, resolved never to return. In the course of his wanderings he came to Thebes—a city of which he knew nothing. There he found everything in confusion. Laius, the king, had just been killed by an unknown wayfarer; the Sphinx was devouring all who failed to answer her riddle. Oedipus answered it and thus destroyed the monster's power, and the Thebans in gratitude made him their king. All was then well with him—or so it seemed. He ascended the throne, and married the widowed queen, Jocasta.

For years—until his children were grown up—he lived in prosperity and happy ignorance, a wise ruler, honoured and beloved. But the Gods had not forgotten. Thebes was smitten with a plague, and the citizens once again looked to Oedipus to succour them.

At this point in the legend Sophocles' play begins. Oedipus has already sent his kinsman Creon to ask Apollo's oracle for guidance, and in the first scene of the play Creon returns with the 'good news' that all will be well once the unknown killer of Laius is discovered and either put to death or driven for ever, as a thing of pollution, from the city. Oedipus eagerly undertakes to find out the criminal.

There is no need for me to go on with the story. By a series of brilliantly-managed incidents and interlinked scraps of cumulative evidence we are made to watch first the vague dread, then the growing terror and finally the ghastly certainty in Oedipus' mind that the guilty man is himself: he it was who killed Laius at that chance encounter on the road; he it is who is now living as the husband of his mother. Only one end is possible for such a tale; Jocasta kills herself, and Oedipus, mad with horror, blinds himself with a pin from her dress, that he may never see again the once-loved things which by his guilt he has defiled—his house, his city, his people, and his children. Led by his daughter Antigone, he leaves Thebes for ever, an exile and a beggar.

This play, with the overtones and undertones of its dark poetry, has haunted the imagination of the world for more than two thousand years. I would not pretend to 'interpret' it, even in the limited way in which I tried to interpret *Ajax* and *Antigone*. The Greeks, as I have said, lived closer to death than we do; they were not cushioned as we are from the primitive things—from the hauntings, the menaces and mysteries, the irrational terrors, the darkness ever lying in wait. All their beautiful rationality and lucidity of thought, which we so justly admire, were only the sun-glitter on the surface of a sea of which the depths were unfathomable and filled with monsters. The play of *Oedipus* moves in these depths. What is human wisdom confronted with the vast Unknowable? Our seeming happiness is poised on a razor's edge (a favourite metaphor of Sophocles); there are things in the best of us which belong to the beast, and the home of one half of our nature is still, perhaps, the haunted wilderness—the wild mountain of Cithaeron, '*my* mountain', as Oedipus calls it, where his parents tried to kill him but failed. And the darkness is only deepened by the deliberately flat and conventional comment which Sophocles put into the mouth of the chorus at the close: *Call no man happy till he has died happy.*

There was a gap of many years between *Oedipus the King* and its sequel *Oedipus at Colonus*, which was almost certainly the last play that Sophocles wrote. The *Oedipus at Colonus* is a play of very great beauty, but I think it is not an easy one for a modern audience to understand without some knowledge of ancient

Greek thought and feeling. Unlike the other plays I have described, it has little incident—little plot in the modern sense of the
word. It is less like a play than a dramatic meditation on a theme—
and the theme itself is a strange one, the sense, namely, that a
man like Oedipus, who has suffered more than any man should
be called upon to endure, and has, by Fate—or Chance (*Tyche*
the 'way things happen')—offended against human law and the
most sacred taboos, can yet, when his long life of anguish is over,
bring a blessing to the place where he is buried. The curse which
has destroyed him becomes a beneficent influence to the city—
Athens—near which he lies. One is familiar with the idea of
learning, or of purification, through suffering: it is to be found in
Aeschylus, and in Keats, and in Shelley and in Shakespeare's
King Lear; but the idea in this play is not quite that. Oedipus
himself has learnt little: he is still a proud and passionate old
man; he can still curse, with terrible effect as the course of the
legend shows, his unfilial sons; he still looks upon himself as
the sport of an incomprehensible and malignant Power. It is not
he who has changed; he is the old Oedipus still; but he has
become a man apart, a man upon whom the finger of a jealous
god has been laid. He, the guiltless guilty one, has acquired
a sort of sanctity, so that his ghost will have the power to
bless.

The play opens with the arrival upon the stage of Oedipus and
the faithful Antigone. In verse which has its own grave music
Oedipus begins:

Child of your old, blind father, tell me, Antigone,
To what place have we come or to what city of men?
Who today will welcome the vagrant with a scanty crust—
Little I need, and with less than that little I am content;
For three masters have taught me patience: grief and time—
My long, long years—and a mind which is noble still.

Finding that they are at Colonus, near Athens, in a copse thick
with laurel, olive and wild vine and filled with the song of
nightingales—a grove which is sacred to the 'dread goddesses,
daughters of Earth and Darkness, the all-seeing Kindly Ones'—
Oedipus cries out that his destiny is fulfilled: his wanderings
are over, for Apollo had foretold that when he came thither he
would find rest at last. Such incidents as the play contains are

provided by the attempt of Creon to get Oedipus to return to
Thebes, his seizure of Antigone and her sister, their swift rescue by
Theseus, the good king of Athens, and one very powerful scene
in which Polynices comes from Thebes to back Creon's attempt,
and is sent away by Oedipus with the curse which is afterwards
fulfilled by his death—as we know from the *Antigone*. Theseus
is persuaded to believe that the tomb of Oedipus will be a blessing
to Athens, and at the end of the play, in response to the flash of
lightning which is the promised sign from heaven, the blind
beggar, suddenly erect and needing no guide, himself guides
Theseus to the spot where he must lie.

The play, like all Sophocles' plays, is haunted by Presences,
but they are no longer malignant as they were in *Oedipus the
King*. The dark gods are there still, but only, as it were, on the
fringes of consciousness. The chorus can still say,

> Not to be born is best; but being born
> That man is luckiest who with all speed returns
> Thither, whence he came;

but the audience know better: they are brought to believe that
such a negation is meaningless, and that human life, however
bitter, yet has nobility and mystery because it is in touch with
the unseen.

There is a device peculiar to Greek drama which I have not yet
mentioned—the Messenger's speech. Partly for practical reasons,
such as the nature of the stage and the scantiness of scenery and
properties, partly for aesthetic reasons, Greek playwrights
preferred scenes of violence—deaths, murders, suicides and so on
—to happen off-stage and to be reported by a messenger. The
suicide of Ajax, which takes place on the stage and is, indeed, the
centre of the play, is exceptional. The device of the Messenger
gave opportunities for imaginative description of a high order,
and Sophocles took full advantage of them. The Messenger's
account of the passing of Oedipus is perhaps the finest example of
such speeches, and I quote it here—throwing over Sophocles'
poetry 'the grey veil (to borrow Shelley's phrase) of my own
words'.

> By the sheer chasm where the brazen steps lead down
> To the rock-roots in the dark, he chose one path

Of the many that branch there, and near the basin in the rock
Where Theseus' covenant with Pirithous has its memorial,
He stopped, midway between it and the Thorician stone—
The hollow pear-tree and the marble tomb.
Then he sat down, and loosing his beggar's rags
Called to his children to bring running water to wash his body,
And for libation. And obedient to their father
They went quickly to the green knoll where stands Demeter's shrine,
And returned and washed him, and put the death-robe on him.

Then suddenly, when all was done as he desired,
The Lord of Darkness spoke in thunder; the girls
Shuddered at the voice, and fell weeping at their father's knees,
Lamenting and beating their breasts for pity and fear.
And he at the sound of their crying
Took them in his arms, and said: 'This day, my children,
Is the end for me. All that was mine is gone, and never again
Will you labour, as you have long laboured, to care for me.
It was hard, I know; yet one word makes your labours light,
Love—the love you had from me as from no other.
But now we must part.'

So the three clung to one another, mingling their tears,
And when at last the passion of their weeping was stilled
There was silence—and in the silence the Voice
Of One who called to him, and the hair of their heads stood up for fear.
Again and yet again the God called: Oedipus,
Oedipus, why do we delay? You tarry too long.
And Oedipus, when he knew it was indeed God's voice,
Asked Theseus to come to him, and said: 'Promise me, friend,
Never to forsake my children, but to do for them
All that the wisdom of your heart prompts you'.

And Theseus promised. Then Oedipus, laying on his children his blind hands,
Said: 'You must be brave as becomes your blood, and go
Out of this place, not asking to witness the things
Which are not lawful for you to see or hear.
Go quickly: Theseus alone may know what is to be.'

Those words he spoke, and we all heard them, and went away
With the two girls, weeping as they wept; and soon after
We looked back—and lo! Oedipus was gone—vanished away.
Only Theseus we saw, his hand over his eyes
As if to screen them from some awful thing
He had seen, and could not bear to see.
And presently he made obeisance, saluting
The dark earth and the heaven in a single prayer.
He alone knows how Oedipus died—No fiery bolt
Killed him, no whirlwind from the sea rapt him away—
But God's messenger came for him, or the dark underworld
Opened in love to receive him, without death's pain;
For his passing was not in anguish or grief, but marvellous
Beyond all telling.

So ends this solemn and beautiful play, on which Sophocles
lavished all the resources of his art—and in which, incidentally,
he was able to give expression to his love for Colonus, where he
was born, in the words already quoted in another context.

> white Colonus,
> Earth's loveliest, where the nightingale's
> Liquid notes most haunt
> The darkness of green glades. . . .

Perhaps the most obvious characteristic of classical poetry,
as of classical art generally, is the firm intellectual framework
within which it delights to move. I say 'delights' because that
framework was not felt as a restriction; on the contrary, it was
felt as a liberation. Classical Greek society, in spite of wide
differences between individuals in wealth, status and intellect,
was a homogeneous society, and the artist could therefore expect
understanding from it. The poet wrote in full confidence in the
validity of the shared experience and the best common thought of
his time. He dealt habitually, and inevitably, with the passions
and beliefs which bind men together, as men—not (as we are
accustomed to find in modern literature) with the idiosyncrasies
which set him apart from his fellows. A Greek writer felt no need
to explain himself; if he was aware of personal oddity, that was
his own affair, and of no possible interest to his public. In classical
Greek literature one finds no rogue elephants, no angry men,

young or old, no experimenters, no exhibitionists. There is
anger in Thucydides, but it is not anger against society or the
constitution of things, but only at the failure of the political
ideas of his admired and beloved hero, Pericles—and against the
vulgar Cleon, who in fact continued them. The Greek poet—
and prosewriters too, though prose being a late development
had not a long course to run before the true classical spirit
declined—was not a man apart, or a clique-leader, or rebel, or
self-styled 'intellectual'; he was (to borrow Wordsworth's phrase)
'a man speaking to men' about subjects universally important
and intelligible, such as food, wine and love (if the poet was a
lyrist), or (if he was a dramatist) about a man's relationship to his
fellows and to God, a subject equally important and intelligible,
however mysterious. The Greek artist, to put it in other words,
was at home in his world and integrated with the society of his
time. One result of this integration, and that not the least important, was, in poetry, the constant recurrence of the *great
commonplaces* of human experience. Sophocles was supreme in his
handling of the great commonplaces, as, in English literature, was
Chaucer, and many of the seventeenth century lyrists.

> Lo, the ook that hath so long a norisshynge
> From tyme that it first bigynneth sprynge,
> And hath so long a lif as we may see,
> Yet at the laste wasted is the tree.
> Considereth eek how that the harde stoon
> Under oure feet, on which we trede and goon,
> Yet wasteth it, as it lyth by the weye.
> The brode river sometyme wexeth draye.
> The grete townes see we wane and wende;
> Then may ye see that all this thynge hath ende. . . .

Only in ages with a shared belief and a firm intellectual tradition
can poets in this way ennoble and irradiate the commonplace.
Almost any page of Sophocles would provide instances; here is
one from the *Oedipus at Colonus*, on the same theme as Chaucer's
—mutability:

> Dear son of Aegeus, only the gods have power
> Not to grow old, never to die; all other things
> Melt at the touch of time's irresistible hand:

Earth's pride, the body's strength, wither away;
When faith falls, the bud of unfaith swells on the tree,
And inconstant as a breath is the friendship of cities, as of men.
Soon or late sweet turns to sour, and bitterness again to love;
And though now all is fair weather for you there in Thebes,
Yet one of the myriad nights or days in time's womb
Will bring you clouds, and those pledges of fair trust,
Some light word spoken, as chaff will be scattered by war.

The classical poet did not need to search for themes; he found them ready to hand, in widest commonalty spread. Old thoughts, yes; but it is the privilege of genius to present old thoughts as fire-new from the mint.

I have stressed the strength of tradition in Greek poetry, and one can trace it unbroken from Homer through the lyrists to the Athenian playwrights—at any rate as far as Sophocles. In Euripides, Sophocles' junior by ten years, there is a change; the old ritual form is still there, the plots are still drawn from the common well of legend and myth; but a new thing, not easy to define, has crept in. Euripides is more sensitive than Sophocles was to the changing spirit of the age with its growing restlessness and doubt, its questioning of the old assumptions. And he leads the change, as great artists are wont to do. He is out to disturb, to play catfish in the bowl of opinion; and disturb he did, as one knows by the ridicule and abuse heaped upon him by the conservative Aristophanes, though in time he was to become the poet his countrymen best loved.

In Euripides' hands, odd things happen to the ancient and time-honoured tales; an action or a situation which once was seen as a majestic or awful symbol of the dark workings of Fate upon the blind and ephemeral life of men, is quietly removed from its ancient context. Husband-murder, for instance, is not an agreeable trait in women, even when it is inspired by a family vendetta: blood, admittedly, must have blood, but what must Clytemnestra really have been like, to do what she did? Or her daughter Electra, living with her peasant protector, and plotting revenge? Alcestis again, in the old story, died, with proper feminine devotion and selflessness, that her husband Admetus might continue to live. Very good—but would it not be interesting (Euripides seems to say) to consider more closely the attitude of mind, the bland and appalling egotism, of the husband who permitted such a sacrifice? And what of Medea, the foreign woman (and thus at a double disadvantage, being neither a Greek nor a man), the sorceress, the slayer of her children? Was not justice—and all genuine human sentiment—in fact upon her side? What, to a thoughtful spectator, is, or should be, the real centre of interest in the horrible tale of the sacrifice of Iphigenia by her father at Aulis? Not, surely, the fateful fact of the deed of blood, but rather the conflict of passions in the victim's heart, her longing for life, her terror of death and her final loving and selfless surrender. Euripides, in short, again and again in his plays was reinterpreting the myths and modernising them. He was inviting his audience, most of whom were already ripe for the invitation, to take a fresh look at them from a different angle.

Educated, at least in part, by the sophist Prodicus, and the friend of Socrates, that acute and remorseless critic of received opinion, Euripides was in the van of the intellectual changes which were beginning to take place in Athenian society; those changes, within half a century of Euripides' death, were to lead to the disintegration of the spirit of classical Greece, but seen as they are in the work of Euripides, who was a true poet and had not lost touch with the past, they give the sense of an enrichment. Euripides was ahead of his age in his attitude towards women and slaves—they were both, for him, human and therefore capable of nobility of heart; in this, perhaps, he was reverting to the better sentiments of the past, but there was another field in which he seems to have been wholly an innovator: this was in his hatred of war. Euripides dwells only upon its tragic aspect, upon its cruelty, futility and waste. Not that he was not a good patriot, in the conventional sense of the word; he loved Athens and was proud of her past and jealous of her future; writing in the course of the Peloponnesian War, he can pour abuse and scorn (in the *Andromache*, for instance) upon Sparta and her ways; but in war itself, in its stark and brutal essence, he saw nothing but ugliness and shame. His *Women of Troy* alone would be proof of this.

Great poet though he was, Euripides was a lesser poet than either Sophocles or Aeschylus. Just as the *Odyssey* is a lesser poem than the *Iliad*, though easier, perhaps, to read because of its incidental beauties, variety of adventure and multiplicity of situation, so Euripides makes a stronger appeal to many modern readers for certain detachable excellencies in his work which none could miss.

There is room here only for a brief word about Comedy—which in effect means the plays of Aristophanes, for the work ot Menander, largish fragments of which survive, including a complete, or very nearly complete, play discovered very recently, falls outside the period I am discussing. In any case, I must confess that what is preserved of Menander, together with the comedies of his Latin imitator Terence, is to me tedious. One cannot recapture the mood to which this sort of writing appealed, or sufficiently recreate in imagination the intellectual and cultural atmosphere which made it desirable, and there is not, in the plays themselves, enough of the stuff of human nature to make them independent of time. What Menander and his peers did for their contemporaries was done very much better for their own as well as for subsequent generations by Molière and Shakespeare. But there has never been a successor to Aristophanes. I do not mean by this that his genius was supreme; it was not, but for us, who do not possess the plays of his contemporaries, it was unique. Moreover, the Aristophanic comedy could not have been developed in any other society or in any other age. The genre itself was as unique as was Aristophanes' personal handling of it.

When and where Greek comedy originated nobody knows; it is said to have existed at Megara and in Sicily before it came to Athens. The word itself may mean either 'revel' songs, or 'village' songs, and no doubt we can accept Aristotle's statement that the germ of it was the phallic impromptu performances in honour of Dionysus, the god of fertility. Greek religion, eminently practical, had the excellent sense to provide for the Dionysiac element in human nature as well as for its loftier aspirations. There is, after all, something to be said for facing facts, and the Greeks' uncomplicated acceptance of a man's animal nature probably saved them a good deal of distress. Exactly what the primitive phallic performances (song and dance) were like one can only guess; but in addition to the symbolic exhibition of male sexuality they appear to have consisted also of personal abuse of all and sundry. In fact, they were an opportunity for the simple worshipper to get a good deal off his chest—much as the Egyptians, according to Herodotus, on their way to Bubastis for the annual festival, would push their boats in to the river-bank at suitable spots to allow the women to hitch up their skirts and shout abuse at their sisters in the vicinity. Religious ceremonial nowadays provides less opportunity for bad language and sexual symbolism.

By a process which cannot be exactly traced these rude but satisfying revels were developed into the admirable art of Athenian comedy, which, for all its elaboration, continued to base itself on the two original elements—phallicism and personal abuse. It is significant that it was at Athens that it reached its acme; Athenian democracy made it possible, for no writer could have aimed his shafts at a 'tyrant' or a governing clique without disastrous consequences to himself. Athens in this respect was free. Aristophanes, being an artist, of course modifies the abusive element, extends its range, and, though he still has his favourite personal butts, gives it social and political point. He abuses not only individuals but political programmes, such as the continuance of the war with Sparta, and philosophical movements such as the speculations and pretensions of the sophists and the revolutionary thinking of Socrates. His handling of these large themes is boisterous and amusing, though many of his jokes, being esoteric, necessarily escape a modern reader. But it is the phallic element in his plays which really make them untranslateable and impossible—despite a gallant attempt to stage the *Lysistrata* recently in London—to play them successfully to a modern audience. For us, sexual jokes must, I think, have an element of surprise in them; they must be somehow allusive, or fetched in a circuit; or they must tickle by contrast with their context. Even Shakespeare's bawdy has inspired a whole volume of elucidation. Greek bawdy was different: it had no subtlety whatever, for the simple reason that the sexual appetite had not yet succeeded in embarrassing its owners. One can fancy a modern playwright working out with infinite innuendo of situation and dialogue an amusing comedy about women in society getting their way by the simple expedient of refusing to go to bed with the men; but I doubt if he would include a scene which showed a foreign ambassador coming with the news that all the agonized men in his town were walking about doubled-up as if they were looking for something with a lantern in the dark.

I have called the art of Aristophanes an admirable art; and so it was. Aristotle in a famous phrase declared that the function of tragedy was by pity and terror to effect a purgation of those emotions. There is no reason in nature why the purgation of other emotions should not be effected by a horse-laugh—which is usually more wholesome than a snicker. Moreover, strange as it may seem to the more departmentalised modern mind, Aristophanes, the purveyor of horse-laughs and cautiously conservative critic of his times, was also a lyric poet of exquisite sensibility and skill, as any reader of the choruses in the *Birds* will remember. The Greeks were good craftsmen, and liked a thing to be well made, if it was made at all, and their sense of beauty was as comfortably at home in a riotous farce as anywhere else.

The Aristophanic comedy was strong meat and needed a certain emotional vitality to make it acceptable. It was also a social phenomenon of great significance, marking as well as anything the wide difference between ancient society and modern. Boys and women saw these plays as well as men—'I'll wager,' says Aristophanes somewhere, 'that they wished they had wings, so that they could fly home while the tragedies were on, and fly back to see the comedies.' Greeks, no doubt, were on all occasions outspoken; but here, at the representation of the comedies, bawdy on a truly tremendous scale was given a public sanction—indeed a religious sanction, for, as I have already said, Dionysus himself was taken to a front seat in the orchestra to make sure he did not miss a word of it—not a word even of the *Frogs*, in which he appears in person as a bemused and second-rate literary critic.

CHAPTER 27

Literature: Science and Philosophy

THE BEGINNINGS OF NONE OF THE GREAT MOVEMENTS OF THOUGHT or of the important steps forward in civilisation can be dated exactly. It is tempting to say—and some people have said—that science, or at least the scientific spirit, first arose in Ionia some six hundred years before Christ; but this is an over-simplification of the truth, due to the nature of that very remarkable efflorescence of speculation and enquiry, which has so much influence upon the world into which Herodotus was born. In point of fact, long before the time of the Ionian philosophers much had occurred in the East, especially in Egypt and Babylonia, without which Greek science might never have arisen at all. The Phoenicians, for instance, had invented the alphabet, an achievement of the intellect of which only familiarity now prevents us from properly appreciating the magnitude. The alphabet was adapted for Greek use about 800 B.C. The Hittites towards the end of the second millennium had discovered the process of smelting iron, a revolutionary discovery; the Babylonians, a little earlier, had gone far in arithmetical astronomy, and the Egyptians, in addition to valuable work in surgery and medicine, had devised a calendar and an advanced system of weights and measures. All this and more provided the bricks for the Greek thinkers to build with. The techniques of science the Greeks found in considerable measure ready to hand, and did not themselves advance them much further, except perhaps in mathematics; what they did was to deduce from these techniques a logical body of scientific knowledge greatly superior to anything which had previously appeared.

Nevertheless the beginnings of Ionian philosophy *look* to the historian like a new thing; and new they were in so far as the speculations of men like Thales and Anaximander of Miletus were a first attempt to explain the working of the universe in terms of natural forces. Under the authoritarian régimes of the great empires of the East, where the masses of the people were kept in ignorance to serve as tools for their masters, the sciences and the techniques of science were for use, and speculation could not be expected to flourish. The ultimate causes of things remained enshrined in myth, and the preservation of myth, with all its attendant ceremonial, was in the hands of a priestly caste; but in the Greek cities of Ionia at the end of the seventh and the beginning of the sixth centuries before Christ conditions were different: there the management of affairs was in the hands of a mercantile aristocracy, eager for expansion and discovery and for the development of new techniques to aid their enterprises. There was an atmosphere of speculative freedom, and a growing confidence not only in the skill, but in the mind, of man and in what it might achieve. Thales, learning his geometry in Egypt, applied it to a means for measuring the distance of ships at sea, and by making use of the Babylonian astronomy foretold an eclipse of the sun. His work was in the first place practical, but his importance in the history of thought lies less in his development of techniques than in his speculative cosmogony. Abandoning myth, he attempted an explanation based on purely rational grounds of how the universe came into being. For Thales, the element out of which everything was made was water; his successor Anaximenes improved upon this by supposing that the four elements—earth, air, fire, water—were all forms of one original indeterminate substance. He also produced the striking theory that fish were an older form of life than mammals; when dry land first appeared out of primeval water, some of the fish adapted themselves to living on land. Hence men have evolved from fish.

The point of interest in the thought of these two men, and in their successors, is not, of course, the particular guess at 'water' or the 'indeterminate substance' being the original material of things, but the fact that it tried to find an original material at all. To reduce Many to One by a process of abstract thinking, to determine the true bases of likeness and difference in a world of apparently inexhaustible multiplicity, is the prime task of intellect. There are still savages, I am told, who have names for every tree but cannot form the concept of *a tree*—nor do I myself know the nature of the mental process by which I consent to include a papillon and a St Bernard under the general name of dog. These Ionian thinkers, then—Thales with water, Anaximenes with the 'indeterminate', Anaximander with fire, Heraclitus with the 'tension' which, as in bow and lyre, kept the physical universe in being—were all seeking some inclusive substance or principle which could explain the constitution of things, and explain it, moreover, without recourse to magic or the gods. They used their eyes and they drew analogies from the way things actually worked in the current techniques of the time; they were rationalist thinkers; much of their knowledge of, for instance, mathematics and astronomy, was already ancient, but they used it in a new way, and for that reason deserve recognition as founders of the Western intellectual tradition.

According to these thinkers life, in some unexplained way, was a product of matter. They came to be known as the atheistic school of Ionia. But there was another group, in which the greatest name is that of Pythagoras, which held different views. This group, living and working in the Greek settlements in Italy, rejected the Ionian materialism and maintained that the first of things was Mind, or Providence, or Soul, which guided and informed the physical world. These two traditions, the religious and the materialistic, continued to act and react upon each other throughout the subsequent history of Greek thought. Pythagoras himself, who was a native of Samos and emigrated to Croton in southern Italy when the Ionian coast was threatened by the advance of the Persians, was a religious mystic, an active and reforming politician, and an eminent scientist, who made great advances in mathematics. His Cosmogony, based upon his theory of Number, I do not profess to understand—unless, indeed, it is intended only to symbolise a certain perfection of harmony and proportion in the constitution of things—and my mind rebels at the notion of peculiar sanctity in the Decad, the mystic Ten, sum of the first four numbers. I have a blind spot with regard to such things, though I can admire the intellectual passion which leads a man to see in any discovered or imagined truth something of the divine, and to sacrifice an ox in worship after the revelation of certain marvellous properties of the square on the hypotenuse.

It is too easy nowadays for the non-scientific layman to accept the findings of the scientist, and to miss the pains and the splendour which led to, and crowned, them. But Pythagoras, like the materialists, did not neglect observation and experiment: he made for instance, important discoveries in acoustics, about which he was set thinking by the chime of hammers on an anvil, as he chanced to hear it on passing a blacksmith's shop—while others of his school conducted experiments in physiology, dissecting and vivisecting animals. The experimentalism of the Pythagoreans was continued by Empedocles, a native of the Sicilian town of Agrigentum, who made the discovery that air was material and could exert force; the simple experiment by which he proved it consisted in showing that a water-clock (a hollow cylinder open at one end and with a small hole at the other) could not be filled by putting the open end into water, so long as the hole at the other end was kept covered by a finger. The discovery was important because it opened a new range of speculation on the validity of the senses as evidence: air, which was invisible, yet had body. If there was one invisible body, there might be others, and the way was open for Democritus and his theory of the atomic structure of the universe. Thus 'ancient science,' as Benjamin Farrington wrote, 'had clearly established the fact that Nature works by unseen bodies. Modern science has progressively devised better methods of seeing the unseen.'

It will be clear from the preceding brief account that in early Geeek thought there was little or no distinction between what we call science and what we call philosophy. The Greeks themselves used the latter term for both, and it is worth remembering that for them it carried a rather different meaning from what it carries for us. Its most general sense is 'love of wisdom', but that does not quite cover it, as *sophia* in Greek includes humbler notions: it also means 'skill', and sometimes even a mere 'trick'. Its corresponding adjective means, not only 'wise' but also, in other contexts 'clever' or 'ingenious.' A thief, a lawyer, a politician or an inventor could, in Greek, all be described as *sophos*, just as well as a man of profound learning or wisdom. This gives a pointer to the origins of 'philosophy' not only in ancient Greece, but (I fancy) anywhere else: it begins with the observation, for practical purposes, of how things work; it invents or improves techniques, and concurrently with its practical uses comes the attempt to generalise, to find a wider and wider application of a particular phenomenon, until it can be described as a law, and then—finally—to discover (or imagine) the single principle which governs the universe. Thus reason and experiment go hand in hand, and so long as they continue to do so, real knowledge grows;

but at times they part company, and reason, growing, so to speak, uppish, fancies that it can manage by itself. From this division many results flow, the chief of them being the rise of 'philosophy' as we understand the term today—a pursuit of great intellectual charm but of small practical value. The division occurred early enough amongst the Greeks, and expressed a revolt from the too close following of the 'mere' evidence of the senses. The most influential of the early rebels was Parmenides of Elea, who proved to his own entire satisfaction that the universe was a single perfect whole, unmoving and immutable for ever. Everything, he declared, either *is* or *is not:* nothing which *is* can change except by the admixture of something else; that 'something else' must be what *is not*—and therefore does not exist. Hence nothing changes. Parmenides and his followers were much pleased with this tiresome but irrefutable argument—irrefutable except by the sort of counter-argument which Dr Johnson used to refute the idealism of Bishop Berkeley. The historical importance of Parmenides lies in the fact that his way of thinking not only provides an illustration of a certain profound characteristic of the human mind (that very odd and complex entity), but also that he opened the way for the most influential of all the Greek philosophers, Plato, who, for better or worse, resolutely turned his back upon experimental science and, despite his love for this many-coloured and varied world, found his final reality in the intense inane.

I have called Plato the most influential of the Greek philosophers, and I think he was, though Aristotle ran him pretty close. Nevertheless there are good philosophers today who do not think much of him—Bertrand Russell, for instance. The hostility to Plato, where it exists, is due chiefly to two things: first, by his rejection of experimental science and contempt of industrial techniques as beneath the dignity of a philosopher, Plato administered a check, from which Greek thought never fully recovered, to scientific invention and the consequent control over matter, towards which the old Ionians had given a promising lead; Plato, in fact, did his best—and it was a good best—to strangle Greek science in the cradle. Secondly, the Platonic philosophy is not a system so much as a method: it contains no body of coherent conclusions; it does not state, but, rather, guides and suggests; it is not a system of thought, but a way of thinking, an attitude of mind. Clearly, if that attitude of mind, that way of thinking, happen to be antipathetic to the reader, Plato will appear an unsatisfactory philosopher. There is a third reason why some readers are hostile to Plato, and that is his expression of certain views which he did—in spite of his generally tentative approach to truth—express with extreme definiteness and clarity: the views, namely, which he held about marriage and the family, and about the authoritarian state. These views, though wholly intelligible historically and within their context, are nowadays distasteful to pretty well anyone of a liberal turn of mind. Nevertheless Plato was so important a thinker and so brilliant a writer, that he obviously cannot be circumvented. He was, moreover, one of the few philosophers—Berkeley and William James are two others that occur to me—whose work is delightful to read by reason of its literary grace and freedom from technical jargon, even for those whose interest is not primarily philosophic.

I have already suggested that Plato's work represents the decadence of the old Greek spirit, and so it does. But the human spirit being what it is, any end is always a beginning. Plato does not belong to Herodotus' world, though he is the child of it, and the temper and substance of his thought spring inevitably from it. Plato, as everybody knows, was a pupil of Socrates, and it is the pupil who has given the master immortality. Socrates wrote nothing; all his teaching was oral, and the image of him we have in our minds today—amongst the most vivid of any man in the ancient world—is due almost wholly to the writings of Plato and of Xenophon—and to a scurrilous scene or two in Aristophanes. How far Plato's presentation of Socrates' thought is a true one it is not possible to say, but that Socrates was a revolutionary thinker there is no doubt at all: it is evident, if from nothing else, from the conservative Aristophanes' guying of him in the *Clouds* and from the fact that the Athenian democracy, supposedly liberal, condemned him to death on a trumped-up charge of preaching atheism and corrupting the youth of Athens. Aristotle in his dry manner tells us that Socrates invented the logical method of induction and 'general ideas', or 'universal definitions'; perhaps he did, though it might be truer to say that he improved, rather than invented, the former, as one cannot assign to one man the invention of an intellectual process which is present, at least in embryo, in any advanced and self-conscious society; and that he not so much invented as concentrated his thought upon the latter, as the movement towards general ideas is the fundamental movement of all philosophy and science, not to say of all thinking whatsoever. Nevertheless, however we define Socrates' peculiar contribution to philosophy, it is evident that the whole effort of his thought was directed to the attempt to get behind accepted and popular attitudes towards morality, government and religion and to reveal the inadequate philosophical basis upon which they stood. In this Plato followed him, and went much further.

Plato was born about 430 B.C., just at the outbreak of the Peloponnesian war which was to destroy the power and splendour of Athens. He belonged to one of the oldest Athenian families and would, in the ordinary course of things, have taken up a political career, had not circumstances and his own temperament prevented him. By nature he was poet and dreamer, with a poet's love of the sensible world and a poet's ability to immerse himself in it and to withdraw from it by turns. One of the most charming of the small poems in the Greek Anthology—

> Bright Star of mine, you watch the skies:
> Would I were heaven, to see you with a thousand eyes—

is his. He grew up in war-time Athens, and it is not hard to understand how with his richly sensuous nature, combined with a soaring idealism and an almost feminine delicacy and sensibility, he was forced to turn away from the growing coarseness and brutality—so vividly described in the grim pages of Thucydides —which were overlaying the life of that once brilliant society. What led him finally to reject an active political career and devote himself to contemplation he himself recorded in one of his letters. 'As a young man,' he wrote, 'I passed through the common stage of supposing that I should enter politics as soon as I became my own master. At the time the situation was that the democratic régime in Athens having fallen into general disfavour, a revolution took place and political power fell into the hands of thirty men. A number of them were acquaintances of mine, and some related to me by blood, and I was invited to support them as they naturally supposed I should approve their policy. Well, I was young, and it is not surprising that I expected them to rid public life of its abuses and introduce a just and decent form of government. I set myself to watch with the closest attention what they would do, with the result that I soon saw that the previous government was a golden age compared with theirs. I was sickened by what they did and withdrew all my support. Not long afterwards there was another revolution and the Thirty Tyrants were driven from office. Once again, though this time with less urgency, I felt the desire to play my part in public affairs; in the generally confused situation much that was distasteful was, of course, going on, and it was only to be expected that in an atmosphere of revolution there should be personal hatreds and reprisals, nevertheless the restored democracy acted on the whole with great moderation. Unhappily however certain influential persons brought an action against Socrates—whom we loved. They sued him on the outrageous and absurd charge of impiety, and the jury condemned him to death.' Plato continues by describing what he sees as the rapid crumbling of all the social decencies and the growing corruption of government, and concludes with the reflection that no system of government anywhere in the world can be good, and humanity can never be free from its misery, 'until true philosophers assume political power, or the governors of states, by some heaven-sent miracle, become true philosophers.'

This is a far cry from sixth-century Greece, from the jolly scoundrelism of a Polycrates and his piratical navy, from the drinking songs of an Alcaeus or Anacreon, or the eager hopes and golden self-confidence of Athens after the defeat of Xerxes; the old, bright, bloody, masculine world had come to an end; Greeks —Athenians—who had always lived gaily under the shadow of death, grieving only for life's transience, now knew that it was not only their individual selves which would go down too soon into the dark: it was their way of life which had died. City life and the old personal and political squabbles were still, no doubt, good enough for the go-getters and the vulgar, as indeed they are in any country and in any age; but they were not good enough for the idealistic and other-worldly Plato, who saw too clearly that the springs had dried up and a radiance had passed away, leaving the world shabby. There was nothing he could do but withdraw into contemplation and fashion for himself and for those who would listen to him a new world of the mind and spirit. Plato was the first philosopher of the spiritual life, the first to find in the unseen the only reality, the first to teach that man's true home is in eternity. It was through the writings of Plato that Augustine was led to Christianity.

But there is more in Plato than religious mysticism. I like to think of him first simply as an imaginative artist and as the inventor and perfecter of a new literary form—the dialogue. The form was beautifully apt both for Plato's mind and for his method. The old philosophers had written in verse: crabbed, difficult verse, somewhat dark and oracular; later philosophers— Aristotle for instance—composed treatises, as rounded and complete as they could make them; but Plato's dialogues, at least the majority of them, have no sense of finality, no conclusion; they are true conversations, artfully directed indeed, but eddying, and progressing, and returning upon themselves 'whither the argument leads', as conversations do. The dialogue moreover gives space and opportunity for different points of view, different approaches towards a problem, and in good hands has a suppleness of movement, a dramatic life and verisimilitude such as the formal treatise can never have.

One must admit that not a few of Plato's *dramatis personae* are yes-men or mere cockshies to be knocked down by Socrates; but not always: many of his characters step from his pages in all the fulness of life—Thrasymachus, for instance, in the *Republic*, the swaggering bully (who had nevertheless 'once actually been seen to blush'), the brash and commonsensical arguer, bludgeoning the company into the belief—not, surely, a wholly stupid belief, and tempting to all of us in our less philosophical moments —that justice is, in the last analysis, a mere convention, deliberately built up by the powerful to protect their interests; or the aged Cephalus, calmly happy to have been released from the turbulence of youth; Agathon the playwright, in the *Symposium*, who, though he yields in the end to the metaphysical exaltations of Socrates, yet delivers a most noble and moving panegyric upon love; the boys playing at knuckle-bones in the *Lysis;* Charmides, the incarnation of youthful temperance; Theaetetus, the apt scholar the movement of whose thought is 'like a stream of oil, flowing silently'. These are a few which spring to mind. Then, in addition to persons, there are scenes, sketched lightly in with a novelist's skill, like the irruption of Alcibiades, not too sober, into the party in the *Symposium*, or the famous scene at the close of that dialogue, where everyone but Socrates succumbs to sleep: 'The others had all dropped asleep or gone home except Agathon, Socrates and Aristophanes, who were still awake and still drinking. Socrates was talking—Aristodemus could not, he told us, remember everything he said, for he had arrived late and was drowsy; but the chief point was that Socrates was trying to make the other two admit that the same man ought to be able to write both tragedy and comedy. They agreed perforce, being in any case too sleepy to follow the argument. Then Aristophanes dropped off, and, finally, Agathon, just as dawn was breaking. Socrates, having put them to sleep, got up and left the house, and after taking a bath at the Lyceum spent the rest of the day as usual. In the evening he went home to bed.'

One could mention many more, such as the arrival of Socrates and his young friend at the house where the sophist Protagoras was staying, or the delightful setting of the *Phaedrus*, with the light talk, somewhat shy and earnest on the part of Phaedrus and smilingly ironic on the part of Socrates, as the two men, strolling together outside the city walls, find the perfect spot where in coolness and shade they can lie on the soft grass and discuss the eternal verities of life and love; or, again, the vivid opening scene of the *Republic*, where Socrates is urged to stay for the pleasure of witnessing a new all-night festival with a torch-race on horseback. It is such scenes and characters, interspersed with rapid personal portraiture—as of Socrates stumping along the streets of Athens and glaring to left and right, under his brows, like a bull, or of the boy Hippocrates, who 'blushed as he spoke, as I could see, for just at that moment the dawn was breaking'—it is these things, together with the constant references to the everyday life of the city, to men working at their trades, to the shipwrights, the dyers and carpenters and cobblers, which—philosophy apart—make Plato so agreeable an author to read. Plato loved life and all the manifestations of it, and he was able in the course of his dialogues —some of them so difficult—to bring the sense of it, fresh and breathing, to his reader's mind. The dialogue he invented was the perfect vehicle for his purpose, moving, it often seems, almost casually and with many obliquities and interruptions towards some speculative goal—What, in fact, *is* Temperance, or Beauty, or Justice?—and, as often as not, breaking off without any final or dogmatic conclusion. Herodotus was the first, Plato the second —and perhaps the last—great prose artist of Greece.

It may seem strange that Plato with his richly sensuous apprecia-tion of the world of nature and man—he writes constantly of love, and not always to use it as an analogy of, or a stepping-stone to, the intellectual love of truth—should have cast aside, in the final reaches of his thought, the world of appearances as a bodiless shadow. The times had much to do with it, and the very delicacy of his sensuous perception helped to make him feel like an alien, while a certain innate austerity in him, a natural temperance and fastidiousness, could not but be outraged by the growing brutality and corruption around him. But whatever the reason, the fact is that the direction of his thought was towards establishing the existence of two worlds: the world of appearances (or of Opinion) in which the ignorant are content to live, and the spiritual world (the world of Knowledge), which is the only home of the wise. He reached his conclusion by way of what is commonly known as his Theory of Ideas, a process of reasoning, which began as a theory of knowledge and ended as something not unlike a religious manifesto. In his Theory of Ideas (or of 'universals') he was following his old master Socrates. 'How is it,' he asked, as Socrates had asked, and as all metaphysicians have asked since; 'how is it that we know?' The savages who name their trees but cannot form the conception of *a tree*, cannot, surely, be said to know them, because knowledge of a thing implies knowledge of its relationship to other things, and in particular to the class of things to which it belongs, to the 'form', or 'idea', or 'universal', in which it shares. This applies to abstract notions as well as to concrete things: we may suppose, for instance, that we know a beautiful face or a just action when we see it; but our knowledge cannot be real knowledge until we know what justice and beauty are, in themselves. Thus far, in his search for 'universal definitions', Plato is easy to follow, especially as his search leads, as his manner is, through so many agreeable by-ways of argumentation and error; but he comes in the end to a strange country on the threshold of which not a few of his readers must pause. Not con-tent with his noble and profound definitions of the great abstract words—Beauty, Love, Temperance, Courage, Justice: unwilling to stop at the image which his subtle thought has enabled him to form of them, he proceeds to tell us that all these things—all the great abstracts, and the objects, too, which we can touch or see in this world—in their essence, or Idea, or Form, have an actual, separate existence, or Being, somewhere in that other, and eternal, world which only the mind can understand and dwell in. In this world are beautiful things; in that world is Beauty itself, immutable and everlasting. Which of the two worlds is reality and which the shadow, we already know.

I enjoy the writings of Plato, but, not being a philosopher, I enjoy them for the wrong reason. When he talks of Ideas—of Forms—as *existences*, as real and actual to the eye of the mind as are their shadows on earth to the eye of the body, I say it is nonsense; yet there is a kind of nonsense which is perhaps preferable, in some respects, to sense. Language is an imperfect instrument, and there is a sort of experience which is inexpressible in logical terms. May one not read Plato's highest metaphysical flights not as statements of belief about the constitution of things, not as inspired guesses like those of the old philosophers of Ionia and Italy at the nature of matter and of mind, but rather as a sort of symbolism, or poetic image, of an habitual experience of his own? I do not find Plato's 'Beauty Itself, immutable and eternal', and all his other Essences, at all nonsensical, if I try to approach them in the same spirit as I should approach, say, Keats' nightingale, not born for death.

The strength of Plato lies in the fact that together with his aspiration towards the world of the spirit he was still able to live, delightedly, in the world of sense. Or not, perhaps, to live; for the City State as he saw it around him had gone awry and was no home for a true philosopher. Yet, at the same time, there was still so much in it that was beautiful, so much in human character —in the young especially—that was still noble and full of promise, that he was never able, and never willing to turn his eyes wholly away. He took, as it were, his love of this world with him into the spiritual world which he created. He never, as St Augustine, for instance, did when he was sickened by the sensualities of his youth, flung it aside as anathema. Both worlds he continued to possess, finding the excellencies of the one only through the transfigured excellencies of the other. This was because he had the mind of a poet as well as of a philosopher; one feels that for all the passion of his search for an intellectual eternity inhabited only by those creatures of his brain, the Ideas, he would nevertheless have understood William Blake's insistence upon Minute Particulars.

Plato's politics, if they are taken in any sort of literal sense, are repellent; but springing, as they do, from his reaction to the collapse of the old ideals of the City State, they are intelligible enough. His ideal Republic leads straight to all the detestable modern totalitarianisms. To say, moreover, as Plato said, that no good government is possible until philosophers are Kings or Kings philosophers, is either rubbish or a truism. It is like saying that none of us will be virtuous until we have attained to virtue. Political theory, in order to be useful, must bear some reference to the facts of human nature, and one fact of human nature is that philosophers are unlikely to have either the wish or the ability to engage in the affairs of government. Nevertheless, there is, I suppose, in this famous saying of Plato one grain of truth: it does, at least, establish a connection between morality and the exercise of power—a connection which, though obvious to modern thought, however much ignored in modern practice, was not apparent in the older Greece. Utopias make fascinating reading, they reveal so clearly both the weakness and the strength of their creators: one of the commonest weaknesses is the touching belief that recalcitrant mankind can be dragooned into righteousness.

Plato in his early manhood believed at least for a moment, that his political ideas might bear some practical fruit. He went to Sicily and tried to educate the young tyrant of Syracuse into philosophical kingship. But he soon returned to Athens, where he founded the Academy—the first of Colleges—where he spent the remainder of his long life, writing and teaching. He died at the age of eighty, as Cicero tells us 'pen in hand.'

The Ionian philosophers had been, in the main, practical men, interested in science as an 'art', or technique, directed to the control of nature for the improvement of the human lot, and founding their cosmologies upon certain observed natural phenomena. They had the same sort of interest in science as Bacon, for instance, had. In addition to specific inventions, such as bronze-casting, the lathe, the key, the level and the square by Theodorus of Samos, or the soldering-iron by Glaucus of Chios, brilliant work was done in the early part of the fifth century in medicine by the school of Hippocrates in Cos. It took Europe more than a thousand years, after the loss of the old Greek learning, to reach a similar point of advancement in the diagnosis and treatment of disease. What would have been the effect upon ancient civilisation if this kind of scientific experiment and enquiry had been con-sistently followed, one can only guess. It might well have led to a technological revolution—for good or ill. But, as I have already indicated, it was checked by the enormously influential teaching of Socrates and Plato. Moreover there was another reason, this time a social one, why experimental science fell into disfavour: this was the increase of slavery during the course of the fifth century. The effect of the increasing employment of slaves in all technical processes was to bring those processes into disrepute as occupations for free men. Engagement in trade or handicraft had been no disgrace in the older Greece. Solon had made a law that no son in Athens should be obliged to support his father in old age unless he had taught him a trade. But by the middle of the fifth century the situation was different, and Plato's contempt of the mechanical arts as a field for intelligent enquiry was in part a reflection of their altered status in society.

The same contempt of the mechanical arts is to be seen in Plato's great successor, Aristotle, a thinker (in my view) to be regarded with awe untempered by affection. The scope of his work was vast, and included metaphysics, cosmology, ethics, politics, biology, logic and literary criticism. But one cannot *read* Aristotle, as one can read Plato; one can go to him only in the spirit of a student, to be improved or depressed; and one returns from the session thankful for two things: first, that so powerful and comprehensive an intelligence should have appeared in the world, and, secondly, that anything of a similar sort should have appeared so seldom. Aristotle's chief contributions to knowledge were in logic (the Aristotelian logic held the field for over two thousand years, but is now, I am told, outmoded) and in biology. His *Ethics*, a famous book, has, I think, nothing to teach us today. Herodotus, if he chanced to read it in Elysium, must surely have smiled, and wondered what had happened to the Greece he knew to render possible so uninspired and cautious a system of morality. The doctrine of the Mean would certainly have tickled him—that doctrine which asserts that every virtue is a mean between two extremes, each of which is a vice. One remembers Bertrand Russell's delightful story of the mayor who, reviewing his policy in a public speech on the occasion of relinquishing office, declared that his constant aim had been to steer the difficult course between partiality on the one hand, and impartiality on the other. Aristotle's *Poetics* is in a different category: this essay—or lecture—dry, difficult and short—is a brilliant piece of work. It is the first attempt at formal literary criticism in Greece—for Plato, though he has much to say about poetry and poetic inspiration (which he considered a kind of madness) says it mostly by the way and always with a view to its moral implications. Aristotle on the contrary tried to establish the *laws* of poetry, as such, in particular of dramatic poetry. The *Poetics* can be useful reading today, when so much of current literary criticism is unrelated to any principles at all, and dependent merely upon taste or prejudice.

I am not competent to speak of Greek mathematics, the branch of science in which, as good judges have declared, the Greek genius was most brilliantly shown. Pythagoras was said to have been the first to make the study of mathematics a 'liberal education'. Plato attached such importance to mathematics that pupils were not allowed to enter the Academy without a grounding in geometry. In Geometry Euclid (who was a few years younger than Aristotle) remained absolute master until the middle of the last century, when some of his initial assumptions were for the first time questioned. Greek contributions to astronomy were hardly less important than their contributions to mathematics. Anaximander (early 6th century B.C.) was the first to suppose that the earth floats freely, unsupported by any other body; Pythagoras (middle of 6th century B.C.) supposed it to be spherical. Anaxagoras (middle of 5th century) discovered that the moon shone by reflected light. Philolaus of Thebes (end of 5th century) denied that the earth was the centre of the universe. Heracleides of Pontus (early 4th century) discovered that Venus and Mercury revolve round the sun, and supposed the earth to rotate on its axis every twenty-four hours. Aristarchus of Samos (310–230 B.C.) put forward the hypothesis that all the planets, including the earth, revolve round the sun, and thus anticipated Copernicus (1500 A.D.). By the third century B.C. the diameter of the earth and the earth's distance from the moon had both been calculated with very fair precision. The distance of the sun was still underestimated by about half.

All these achievements, it will be noticed, were in the realm of pure science—Euclid himself refused to recognise any practical value in geometry. Advances in applied science were nugatory or non-existent.

PART FIVE

The City State

CHAPTER 28

Democracy in Athens

I BROKE OFF MY SKETCH OF POLITICAL DEVELOPMENT IN ATHENS at the reform of Solon (640-560 B.C.), and the coming to power of Peisistratus. Without the work of Solon the subsequent establishment of Athenian democracy would hardly have been possible, but the real architect of that democracy was Cleisthenes.

The rule of Peisistratus had been wholly beneficial to Athens, especially to the peasant-community; but underneath the quiet exterior of things, the old aristocratical ambitions were still smouldering. At Peisistratus' death they burst into flame again. His son Hippias, who had none of his father's ability, was forced after a brief period of rule to leave the country, and at once entered, as the Greek manner was, into friendly relations with the Persian King. Athens was free—but without a government; so the familiar struggle began again. This time the two rivals for power were Cleisthenes and Isagoras; Isagoras won the first round, but spoiled his chances of ultimate success by calling in a Spartan army to support him, banishing seven hundred families whom he knew to be hostile, and dissolving the Council. It was the presence of Spartan troops on the Acropolis, much more than the savage sentences of exile or the dissolution of the popular Council, which roused the anger of the Athenians; in the comparatively peaceful and prosperous days under Peisistratus the men of Attica with their growing trade and influence, and a certain semblance of popular government bequeathed by Solon and preserved, at least in form, by Peisistratus had come to look upon themselves as the leaders of Ionian Greece and their pride was outraged by the sight of a foreign army on their sacred Hill. It was the moment for Cleisthenes to act. He did so, promptly— it was about the year 510 B.C. The Spartan force—not a large one —was blockaded and within a few days forced to surrender. Isagoras disappeared from history, and Cleisthenes had the way clear for his revolutionary reforms. Like Solon, but unlike almost

every other Greek in history, Cleisthenes had no wish for personal
power; his reforms were directed solely towards the benefit, as
he saw it, of his City. It is to be regretted that we know nothing
of the personal life of this remarkable man: he did not even leave
verses behind him, as his great predecessor did.

Cleisthenes' problem was a purely practical one. The Athenians
were ripe for self-government of a sort, and the problem was,
quite simply, how to ensure in the course of it that the great
families, or clans, did not continue to make a nuisance of themselves by competing for power, as they had done all over Greece
after the period of the kings. The division of Attica, which had
existed from far back into antiquity, into four tribes each with
its three 'brotherhoods' and ninety clans, all based upon the ties
of blood, naturally led to a conflict of loyalties, and it was
Cleisthenes' object to resolve the conflict by redirecting the
loyalty of every Athenian to the community as a whole. This
obviously desirable end one would expect to be reached only
after a long period of development and change; Cleisthenes,
however, brought it into being almost overnight and by entirely
artificial means. He devised, so to speak, a blue-print for patriotism: and the extraordinary—and surely unprecedented—thing
was, that it worked. That Cleisthenes should have seen what
practical steps were necessary is hardly more remarkable than that
his fellow-Athenians should have been willing, at that moment in
their history, to take them. It argues a political intelligence of
a high order—a political intelligence not, on this occasion,
rendered useless by passion.

Cleisthenes, at a stroke, abolished the four ancient tribes,
and created ten new ones in their place, each with its patron
saint, or eponymous hero, sanctioned by the oracle at Delphi.
This may seem arbitrary rather than revolutionary, but the point
was that each of the new tribes was divided into three sections,
widely separated over Attica. Thus the old territorial loyalties
of the Hill, the Plain and the Coast were destroyed. At the same
time Cleisthenes created a new unit of local government, to take
the place of the old parishes or 'ship districts': this was the deme,
or village. There were over a hundred of them, divided into ten
groups to correspond with the ten tribes. Membership of the
deme was made hereditary, so that a family kept the name even
if it went to live elsewhere. This was a further blow at the

influence of the blood-tie; every Athenian was henceforth supposed to be known, not, as formerly, as the 'son of So-and-So',
but as 'So-and-So *of Paeania*', or whatever his deme might be.
As no Greek could do without his local sanctities, the demes,
like the tribes, were given their eponymous heroes.

Such in outline was Cleisthenes' blue-print for the political
reorganisation of Attica. How did the new democracy function?
and what was the political connection between the demes and the
central government in Athens? The People were the supreme
authority, and they—or as many of them as cared to attend—gave
in the Ecclesia (Assembly) their sanction or refusal to all measures
of policy. As the numbers in the Assembly precluded the possibility
of useful debate, all business was previously discussed in the Boule
(Council) and passed on to the Assembly for ratification. The
Council consisted of 500 annually elected members, 50 from each
tribe; it was divided into ten committees, one of which was on
duty for the tenth part of each year. From these committees a
President was chosen by lot every day, and to him, as acting
head of the government, were entrusted the state archives, the
keys of the Acropolis and the state seal. He was not eligible for
re-election. In addition to preparing resolutions for the Assembly
on matters of general policy, the Council was responsible for
finance and received an account from all outgoing civil officials
of their tenure of office.

The method of election to the Council was peculiar and points
to one of the chief differences (apart from mere scale) between the
ancient and the modern democracy. The ancients fully realised
the necessity of representative government, but at the same time,
with their characteristic distrust of the expert and their belief
that any man of ordinary intelligence was as capable as his
neighbour of public work, they wished to open the way to
political responsibility to as many people as possible. The Athenian
ideal was government by intelligent amateurs, none of whom
should hold office long enough to make them feel like profes-
sionals. With this ideal in mind they appointed their officials
annually, and by a curious mixture of chance and choice. For
membership of the Council the demes, on a proportional basis,
elected such candidates as they thought most suitable, and from
the list of candidates, elected for merit, the 500 Councillors were
then chosen by lot. In the same way the nine Archons ('Govern-

ors', originally law officers) were chosen by lot out of 500 candidates elected for merit by the demes, and also the 'Judges', or jurymen, who were first elected by the demes, sent up to Athens, and there drawn for by lot according to what legal business had to be done. Of judges in the modern sense the Athenians had none, once Solon had constituted the great popular court of the Heliaea, consisting nominally of the whole people; after that the business of the archons was confined to matters of procedure. The Heliaea was subsequently split into a number of smaller courts, consisting of hundreds rather than of thousands, and it was to the members of these courts that the power of judgement belonged. Any citizen was allowed by Solon's judicial reforms to bring an action. The accused had to make his own defence, and this in course of time led to the rise of professional speech-makers, who for a fee would compose a defendant's speech, to be learned by him by heart and delivered as his own. Many of these speeches survive from the fourth century and the conception of law which they convey to a modern reader is, to say the least, curious. Much of their matter is, as evidence, entirely irrelevant, being based upon such arguments as that the defendant, having done the state good service in the past, is therefore presumably innocent, or at any rate deserves acquittal. This, however, is a criticism by the way: Solon's decision to make the people as a whole the repository of justice was perhaps the most important single step forward towards a democratic régime. It was human nature—and Greek human nature, at that— which sometimes perverted its fair intention. At a Greek trial the prosecutor proposed the sentence, and the defendant (as we learn from Plato's *Apology of Socrates*) was allowed to propose an alternative. The court decided between the two. The very considerable body of Greek forensic literature which survives is interesting and valuable, for the light it throws upon certain aspects, often murky, of everyday life in fourth-century Athens, but considered as literature it can be tedious. Demosthenes, I suppose, deserves his high reputation as an orator: he was certainly copious, and knew how to coin a phrase; but most of his speeches make somewhat sad reading today. His self-righteousness, his exaggerated touchiness, his absurdly blind and old-fashioned form of patriotism—wishing back, in golden periods, a time which has irrevocably gone—all make the attempt to read him a task rather than a pleasure. One can enjoy a small speech such as he composed against Conon—a young tough who had committed the dreadful crime of knocking down an enemy in the street, and, as he jumped on his prostrate body, of flapping his elbows and crowing like a cock; but one reader, at least, struggling through the famous and immensely long indictment of Meidias finds his sympathy with the accused, who hit the orator in the eye, on a public occasion, in the theatre of Dionysus.

The only department of Athenian state affairs which was not run by amateurs was the military. Not even an Athenian could believe that pretty well anybody might be as good a general in the field as his neighbour. Athenian army commanders were all elected for merit; originally there were ten of them, one elected by each tribe to command the tribal unit, and on that principle the army was organised at Marathon. Later however, though the number of generals remained at ten, they were appointed not by tribal vote but by the people as a whole. All generals might be re-elected for further terms of service, and they were the only public servants in Athens who were not subject to scrutiny at the end of a year of office. There was no distinction between 'general' and 'admiral', any commander being liable to service either by sea or land. The political power of the military commanders was great; being trusted and experienced men, not appointed by lot, they could exert pressure and influence on the Assembly. Pericles, apart from his genius for leadership, exercised his thirty years of dominance over Athenian policy by virtue of his military office. Technically, he had no more power to direct policy than any other Athenian citizen, in or out of office, and he had to *persuade* (and disastrously succeeded in persuading) the Athenian people to embark on their expansionist policy and to undertake, and to continue, their war with Sparta.

All Athenian citizens served as a matter of course when occasion arose, with the fleet or the army, poorer classes as light-armed troops, the richer as hoplites (heavy-armed infantry) or cavalry providing their own equipment. In the fleet the oarsmen were either foreign mercenaries or slaves, only the crew of a trireme (20 strong) and the party of ten marines being free citizens. With each trireme on service went the trierarch, a wealthy citizen who had been required by Athenian custom to fit out the ship and maintain her in good order. Only the hulls and a part of the rigging were provided at the expense of the state.

The mention of the trierarchs suggests an important difference between the old Greek democracy and the democracies of the modern world. The difference concerns the Greek attitude towards public finance in general; and, by implication, towards the nature of the relationship between the state and the individual. In the Western World today the interests of the individual are supposed to be paramount, and the state exists to protect and to further them. For this protection and for the provision of certain amenities which he would not otherwise possess, the individual pays—reluctantly—a certain proportion of his income in various forms of taxation. In the Greek democratic communities the position was reversed: the Greek view was always that the state came first, and that the individual existed only to serve it—which service was not so much a duty as a privilege. Hence the (to us) extraordinary institution of *liturgies*.

In Athens—and probably in most of the democratic states— resident aliens who, since Solon's time, had been encouraged to take up residence, provided that they were skilled craftsmen, and slaves who had bought, or been given, their freedom, paid a poll-tax to the state; but the free citizens paid no direct taxes whatever, except in war-time. How then were the public services paid for? The answer is, by the liturgies, an institution which, to the modern mind, seems too Utopian to be true, and is impossible to understand as existing amongst the hard-headed and fiercely self-regarding Greeks unless one first understands the nature and quality of their feeling for the state. Wealthy Athenians not only paid for, but competed for the privilege of paying for, certain public services out of their own pockets. This was the 'liturgy', or 'service'. The fitting-out and maintenance of ships for the navy, the arrangements for festivals and public games, the production of plays, and all other such national jamborees, were paid for voluntarily by individuals who chanced to be able to afford it. No compulsion, no persuasion even, seems to have been needed to raise this money; to provide it was a pleasure and an honour. I have said enough elsewhere about the Greek love of home; nothing illustrates it more vividly than this; a Greek belonged to his community in a far more intimate and personal way than is possible in the modern world; it was an extension of himself, and necessary to his being. He *wanted* his city to be not only powerful amongst its neighbours, if such a thing were possible, but beautiful to look at. The artistic and intellectual eminence of Athens in the fifth century was as much a matter of personal pride to her individual citizens as was her growing wealth and material dominion. It is better, said Pericles, to be a poor man in a splendid city than a rich man in a needy one—and that, on the lips of a Greek, was no pious platitude, but a statement of fact. The actual buildings which made Athens beautiful, and of which the ruins still stand on the Acropolis, make, unfortunately, a different story: those buildings were not paid for by liturgies; they were paid for by the tribute money belonging to the Confederacy of Delos, which Athens filched for her private use. So hard it is to retain one's honesty and ideals in face of commercial prosperity and military success. A further illustration of the Greek sense of community in the best days is the absence of personal ostentation. Demosthenes remarks that a stranger on coming to Athens and having duly admired the splendour of the public buildings, might well ask to be shown the houses where Themistocles or Aristides or others of the great men of old used once to live—and how surprised he would be to find that his guide did not even know where they were, or how to distinguish them from all the other modest dwellings in the neighbourhood.

> *Privatus illis census erat brevis,*
> *Commune magnum —*

so Horace put it in a neat phrase, as he dwelt admiringly in imagination on the very real austerity of Athens in contrast with the vulgar and ostentatious use of private wealth in his contemporary Rome. The Greeks may be justly accused of most of the crimes in the Newgate Calendar, but they were never, in their great days, vulgar. It is one of their chief titles to the homage of posterity.

It will be seen from the foregoing sketch that the Athenian democracy, of which the foundations were laid by Solon and the superstructure built by Cleisthenes, and which was modified though never changed in any important respect by succeeding statesmen, possessed what in Athenian eyes were the essential merits of giving to as many people as possible an active share in the business of government, and at the same time of leaving the individual free to manage his personal concerns in his own way. Though possible only in the dimunitive communities of ancient Greece, so largely self-sufficient, and free from the economic complexities of the modern world, it was a brilliant political experiment and succeeded in providing, for a brief period of some sixty or seventy years, much of the necessary background for what the Athenians felt to be the 'good life'. It gave them 'activity', as Aristotle defined virtue, 'along the lines of excellence.' Nevertheless in the face of all the impassioned cries for 'freedom' and self-government which have echoed down the ages, it is as well for a detached observer to ask, 'Whose freedom?' One must remember that the Athenians, though they were justly proud of their free institutions when they compared them with the Oriental despotisms or with the narrow oligarchies and 'tyrannies' which they could see around them, or remember, in other parts of Greece, were none the less enabled to live the life which satisfied them—a life of active and constant participation in public affairs, of gaping in the law-courts, shouting in the Assembly, arguing in the Council, idling and talking—forever talking—in the market place—in no small degree because the dirtiest work was done for them by slave labour. This is hardly, I suppose, a thing to deprecate or to be surprised at; it took more than eighteen centuries of Christianity to abolish the institution of slavery, and even now it lingers. In the ancient world it was universal and unquestioned. Aristotle speaks of races and classes of men who are 'by nature' slaves—much as he speaks of the 'justness' of a war when it is waged against men who are 'natural subjects' but refuse to recognise that patent fact.

In Athens during the time of Pericles there were probably about 100,000 slaves, a number not very different from the number of the free population, including women and children. Few of them were Greeks; most were kidnapped or bought somewhere in Thrace or Asia Minor, by speculators, brought to Athens and sold again in the slave-market. Women slaves may at certain periods have been Greek, for it was Greek military practice on the capture of an enemy town, to butcher the men and sell women and children into slavery.

Zimmern in his invaluable book *The Greek Commonwealth* made an eloquent plea for the Athenians in their treatment of the slaves, and would have persuaded us of the falsity of the common view that Athenian civilisation rested upon slave labour. He would regard the slaves in Athens—all except those who were employed in the mines at Laureion—as 'fellow-workers', hardly as slaves at all, and presents the treatment they received as yet another instance of the enlightenment and humanity of Periclean Athens. There is no doubt whatever that a large proportion of the slaves in Athens were employed in work of a kind which one does not associate with slavery. Athens, as her commercial activities grew, needed men; as we have seen, she encouraged foreigners who were skilled in a trade to settle in the city, and gave them many of the privileges of citizenship; and she also needed the work of her slaves in craftsmanship and industry. Slaves worked side by side with free citizens at the same tasks, at building, or metal-working or whatever it might be. They held posts as clerks and accountants. They were indistinguishable in dress and appearance from their masters; they were allowed to own money, and—most important of all—the best of them lived with a prospect of ultimate freedom, which they might either purchase with their savings or obtain as a legacy in their master's will. Pasion, the immensely wealthy fourth-century banker, began life as a slave.

All this is indisputable, as is the fact that many household slaves, if they chanced to have a good master, lived as members of the family and happily enough. But it is easier to collect facts about the past than to interpret them: the Greeks were not a humane people; cruelty and indifference to suffering is no doubt a universal trait in human nature, but with us today it is at least disguised; with the ancients it was still open and unashamed. The Athenians needed their slaves: they needed them not only for the dirty work but also for assistance in many honourable tasks, and they knew well enough—who wouldn't?—that a slave who is treated like a beast cannot be expected to do well the work of a free man in industry and the crafts. It may well have been self-interest as much as virtue which led them to make their slaves' lives tolerable. And there remain the slaves who were employed in the silver-mines. There may have been some 20,000 of these; they were selected in the slave-market—all those who seemed too stupid or too recalcitrant to be taught a craft. Sent to the mines, they worked there, in continuous shifts day and night, until they died. The

mine-shafts (still existing) were two to three feet wide and two
to three feet high; the slaves worked naked and in chains by the
light of oil-lamps. They had nothing to look forward to but death.
This fact, it seems to me, is not difficult to interpret; and the
callousness to human suffering which it indicates is in no way
softened by that other fact, that other slaves were treated better,
or even well. 'Societies,' wrote Zimmern, 'like men, cannot live
in compartments. They cannot hope to achieve greatness by
making amends in their use of leisure for the lives they have
brutalised in acquiring it.' On the contrary: societies, like men, do
habitually live in compartments; in both there are certain patches
of darkness—or patches of light; the pure white radiance is still
reserved for eternity. Even the cultivated society of eighteenth-
century London, in spite of the background of the gin-shops,
the squalor, the public hangings and the slave-trade, had its
elements of graciousness and charm. There is no need to explain
away the one in order to recognise the other.

Athens was at the pinnacle of her greatness when Herodotus
went to live there about the year 447 B.C., though even then there
had been dropped into the wide arable land of events the seed
which was to grow into a poison tree and destroy her. That seed
was the imperialist policy first set in motion by Themistocles and
Aristides after the defeat of Persia and later intensified by Pericles.
There is no need here to trace in detail the complex of events
which attended the rise and consolidation of the Athenian empire.
The general pattern is sufficiently well known. It began with the
vision of Themistocles which foresaw the necessity of sea-power
for Athens, if she was to survive. After the retreat of Xerxes the
Ionian and Aeolian communities of the Asiatic coast, together
with most of the Aegean islands and certain settlements on the
northern Aegean, formed a voluntary maritime federation under
the leadership of Athens, with the object of protecting themselves
from any further attack by Persia and also of continuing raids on
Persian territory to recoup themselves for the expenses of the
war. Some members of the federation, which was known as the
Confederacy of Delos because the common treasury was set up
in that island, contributed ships, others money. The members
met periodically in Delos to discuss policy, and it was soon
apparent that the influence of Athens over the greater number of
the smaller states represented gave her effectual control over the

deliberations. Nearly all the members except two or three of the larger islands followed one another in converting their contribution from ships to money, which was what Athens wanted; then, suddenly, about the year 458 B.C., Athens, feeling herself already mistress of the confederacy in fact though not in name, transferred the treasury of the League from Delos to her own Acropolis. It was an act of open tyranny, and in every way inexcusable. Granted her power, which was great, it transformed at a blow the Delian League into the Athenian empire. Pericles at that moment was at the beginning of his long career of dominance.

Pericles' policy was further to democratise the Athenian government and at the same time to increase in every possible way the extent of Athenian territorial dominion. He dedicated himself to what he saw as the sacred task of making his Athens the acknowledged Queen of the Grecian world, supreme in wealth and power, unrivalled in external beauty, the model of political liberty, the central flame of Greek intellect and culture at which lesser communities might gratefully kindle their little lamps, and an example to all the world of that passionate and personal devotion of her citizens which is the only true patriotism. That he was a remarkable man is not to be doubted. Somewhat cold and aloof (so it is said), unwilling to mix much in society outside his own brilliant inner circle, friend and pupil of the free-thinking philosopher Anaxagoras, personally incorruptible to a degree unprecedented in a Greek, he was out of the usual run of Greek soldiers and politicians. But whether he was Athens' greatest statesman, as so many modern writers have maintained, is highly questionable. It is as easy to charge him with responsibility for the ruin of Athens as to praise him for her brief hour of splendour. Empire—and it was empire that Pericles wanted and in large measure achieved—was incompatible with the essential virtues of Greek civilisation. That civilisation could flower only in small, independent and, so far as possible, self-sufficient communities. The proper movement of Greek political thought was, as I have said elsewhere, towards free institutions and democratic government; nevertheless, in the course of their long history, Greeks had *lived well* under their tyrants and their oligarchies (there was a strong oligarchical party even in Athens during the time of Pericles) simply because it was *their own* community which submitted, for the time being, to the control of the tyrant or the political bosses of the moment—and who could know what the morrow might not bring? Even when they grumbled at personal oppression, they rejoiced in the independence of the state, and it was up to them, they felt, to take the current when it served and cut the throats of their oppressors. Empire was a very different matter; the word was as abhorrent to the ordinary Greek as the name of King came to be in Rome after the expulsion of the Tarquins. The Athenians, of course, gloried in it while it lasted; but they were only preparing their own destruction. Normal Greek feeling against the imperial City was too strong to be long denied; that, added to the commercial rivalry of the other great trading communities, led by Corinth, and the natural jealousy of Sparta, brought on the Peloponnesian war. The war was fought with the utmost savagery and dragged on for twenty-seven years. At the end of it the Athenian empire had melted away, and Athens, though she remained for centuries the intellectual and artistic centre of the Mediterranean world, never again counted in politics for anything at all. Her defeat was the end of a volume of Greek civilisation. The confident morning of the whole Greek world was gone for ever, and the shadow of Alexander, the young military genius from the wild mountains of Macedonia, the buccaneer who slept with the Iliad under his pillow and wished he could have been born a Greek and not a barbarian, was already darkening the horizon.

Scholars have often written as if Periclean Athens and Greek civilisation were, so to speak, synonymous terms. I do not subscribe to this view. Nevertheless Athenian society at that time did have a peculiar brilliance unsurpassed, perhaps, by any other at any time in history. The mere list of contemporary names is impressive: Pericles himself, Sophocles, Pheidias the sculptor, Euripides, Anaxagoras, Socrates, the painter Polygnotus, Gorgias and Protagoras the sophists (professional teachers of philosophy and the arts), Aristophanes, Thucydides, not to mention Herodotus, the honoured guest, and possibly the most brilliant of them all. It is surely a company unrivalled in intellect and creative power. In spite of the deep-seated conservative element in Greek life and thought, it was an age of very rapid development and change, and at the same time of remarkable intellectual tolerance. Men could say what they liked in public, and they said it in no uncertain terms. In the middle of a desperate war which involved the very existence of the community, Aristophanes could curse the warmongers in his stage-plays and publicly plead for peace—and Euripides could write the *Women of Troy*. The name of no statesman or public figure was sacrosanct: Pericles himself came in for ridicule from Aristophanes and others. There was an attempt at one time to get the great man ostracised, but it failed, and his oligarchical rival was banished instead; the comic playwright Cratinus, referring to the incident, wrote: 'Well, the judgement is over—and here comes the squill-headed God Almighty, with the Odeon on his cranium'—not courteous words, but hardly possible in any but a liberal society. Pericles, by the way, had an oddly shaped head: it went up into a peak on top, and he seldom (we read) ventured abroad without a helmet, to modify the effect of this on the beholder.

Ideas were stirring, as never before in a Greek community; we know too little directly about the sophists, because our chief source of information about them is Plato, who detested them; but there seems little doubt that the best of them at least, were men of ability and capable of bold and fruitful speculation. They kept thought on the move, lecturing in public and private on politics, language, ethics and religion, and acting as a constant stimulus to the quick wits of Athenian youth. In outward aspect Athens had never before been so beautiful; the genius of her architects, sculptors and painters was devoted wholly to her service. The public function of the arts was indeed one of the great things about this age. In the modern world the arts are for the delectation of a few, and in their hours of privacy—or were so until yesterday, when certain new popular arts began to arise. In ancient Athens as in Greece generally all art was popular art and offered not to individuals but to the community as a whole; its patron was the whole body of the people—or, if one cares to put it in another way the goddess Athena herself. It was produced for the city's glory; Pheidias did not make his statues for a wealthy client to buy; he made them, on a commission from the state, for the honour of Athena and to adorn her temple, just as Sophocles and his fellow playwrights wrote their plays to add a lustre to the festival of Dionysus. The artist in Athens was the servant of the community, as the military commanders were, and the civil officials. The artist was honoured, but less honoured than the soldier: Aeschylus, when he wrote his own epitaph, did not mention his poetry, but only the fact that he had fought for his country at Marathon. I suppose the principal reason for the debasement of certain forms of popular literature and entertainment today is the discovery that they can be made to pay; the Greeks were blessed in that they never made, or apparently wished to make, that melancholy discovery. Hence the intellectual integrity of their art, and its consistently noble austerity.

That the Athenian public, many—possibly most—of them illiterate, as the story of Aristides and the potsherd suggests, could not only follow intelligently, but rejoice in, such complex and difficult works as, say, the *Agamemnon* or the *Oedipus at Colonus* or the *Hippolytus* of Euripides, is sufficient evidence of a taste and intelligence far beyond what any formal education can give. That they did rejoice in them is indisputable, just as they rejoiced in the uproarious farces and political skits of Aristophanes, passing from the one to the other as naturally and easily as Chaucer could pass from the Knight's to the Miller's Tale and remain in both wholly true to himself. Periclean Athens, with its play of intellect, its ceaseless activity in the spheres of action—politics and fighting—which the normal Greek most keenly enjoyed, with its careers open to talent, its increasing material prosperity, its external beauty, its pride in the artistic and intellectual leadership of Greece, its vivid sense of community, its opportunities (despite all these goings-on) of leisure beyond anything imagined or desired in the modern world, was indeed a good place to live in, provided that one was not a slave—or a woman.

'We do not,' as Thucydides represented Pericles as saying, 'envy the political institutions of our neighbours: on the contrary, our form of government, far from being copied from abroad, is an example to the world. We call it democracy. In private disputes all enjoy equal advantages before the law; we choose our magistrates with an eye only to their merit, and party affiliations have no influence upon our choice, nor, provided that a man can worthily serve the state, is poverty or obscurity any bar to his promotion. In private life we are not jealous or suspicious of our neighbour; we cheerfully let him follow his bent, eyeing him with no gloomy or reproachful looks. Our personal affairs are free from prying criticism; in public service respect for the law keeps us on the straight path, and no laws have more influence upon us than those which help the oppressed, and the unwritten laws the transgression of which all men know is shameful. More than any other people we have wisely provided, by means of games and annual religious festivals, opportunities of relaxation from our labours—and how different are we from our enemies in our approach to the business of war! Our city is no close preserve; unlike Sparta we do not drive strangers away or prevent them from learning or seeing amongst us what might do them good; our trust is not in the secret build-up of military strength, but simply in our courage when the day for action comes. Some states subject their fighters to a laborious training from early youth onwards, hoping thus to make them brave; we, on the contrary, live easy lives yet are as ready as they to face peril when we must.

'And have we not much else besides upon which to congratulate ourselves? We love beauty, but can temper that love with a certain austerity; we cherish intellect, but maintain our manly vigour. With us, business and politics are not mutually exclusive spheres: any one man may be equally capable of both. Other people may call a man who plays no public role simply a person who happens to enjoy his privacy: *we* call him a useless clod. Moreover we *discuss* state policy; and argument, with us, is no bar to action; we never feel that ignorance is a help to courage, or that the proper exercise of reason is necessarily accompanied by hesitation. Those, surely, must rightly be judged excellent who, with the clearest knowledge of the difference between hardship and pleasure, yet never shrink from peril, however well they know what it involves. We are more generous than other men; for we win friends not by accepting benefits but by conferring them. . . . In a word, I would say that our Athens is an education to the rest of Greece, and that nowhere else can a member of the community offer the state his service in so many different ways, or with a happier versatility.'

That famous passage from Thucydides, in which he professes to record the speech which Pericles made in honour of the Athenian dead at the close of the first year of the Peloponnesian war, has been praised by many scholars as the noblest expression of the Athenian ideal, and few readers would deny its excellence. Nevertheless, self-praise is seldom the best praise, even in war-time when it is spoken to strengthen national morale; and I for one cannot but detect in Pericles' words something declamatory, as

Matthew Arnold confessed to detecting 'something declamatory' in 'Wordsworth's great Ode'.

Athens at the beginning of the Peloponnesian war was on top of the world; but for anyone familiar with Herodotus' account of the older Greece it is hard not to feel that her forward leap, in many ways so remarkable in the history of civilisation, was not altogether towards better things. A certain hardness, a feverishness almost, has crept into the life of the most civilised community in Greece; the City, now, has become all in all. The old country pieties, the old simplicities, are going, or gone. With the almost oriental seclusion of women the graciousness of society has suffered a decline; Greece had always been a man's world, but women, within their sphere, had nevertheless counted for much; now they counted for nothing whatever—unless like Pericles' Aspasia, they are *hetaerae*, or high-class whores. The age-long conservatism of Greek life, based on the land, the family, the ancient sanctities of place, is being undermined. New men, like Cleon the tanner, are beginning to come to the top, and their voices are more strident than of old. Belief is crumbling; clever young men crowd the lecture-rooms of the sophists, eagerly learning to 'make the worse appear the better cause.' Slavery, which inevitably saps the vitality of the nation who uses it, is on the increase. All these things help to explain the sense one has of an almost hectic quality underlying the charm, the brilliance, the intellectual supremacy of Periclean Athens. Pericles, after all, was impelled to *justify* to his fellow Athenians the position which Athens had attained and was fighting to hold; he justified it nobly, in memorable words, but the need to do so would hardly have been felt in an older time. Perhaps what contributed most of all to the social decline of Athens in this period was the very thing that Pericles in his Funeral Speech laid most stress upon as the cause of her pre-eminence—her democratic institutions. A passionate concern with politics was (and is) a defect as well as a virtue in the Greek character; by the middle of the fifth century it was becoming an obsession. Office had been thrown open by Pericles to all free citizens; pay had been introduced for members of the Council and for jurors; poverty, obscurity, the need for attention to business or trade, were no longer any bar to participation in public life, and the men of Athens seized the opportunities offered them with a fierce joy. From one point of view it was, no doubt, magnificent; from another it was less so, and one is tempted to guess that democratic Athens was becoming a city of busybodies, of 'men who,' as a hostile speaker in Thucydides put it, 'can neither rest themselves nor let anyone else rest'. Few forward steps in the history of civilisation have been without their accompanying shadow, and it is a not insignificant fact that the age in which all over Greece democracies were springing up coincided with a sudden silencing of the lyric poetry which had been one of the most characteristic and beautiful expressions of the older order.

It would be no less ungenerous than absurd to seek to belittle the achievement of Athens in the age of Pericles; but at the same time it is as well to recognise that the brilliance of that age was only a sort of Indian summer in the history of Greece. The best was already past. The Greeks were incapable of organising an empire, and Athens in her attempt to do so flouted what was deepest and most characteristic in the genius of the Greek people as a whole, including her own, and thus prepared her own destruction; and with the death of Athens as a political power something else died too—something which can only be described, however vaguely, as the essential spirit of Greece. Men's eyes began to turn away from the familiar world, and to seek another—a spiritual—world, in which they hoped to find reality and permanence. It might not be too extravagant to say that when the Long Walls of Athens were pulled down by the orders of Sparta, the modern consciousness was born. The Athenians, the most quick-witted of the Greeks, were not originators: their genius consisted rather in taking over ideas and carrying them to a previously unattained level of excellence. It was the Ionians of Asia Minor who took the first steps in philosophy; I do not know who first thought of popular government—the urge towards it existed, ideally, in most of the peoples of Greece—though it was certainly Athens which brought it to the highest point of its development; Athenian architecture, noble though it was, was by no means unrivalled by the rest of Greece, and it was at Corinth that some of the most important technical innovations originated; the coins of Athens never approached in beauty of design and execution the coins of Syracuse; throughout her history Athens had no lyric poets of eminence; in the art of history Herodotus of Halicarnassus opened the way for Thucydides—who never came near him in depth or humanity. The one thing which Athens originated was the poetic drama: this was a native growth, and remains amongst the chief glories of the ancient world.

For centuries after her defeat by Sparta Athens remained the cultural centre of Greece, and something of the glow from the part she had played, so long before, in the Persian wars lingered on. The work done there in philosophy and science, in the Academy and the Lyceum, during the fourth and third centuries, and in the great religious and philosophical schools of the Stoics and the Epicureans, was of primary importance to the progress and development of Western thought; but the long cultural pre-eminence of Athens should not blind us to the fact that it was achieved at the expense of much that was precious throughout Greece in an older and simpler age. Greek thought, Greek art, Greek literature, are still a potent, even when unrecognised, element in western culture; and Athens did more, perhaps, than any other single Greek community to advance them; but the finest flowering of Greek life was in an earlier time, during the great formative period of the seventh and sixth centuries, described by Herodotus with so rich a humanity and wisdom and so delicate an interplay of light and shade.

CHAPTER 29

Aftermath

IT IS NOT MY PURPOSE TO TRACE IN ANY DETAIL THE TEDIOUS AND involved course of Greek affairs between the end of the Peloponnesian war and the conquests of Alexander the Great. All Greece, when Athens fell, knew that it was the end of an epoch; her defeat by Sparta was felt to mean the end of the City state, as Greece had come to know it and to glory in it. The failure of Athens was not only a military defeat; it was also the failure of her ideals. In the desperate struggle for survival during the long years of war she had become, as Murray put it, a byword for brutality. On the night when the State galley entered Piraeus with the news of the destruction of the fleet at Cynoscephalae, 'no one' wrote Xenophon, 'slept. They wept for the dead, but more bitterly they wept for themselves, remembering what things they had done to the people of Melos, to the people of Histiaea and Scione and Torone and Aegina, and to many more of the Hellenes'. The grief, and the fear, were not confined to Athens. The whole of Greece knew that something which had once been good had gone for ever. The City state lingered on for a generation or two, but only as the shadow of its former self, for the best minds began to reject the old, full life of the citizen and to turn away from politics. The times were ripe for a new order.

The new order came, as everyone knows, from barbarous Macedon. So much legend has gathered round the personality of Alexander the Great, that it is harder in his case than in that of any other dominating figure of the past to know what he was really like. Was he a military genius only, an incredibly successful, bloody-minded adventurer? Or had he really a vision to the realisation of which his conquests were but the means? The answer, I fancy, must depend largely upon prejudice, influenced in some degree by the few intimate personal details which ancient writers have credibly recorded: his pink-and-white complexion, for instance, his extravagant good looks, his fragrant sweat (so

Plutarch tells us) his addiction to heavy drinking, and insensibility to feminine charm.

On the whole, however, we must rest content with the record of what Alexander did, and continue to guess at the motives for it. He was from the first an extraordinary boy; at the age of twenty, finding himself King of Macedon and not free from a suspicion of complicity in the murder of his father, with no money and a load of debts, surrounded at home by a pack of jealous and turbulent nobles and hemmed in by hostile tribes on the north and on the south by a Greece torn with faction and uncertain whether to submit or to fight for the shadow of its ancient liberties, he first set his own house in order, got himself acknowledged as master and leader of all Greece, and then set out, with an army he could not afford to pay, to the conquest of the world. He overran the whole Persian empire and crossed the Hindu-Kush into India, finally reaching the Ganges, having already sailed down the Indus with a fleet of ships into the Indian Ocean.

Alexander had had many tutors in his boyhood, and one of them was Aristotle, who had never moved from the accepted Greek notion of City-state politics; he is said to have advised Alexander, after his carreer of conquest had begun, to use his native Macedonians and Greeks 'like a leader', but the conquered Persians 'like a master'; but it is to Alexander's credit that he ignored this stupid advice, for he knew, as Aristotle never did, that the day of the City-state had passed irrevocably. A new conception of international relationships was about to dawn. That conception has been called by historians 'the marriage of East and West'. The phrase may stand, for it was Alexander who first broke down the old Greek assumption that the earth was peopled by two sorts of men only: Greeks—and the rest. He soon discovered that the noblemen of Persia were not savages, but were the heirs to an old and rich civilisation from which the Greeks might learn much. India opened his eyes still further; he did not penetrate far into that fabulous country, but he found there one ruler, at any rate— Porus—who had all the attributes of a King. Conquest must come first, and conquest came; but Alexander kept the ideal of a larger and richer unity which was to succeed it, many disparate but complementary parts contributing to a vast and varied whole. The parts were to contribute not only by cultural but by commercial means; for when Alexander had a new harbour capable of accommodating 1,000 ships constructed on the Euphrates at Babylon, and sent his admiral Nearchus to survey the ocean coast from the Indus to the Persian Gulf, his object can only have been to establish shorter and better trade routes between East and West, while many of the seventy new towns he is said to have founded were without doubt sited to serve as trade-centres or clearing-stations. He did much, moreover, to obliterate the distinctions between Greek and 'barbarian' by leaving Persian governors in control of conquered provinces and himself adopting (to the indignation of his troops) Persian dress and much of the court ceremonial of an oriental potentate. This last might indeed be interpreted in more than one way—as mere megalomania, or as one element in the grand design of an ultimate union between East and West.

One world: an association of nations enriched by commerce, with facilities for intercommunication by land and sea, each member retaining its ancient learning and culture and at the same time (an essential, this, in the vision of a man who knew his Homer by heart and fancied that Achilles' blood ran in his veins) purified and enlightened by the clear flame of Greek thought, and all subject to a single King—it was a grand conception, if indeed it was Alexander's, as it well may have been. The idea still exercises us, in one form or another, and it is still unrealised.

When Alexander died, in 323 B.C., at the age of thirty-two and after a reign of twelve years, the enormous empire he had tacked together fell to pieces, his generals fighting amongst themselves for possession of the bits. But the work of conquest had not been wasted: Greek culture was firmly established throughout the Near East, and through the newly-founded towns elements of it, at least, were spread over the continent almost as far as India. Alexandria, the most famous of the cities founded by the conqueror, became under the reign of the Ptolemies (the first Ptolemy was one of Alexander's most distinguished generals) the new centre of Greek culture and learning, in succession to Athens. Meanwhile the star of Rome was in the ascendant. Greece fell to the Roman legions in 146 B.C., but, as a Roman poet put it, she 'took her conquerors captive'. Greek philosophy, Greek learning, Greek taste, and a knowledge of the Greek language were for many generations a necessary part of the equipment of every educated Roman. Rome took over and modified the principles of Greek architecture, sculpture and painting, and in Roman literature every form was imitated from Greek originals, except one—the native 'satire' or medley. Thus, even in the somewhat turbid intellectual atmosphere of Rome, the luminous spirit of Greece continued to act as a leaven and to exercise a formative influence. When Rome fell, the light was put out, but only temporarily. It was rekindled by the devoted work of Renaissance scholars, and is still today a light by which we can see many things worth seeing, if, indeed, we wish to see them and do not prefer a more comfortable darkness.

THE PROGRESS OF HERODOTUS' REPUTATION AS A HISTORIAN HAS been a curious one, and it is only in the present century that the value of his contribution to history has been properly appreciated.

Ancient opinion, as in the Greek writers Ctesias (400 B.C.), Isocrates (380 B.C.), Diodorus (59 B.C.), Lucian (A.D. 160) was hostile, mainly on the ground that he was a 'mere 'storyteller and not fit for contemporary reading because of his antiquated superstitions. Plutarch (A.D. 80) disliked him for his 'malignity', by which he meant the bias shown in his work in favour of Athens and against Boeotia and Corinth.

Of Latin writers, Cicero (more kindly) called him the Father of History.

The first English translation of Herodotus was a version of his first two books by 'B.R.' in 1584.

Until the 19th century Herodotus was more or less neglected by European scholars; then German scholars, notably Niebuhr and Kirchhoff, began to turn their attention to him. Their judgement was that he was not much more than a purveyor of popular tradition. The English scholar Sayce argued that the matter of the *Histories* was probably drawn from written sources, and that Herodotus had wilfuly concealed his obligations.

The first appreciation of his real merit was by the French scholar Amedee Hauvette at the end of the century. About the same time archaeological research in Egypt and better facilities for travel in Greece led to the invaluable studies of J. G. Fraser for his edition of Pausanias—all tending to vindicate Herodotus. Herodotus' mastery of his material and originality of outlook were further stressed by R. W. Macan in his edition of the *Histories* (1895 and 1908). Serious interpretation of Herodotus' literary and artistic purpose was not evident before the present century. Until about eighty years ago he was thought, on the evidence of minor omissions and errors, to have collected his material mainly from gossip and from travellers, himself not having travelled at all. This view has been succeeded by a universal movement towards respect for Herodotus' honesty and intelligence.

I append a chronological list of English translations . . .

Isaac Littlebury	1709
William Beloe	1791
G. Lempriere	1792
P. E. Laurent	1827
Isaac Taylor	1829
Henry Cary	1847
George Rawlinson	1858-60
G. C. Macaulay	1890
A. D. Godley	1921-4
J. E. Powell	1949
Aubrey de Sélincourt	1954

Of the more recent of these, Rawlinson's translation in 4 volumes, enriched with invaluable notes and essays founded upon wide reading and first-hand knowledge of the topography, was an epoch-making book. The translation, with very brief notes, is included in *Everyman's Library* (Dent: 2 vols). Godley's translation is published in the *Loeb Classical Library* (Heinemann) and is a fine and scholarly work. Powell's translation (Cambridge Press) is also the fruit of ripe scholarship, but some readers may be irked by the old-fashioned English which the translator has deliberately employed. My own translation is published in the *Penguin Classics*.

The Story of Rhampsinitus

RHAMPSINITUS POSSESSED A VAST FORTUNE IN SILVER, SO GREAT that no subsequent king came anywhere near it—let alone surpassed it. In order to keep the treasure safe, he proposed to have a stone building put up, with one of its walls forming a part of the outer wall of his palace. The builder he employed had designs upon the treasure and ingeniously contrived to construct the wall in such a way that one of the stone blocks of which it was composed could easily be removed by a couple of men—or even by one. When the new treasury was ready, the king's money was stored away in it; and after the lapse of some years the builder, then on his death-bed, called his two sons and told them how clever he had been, saying that he had planned the device of the movable stone entirely for their benefit, that they might live in affluence. Then he gave the precise measurements, and instructions for its removal, and told them that if only they kept the secret well, they would control the Royal Exchequer as long as they lived. So the father died and his sons lost no time in setting to work; they came by night to the palace, found the stone in the treasury wall, took it out easily enough and got away with a good haul of silver. The king, on his next visit to the treasury, was surprised to see that some of the vessels in which the money was stored were no longer full, but, as the seals were unbroken and all the locks in perfect order, he was at a loss to find the culprit. When the same thing happened again, and yet again, and he found that each time he visited the chamber the level of the money in the jars had still further fallen (for the thieves persisted in their depredations), he took the precaution of ordering traps to be made and set near the money-jars. The thieves came as usual, and one of them made his way into the chamber; but, as soon as he approached the money-jar he was after, the trap got him. Realising his plight, he at once called out to his brother to tell him what had happened, and begged him to come in as quickly as he could and cut off his head, lest the recognition of his dead body should involve both of them in ruin. The brother, seeing the sense of this request, acted upon it without delay; then, having fitted the stone back in its place, went home taking the severed head with him. Next morning the king visited his treasury, and what was his astonishment when he saw in the trap the headless body of the thief, and no sign of damage to the building, or any apparent means of entrance or exit! Much perplexed, he finally decided to have the thief's body hung up outside the wall, and a guard set with orders to arrest and bring before him anyone they might see thereabouts in tears, or showing signs of mourning. Now the young man's mother was deeply distressed by this treatment of her dead son's body, and begged the one who was still alive to do all he possibly could to think of some way of getting it back, and even threatened, if he refused to listen to her, to go to the king and denounce him as the thief. The young man made many excuses, but to no purpose; his mother continued to pester him, until at last he thought of a way out of the difficulty. He filled some skins with wine and loaded them on to donkeys, which he drove to the place where the soldiers were guarding his brother's corpse. Arrived there, he gave a pull on the necks of two or three of the skins, to make them hang down, and untied the fastenings. The wine poured out, and the young man started to roar and bang his head, as if in despair of knowing which donkey to deal with first, while the soldiers, seeing the wine streaming all over the road, seized their pots and ran to catch it, congratulating themselves on such a piece of luck. The young man swore at them in pretended rage, which the soldiers did their best to soothe, until finally he changed his tune, and, appearing to have recovered his temper, drove the donkeys out of the roadway and began to rearrange the wine-skins on their backs. Meanwhile, as he chatted with the soldiers, one of them cracked a joke at his expense and made him laugh, whereupon he made them a present of a wine-skin, and without more ado they all sat down to enjoy themselves, and urged their benefactor to join the party and share the drink. The young man let himself be persuaded, and soon, as cup succeeded cup, and the soldiers treated him with increasing familiarity, he gave them another skin. Such a quantity of wine was too much for the guards; very drunk and drowsy, they stretched themselves out at full length and fell asleep on the spot. This was the young man's chance: waiting till the dead of night, he took down his brother's body and—to show he had the laugh of them—shaved the right cheek of each of the guards. Then he put the corpse on the donkeys' backs and returned home, having done successfully what his mother demanded.

The king was very angry when he learnt that the thief's body had been stolen, and determined at any cost to catch the man who had been clever enough to bring off such a coup. I find it hard to believe the priests' account of the means he employed to catch him—but here it is: he sent his own daughter to a brothel with orders to admit all comers, and to compel each applicant, before granting him her favours, to tell her what was the cleverest and wickedest thing that he had ever done; and if anyone told her the story of the thief, she was to get hold of him and not allow him to escape. The girl obeyed her father's orders, and the thief, when he came to know the reason for what she was doing, could not resist the temptation to go one better than the king in ingenuity. He cut the hand and arm from the body of a man who had just died, and, putting them under his cloak, went to visit the king's daughter in her brothel. When she asked him the question which she had asked all the others, he replied that his wickedest deed was to cut off his brother's head when he was caught in a trap in the king's treasury, and his cleverest was to make the soldiers drunk, so that he could take down his brother's body from the wall where it was hanging. The girl immediately clutched at him; but under cover of the darkness the thief pushed towards her the hand of the corpse, which she seized and held tight in the belief that it was his own. Then, leaving it in her grasp, he made his escape through the door.

The cleverness and audacity of this latest exploit filled the king with astonishment and admiration; soon after the news of it reached him, he sent to every town in Egypt with a promise to the thief, should he give himself up, not only a free pardon but of a rich reward. He was taken at his word; the thief presented himself, and Rhampsinitus signalized his admiration for the most intelligent of all mankind by giving him his daughter in marriage. The Egyptians, he said, were the cleverest nation in the world, but this fellow beat the lot.

The Story of Zopyrus

CONVINCED, THEREFORE, THAT BABYLON WAS NOW DOOMED TO destruction, Zopyrus went to Darius and asked him if the capture of the city was really of supreme importance to him, and, on being told that it was, set himself to devise a way of bringing it about by his own sole act and initiative; for in Persia any special service to the king is very highly valued. Accordingly he passed in review every scheme he could think of, and finally decided that there was one way only in which he could bring the place under, namely by maiming himself and then going over to the enemy as a deserter. Taking this dreadful expedient as a mere matter of course, he at once put it into practice, and there were no half-measures in the way he set about it: he cut off his nose and ears, shaved his hair like a criminal's, raised weals on his body with a whip, and in this condition presented himself to Darius. Darius was shocked at the sight of a man of Zopyrus' eminence so fearfully mutilated, and springing from his chair with an exclamation of horror, asked who it was that had inflicted this punishment upon him, and what Zopyrus had done to deserve it. 'My lord,' Zopyrus answered, 'there is no one but yourself who has power enough to reduce me to this condition. The hands that disfigured me were none other than my own, for I could not bear to hear the Assyrians of Babylon laugh the Persians to scorn.'

'You speak like a madman;' said Darius; 'to say you did this horrible thing because of our enemies in the beleaguered city, is merely to cloak a shameful act in fine words. Are you fool enough to think that the mutilation of your body can hasten our victory? When you did that to yourself, you must have taken leave of your senses.'

'Had I told you of my intention,' Zopyrus answered, 'you would not have allowed me to proceed. So I acted upon my own initiative. And now—if you too will play your part—we will capture Babylon. I will go as I am to the city walls, pretending to be a deserter, and I will tell them that it was you who caused my misery. They will believe me readily enough—and they will put their troops under my command. Now for your part: wait till the tenth day after I enter the town, and then station by the gates of Semiramis a detachment of a thousand men, whose loss will not worry you. Then, seven days later, send 2,000 more to the Nineveh gates and, twenty days after that, another 4,000 to the Chaldaean gates. None of these three detachments must be armed with anything but their daggers—let them carry daggers only. And then, after a further interval of twenty days, order a general assault upon the city walls from every direction, taking care that our own Persian troops have the sectors opposite the Belian and Cissian gates. It is my belief that the Babylonians, when they see that I have done them good service, will increase my responsibility—even to trusting me with the keys of the gates. And after that—I and our Persians will see what must be done.'

Having given these directions to the king, Zopyrus fled towards the gates of Babylon, glancing over his shoulder as he ran, like a deserter in fear of pursuit. When the soldiers on watch saw him, they hurried down from the battlements, and opening one of the gates just a crack, asked him his name and business. Saying he was Zopyrus and had deserted from the Persian army, he was let in, and conducted by the sentries to the magistrates. Here he poured out his tale of woe, pretending that the injuries he had done to himself had been inflicted upon him by Darius, and all because he had advised him to abandon the siege, as there appeared to be no means of ever bringing it to a successful conclusion. 'And now,' he added, 'here I am, men of Babylon; and my coming will be gain to you, but loss—and that the severest—to Darius and his army. He little knows me if he thinks he can get away with the foul things he has done me—moreover, I know all the ins and outs of his plans.'

The Babylonians, seeing a Persian of high rank and distinction in such a state—his nose and ears cut off and his body a mess of blood from the lash of whips—were quick to believe that he spoke the truth and had really come to offer them his services, and in this belief were prepared to give him whatever he asked. At once he asked for the command of some troops, and, when the request was granted, proceeded to put into practice the plan he had arranged with Darius. The tenth day after his arrival he marched his force out of the city, and surrounded and killed the first detachment of a thousand men which he had instructed Darius to send. This was enough to show the Babylonians that his deeds were as good as his words; they were in high glee, and ready to put themselves under his orders in anything he might propose. After waiting, therefore, the agreed number of days, he picked another party from the troops in the city, marched out, and made mincemeat of the two thousand Persians which Darius had posted by the Nineveh gates. As a result of this second service, the reputation of Zopyrus went up with a jump and his name was on everybody's lips. The same thing happened with the four thousand—once more, after the agreed interval, he marched his men out through the Chaldaean gates, surrounded the Persians there, and cut them down to a man. This was his crowning success; Zopyrus was now the one and only soldier in Babylon, the city's hero, and was created General in Chief and Guardian of the Wall.

And now Darius did not fail to do his part: as had been agreed, he ordered a general assault upon the walls from every direction— which was the signal for Zopyrus to reveal the full extent of his cunning. Waiting till the Babylonian forces had mounted the battlements to repel Darius' onslaught, he opened the Cissian and Belian gates and let the Persians in. Those of the Babylonians who were near enough to see what had happened, fled to the temple of Bel; the rest remained at their posts until they, too, realised that they had been betrayed.

Thus Babylon was captured for the second time, and Darius after his victory—unlike Cyrus, its previous conqueror—destroyed its defences, pulled down all the city gates, and impaled the leading citizens to the number of about three thousand.

In the judgement of Darius no Persian surpassed Zopyrus, either before his time or after, as a benefactor of his country, except only Cyrus—with whom nobody in Persia has ever dreamt of comparing himself. We are told that Darius often said that he would rather have Zopyrus without his frightful wounds than twenty more Babylons. He rewarded him with the highest honours, giving him every year the sort of gifts which are most prized amongst the Persians, and, amongst much else, the governorship of Babylon, free from tax, for as long as he lived.

Bibliography

A full bibliography covering so large a subject would hardly be possible. Indeed, of many of my debts I am no longer even aware. The following is a short list of books to which I am especially, and gratefully, indebted.

GEORGE RAWLINSON	*History of Herodotus*, 4 vols., Murray, London, 4th edn., 1880.
J. L. MYRES	*Herodotus, Father of History*, Clarendon Press, Oxford, 1953
J. B. BURY	*The Ancient Greek Historians*, Macmillan, London, 1909. *History of Greece*, Macmillan, London, 3rd edn., rev. Russell Meiggs, 1951.
M. I. FINLEY	*The Greek Historians*, Chatto & Windus, London, 1959. *The World of Odysseus*, rev. edn., Chatto & Windus, London, 1956.
N. G. L. HAMMOND	*A History of Greece*, Oxford, Clarendon Press, 1959.
H. D. F. KITTO	*The Greeks*, Penguin Books, London, 1951.
W. T. EARP	*The Way of the Greeks*, Oxford, Clarendon Press, 2nd impr., 1930.
GILBERT MURRAY	*Five Stages of Greek Religion*, London, Watts, Thinker's Library, 1935. *The Rise of the Greek Epic*, Oxford, Clarendon Press, 4th edn., 1934.
C. M. BOWRA	*Greek Lyric Poetry*, Oxford, Clarendon Press, 2nd rev. edn., 1961.
C. ALDRED	*The Egyptians*, London, Thames & Hudson, 1961.
T. TALBOT RICE	*The Scythians*, Thames & Hudson, London, 1957.

A. ZIMMERN   *The Greek Commonwealth*, Oxford, Clar-
                    endon Press, 1911.
R. GHIRSHMAN   *Iran*, Penguin Books, London, 1954.
R. LATTIMORE   *The Poetry of Greek Tragedy*, Baltimore,
                    Johns Hopkins Press, 1958.
B. FARRINGTON   *Greek Science*, Penguin Books, London,
                    1953.

Index

383